SOVIET ANTIRELIGIOUS CAMPAIGNS AND PERSECUTIONS

Also by Dimitry V. Pospielovsky

A HISTORY OF SOVIET ATHEISM IN THEORY AND PRACTICE, AND THE BELIEVER
Volume 1: A HISTORY OF MARXIST-LENINIST ATHEISM AND SOVIET ANTIRELIGIOUS POLICIES
Volume 3: SOVIET STUDIES ON THE CHURCH AND THE BELIEVER'S RESPONSE TO ATHEISM (forthcoming)

THE RUSSIAN CHURCH UNDER THE SOVIET REGIME (*2 volumes*)

RUSSIAN POLICE TRADE-UNIONISM: EXPERIMENT OR PROVOCATION?

RUSSIA'S OTHER POETS (*co-editor and co-translator*)

Soviet Antireligious Campaigns and Persecutions

Volume 2 of A History of Soviet Atheism in Theory and Practice, and the Believer

Dimitry V. Pospielovsky
Professor in Modern European and Russian History
University of Western Ontario, Canada

MACMILLAN
PRESS

© Dimitry V. Pospielovsky 1988

All rights reserved. No reproduction, copy or transmission of this publication may be made without written permission.

No paragraph of this publication may be reproduced, copied or transmitted save with written permission or in accordance with the provisions of the Copyright Act 1956 (as amended), or under the terms of any licence permitting limited copying issued by the Copyright Licensing Agency, 33-4 Alfred Place, London WC1E 7DP.

Any person who does any unauthorised act in relation to this publication may be liable to criminal prosecution and civil claims for damages.

First published 1988

Published by
THE MACMILLAN PRESS LTD
Houndmills, Basingstoke, Hampshire RG21 2XS
and London
Companies and representatives
throughout the world

British Library Cataloguing in Publication Data
Pospielovsky, Dimitry V.
Soviet antireligious campaigns and
persecutions.—(A history of Soviet
atheism in theory and practice, and the
believer; v. 2).
1. Religion and state—Soviet Union—
History—20th century
I. Title II. Series
322'.1'0947   BL65.S8
ISBN 978-0-333-44674-4   ISBN 978-1-349-19002-7 (eBook)
DOI 10.1007/978-1-349-19002-7

This modest summation of the persecutions of faith in the USSR is dedicated to Alexander Ogorodnikov, Leonid Borodin, Valeri Senderov, Deacon Vladimir Rusak and countless other Christians persecuted for their faith and for spreading the word of God in the face of militant atheism.

Contents

General Introduction to the Three-Volume Work	ix
Acknowledgements	xvi
Preface	xviii

1	The Early Persecutions, 1971–21	1
2	Contempt and Hate Propaganda, 1919–39	19
3	Persecutions, 1921–41	47
	The NEP Era (1921–8)	47
	1929–41	61
4	An 'Interlude': From 1941 to Stalin's Death	91
5	Renewal of the Incendiary Propaganda, 1958–85	98
	Under Khrushchev	98
	After Khrushchev	108
6	Persecutions under Khrushchev	**121**
	The Closure of the Churches	122
	Demoralizing the Remaining Parishes	128
	Monasteries and Pilgrimages	135
	Parents and Children	142
7	Persecutions after Khrushchev	**145**
	The Closing of Churches	146
	The Orthodox	146
	The Old Believers	151
	The Roman Catholics	152
	The 'Unregistered' Ones	154
	The Uniates	157
	The 'True and Free' Adventists	157
	The Evangelical Christian Baptists	159
	The Pentecostals	162
	Persecutions of Clergy and Laity	163

Epilogue	**188**
Appendix 1	193
Appendix 2	213
Notes and References	229
Bibliography	260
Index	265

General Introduction to the Three-Volume Work

Religious belief and the Churches have survived in the Soviet Union in the face of almost seventy years of continuous persecution, unprecedented in history in intensity, although varying in degree and thrust, depending on the external and internal circumstances. According to approximate calculations, given in our book on the history of the Russian Orthodox Church under the Soviets, the toll of Orthodox clergy has been in the region of 40 000 priests, probably as many monks and nuns, and incalculable millions of lay believers. The number of functioning Orthodox churches has been reduced from over 60 000 (this includes parish and monastic churches and institutional chapels) before the revolution to less than 7000 in the late 1970s. Other religions, except perhaps the Baptists, have seen the numbers of their churches and temples reduced by at least the same proportion. And yet in the last decade and a half or so, more and more voices in the Soviet Union have been heard claiming not only religious survival but even revival, primarily of Christianity and Islam. According to all oral evidence, both of Soviet-Russian clergy remaining in the Soviet Union and of recent émigrés, this neophytic phenomenon is almost entirely limited to those under 40 years of age, while their parents mostly remain outside any religion. Hence, whatever the numbers and proportions, the current 'churchification' of the intelligentsia is largely not a carry-over from one generation to the next, nor is it a simple revival of a tradition, because the tradition of the Russian intelligentsia, at least since the 1860s, has been predominantly one of a rather passionate atheism and positivism.[1]

The main purpose of this study is a step-by-step presentation and analysis of the changing styles, strategies and tactics of the

---

1. See *Vekhi*, a collection of essays on the Russian intelligentsia by N. A. Berdiaev, S. N. Bulgakov, M. O. Gershenzon, A. S. Izgoev, B. A. Kistiakovsky, P. B. Struve, S. L. Frank (Moscow, 1909; repr.: Frankfurt/M.: Possev, 1967). Also: Jeffrey Brooks, '*Vekhi* and the *Vekhi* Dispute', *Survey*, vol. 19, no. 1 (86) London, Winter 1973.

never-ending Soviet attack on religion and on believers. This will include as detailed and documented an account as possible of the direct persecutions, of which the most massive occurred in the following periods and under the following pretexts:

February 1918 to late 1920. A bloody attack on the clergy and active laity was conducted under the pretext of their opposition to communism, their real or alleged sympathy for the Whites, and the resistance of lay believers to the nationalization of all church property in accordance with the Soviet decree of 23 January 1918.

1921 to 1923. This wave of arrests of clergy and laity, with executions of some of the most influential and popular church leaders, was officially motivated by their resistance to the confiscation of all church plate of any value, including liturgical vessels.

1922 to 1926. Persecution of the traditional Orthodox Church and her faithful clergy and laity for their refusal to join the state-supported Renovationist schism.

1926 to 1927. Arrests, exile and imprisonment of masses of bishops, as well as some regular parish clergy faithful to them, for an attempt to elect a patriarch secretly.

1928 to 1934. Arrest and liquidation of clergy and lay activists for refusing to accept Metropolitan Sergii's wording of the Declaration of Loyalty to the Soviet State and for breaking administrative connections with him.

1929 to 1930. The beginning of mass liquidation of rural parishes and their clergy and lay supporters under the guise of the collectivization and 'dekulakization' campaign.

1933 to 1934. Destruction of the remaining monastic communities and the liquidation of monks and nuns, along with many members of the urban and rural clergy, particularly renowned preachers and spiritual fathers.

1936 to 1939. Almost total liquidation of religious temples, clergy and active lay believers of all faiths.

1959 to 1964. Khrushchev's physical attack on the Church and all other religious faiths, closure and destruction of the majority of the temples reopened during the religiously 'tolerant' era of 1941 to 1957, arrests and deportations of large numbers of clergy and laity – all under the pretext of imminent construction of communism, incompatible with faith in the Supernatural.

These are just highlights of the most massive attacks, which will be accounted for and discussed in greater detail in their proper context.

The other aim of this study is to trace the continuing religious life in the country: how the believers preserve their faith and even multiply their numbers in these conditions; how, if at all, they are affected by this aggressive state atheism and antireligious propaganda; finally, how and why there is growing movement of adult baptisms and return to the Church after all these years of concerted attack, and this despite the absence of any organized religious education.

Finding sources for this study was a complex and uneven process. There was no problem in locating masses of the officially printed Soviet antireligious propaganda of all categories: from the allegedly scholarly studies of the Soviet 'religiologists' to the primitive attacks on religion in the mass press and, in particular, in the Soviet specialized general circulation antireligious journals, newspapers, brochures and books. The available data on the direct Soviet persecutions of the Church are more difficult to assemble. Only a very small percentage can be obtained from official Soviet publications. Official admissions of persecutions have been made only where they could be blamed on the Church's hostility 'to the young Soviet republic' (the Civil War Years), or on the believers' resistance to the implementation of Soviet laws on the nationalization of church property or confiscation of church valuables (1918 to 1922), or, finally, on Stalin's excesses. But even the gross understatement is the rule. Therefore, most of the material on persecutions comes from testimonies of witnesses, unofficial letters and secret diocesan reports smuggled abroad, the multiple *samizdat* publications of the last two decades (which even include, on occasion, internal secret party documents not meant for print, with open admissions of persecutions) and statements (written and oral) by the émigrés from the Soviet Union of all periods.

Most of the existing Western studies of Soviet atheism limit themselves to the official Soviet sources. Only a small minority of Western scholars, such as Professor Bohdan Bociurkiw, the Rev. Michael Bourdeaux and his co-workers at Keston College, make wide use of *samizdat* in reporting persecutions of religion in the Soviet Union; however, in most cases these relate to the post-Stalin era. This study uncovers a considerable volume of direct witness and documentation on the persecutions of the 1920s and 1930s, dispersed mostly in masses of Russian émigré publications and archival collections pertaining to the time, and largely forgotten and ignored until now. This author firmly believes that only a combination of the material from the official Soviet literature with the information collected in the above fashion, followed by a systematic study of the persecutions during each separate period of Soviet history in question, will enable the reader to gain a realistic picture of the true horrors and magnitude of the permanent Soviet war against the Church.

As for the life of the Church and the believer under these conditions, their attitudes, and the religious revival of the last decades, here again most of the information comes from *samizdat*[1] from all decades of the Soviet era, as well as from interviews with Russian churchmen and religious intelligentsia, both those who remain in the USSR and recent émigrés. The wartime émigrés and documents of the German occupying forces during the Second World War are also very important sources for the religiosity of the life of the Church from the 1920s to 1940s.

Soviet-Russian fine literature (the *belles-lettres*), particularly of the last decade-and-a-half, has ever more frequently reflected the growing interest in matters spiritual, the Church, and Christian ethics of times past and present. This source has also been tapped for the current study.

The objective Western reader may be bewildered occasionally by the obvious 'disproportion' of credibility rendered by this author on the one hand to the official Soviet data, and on the other, to the unofficial data of *samizdat* and the testimonies of Soviet believers. The 'bias' of this book is to give more credence to the latter and to doubt the former, even to present evidence showing its mendacity whenever possible. There are several reasons for this 'inequity'. First of all, there is the old Russian saying: the one who has not been caught by the hand is

---

1. Although the term *samizdat* appeared only in the early 1960s, the Church, the theologians and other church authors have used similar methods for the writing and dissemination of their literature from the early 1920s, after the regime had deprived the Orthodox Church of printing presses, to the present day.

not a thief. The reader will soon see that the official Soviet claims, declarations, the writings of the Soviet 'scientists' of atheism or, as the Soviets call them, 'religiologists', will constantly be 'caught by the hand', mostly by comparing contradictory and mutually exclusive statements and claims made by such authors and institutions in different years, under different circumstances although relating to the same events or periods. Second, the believers, and the dissidents with their *samizdat*, are the parties under attack; they have to weigh carefully every statement they make. They are taking tremendous responsibility for every one of them. One is not likely to make frivolous irresponsible statements when the price for any 'disseminated information' that contradicts the general line of the communist party of the given moment is loss of a job, of the right to receive education, of liberty, and even of life on occasion. Although errors of transmission of information and even errors of judgement may still occur, deliberate misinformation emanating from the religious[1] and *samizdat* circles in general is very unlikely.

The study will be far from exhaustive in its coverage, for the following reasons. First, there is no way to achieve a quantitative analysis or to assess the degree of religious or atheistic penetration in the whole country, categories of believers, etc., our sample of interviewees being too limited in numbers and categories. Second, we have extremely little information on the parallel processes (if there are any on any comparable scale) among the common workers and peasants; further, as our interviewees as well as *samizdat* writings are limited almost exclusively to the intelligentsia, and predominantly to that of Moscow, Leningrad and half a dozen other major cities, we are forced to concentrate our study and analysis predominantly on the Russian Orthodox Church, for this is the Church which most of the neophytic intelligentsia join; and it is her theology, traditions and legacy which are discussed and deliberated in almost all *samizdat* religious and religio-philosophic documents, as well as in the Christian-orientated works of some officially tolerated literary and artistic figures. In addition, although there are plenty of *samizdat* documents of the

---

1. This, of course, excludes official public statements by the official spokesmen of the Churches, especially when they are made for the Western media.

unofficial branch of the Baptist Church and of the Pentacostalists coming from the Soviet Union, they are limited to petitions against persecutions, reports on persecutions and imprisonments, collections of prayers and hymnals. Being neither an intellectual nor a theological phenomenon, the sects simply have not provided us with material which could be analyzed, generalized and conceptualized.

Although in the chapters on religious persecutions and antireligious propaganda the study will give brief accounts of attacks on religions other than the Orthodox Church, the concentration is on the Orthodox Church in all parts of the work, whether it is the study of Soviet atheism and its attitudes to the Orthodox Church or of the life of the Church and the believers. The reason is that Orthodoxy is the national and historical Church of the three core peoples of the Soviet Union: the Great Russians (or Muscovites), the Ukrainians (or the Little Russians),[1] and the Belorussians. In contrast to the multireligious scene in North America and to the supranational character of the Roman Church in the traditionally Roman Catholic nations of western Europe, Orthodoxy (using the vernacular and possessing no extra-territorial centralized Church administration) is not only a religion but a way of life, the very cultural matrix of the daily life in the countries where it has become the national Church. Russian literature, art, folk traditions, habits (where they survive), and attitudes have been formed or at least saturated by Orthodoxy from within. Therefore, the atheistic revolt of Marxist Bolshevism had to match Orthodoxy in its totality in order to crush it as the national way of life. Being only institutionally and ideologically antireligious as is Marxism in most other East European states, to allow a broader scope of religious toleration than in the USSR (in all cases except Albania) would not be effective. The attack had to be so total as to shatter the entire national culture in all its aspects. Hence the attempts of contemporary Russian nationalists to reconstruct Russian culture, Russian art, literature, inevitably brings a revival of Orthodoxy, of elements of Orthodox culture. That is why Orthodoxy is so central to any

---

1. The terms 'Great' and 'Little' Russians are of Byzantine origin, wherein the core area of a nation was called 'Little' while the zones of its later imperial expansion received the appellation 'Great'.

study of Russian nationalism. In fact this work, along with its predecessor, *The Russian Church Under the Soviet Regime* (St Vladimir's Seminary Press, 1984), is a rather bulky 'introduction' to a study of Russian nationalism and its relationship to the Orthodox religious revival, which is yet to be written.

This study is historical, hence the philosophy and the philosophical legacy and ideology of Marxist-Leninist atheism are only briefly discussed in a single chapter in the first volume. A philosophically inclined reader interested in a more profound study of the philosophical and ideational roots and concepts of Marxist-Leninist atheism is strongly advised to read James Thrower's *Marxist-Leninists 'Scientific Atheism' and the Study of Religion and Atheism in the USSR*. Dr Thrower's use of inverted commas in the title of his book has the same connotation as this author's preference for the term 'High Brow' Atheism instead of 'Scholarly' or 'Scientific'.

Acknowledgements

Although all the errors and shortcomings in this work are solely my own responsibility, a number of individuals and institutions have greatly contributed to its 'delivery' if not to its 'birth'. Without their help the 'child' would have had many more defects and the birth would have been much more painful.

First, I owe my thanks to Dr Edward Manukian. Chapter 1 of Vol. 1 is largely his work. As a professional Marxologist with the equivalent of a doctoral degree in philosophy from Leningrad University, he was the right person to write the theoretical chapter. My son, Andrew Pospielovsky, a fourth-year Russian history honours student at the University of Western Ontario at the time of this writing, compiled the bibliography, the Appendix on Soviet antireligious legislation and the index for the first volume, wherefore I owe him many thanks. I should also express my deep gratitude to the Social Sciences and Humanities Research Council of Canada and the University of Western Ontario Academic Development Fund, without whose grants the research that went into writing this study would have been impossible. I owe my thanks to the administration and staff of the Hoover Institution Library and Archives, the Bakhmeteff Russian Émigré Archives at Columbia University, the Dr Lieb Archiv at the Basel University Library, the Widener Library and the Russian Research Center at Harvard University, the Library of Congress and the Kennan Institute for Advanced Russian Studies. Most of the illustrations in this volume have been found at the Hoover Archives, some at Harvard. I should like to thank both institutions for allowing me to use them. Much of the first-hand information in this study would simply not have been there had it not been for the willing co-operation of scores of recent Russian émigrés and other persons directly involved in the life of the contemporary Church in the USSR, who had granted interviews or wrote letters about their experiences to this author. I am particularly grateful to Fr. Alexander Garklavs of Sts. Peter and Paul Orthodox church, Buffalo, N.Y., for providing me with the Metropolitan Sergii (Voskresensky) memoranda to be found in Appendix 1 of this volume. The murdered Metropolitan was Alexander's godfather and the mss. have been kept in his adopted father's, Archbishop John (Garklavs) of Riga and Chicago, personal archives. Fr. Alexander is a war orphan.

SOME TECHNICAL POINTS

Italics. Unless otherwise noted, all italics within quotations are in the original. The exceptions are the normal use of italics to indicate a title or a foreign term.

Transliterations. Generally, the Library of Congress system is used, with the following exceptions:
In personal names 'sky' ending is used instead of 'skii'; 'ya' and 'yu' are used in personal names to depict 'ю' and 'я', instead of 'ia' and 'iu', e.g. Yaroslavsky, not Iaroslavskii.
'X' is used to transliterate the Russian 'ks' throughout.
A single apostrophe (') is used for both soft (ь) and the hard (ъ) signs.

The Calendar. Prior to February 1918 the Julian Calendar was used in Russia, which was thirteen days behind the Western Gregorian one in the twentieth century. Wherever the Old Calendar is used, it is indicated as o.s., i.e. old style.

Abbreviations. These are noted in the appropriate places in the main text and in the notes and references whenever a certain title is used more than two or three times. For example, *Bezbozhnik u stanka* becomes *Bezbust*. Similarly, such oft-repeated publication cities in bibliographical references as Moscow, Leningrad, St Petersburg, Petrograd, New York becomes respectively: M., L., Pbg., P., N.Y.

DIMITRY V. POSPIELOVSKY

Preface

'The Bolsheviks come out against religion not only because of the counter-revolutionary positions of the Church, but also because of the programme and principles on which the Bolsheviks stand.'
(*Nauka i religiia*, no. 12, 1985)

This book deals with the day-to-day application of the Marxist-Leninist antireligious theories and policies catalogued, discussed and analysed in the previous volume. The structure of this volume is of necessity monotonously repetitious, alternating between chapters on direct persecutions and those dealing with the type of propaganda that is meant to stir up antireligious feelings, or at least to evoke in the reader, listener or viewer a feeling of contempt towards the clergy and the believers. Such propaganda aims at depicting the believers as social misfits less than human – or 'vermin', to use Lenin's phrase. Once this effect is achieved, injustices and cruelties towards the clergy or the believing laity are accepted on the same level as cruelty to animals, or even more tolerantly than cruelty to animals. One does not despise an animal for being an animal, but one tends to despise a human being for behaving in a way unworthy of human dignity. Hence the first step towards conditioning society to condone or at least passively tolerate the persecution of groups of defenceless people is to degrade their image so that they appear less than human. And that was the purpose of the mass antireligious propaganda, especially during the periods of mass persecution campaigns: 1920s, 1930s, and 1959 to 1964. Each one of these periods was preceded and accompanied by an intensified propaganda of contempt and hate.

Each chapter in this volume deals with persecutions or propaganda in a certain historical period. It is hoped that the juxtaposition of the propaganda and persecution chapters will reveal their consistent and systematic interrelationship. The intention of this volume is to demonstrate that in no period of Soviet history did either the persecutions or hate-and-contempt propaganda against the Church and the believers ever cease completely. Both are found in the Soviet Union today. Their forms, intensity and degree of overtness or covertness vary from period to period, and from one confession to another, depending on the situation inside and outside the USSR and other policy considerations.

The many sources, method of collection of material, and all the acknowledgements gratefully mentioned in Volume 1 of this series apply equally to Volume 2.

My particular gratitude is owed to the following persons: Mrs Pamela Hutchins-Orr for her excellent style editing, Mrs Deborah Kostoff for her excellent and dedicated typing and proof-reading of the text, and to my son Andrew for again compiling the appendices and the bibliography for this volume.

1 The Early Persecutions, 1917–21

'We must combat religion – that is the ABC of... Marxism. The combatting of religion... must be linked up with the concrete practice of the class movement... eliminating the social roots of religion...'
(Lenin, *Collected Works*, vol. 15)

The Church was the object of persecution from the earliest days of the revolution. The first phase, roughly between 1918 and March 1921, was part of the Red Terror of the War Communism era. Thousands of clergy and faithful laymen were murdered or persecuted in those years. The pretexts for this were several. The principal ones were suspicion of collaboration with the enemy during the Civil War, the Patriarchal anathema pronounced on the Bolsheviks (which was seen to undermine the prestige of the new regime in the eyes of the largely religious population), sermons which blamed fraternal carnage on the Bolsheviks for causing it and on Marxist materialism for justifying it, and lastly, resistance to the implementation of the 23 January (5 February) 1918 Decree on the Separation of Church and State, particularly attempts to confiscate churches and church property.

Resistance to confiscation and to the closure of monasteries was mostly organized by lay congregations and monastics, assisted by the local parish priest and bishop. All these people were subject to arrest and terror; monks and nuns were often killed where religious houses were closed or confiscated. In many cases the tortures, murders and vandalism were the autonomous initiative of local anarchistic bands of army or navy deserters calling themselves Bolsheviks.[1]

Later, when the Russian Orthodox Church adopted a policy of civic loyalty to the Soviet regime, her leaders repeatedly declared that their earlier hostility had been motivated by the bloodiness of these roaming partisan forces, and was not directed against the new Soviet State *per se*. The Church explained that she now realized that the central Soviet

Government was not responsible for the behaviour of these local forces, but since the new government had not condemned them the church had assumed that they had government sanction.² The fact remains that the Soviet regime has never, to the present day, disowned these forces or disassociated itself from them. On the contrary, many of their conveniently dead leaders such as Chapaev or Shchors have been immortalized in books and films.³

The earliest and most detailed account of anti-Church terror in the Soviet Union is contained in A. A. Valentinov's now generally forgotten *Black Book*, first published in English and German in 1924. The author recounts many examples of murders occasioned by alleged collaboration with the 'enemy' during the Civil War. The following illustrations show the flimsiness of such allegations.

Germorgen, Bishop of Tobolsk, was murdered on 16 June 1918 by drowning. He and other political detainees in the Tobolsk prison were herded into a river steamer on the excuse that they were being evacuated because of approaching White forces. Rocks were hung around the necks of each, and all were pushed off the deck. Before the revolution, Germorgen had been in trouble with the tsarist establishment for actively opposing Rasputin and for having begged the Tsar to remove him from court. In 1918 the Patriarch, in response to the Bolshevik terror, appealed to his flock to organize religious processions in the cities and villages around the country. In Tobolsk, Bishop Germorgen was warned by the Soviets that he would be arrested if a procession took place. Tobolsk was a sensitive area because Nicholas II and his family had been held there before being moved to Ekaterinburg on 27 April; therefore the authorities were particularly wary of any public demonstration. The Bishop ignored the warning, and on Palm Sunday 28 April there was a great procession from the Cathedral and around the walls of the city with banners and hymns. Before the house of the Romanovs the Bishop raised his arm and gave his blessing to the Royal family. This was also the occasion of Germorgen's last sermon, in which he said: 'I feel my passion days are approaching . . . Therefore I beg you all to lend me support by your prayers in these days,' just as Jesus had asked His apostles to stay awake and pray for Him. He was arrested the following Holy Week. The Soviet government promised to release him for a ransom of 10 000 rubles, later increasing it to 100 000. When the money was collected and submitted, the delegation of notables and clergy which had come to collect their bishop disappeared behind the prison walls and apparently shared his fate.⁴

Another very popular bishop savagely murdered during the Civil War was Ioakim, Archbishop of Nizhni Novgorod. This was a remarkable man, a scholarly theologian, a compelling orator and an energetic missionary who had been very successful in returning whole villages of Old Believers to the Orthodox Church during his tenure as Bishop of Orenburg. There is no information on Ioakim's political views but he seems to have opposed even the first, February Revolution, for he spent some time in gaol under the Provisional government. During the Civil War he appeared in Crimea, which suggests some connection with the White Forces. In any case the Reds murdered him by hanging him head down from the iconostasis above the central 'Royal Doors'.⁵ The clergy in Crimea suffered terrible persecutions even before the White Army began its first operations in northern Caucasus. A priest, Ugliansky, was murdered by the Red Guards on the grounds that he used green rather than red ribbons on his church icon lamps. Churches in Simferopol, Feodosia and other Crimean cities were desecrated and many of their clergy brutally murdered.⁶

The first two martyr-priests in the Petrograd area were Ivan Kochurov, an Orthodox missionary in the United States on a visit to Russia, and Filosof Ornatsky, an eminent Petrograd priest whose two sons were Imperial Guards officers. Ornatsky refused to be intimidated even by the arrest and later execution of his sons. He was arrested in the spring of 1918 after serving a public requiem for victims of Bolshevik terror. When a procession of several thousand faithful, carrying banners and singing hymns, proceeded to the prison to plead on his behalf they were assured that the priest was safe and his life was not in danger. But such was not the case, for he was shot that night, according to the evidence of a *Che-Ka* driver who was employed to drive Ornatsky and thirty-two other victims to the site of execution on a cliff overlooking the Gulf of Finland. When they arrived the priest asked permission to perform a brief funeral service and each of the victims received his blessing before being shot. All the executed, including the priest, fell straight into the sea below.⁷

Father Vostorgov in Moscow was an outstanding teacher,

missionary and church activist. He had mastered Persian and served for some time as an Orthodox missionary in Iran converting local Nestorians (including three bishops) to Orthodoxy. His sermons were famous, and as an internal missionary he had preached in churches as far apart as Kamchatka on the Pacific, Manchuria and Moscow. In 1913 he established in Moscow the first theological college for girls in Russia. He was a convinced monarchist, made fiery anti-Bolshevik speeches at the 1917–18 *Sobor* and made his church of St Basil in the Red Square a centre for right-wing elements. His great popularity as a pastor among regular Moscow parishioners forced the Bolsheviks to stage a blackmail operation in order to arrest him, allegedly on the grounds of black-marketeering. A Bolshevik *agent provocateur* convinced him to negotiate a private sale of the Moscow diocesan residence after the property had already officially been nationalized. The Church needed money badly after the nationalization of her bank accounts in January 1918. On 23 August 1918 Fr. Vostorgov was shot, along with the local Roman Catholic priest Lutoslawski and his brother, two former tsarist ministers (N. Maklakov and A. Khvostov), an Orthodox bishop Efrem, former State Council Chairman I. Shcheglovitov, and Senator S. Beletsky. Fr. Vostorgov conducted a short funeral service, and preached a brief sermon to the victims, calling on them to face death bravely 'as their last sacrifice of atonement, with faith in God and in the coming regeneration of Russia', after which each victim came forward to be blessed by the bishop and by Fr. Vostorgov. Then the latter turned to the executioners with the words, 'I am ready', and was shot.[8]

The material in Valentinov's book on this period is based on the various investigations carried out by Whites and foreign observers immediately after the reconquest of certain territories. The accounts are full of horrid details. They deal mostly with territories which had changed hands several times in the course of the Civil War.

During the less-than-one-year occupation of the Stavropol diocese in 1918 the Bolsheviks killed at least fifty-two Orthodox priests, four deacons and four readers. Since in this diocese, with its large Moslem and Old Believer minorities, the Orthodox were not an overwhelming majority of the popula-

The Early Persecutions, 1917–21

tion, these numbers may represent over 20 per cent of the diocesan priesthood.

The pretexts for the persecutions were many and various: liberal and bourgeois sympathies, condemnation of bolsheviks in sermons, Te Deum services for a passing White Army detachment, protests against blasphemies.

Of some twenty concrete cases of murders of priests in the Stavropol Diocese described in some detail in the book, only ten could be suspected of collaboration with the enemy and then only in the form of prayers. Priest Alexander Podolsky was murdered for having conducted a Te Deum service for a Cossack regiment prior to its attack on the Bolsheviks. The Bolsheviks subsequently tortured and then murdered the priest. When a peasant came to take and bury his body, he was likewise shot dead on the spot by the Red murderers. Fr. Alexei Miliutinsky was murdered for telling Red Army soldiers that they were leading Russia to disaster and for offering prayers for the victory of anti-Bolshevik Cossacks. Prior to his murder he was severely tortured and partly scalped.

In addition, there are reports of murders of completely apolitical and even left-wing priests, for example:

> Priest Ivan Prigorsky, a man of extreme left convictions, was dragged out of the church on the Great and Holy Saturday, brought to the square in front of the church, where Red Army men attacked him, cursed and beat him, mutilated his face, and then killed his half-dead bleeding body.[9]

In the Diocese of Perm', north-west Urals, during a few months of Bolshevik rule in 1918 at least forty-two churchmen were murdered, according to the diocesan bishop. A Che-Ka official who defected to the Whites early in 1919, claimed that the Che-Ka had executed 550 persons in the same province in 1918; the above forty-two Orthodox churchmen represent 8 per cent of the victims in a province where the Orthodox clergy constituted no more than 0.0005 of the total population, owing to very sizeable non-Orthodox minorities there (Old Believers, Moslems, and even Shamanists and Animists). The same source reported that there were secret instructions from Yakov Sverdlov (then 'president' of Soviet Russia) in June 1918, ordering the wide use of hostages consisting of industrial entrepreneurs, members of the Liberal and Menshevik parties and clergy. 'Very many hostages were taken out but very few survived.'[10]

Bishop Germorgen's murder was undoubtedly connected to Patriarch Tikhon's 19 January (1 February) 1918 excommunication of Bolshevik leaders and the spate of religious processions which it generated. There were many more murders as a result. One of these took place in the town of Chernyi Yar on the Volga. The victim was a leading lay missionary, Lev Z. Kuntsevich. Such huge crowds arrived at the church to hear the Patriarch's encyclical that Kuntsevich was forced to proclaim it outside the church. Unfortunately the Civil War front was not far away, which made the Bolsheviks particularly sensitive to such demonstrations of implied hostility to them. Kuntsevich was arrested and publicly shot in the city square in July 1918 before the eyes of his wife who had been assured only minutes earlier by the prison authorities that her husband would soon be released.

Andronik, Archbishop of Perm', was arrested immediately after the rite of anathema was performed in his packed cathedral. Several different versions of his death circulated among the local population. A widely held story that the *chekists* first tortured him by cutting out his cheeks and plucking out his eyes and then paraded him through the streets before burying him alive, is probably related to another priest who resembled the bishop in appearance. According to the Tobolsk diocesan journal, Archbishop Andronik was last seen alive in prison in December 1919. He must have been murdered soon after that. Two Latvian chekists, later imprisoned, have stated that Andronik's arrest had the consent of a sizeable number of the local industrial workers. The Che-Ka took advantage of this rare case of popular support and followed it up with mass murders of Perm' clergy, including the vicar-bishop Feofan of Solikamsk. The All-Russian Church Sobor, still is session in Moscow at the time, requested and gained permission of the central Soviet Government to send its investigating team to Perm'. After the completion of the investigation when the team was returning to Moscow, a Red Army detachment boarded the train and massacred the bishop and all his assistants. Presumably the documents they carried with them were destroyed by the raiding party.[11]

There are numerous reports of murders committed in reprisal for sermons critical of Bolshevik terror, preaching that the laws of God are above those of men and advising Christians to give priority to the former in their choice of behaviour.

Bishop Makarii of Viaz'ma was a brilliant preacher much loved by the local population. His sermons were favourite topics of conversations in that small provincial town situated between Moscow and Smolensk. The local Bolsheviks decided to put an end to this, and one evening in the summer of 1918 he was arrested. At first they kept him in the dungeon of the local Revolutionary Committee building where he was regularly beaten and otherwise insulted. But the bishop was too popular to be disposed of locally, so he was transferred to Smolensk and there murdered with fourteen other persons in a field outside the city. At the site he was praying for the victims, and whenever he saw that one of the victims was losing heart, he approached him, blessing him with the words: 'Depart thou in peace!' A soldier who was ordered to carry out the execution later recounted the details of the murder to his doctor. The soldier was suffering from a mild case of TB; the doctor prescribed him the proper treatment and regime and was certain the man would soon recover; instead his health kept deteriorating. It was then that he confided to the doctor that he simply could not live any longer with the burden of having murdered a saint. According to his story, when the bishop approached him in the field, he gave the soldier a blessing with the words; 'My son, let thy heart not trouble thee. Carry out the will of the one who sent you here.' Then having come to the spot where he was to be shot, he prayed: 'My Father, forgive them for they do not know what they are doing. Accept my spirit in peace!' The soldier was convinced of the bishop's sanctity, for in the darkness of the night the bishop had sensed the disturbed state of the soldier caused by the realization that his 'client' was the popular bishop. Ever since then the soldier periodically saw in his dreams the bishop blessing him in silence. 'But how can I go on living in the Lord's world after this?' he asked; and within a few months of giving this account to his doctor he died of consumption.[12]

Nikodim, Bishop of Belgorod, serves as a perfect illustration of murders for purely spiritual sermons. He deliberately kept aloof from any politics, but 'in his sermons condemned acts of violence, plunder, murder; he appealed to his flock to faithfully follow the teachings of Christ and give them priority over those of men'. The local Che-Ka commandant, Saenko, personally arrested him at Christmas 1918. The bishop was so popular, however, that the population became violent in demanding his immediate release. Saenko at first gave in, warning the bishop to stop his sermons. But the same evening the bishop made his usual sermon after vespers, whereupon he was re-arrested. When a local priest's wife went to plead on the bishop's behalf, Saenko killed her on the spot. The following night the bishop was secretly murdered in the prison yard. The bishop's hair and beard were shaved off, he was disguised in a soldier's uniform and thrown into a common grave outside the town the same night. But the people found out and for a long time held daily requiems there.

The abnormal suspiciousness of the Bolsheviks, which demonstrated their insecurity, is shown by the massacre of the Astrakhan' clergy and their bishop, Leontii. This apparently happened in 1919 when Astrakhan' was in the immediate rear of the Red forces and all available space was taken up by wounded Red soldiers. The Soviet authorities at first cooperated, publishing his appeal in the local paper, which ended with the words: 'I was naked and you have clothed me, I was ill and you looked after me.' But the local Che-Ka commandant, Atarbekov, interpreted this quotation as an attempt to undermine the authority of the Soviet Government and shared these suspicions with Kirov, the chairman of the local Revolutionary Committee, who agreed with Atarbekov and gave him a *carte blanche* for terror. (Kirov's immediate boss at the time was Stalin.) Within days the bishop and most of the Astrakhan' clergy loyal to him were 'liquidated'.[13]

The Valentinov book cites numerous cases of priests killed for their sermons, of which we shall reproduce but two of the most blatant savage cases. A Kharkov priest, Mokovsky, was executed for criticizing the Bolsheviks in his sermons. When his wife came to Che-Ka asking for the release of his body for a Christian burial, the executioners grabbed her, chopped off her arms and legs, pierced her breasts, and killed her. In the Donets Coal Basin the priest, Dragozhinsky, in the village of Popasnaia was executed for a sermon on religion and atheism in which he quoted the words which Julian the Apostate pronounced on his death bed: 'Thou hast vanquished, the Galilean.' The Bolsheviks saw in this a hint that they were the apostate who would have to repent.[14]

Most common were seemingly senseless murders and desecrations of churches. The new ideology saw religion as a serious threat; its vitality maddened and perplexed the Bolsheviks, and they feared its power over the hearts and minds of the population. The Che-Ka commandant Saenko expressed this fear when he is alleged to have shouted at the time of Bishop Nikodim's arrest: 'It is owing to the priests and monks that the revolution has failed.' In 1919 the success of the revolution was still uncertain, and the Church was an important centre of resistance to Marxist ideology as they continued to warn that the preachers of the new secular paradise were false prophets and their promises were lies. It was in this context that savage brutalities against the Church were carried out by the Bolshevik gangs.

Among the most glaring illustrations of this was the case of the Metropolitan Vladimir of Kiev, the first bishop killed by the Bolsheviks. He was a man of forceful personality who had made himself unpopular with the Tsar by consistently opposing the influence of Rasputin at court. For this reason he was removed from Moscow to Kiev in 1915. Earlier he had earned the label of 'reactionary' by condemning the 1905 Revolution in opposition to the liberal Metropolitan Antonii of St Petersburg. By 1917 he was embroiled in conflicts with local Ukranian nationalists, urging him to break with Moscow, and with a Ukranian bishop living in retirement in the Monastery of the Caves who had ambitions to replace the Metropolitan and was urging the Ukranian monks to turn against him. This may account for the fact that the monastery did not actively defend the Metropolitan when, on 25 January 1918, a group of Red Army men led by a commissar came to the monastery and began to agitate the monks against M. Vladimir. The Metropolitan was severely beaten and abused by the probably intoxicated armed Bolsheviks, dragged out behind the monastery gate and shot. A passer-by witnessed the scene. The Metropolitan first asked permission to pray, knelt, raised his arms and said: 'Oh Lord, forgive my transgressions both voluntary and involuntary and accept my spirit in peace.' Then he turned toward the murderers, blessed them with the words

'May the Lord forgive you.' Shots were heard in the monastery. Next morning his body was found in a pool of blood. The body was badly mutilated, evidence of torture prior to the murder or as a form of protracted death. On 20 February 1918, *Izvestia* reported the murder, denying Soviet responsibility for the act.[15]

The murder of M. Vladimir could be explained as an act of local revolutionary vengeance against a convinced enemy of the revolution. There were many such vicious random incidents throughout the countryside. However, many murders had no apparent cause or reason, such as those which took place on 14 January 1919 in the Estonian University town of Tartu, when retreating Soviet troops arrested anyone they could find and killed twenty detainees. Among them was Bishop Platon (Kulbush) of Tallin who was discovered to have had seven bayonet gashes and four bullet holes in his body. With him were two Orthodox priests (Russian and Estonian), a Lutheran pastor and sixteen laymen.[16]

Monasteries were the targets of Bolshevik terror as early as 1918. One of the first to be plundered was the Holy Mountain Monastery near Kharkov. In a nearby *skete* in the village of Gorokhova a monk Izrail' was murdered for refusing to hand over the keys of the *skete* cellars. In the same area a religious procession was attacked when it rested for the night on its way: two priests, a deacon, the owner of the cottage where these clerics stayed, and the landlord's daughter were attacked and killed in the night.

One Red soldier wrote to his family that having entered the Don region in February 1918, the Reds were killing priests left, right and centre: 'I also shot a priest. We are continuing to chase these devils and killing them like dogs.'

Prior to killing an 80-year-old monk-priest, Amvrosi, the Reds savagely beat him with rifle-butts. Fr. Dimitri, a priest in the same city, was brought to a cemetery, undressed, and when he tried to cross himself before execution, a soldier chopped off his right arm. An old innocent priest who tried to prevent the execution of a peasant was beaten and sliced up with swords. In the Holy Saviour Monastery a Red Army detachment arrested and killed its 75-year-old abbot by first completely scalping him and then chopping off his head. In the Kherson Province a priest was found to have been killed by crucifixion. In a Kuban' Cossack village an eighty-year-old retired priest was forced to put on female dress, brought to the village square and ordered to dance. When he refused, the Reds hanged him on the spot.[17]

Whenever chekists arrived in a village they almost invariably vented their rage on the priest. It did not matter to them whether he was merely a harmless old man, or whether he was the local benefactor, like Fr. Yakov Vladimirov in the Kuban' Cossack village of Plotavy. He had raised his parishioners' standard of living considerably above that of their neighbours by teaching them advanced methods of agriculture and bee-keeping. His only 'crime' was his popularity and spiritual charisma. One day a group of chekists arrived at the priest's home asking him for overnight hospitality. They told Fr. Yakov they wished to discuss some business with the village community (*mir*) the following day, and asked him to spend the night at the village school, so that the village would not think that the chekists were corrupted by the priest during the night. The priest complied. The villagers, suspecting that all was not well, protected him at the school by a bodyguard of sixty persons. In the morning the chekists politely thanked the priest's wife for her hospitality and went to the meeting. After it they walked out with the priest. The villagers followed but soon saw a machine-gun pointed at them by an armed detachment, and a freshly dug ditch. The priest realized his end was coming and crossed himself. The chief chekist took him by the hair and shot him in the face over the ditch. Another chekist grabbed the priest's wife and her 15-year-old boy. The mother was shot before the boy's eyes. Then the chekist looked at the boy and said: 'I don't think you should live having seen all this. Sit down and take your boots off.' The boy did as he was told and was also shot. But there was another, 12-year-old, son. The chekists mistook another boy for him and shot him. The real son, Vania, was warned by the villagers and hidden away.

Many of the murders were plain exercises in sadism: for instance, the Voronezh *chekists*, as a punishment for praying for the victory of the Whites, did not hesitate to boil seven nuns in a kettle of tar.

The accumulation of such acts of terror across the country moved the Arkhangelsk City Union of Orthodox Clergy and Laity to appeal to the Paris Peace Conference for intercession on behalf of the Church in Russia. The appeal was based on a document which they had presented to the Provisional Government of North Russia (headed by the socialist Chaikovsky) on 19 April 1919. It stated among other things that:

> The regime of people's commissars not only seals up temples, but also turns them into tea-rooms, army barracks and even cinemas. Drunken orgies take place in desecrated churches. The clergy is submitted to abuse and tortures ... Fr. Shangin was murdered and his body cut up into shreds ... Arch-priest Surtsov was submitted to beatings for several days, then he was shot and his body thrown into Pechora River. In the town of Pechora an old retired priest, Rasputin, was first tied to a telegraph pole, then shot dead and given to the dogs to eat. In Seletsk Afanasii Smirnov, a psalmist, was executed for having served a funeral litany over the body of a dead French soldier.[18]

Other acts of terror against the church were perpetrated in connection with the nationalization of church property by the decree of 23 January (5 February) 1918. Many times Red troops opened fire on the crowds surrounding their church in its defence. They also fired on the religious processions ordered by the Patriarch and the All-Russian Sobor as a protest against the persecution of the Church and as demonstration of support for the Church. Many thousands were killed in this way, especially in the spring of 1918. There are well-documented reports of shooting down religious processions in Voronezh, Shatsk (Tambov Province), and Tula (where thirteen people were killed and many wounded, including Bishop Kornilii).[19]

The Church was harassed in the performance of its religious function. For instance, having secularized the registration of marriage and divorce, local Soviet governments began to force the clergy to remarry those whose earlier church marriages had been annulled by civil divorce. The church was only willing to remarry those whose divorce conformed to the religious canons. This was in opposition to the Soviet position that 'Clergymen of all Confessions ... may not refuse a religious wedding to those who wish to have one after the conclusion of the obligatory civil contract.'[20] This contradicted the Soviet decree on the separation of Church and State. The Church was finally relieved of these pressures when the Patriarch and his Synod signed a declaration in May 1920, relegating all *formal* marriage and divorce proceedings to the civil authorities.[21]

Religious persecution was not limited to the Orthodox Church, although it was the most prominent target. The official pretext was that the Orthodox Church had been the State Church in Tsarist Russia, and thus was a 'legacy of the reactionary past', and officially it was the reactionary class enemies who were being persecuted, not the Church as such. Obviously other religions of the Empire could not be suppressed in this context, but as champions of an alien ideology they were all ideological enemies of socialism in the long run. Many instances of brutality directed against Roman Catholic and Protestant clergy can be cited. For example, a Roman Catholic priest, Krapiwnicki, celebrating the Corpus Christi service in Stavropol in 1918, was dragged out of his church during the service and brought to the local Red commandant; he would have been executed had it not been for the intercession of the local Polish consul.[22] Archbishop de Ropp of the Roman Catholic Diocese of Mogilev was arrested in April 1919, although he was one of the most moderate of the Roman bishops in Russia and had advocated loyalty to the new regime and acceptance of its laws. In November of the same year he was exchanged by agreement with the Polish Government for Radek, the Polish-Jewish communist then under arrest in Poland.[23] De Ropp's arrest was an act of retaliation for the Papal protest against the persecution of the Orthodox Church in Russia.

In view of the fact that the non-Orthodox faiths had enjoyed only limited rights in pre-revolutionary Russia and this could have been expected to bear a grudge – against the Orthodox Church, the messages of sympathy to the latter as a Church suffering particular Bolshevik persecutions, issued by the Roman Catholic, Evangelical and Lutheran Churches, as well as by the Jewish Rabbinate of Petrograd and the Muslim Imam, gave a significant moral support to the Orthodox.[24] All of them speak only about the sufferings of the Orthodox Church, not of their own, which indicates that indeed there was no comparison between the magnitude of the persecution to which the Orthodox Church was subjected and the hardships endured by other religions in the country. If one bears in mind that less than two years earlier all these religions had been under various degrees of pressure from the Tsarist Government, where the Orthodox Church was the established State Church, it becomes clear that they were of the opinion that the sufferings of the Orthodox Church after the revolution went beyond the hardships they had suffered under the Old Regime. Yet, as Valentinov's book bears witness, the Bolshevik treatment of the different faiths varied from place to place. In Kharkov the two men in charge of religious affairs in the Soviet Executive Committee were two Jews, Kagan and Rutgaiter, who forbade the clergy to baptize, wed or bury anyone without the express permission of these two Bolsheviks:

> For non-fulfilment of this order the clergy faced the Military-revolutionary Tribunal [court martial]. Its strict fulfilment meant that infants died unbaptized and corpses decayed while the relatives waited for permission to bury them in church.[25]

The report on the situation in south-eastern Ukraine (the Lugansk-Konets area) states: 'The Bolsheviks did not bother other confessions except in the case of the Jewish "bourgeoise" who were forced to perform communal work on Saturdays.'[26] In contrast, the report on the North-Caucasian area (the provinces of Stavropol and Black Sea) says: 'The Red Army violated not only the Orthodox clergy, but also those of other religions as well.'[27] Returning to Lugansk, there is an interesting account of how the Bolsheviks in the City Soviet suggested converting some Orthodox churches into cinemas and civic centres. When one of the members of the Soviet, apparently in an attempt to save the churches, suggested converting the local synagogue into a public bath, the whole question was shelved by the presidium, and the Orthodox churches were spared.[28] It would therefore be safe to conclude that while the attack on the Orthodox Church during the War Communism was a concerted action of the Soviet Regime, in addition to individual actions of local Bolshevik forces, attacks on other religions were individual acts of local Bolsheviks.

An official Church source of that time gave the following incomplete data on the persecution of the Church between June 1918 and January 1919:

The Early Persecutions, 1917–21

Killed: one metropolitan, eighteen bishops, 102 priests, 154 deacons, 94 monks and nuns;
Imprisoned: ... Four bishops, 211 priests, both married and monastic;
sequestered real estate from 718 parishes and fifteen monasteries;
closed 94 churches and 26 monasteries;
desecrated 14 churches and nine chapels;
forbidden eighteen religious processions;
dispersed by force 41 religious processions;
interrupted church services with insults to religious feelings in 22 cities and 96 villages.

These data do not include the Volga and Kama Regions and several other parts of the country.'[29]

By 1921 the figure of liquidated monasteries and convents rose to 573,[30] more than twenty times the January 1919 figure. Monasteries were being liquidated on the pretext that they were parasitic communities. The Patriarch tried to offset this argument by turning most of the remaining monasteries into monastic working communes, on the model of the voluntary Orthodox Christian agrarian communes which were in existence long before the revolution.[31] The regime responded by accusing the Church of attempting to create her own 'state and her separate economy within the worker-peasant state', and forbade the creation of Church communes.[32] The aim was obviously to deprive the Church of any stable institutions. Monasteries, in any form, were particularly undesirable from the regime's point of view, owing to their traditional spiritual and intellectual prestige, and their role as centres of mass pilgrimages. Potentially they could become co-ordinators and centres of religious and generally Christian action (similar to the monasteries of contemporary Poland). Owing to the peculiar aura of the monasteries, it would be wrong to extrapolate from the numbers of their closure (its rate in the total number of monastic communities exceeding 50 per cent) to other aspects of church life, and individual parish churches. In the process of the liquidation of monastic communities many brutalities, murders and mass executions of monks and nuns took place. Thus, the number of clergy killed for their faith in the period from 1919 to 1921 must certainly have exceeded by far the incomplete estimate of 330 clergy and monastics killed in the first year of communist persecutions.

Although, as we have seen, the Church had declared her neutrality in the Civil War and her neutral loyalty to the Soviet government as early as 1919, she had tried to normalize relations with the new state by accepting the official government explanation that the central Soviet government bore no responsibility for the above 'local atrocities'. Later Soviet authors would admit central responsibility for the early persecutions. Yaroslavsky justified them by the fraudulent charge that Patriarch Tikhon had given his blessing to the anti-Bolshevik forces: 'We fought with arms and weapons against the church which used weapons against us.' And he held the whole national Church responsible for the wide participation of those local clergy in White occupied territory who fought with the White Army, and formed the so-called 'Jesus regiments' made up entirely of clergy.[33] These were acts of local initiatives for which the Patriarch bore no responsibility. Second, none of the documented acts of brutalities towards the clergy and believers related to members of these regiments. Third, only a few victims had given even oral support to anti-Bolshevik forces. Fourth, 'fighting with arms' does not mean slicing up unarmed people, scalping and torturing them, or killing priests' wives and children.

How did the churches and most of the clergy and monastics survive this first onslaught? Some answer to this question can be had from the following passage relating to the Lugansk area:

> The population of the village of Avdeevka protected their church and clergy from plunder. Likewise, in response to the decree on the separation of Church and state these villagers resolved at their communal meetings to sustain the church and its clergy by dues and pledges. In the village of Grishino the population ignored the Soviet ban on a Te-Deum service, subsequently physically protecting their clergy from Bolshevik reprisals. In the city of Iuzovka (currently Donetsk) the miners and industrial workers ... called a public meeting even before the Bolsheviks entered the city, and issued a resolution that if the Bolsheviks showed disrespect for the clergy and the Church, the workers would rebel. The

The Early Persecutions, 1917—21

resolution was handed to the Bolsheviks, whereby the Church and the clergy were saved.[34]

The same report mentions that in other places the population was so cowed by the terror that it remained passive, only secretly grieving over the brutalities against their Church. In some cases weak clergymen were too ready to fulfil any orders from Bolshevik bosses.[35]

In the major cities it was the co-operation and action of the laity which saved the churches there. In Petrograd in January 1918 Alexandra Kollontai, the Bolshevik commissar for social welfare, sent armed troops to the Alexander-Nevski Monastery to confiscate it, allegedly for social welfare purposes. Such huge crowds gathered to defend this religious centre that even fire opened by the Red sailors, killing a priest, could not disperse them. Following this incident a religious procession with Metropolitan Veniamin of Petrograd at its head marched through Petrograd with several hundred thousand people participating. Thereafter Leagues of Laymen began to be formed in many cities to defend the Church. Over 60 000 volunteers joined the league in Petrograd, and a similar number in Moscow. This represented 6 to 10 per cent of the (then reduced) total population in each city. The leagues were particularly active in preventing state agents from taking over monastery buildings which were now officially nationalized. According to contemporary Soviet press reports, in the four months of February to May 1918 alone 687 persons were killed in the clashes between these leagues and the government.[36]

These *ad hoc* actions by laymen saved the Church in those years; in contrast to the disenfranchised clergy, the leagues consisted of working people who could not be easily ignored by the Soviets.

In conclusion, while large sections of the population were relatively indifferent to their national Church, where the population stood up united in defence of their faith, their resistance on behalf of the Church was sufficiently large-scale to protect a substantial number of churches and clergy and some 30 per cent of the monasteries and convents from destruction or liquidation. Yet the fact that in so many places Bolshevik attacks on the Church were not opposed indicates a considerable religious decline. The last Russian army chaplains confirm that when the February Revolution made soldiers' attendance at services and acceptance of the Sacraments voluntary, both declined from 100 per cent to 10.[37] Later, abhorrence of Bolshevik atrocities resulted in a noticeable increase in Church attendance beginning from the lowest point in 1916–17.

In the context of persecutions in the early years of the Revolution there is very little to be said about religious denominations other than the Orthodox. The leader of the Russian Evangelicals at that time, Ivan Prokhanov, wrote that the Bolsheviks:

> declared their opposition to the ... Greek Orthodox Church, but generally speaking in the beginning they showed a friendly spirit to the Evangelical movement and various other religious organizations and sects ... which were persecuted under the Czar's regime.[38]

An expert on the history of Russian and Soviet Moslems distinguishes four periods in the Soviet Moslem policies. The first one, 1917 to 1920, was marked by broad tolerance and included the Soviet Government's appeal of 24 November 1917 'To All Toiling Moslems of Russia and the East'; promising them full religious rights and support in the new socialist state.[39]

2 Contempt and Hate Propaganda, 1919–39

The beginning of the systematization and centralization of Soviet antireligious propaganda should be attributed to the birth in 1919 of the first specialized antireligious monthly, *The Revolution and the Church* (*Revolutsiia i tserkov'*, henceforth *RiTs*), published by the People's Commissariat of Justice,[1] followed in 1922 by the short-lived *Science and Religion* (*Nauka i religiia*, henceforth *NiR*), edited by the renegade priest Gorev-Galkin, and specializing in condemning the Church for resisting the state confiscation of sacramental objects from the churches, allegedly to alleviate the famine.[2] It was replaced in the same year by *Bezbozhnik* (The Godless), a wide-circulation paper at first published thrice monthly, later becoming a weekly.[3]

The contempt-and-hate campaign in the very first issues of *RiTs* attempted to represent the Church, the Orthodox Church in particular, as a fraud, and to sow division by singling out the Orthodox Church for attack while presenting the Protestant sects (the Churches formerly oppressed by the tsars) as hard-working and loyal, and Moslems as supporting the Soviets.[4]

One of the first signs was the government decree of 1 March 1919 (reconfirmed in August 1920), regarding 'the complete liquidation of the cult of corpses and mummies', ordering the opening-up and public exposure of the saints' relics. The Soviet media was particularly eager to present the relics of St Sergius of Radonezh of the fourteenth century, Russia's most revered national saint, as fraudulent. It claimed that there was nothing but cotton-wool, hair, rotten bones and dust in his shrine. Witnessing this,

> Believers no longer weep, don't fall into fits of hysteria, and don't hold a grudge against the Soviet government anymore. They see there has been no blasphemy... Only an age-old fraud has been made naked in the eyes of the nation.[5]

Quite the opposite story concerning the same relics comes from the monks of St Sergius-Trinity Monastery, the home of these relics, who were present when the shrine was opened (a learned monk, a bishop in retirement, and the rector of the seminary at that monastery). According to them, when the relics were exposed the partly decayed vestments and the pieces of cotton-wool which the pilgrims traditionally leave on the relics to be taken back home to rub and bless family members, especially in sickness, were removed; underneath, there was the excellently preserved body of the saint. The masses of believers who had crowded the church fell on their knees in prayer. Outside the church the mobs pulled down from his horse Comrade Shpitsberg, the Bolshevik commander of the nationalized monastery, and beat him up, along with the soldier who had lied to the pilgrims, saying that the relics had rotted away. Another, similar, episode concerning the relics of two saints in the city of Vladimir (twelfth and thirteenth centuries respectively) led the doctor who had acted as the medical state witness to a reconfirmation of his faith, according to his own testimony.[6]

Nevertheless, there were cases of finding nothing but cloth, rotten bones and dust in place of relics. Such was the case, if Soviet official versions are to be believed, of an eighteenth-century saint, Tikhon of Zadonsk, and some Novgorodian saints. The typical *RiTs*'s moral after one of such reports was: 'Thus the spiritual fathers have been deceiving the nation . . .' But a few issues later it reports a trial of the Novgorod clergy including Bishop Alexii, the future Patriarch of Russia, accused of having purged the Novgorod relics of all external objects prior to the government commission inspection. At the trial Alexii stated that most of the relics survived only in the form of scattered bones, and, to the surprise of his judges, confirmed that the Church did not teach that the bodies of saints must necessarily be immune to decay, and conversely, 'non-corruption of the body is in itself not a sign of sainthood'.[7]

Toleration of miracles would have meant a tacit admission that there was a sphere of supernatural or at least rationally inexplicable phenomena, inconsistent with Marxian materialism. According to a reliable witness, manifestations of the supernatural had often occurred in the early postrevolutionary years in the families of fanatical communists actively hostile to the Church, where some family members were practising Christians. The most common reports of miracles at that time concerned the sudden renovation of a family icon: an old darkened icon with a hardly discernible image, would suddenly, before the very eyes of the communist, begin to shine with fresh colours as if it had just been painted. This often led some atheistic communists back to the Church. The source comments: 'The Lord clearly responded to the prayers of the repenting and suffering Russian people, manifesting Himself to them.'

The same witness, Leontii, a Kiev monk with a graduate theological degree who had become a bishop during the Second World War and ended his days as the Orthodox bishop of Chile, reported other miraculous manifestations appearing publicly to thousands of people and causing violent reactions from the Soviets:

> the most amazing was the renovation of the Sretenskaia church at the Sennoi Marketplace. The church had two goldplated domes ... which with time became completely tarnished as if covered by a grey paint ... Then one autumn evening a Jew living near-by saw such burning brightness of the long-forgotten gold of the domes, that he thought the church was on fire and called for ... the fire brigade. But instead of fire it was found that it was the sudden brightening of the domes. The light shone and moved in patches from place to place on the domes as if tongues of fire. By next morning there was already a huge crowd in front of the church. The police were helpless ... The news reached me by noon. I hopped on a tramway, but a long distance before the church the tram had to stop because of the crowds. With difficulty I reached the place on foot and watched the wonderful miracle for several hours. The progression of renovation of the gold plate continued for three days ... There arose a mood of unusual general religious euphoria in the city. It was a great moral boost for the believers ... and a catastrophe for the antireligious propaganda ... The following day ... two articles in a local newspaper, one of

them signed by members of the Academy of Sciences, stated that the phenomenon was caused by a rare air wave containing a peculiar electric discharge . . .

Later it became known . . . that the GPU forced the academics to sign the article. If the renovation phenomenon is natural, then why were the gold-plated market billboards not similarly renovated? . . . Several months later the Soviets dynamited the church.

The author described a similar renovation of both the domes outside and of the frescoes inside another church in Kiev. And again, shortly afterwards this church (of the Holy Jordan) was dynamited.

The other event which, according to Bishop Leontii, became known in the whole Ukraine and other parts of the Soviet Union, occurred in a village near Vinnitsa. When by order of the provincial Soviet its representative came with a detachment of mounted police to the village of Kalinovka to close a local church, he was met by hostile crowds. The crowds were too big for the police to force their way, and they retreated. Not far from the church there stood a traditional Crucifix at a crossroads. The retreating policemen, frustrated by their failure, suddenly let out a volley of fire at the Crucifix:

> Of all the fired bullets only one hit the target: Christ's collarbone. Suddenly blood gushed forth from the wound. One of the firing policeman lost control of himself and fell off the horse. Others took off. The crowd fell on their knees and began to pray before the bleeding Jesus. The news spread, and by evening there were already several thousand pilgrims. In the following few days detachments of police came twice with the order to hack the Crucifix down, but each time they returned without fulfilling the order. They said an inexplicable force prevented them from approaching the Crucifix. Articles in the local newspaper tried to explain the phenomenon by claiming that there had been an accumulation of water in the wooden cross behind the metallic figure of Christ. Once the bullet hit the metal the water, having acquired the rusty colour of the metal, began to seep through.

But the blood from the Crucifix was running for several days. Huge crowds of people were coming to the Crucifix, bringing their own crosses and setting them up next to it. People came in processions and prayed before the Crucifix, dipping their kerchiefs into the miraculous blood. Day and night religious singing was heard and burning candles were seen on the spot, although priests were absent for fear of reprisals. Many atheists rediscovered their faith in God there.

Needless to say, at the very first opportunity the Soviets destroyed the bleeding Crucifix and all the adjacent crosses.

The Soviet account of the same events was quite different. Unable to explain the renovations of icons, a Soviet text simply calls them fraudulent machinations of priests and *kulaks* to dupe the poor peasants. The Kalinovka bleeding-Cross story is left unexplained. It is simply stated that a commission of experts produced a report that the dark fluid coming out of the bullet hole in Christ's rib was not blood. The story depicts the pilgrims as drunkards, good-for-nothings and illiterate fools. Allegedly the Cross simply disappeared after the churchmen and other interested elements had made enough money from the pilgrims. The mass kissing of the Crucifix was said to result in several thousand outbreaks of syphilis and mass robberies. The syphilis story's purpose is clearly to show the believers as moral scum of the nation.[8]

Variations on the same theme were attacks on theology and the seminaries, perhaps to give a rationale for the regime's continuing refusal to allow the Russian Orthodox Church to reopen theological schools. A 1923 *RiTs* editorial claimed that 'it is hard to imagine anything more repulsive than these hundreds and thousands of corrupt young men and those who are being corrupted to the marrow of their bones scoffing at the believing simpletons'. The article maintained that none of the seminarians, whether Orthodox or Catholic, believed in the teachings which they used in order to exploit the dark masses.[9]

But in the early stages the Soviets preferred to divide and rule, attacking primarily the hierarchy of the Orthodox Church as a tsarist, reactionary and counter-revolutionary legacy. Thus one report says how a Soviet propagandist for the Church–State separation came to a village church, and gaining the approval of the majority of parishioners addressed them with a speech attacking the Church as an organization in which the clergy had been usurping power ever since the Nicean Council's resolution that no laymen should teach in church. He attacked the clergy which he claimed 'enslaved the lay believers', and his appeal was not to close and discontinue churches but to take the churches over from the clergy.[10] Another report praises a rural parish which refused to accept a priest sent to them by their bishop but elected as their priest a former psalmist 'who stands for the Soviet power'. Their resolution (7 January 1920) stated that the parish did not recognize the authority of any patriarchs or bishops over them and would physically defend their elected priest. They had even addressed a letter to Lenin to that effect, and their right to control the temple and run it was subsequently confirmed by the People's Commissariat of Justice.[11]

The first (and only?) issue of *NiR* opened with an editorial condemning Patriarch Tikhon and his clergy for having 'sold their teacher', Jesus, 'to the tsar and capitalists'. The journal implicitly supports the Renovationist-Living Church schism by declaring: 'Everything that is alive in the church has risen against them', that is, against the Patriarch and those who remained loyal to him. And indeed the leading priests and ideologists of the schism – Kalinovsky, Krasnitsky, Vvedensky, Belkov – are found among the contributors to this antireligious publication, which passed itself off as being only anti-Tikhonite, on the grounds of the Patriarch's resistance to the state confiscations of sacramental church objects, allegedly to rescue the famine-stricken.[12]

But we know from Lenin's secret letter to the Politburo that his intention to confiscate church valuables was far from philanthropic. He wanted to provoke a major conflict with the Church, using the famine situation in order to represent the Church as a heartless, selfish institution, and thus to decrease her national prestige. Hence his ban on any Church participation either on the famine-aid committees or in the money and valuables collection campaigns.[13]

To give the impression that it only separated the sheep from the goats, *NiR* printed the cartoon opposite, showing a compassionate parish priest handing a chalice over to a starving old man on the left, then being anathematized by the Patriarch on the right. This was followed by a letter from a priest favouring the giving-away of all church treasures,

A humble village priest gives away the church gold to the starving one.

who be Q. ought to anathematized?

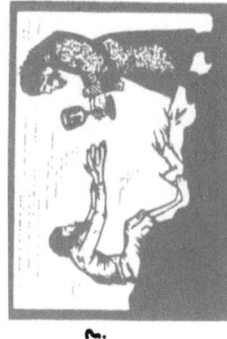

But the 'Princes of the Church' anathematize the poor priest for his love for the common folk.

including the sacramental vessels. The letter quotes relevant canons which forbid use of the vessels for personal secular purposes, but not for charity. All Church fathers and the official book of Church law, the letter continues, say that the Church has no use for gold and 'The wealth of the Church is the wealth of the paupers'. This, apparently renovationist, priest condemns the Patriarch, that is the Church establishment, as if to support the trial (reported in the same journal) of fifty-four Moscow clergy and laity for offering resistance to the state requisition teams. The report tries to tarnish the reputation of the Patriarch, who was brought to court as a witness. But the courage of Patriarch Tikhon was apparent when he took all the responsibility upon himself:

> It is I who wrote the order [to withhold the sacramental objects from the requisition brigades] ... I personally composed it ... Why should it matter who helped me if I am responsible? I've signed it, and I am responsible.

At the end of his statement the Patriarch disclosed the reason for his resistance: 'Had the Church ordered the giving-up of the treasures, then it would not have been an act of sacrilege.' As we know from Lenin's letter and the consequences of the confiscations, the Patriarch, quite justifiably, did not trust the good intentions of the state, especially after it had forcibly closed the Church's 'committee in aid of the famine-stricken' and had forbidden the Church to continue the collections or to undertake any other actions in their favour.[14]

The same journal published a pseudo-document, allegedly the Patriarch's secret encyclical addressed to all Russian bishops. It appeared under the heading 'From an Apocrypha File', and there is a note in minuscule print at the bottom of the page explaining that apocrypha means 'not a genuine work but recommended by the Church for pious reading'; but the average reader would hardly look at the note at the bottom of the page. The fraudulent text, written in the high Russo-Slavonic style of many church documents, is full of monarchist zeal and praise for the White émigré clergy (the Karlovcians); it condemns and excommunicates all those who would even voluntarily donate any church utensils or vestments for the famine-stricken. The gist of the concoction is that the Church is indifferent to the suffering and deaths of millions, even happy about the prospect that this economic catastrophe may weaken the Soviets and bring the day of restoration of monarchy closer. Instead of giving his signature as the real author of the parody, Mikhail Gorev calls himself only a 'copier', while placing Patriarch Tikhon's name as the author. The aim of the piece is obvious: to confuse the readers, to leave the impression that such a document was indeed written by Patriarch Tikhon, and to intensify the rift between the Renovationists and the Patriarchal Church.[15]

This article at least admits that it is not genuine. The leader of the League of the Militant Godless (LMG) did not do even that when he deliberately lied to his audience at the LMG's Second Congress that 'The Church ... under the leadership of Patriarch Tikhon blessed the counter-revolutionary rebellion against the Soviet Power.' The truth was that Tikhon had refused to give the blessings to the Whites or Reds, because the Church could not participate in a divisive fratricidal war.[16]

By the late 1920s, Soviet antireligious propaganda became less selective in its attack on the Church. In 1927, on the eve of the wholesale assault on all faiths, it began to publish a series of articles with insulting and vulgar attacks against the very same Renovationists whom it had presented so sympathetically only five years earlier. Now they were particularly attacked for their duplicity, for modernizing their appearance, their ritual, and for pretending to be friends of the Soviet social system so that their 'product' will sell:

> The petty commercial bourgeoisie wants to live ... to enjoy savoury foods, to make use of every cleavage ... in the Soviet system in such a way as to make a profit without falling into the hands of the GPU ... It is for this 'delicate business' that it needs a god ... to make black look white.[17]

This is followed by articles denouncing in equally vulgar terms Judaic and Moslem reformism, parallelling the Renovationist Schism in the Orthodox Church, and presenting them all as cheaters, greedy money-makers, capitalists' henchmen, enemies of the working class. The context of the attack is that the reformists' potential may be more dangerous to the Soviet system owing to the fact that their hostility and extraneousness to the 'new society' is less obvious.[18]

The antireligious literature of the time often attacked

Christianity, in particular Orthodox Christianity, for allegedly fomenting anti-semitism;[19] yet their anti-Judaic propaganda has a poorly concealed anti-semitic bias in full accord with Marx's original definition of Jews as a commercial stratum in capitalist societies. A cartoon in *Koms. pravda* depicts a Jewish shopkeeper and a rabbi discussing a deal. The caption reads: 'A good private shop and a good commission strengthen the Lord's presence in the heart of a man.' There was an assault on private enterprise in 1929 and these cartoons were obviously meant as hate-and-contempt propaganda. An example of this is the cartoon of a Jewish-looking businessman leading one-eyed Jehovah on a leash, walking hand-in-hand with a tsarist gendarmerie officer, the inference being that a Jew and a capitalist are synonymous.[20]

The campaign against clergy, singling out for attack only the clergy of the established Patriarchal Orthodox Church with an obvious aim to break first the spine of the national Church, gradually became less differentiated by the mid-1920's, followed by a general assault on the clergy of all religions, beginning roughly in 1927. The leitmotif of the early attacks is the connection of the Orthodox Church with monarchy and the ruling classes. After Patriarch Tikhon's encyclical on political neutrality and disengagement of the Church, Soviet propaganda took the line that the encyclical was only camouflage, and that the real essence of the Church is 'belief in an autocratic bourgeois-aristocratic power', which the clergy simply dares not admit openly to the toilers. The propaganda then began to make ample use of the statements of some hierarchs and the church press on the territory held by the Whites, and later of the monarchist right-wing statements of the émigré clergy of the so-called Karlovci Schism (in Yugoslavia), largely concealing the fact that this schism had been disowned and declared illegal by both Patriarch Tikhon and his successors.[21] However, after the Orthodox Church had gone out of her way to assure the regime of her loyalty, to replace the qualified civic loyalty of Patriarch Tikhon by the wholesome and positive loyalty of Metropolitan Sergii (1927), A. Lunin, one of the leaders of the LMG, ridiculed Metropolitan Sergii for turning 'Jesus into a Marxist'. This was a sneering comment on Sergii's enforced 1930 interview with foreign correspondents in which he denied any religious persecution and stated

Contempt and Hate Propaganda, 1919–39

Bourgeois: Jehovah, you must gather your whole people, find your lost children who are hiding here somewhere. The colonel will help us. (*Bezbozhnik u stanka*, no. 1, 1924)

that Christianity shared many social goals with Marxism. Lunin takes to task local atheists swayed by the 'trick' of Church loyalty and tolerating clergy activities in reopening the formerly shut churches.

Needless to say, the term used for all clergy by the late 1920s became the pejorative 'pop', which in the early 1920s was applied only to the clergy loyal to the Patriarch. Lunin called for continued vigilance and resistance to the 'pops' and for an end to public debates with the clergy on religion and atheism. Otherwise, 'not only all closed churches will be reopened, but hundreds of new ones built'. Apparently public debates between believers and atheists, so fashionable in the early-to-mid-1920s, began to alarm the atheistic establishment, which by the end of the decade was seeking excuses to end them. The 'scholarly' and 'methodological' *Antireligioznik* found no other logical argument against the debates except that they allegedly 'do not satisfy public demand. The godless masses are trying to solidify their proletarian ideological positions by profound study and serious preparation', which apparently could be undermined by effective arguments of the clergy, for the article attacked the appearances of a local Renovationist bishop and preferred talks by sectarian deserters to atheism. And then suddenly the article turned to an attack on Baptists, labelling their leaders and activists 'lackeys of capitalism', traitors refusing to bear arms on the side of the Soviets in the forthcoming final war against capitalism.[22]

Only a few years earlier no less a person that Piotr Krasikov, the editor of *RiTs* and the head of the Commissariat of Justice Department of Cults, sympathetically called a sectarian group 'Toiling Sectarians' in an editorial which dealt with the New Israel sect. This sect had resolved at its 1922 congress to support the Soviet regime as aiming at communism, and to amalgamate all members of the sect in agricultural communes as a practical base for strengthening the cause of the 'future All-Russian Communist Congress'. Krasikov's comment on the sectarians and their resolutions was that although the idealistic religious *Weltanschauung* obscures their full vision of Marxism, Communism and materialism, these sectarian peasants were instinctively heading in the right direction:

> The ideals of the sectarians ... have only vaguely ... reflected their real class and mankind's interests, inasmuch as all religions do in the positive part of their teachings.

He welcomed their decision to support and, particularly, their decision to establish farming communes, which initiative, in his opinion, the Soviet Government should fully support.[23]

However, in 1929 the central organ of LMG, reporting on an agricultural co-operative of a priestless Old Believer sect, demanded that the sectarians be expelled from farm management;[24] and in 1931 *Antireligioznik* presented absolutely all forms of behaviour and policies of the Churches and sects as insincere, aimed at subverting the Soviet system, whether openly anti-Soviet or pro-Soviet. The above sect of New Israel and its communistic agricultural communes, like those of other sects, are condemned as but a manoeuvre to adapt to the new conditions. The Central Council of Baptists' statements that Jesus was 'the founder of the teachings of contemporary communist parties', and the same ideas echoed by the Adventists are, according to the article, but insincere attempts to curry favour with the Soviet system. The peasant anti-alcoholic Churikov sect (which remained on the fringes of and in communion with the main-line Orthodox Church) and its communes in the Leningrad, Moscow and other regions, had portraits of Marx and Lenin placed next to icons. All this was declared by the article to be devious masks whereby the religions try:

> to retain their influence over the toiling masses ... and to conceal their real counterrevolutionary essence ... But all these attempts are in vain ... the toiling masses will tear off this mask and will put an end to this masquerade of 'pops' and sectarians. The duty to the godless is more forcefully to unmask the class essence of religion, to speed up the final liquidation of this sworn enemy of the workers and of socialist construction.[25]

If this is an ostensibly 'scholarly-methodological journal', what can then be expected of the mass atheistic press, aimed at heating up a hate campaign against religion? For example, the illustrated fortnightly *Bezbozhnik* in its treatment of the Churikov peasant teetotallers admits that their commune is highly productive and wealthy, but claims that this is achieved by 'unpaid slave labour' of the sect members. Nothing could be further from the truth. Churikov was deeply loved among workers and peasants, and especially their wives, for his effective anti-alcoholic drive.

A petty-merchant from the Volga area, Churikov, with the support of a grand duchess and the Metropolitan of Petersburg, began to set up working Christian communes of sobriety in the vicinity of Petersburg. He had a particular gift for curing literally thousands of alcoholics by prayer, sermon, and appeal for love of God and man and working for the communal good. In 1916 his commune was one of the first agricultural settlements in Russia to acquire a tractor. His agricultural techniques were modern and highly productive. Everybody prospered and by 1927 his fourteen agricultural communes contained over 10 000 people. He preached 'Christ's socialism' and practised what he preached. It was apparently the inability of the state collective farms to compete with Churikov's communes morally and economically that caused the mounting attacks against him, his eventual execution in 1930 along with his chief lieutenants, and the dissolution of his communes along with all other religious farming communities in the country. Prior to that, the Soviet press had led a campaign of slander against the saintly old man, depicting him as a lecher and glutton, enjoying women and luxury foods, while the rest of the commune was forced to fast.[26]

Once collective farms replaced the religious communes and the state forced the latter into liquidation, Soviet propaganda transformed the same sectarians and other religious commune-builders from prosperous builders of agricultural associations into destroyers of the same communes. In one case, we are told, upon the dissolution of their commune the Churikovites all joined a newly formed collective farm. They managed to have their former leaders elected administrators of the *kolkhoz*, but then they began to sabotage the harvest, leaving crops under the snow in the fields, feeding grain to the pigs, etc. With 'the help of religion' the sectarian *kolkhoz* administrators were teaching their members to pilfer farm property and equipment. Thus, from scrupulous and hardworking farmers and honest peasants (see Krasikov above) the sectarians were 'transformed' into wreckers of Soviet collectivization. Similar allegations were made regarding Orthodox and other clergy, for allegedly penetrating collective farms and wrecking them and their harvests from within.[27] The year is very convenient – 1933, the year of the massive famine; so, it was very convenient to blame the religions for that state-organized famine.

We may remember how Krasikov was talking about 'the

toiling sectarians', the sectarian peasants with their instinctive sense of justice ... Well, eight years later sectarianism was transformed by Soviet propaganda into an agency of 'the Russian bourgeoisie'. Similarly the alleged hero and patron of the sectarians, Kerensky, the head of the Provincial Government who had abolished the death penalty and released all even vaguely political prisoners, was transformed into 'Kerensky the executioner'.[28]

It was at least as early as 1925 that the Soviets began broadening their antireligious front, gradually embracing the Renovationists and the sectarians in their overall attack. Apparently they thought that the Orthodox Church had been institutionally sufficiently weakened through the schisms and terror to allow a more general antireligious assault. On the other hand, work had to be found for the newly founded League of the Godless. The sectarians began to feel insecure in the new climate. In contrast to the Orthodox, who had at first tried to take a stance of benevolent neutrality towards the Soviet State, and even when forced to declare total loyalty in 1927 still continued to stress the Church's incompatibility with Marxist communism, the sectarians responded to the first assaults by trying to assure the regime that they were close allies of communism. An article to this effect by a Tolstoyan was co-signed by leading personalities of the Baptist, Evangelical, Adventist, Dukhobor, and Molokan sects. But it was useless: 'The Godless' rebuffed them, claiming bourgeois and aristocratic roots of schismatic and sectarian movements in Russia's past (class enemies), incompatibility of Christianity with Marxism, and therefore even if sectarian communes were prosperous, 'they cannot be exemplary' because of their ideology. These were the first signs of clouds gathering against the sectarians, attacks on whom became particularly vicious from 1933.[29] There may have been several reasons for that: first, the need to justify the liquidation of sectarian farm communes and co-operatives; and second, owing to the decimation of Orthodox clergy and the closing of so many rural Orthodox churches, the non-hierarchical sects begin to fill the vacuum. And precisely because they do not depend on a centralized hierarchy for ordination and appointment and their unelaborate services can be performed at any home with almost no preparation, they are more difficult to control and to liquidate, and for this reason provoke the wrath of the totalitarian regime.

We have already mentioned the change in attitude to the Moslems. With the attack on the 'bourgeois-nationalist' deviations in the Communist Party towards the end of the 1920s, including the Pan-Turkic communist movement of Sultan Galiev, the Soviets began their frontal attack against Islam. They attacked Sultan Galiev's theory that Islam, being the youngest of the great religions and having stronger 'civic-political motives' than other faiths, should be treated more cautiously by the communists, and that there should be only very limited antireligious propaganda and no direct attacks on Islam in the Turkic-Moslem areas of the USSR. The supposedly scholarly-theoretical monthly *Antireligioznik* (The Antireligious) by 1930 rejected such exceptions and insisted that Islam should be seen as a class foe of the toiling masses and attacked just as indiscriminately as other religions.[30] The earlier attacks on religious modernism-renovationism, which had begun in 1927 and included Islamic reformism, should be seen as a preparation for the frontal assault on Islam. The point is that the Moslem reformists, emphasising women's role in the mosque, for instance, had been a part of the Turanian (pan-Turkic) movement of the pre-revolutionary epoch: a movement which allied itself with Lenin and the Communist Party in the course of the Civil War after Lenin's appeals to the Moslems and his promises of national autonomy and religious freedom to the Moslems. Thus we see a direct connection between the incendiary, name-calling and label-sticking attack in the press (1927) and its realization in terror (1929 on). In the case of Islam it is directly linked with the physical annihilation of the 'Islamic' nationalistic communists of the Tatar-Turkic areas of the USSR.[31]

The decade of the 'final solution' of all religions opens with a typical editorial in the fortnightly *Bezbozh.* entitled: 'Let the Five Year Plan Slam Religion on the Head'. After naming priests and sectarian leaders as chief subversive agents undermining collectivization, the article concludes: 'The plough and famine gave birth to gods, while the tractor, the kolkhoz and prosperity hit gods. They hit them very hard.'[32] But where is the prosperity?

As prosperity evaded the socialist economy, religions began

Contempt and Hate Propaganda, 1919–39

Hail to the Five-Year Plan!

The caption over the poster reads: THE FIVE-YEAR PLAN IS A PRACTICAL PROGRAMME OF STRUGGLE TO SMASH RELIGION. (*Besbozhnik u stanka*, no. 22, 1929)

to be used as scapegoats: priests and sectarian 'kulaks' were accused of deliberately wrecking the harvests, sabotaging collective farms, and other crimes. Favourite scapegoats for poor productivity and harvest failure were religious feasts, which allegedly brought high absenteeism and drunkenness in the villages.[33]

Lenin's dictum that religion is 'moonshine' begins to be interpreted literally in these years, shifting the emphasis from religious feasts causing drunkenness, to religion itself being the dope, organically linked to alcohol, and aimed at keeping man in a constant stupor. Such writings were often accompanied by blasphemous cartoons, such as depicting God getting drunk on communion wine and ending up in a Soviet sobering station where he is treated by hypnosis.[34]

Obviously, from treating religion as a form of stupor there remains only a short step to approaching it as a mental disorder. And it was in the 1930s that *Bezbozhnik* began to depict religion as something intrinsically linked to various forms of psychic perversions and deviations, and even to criminal behaviour,[35] presaging the boundless schizophrenia theories of Professor Snezhnevsky by some two decades,[36] and their application to religion proved to be much greater than predicted by the 'Marxist classics'. It was therefore necessary to find other rationales, besides the class and economic ones, for this phenomenon. Mental deviation, criminal behaviour, alcoholic delirium could well serve the purpose: hence, the victory of the Yaroslavsky line in favour of a multifaceted attack on religion and believers.[37] At first Yaroslavsky appeared to be defending the right of religions to some degree, when he attacked *Bezbozhnik u stanka* (the Work-Bench Godless, henceforth the *Bezbust*.) for promoting such slogans as: 'Down with that crap – religion!', carried in one of the public antireligious demonstrations. *Bezbust*. retorted that it hurled insults at religion, not at believers as persons. It is the religious ideology that should be attacked, not the clergy. It was of this personal attack, they argued, that Yaroslavsky was guilty, since he substituted anti-clericalism (ridiculing, abusing, and insulting the clergy) for atheism. Likewise, they claimed the antireligious struggle should be led only by the party and by the industrial proletariat, not by the whole nation which Yaroslavsky was trying to mobilize and recruit into his League of the Godless.[38] Thus, as his publications confirm, Yaroslavsky's protestations were but a facade in his struggle to destroy his rivals and monopolize the antireligious front, using all methods possible in order to whip up the nation into an antireligious frenzy. In practice, both *Bezbozh.* and *Bezbust.* resorted to primitive blasphemies, insulting any believer, with, for instance, cartoons depicting the Nativity as an adulterous three-party romance with the Virgin Mary. Caricatures of such type were a common occurrence in the journal.[39]

The same song was sung by the general mass media, including the youth daily *Komsol'skaia pravda* (henceforth *Koms. pr.*) and *Krokodil* (Crocodile) the chief Soviet satirical magazine. *Krokodil* depicted the clergy as alcoholics, lechers and money-grabbers, at least from 1922. Almost no issue appeared in 1923 without at least one caricature of the clergy or the Church. The *Koms. pr.* 1929 anti-Christmas campaign practically equated religion with drunkeness. Its parody on the Christmas Tree is decorated with a Gospel, next to which is a criminal with a knife, followed by a bottle of vodka hanging from a tree branch, and a Bethlehem Star with a cross inside it crowning the ugly company.[40]

Thus it is hardly possible to speak of any differentiation in styles, methodology and approach in different Soviet atheistic periodicals. As we have shown, even 'sophisticated' theoretical and methodological journals were prone to publishing direct hate propaganda against religions and believers. It would be more accurate to differentiate between different periods in Soviet antireligious attacks, always keeping in mind what was going on in the country as a whole in each particular period, and how certain types of antireligious attacks in the press related to practical policies regarding the Churches and believers.

There may have been some uncertainties as to which course to take in 1925, hence the possibility for debate between *Bezbozhnik* and *Bezbust.* It was the year of the birth of the League of the Godless as an organization of the masses and of the addition of the illustrated fortnightly *Bezbozhnik* to the weekly newspaper by the same name which had been appearing since 1922. Thus, Yaroslavsky's line was winning, his empire growing, and *Bezbust.* might have been waging rearguard battles against its rival. It was a battle over immediate tactics, rather than principles, as excellently illustrated in two articles by Yaroslavsky's deputy editor, Anton Loginov. He writes: 'it's common knowledge that religion is opium, . . . poison, stupor, moonshine, and yet we are not supposed to insult believers' feelings. Why should we say one thing and do another?' And then he answers this rhetorical question simply by saying: 'Not every stab at religion serves the aim of struggle against it ... every "persecution of the faith" builds up religious fanaticism.' He describes Komsomol and LG members' raids on churches: blasphemous shouts during the service; letting out a pig in the middle of a church. He condemns these methods only because they are counter-productive, not because he preaches any genuine respect for believers or their convictions.[41] Obviously, this philosophy does not preclude any change in methodology should it be seen to be more practical or should there be an order from higher authorities to do so. In principle, therefore, there is nothing unusual when the same publication which in 1925–6 preached some restraint and selectivity, a short time later unleashed the most vulgar and nihilistic attacks on religion and believers.

The nihilism included a campaign against iconography and church architecture begun in 1928. The People's Commissariat of Education boasted of having convinced the department dealing with historical monuments to reduce the list of architecturally precious churches under its protection from 7000 to 1000, automatically condemning 6000 church buildings to future destruction. LMG officials boasted of public burnings of thousands of icons. The conclusion of a plenary session of the LMG Central Council was that such destructions, as well as public abuse of priests, are proper where they serve the purpose of antireligious struggle, but they are wrong where they result in support for religion. The city of Vladimir, whose church architecture and frescoes are among the world's most beautiful, is described in *Bezbozhnik* as a city disfigured by the ugliness of the multiple churches. It is often stated that icons are harmful because their Jesus 'is a model for slaves and a patron of executioners'.[42] Such writings would be a premonition of and rationalization for the forthcoming mass closures and destruction of churches and of religious art along with them. In fact, the *Bezbozhnik* pages begin to be filled with photographs of disfigured churches, turned into clubs, shops, factories and garages, with appropriate boasting captions.[43] The illustrations on pp. 39–41 are a witness of that 'achievement'.

The LMG concept of beauty: the Leningrad Putilov factory church on the left transformed into a workers' club on the right. The author, Oleshchuk, presents this as a model to be emulated.
F. Oleshchuk, *Kto stroit tserkvi v SSSR* (M.-L.: Moskovskii rabochii, n.d.) 24.

The Moscow Christ-The-Saviour Cathedral before its destruction in 1931

1931: Ruins of the Christ-The-Saviour Cathedral

As early as 1926 Loginov insisted on the replacement of an areligious by an antireligious school; his antireligious attacks were no milder than Kostelovskaia's of *Bezbust*. In 1928 at the Fifteenth Party Congress Stalin took the Party to task, calling for its participation in a more active and persuasive antireligious propaganda.

Along with the campaign for antireligious education a campaign was led against schoolteachers of the old intelligentsia. It was asserted that they were active anti-Soviets and 'clericalists', surreptitiously allowing priests to contact and spiritually influence schoolchildren. Reports appeared about individual (always named) schools where the majority of teachers were members of the former gentry, sons and daughters of priests, merchants, *kulaks* and other 'non-socialist' classes. In those years of de*kulak*ization and collectivization this meant invariably that such teachers would be sacked and, in most cases, imprisoned or exiled.[44]

As we have seen, 'all-persuasive' translates as all means to be used against religion, including the hate-the-clergy line of Yaroslavsky, the class-enemy line of Kostelovskaia, and Lunacharsky's concepts of a hostile cultural phenomenon. But hate-the-clergy is seen as effective in dividing the ranks of believers without, allegedly, insulting the latter's personal feelings. Henceforth, Kostelovskaia's *Bezbust.* was forced to adopt this anti-clergy emphasis and specialize in it, until the closure of the journal and its absorption by the illustrated *Bezbozhnik* in 1932. Ironically, only five to six years earlier *Bezbust.* had argued that such an 'unprincipled' antireligious line played into the hands of religions.

Even as it was declared that 'the forms of antireligious work must be brought closer to the masses', all forms of attack were being used, especially hate and contempt directed at the clergy. Clerics were depicted as 'direct agents of private capital' at the height of the campaign against the *kulaks* and private enterprise. Articles on the Orthodox and the sects appeared under such captions as: 'No favours to the class enemies ... The enemy does not sleep!' and 'Militant godless, don't you take off your weapons before the resisting enemy!' At the same time, attacks against sectarian collective farms condemned them not for inefficient work or poor productivity, but because they prevented the penetration of antireligious propaganda into their midst. Hence they must be abolished (and abolished they soon were, as we know). Another antireligious page in *Koms. pr.*, in the relatively calm year of 1931, appears under the caption: 'The Orthodox and the Sectarians are agents of the Exploiting Classes'.[45]

Koms. pr. instructed its readers to sacrifice their family ties for the sake of atheism: no compromise with family religious traditions for the sake of family unity or loving pity for the old grandmother. Pity should not stand in the way of building socialism: 'You must beat religion on the head every day of your life in all its expressions in daily life.'[46]

This new sinister turn was often reflected in the pages of *Bezbozhnik* in the 1930s, which at the same time became less and less dynamic, publishing only a routine of hate and insults without any originality or search for new approaches. The still lingering *Bezbust.* published a vicious attack on practising believers among top Soviet scholars in the prestigious Timiriazev Academy of Agricultural Sciences, menacingly (in this climate of mounting terror) citing their names,[47] and stressing that one of them, Professor Borisov, was even a practising Orthodox priest. The article was unscrupulous in its use of slander and name-calling.

The 1929–30 purge of the Russian Academy of Sciences illustrates how such labels translated into sinister deeds in those days. Close to 100 leading scholars of the nation (from mathematicians to historians, from chemists to orientalists . . .), their assistants and most talented graduate students, were arrested on forged charges and given sentences ranging from three years of internal exile to the death penalty. Most of them had been practising believers; some were Orthodox clergymen who combined their scholarly research with pastoral or monastic functions. A case in point, showing the devious methods used by the investigation, concerns the famous historian Sergei Platonov, also arrested at the time. Provocatively he was asked by the investigator how he, Platonov, being so religious, could appoint Kaplan, a Jew, to the directorship of the Pushkin House. 'What do you mean, a Jew?' asked Platonov: 'He is married to Professor Shakhmatov's daughter and, wearing a cassock, he reads the Psalter in the church every lent.' This information was sufficient to send Kaplan off to a concentration camp for five years.[48] It is in this light that more and more reports on believers, with their names and biographies appearing in the atheists' press, become particularly sinister in meaning: for example, a photograph of a classroom in which one of the girl pupils is writing on the board the names of those classmates who were seen attending the church at Easter.[49]

Any methods were now justified, any strategy, any tactic, as long as it promised immediate results and whipped up antireligious frenzy. Consequently, the crude anti-Christmases and anti-Easters which the Komsomol and early societies of atheists used to organize in the early 1920s, and which were later condemned by the Soviet press as too crude and ugly to be effective, were now also renewed.

Here is a description of one such 'Komsomol Christmas' of 1923 in the city of Gomel. It began by a mock trial of gods in a city theatre. The defendants were stuffed scarecrows representing the gods of different religious, as well as the clergy: Orthodox, Catholic, Jewish. The judges were proletarian komsomols. The verdict: all gods and clerics must be burned at the stake. The whole mass poured out into the streets of the city with torches and scarecrows in their hands and shouted, 'Away with the churches, away with the synagogues!' The effigies were then publicly burned in a city square. All this happened on Christmas Day.[50] By the mid-1920s, parades were replaced by similar meetings, but only behind closed doors, and accompanied by antireligious lectures and poetry readings, as well as by articles in the atheistic journals. One typical article condemns Christian feast days as serving the interests of the exploiting classes alone, because the Christian Christmas message of peace and goodwill does not distinguish between the working classes and the capitalists, and there can be no peace as long as the latter remain, as long as strikes go on in the West. The article then vulgarly ridicules a church service as 'a pop's speech embellished by an artistic entertainment of song and recital, and concluding with an angelic resolution for general acceptance and fulfilment'.[51]

It is around 1928–30 that the same tone and type of attack on religious feasts was resumed. Blasphemous public parades were renewed, such as an LG parade in 1927 on the tenth anniversary of the October Revolution, with mock-bishops, generals and capitalists whose effigies were then publicly burnt.⁵² Now these parades, when organized at the time of Christmas and, particularly, Easter services with the traditional Easter processions at midnight around the church, make the holding of the Church celebrations almost impossible. For instance, announcements of anti-Easter campaigns state that the parties will begin at eleven p.m. (the time of the beginning of the Nocturns in the Orthodox Paschal celebration) and will continue until the early morning hours, with open-air shows of antireligious films, orchestras and dancing in the square facing churches. Appeals are made to bakeries not to bake traditional Easter cakes. However, in the few cases where the results are reported, it is admitted that 'some churches' were packed to bursting (that is, there were several thousand people in each church), while the anti-church celebrations attracted from 100 to 600 people.⁵³ The new element in the anti-feast demonstrations is that they must also promote socialist competition in the fulfilment of the five-year plans and condemn religion, clergy and church feasts for the alleged subversion of this economic struggle.⁵⁴

The terror that escalated throughout the 1930s and resulted in 1939 in the physical destruction of the whole Church, and all organized religion in the country, left no more room or reason for debates on strategies and tactics of the antireligious struggle. The terror at the same time demonstrated the recognition of the failure of the verbal struggle, especially when Yaroslavsky was forced to admit towards the end of the decade that over 50 per cent of the population still believed in God. *Bezbozhnik* of course joined the chorus condemning Trotsky, Bukharin and other 'traitors of the communist course' in the 1930s, and lost its own voice like the rest of the Soviet press.⁵⁵ All that was left for *Bezbozhnik* to write about in 1939–40 were drab articles like 'Stalin on Religion', praise for the five-year plans, and appeals to the LMG members to be good patriots. In the words of one Western scholar:

> Yaroslavskii acknowledged that it was necessary to exercise caution ... and a policy of deep, insistent, and patient persuasion was stressed ... Two decades of experience had produced a chastening effect on the *antireligiozniki*.⁵⁶

This is academism at its ivory-tower best: hastening indeed, when in a territory of 22 million square kilometres there remained only several hundred of the original fifty thousand Orthodox churches, four bishops out of the original 300, some two to three thousand priests out of the original 45 000. All other religions were hit similarly. The only thing that remained for enthusiasts of atheism to do was to spy out individual believers and denounce them to the NKVD. The Church had to be revived first, so that there would be an object for attack; while the vulgarity of the attacks of the 1920s and early 1930s had to wait for the Khruschev era and its new assault on religion.

3 Persecutions, 1921-41

'To be a priest today means being a martyr.'
(E. MacNaughten, 'Informal Report of Religious Situation in Russia')

THE NEP ERA (1921-8)

The New Economic Policy (NEP) was launched by Lenin at the end of the 10th Party Congress in March 1921 in response to the economic catastrophe which the War Communist system had brought to the country. It was also a compromise with the general population: the country was torn by massive popular rebellions against Bolsheviks, among which the most famous were the Kronstadt Sailor Rebellion of February–March 1921 and the Antonov Peasant Rebellion of 1921–2 engulfing most of the Russian Central Black Earth provinces.[1] NEP ushered in an era of limited free enterprise in industry, trade and agriculture, a relative relaxation of ideological controls over the intelligentsia. The regime was trying to appear respectable to the eyes of world public opinion in order to be diplomatically recognized internationally and thus to win for itself a place in the international markets. Obviously, in these conditions it was not in the regime's best interest to continue the war communist policy of murdering churchmen without formal trials and plausible accusations. The fact that the persecution of the Orthodox Church continued throughout the years of the NEP (1921–8), although under more 'respectable' pretexts, indicates that destruction of religion, at least as an institution, was a high priority on the communist ideological agenda of the Soviet Government.

There were two mutually interrelated antireligious strategies adopted by the regime in these years. One was under the pretext of the campaign to confiscate church valuables, allegedly in order to import food from abroad to feed the famine-stricken areas. The other was connected with the government-encouraged and -supported Church schism, the government's legalization of the schismatic group as the only legitimate Orthodox Church, and the subsequent persecution of those who refused to recognize the schism.[2] The period ended with the Declaration of Loyalty which the regime forced Metropolitan Sergii, the patriarchal deputy locum-tenens, to sign in 1927, and with the subsequent persecution of those churchmen (predominantly bishops) who refused to recognize the terms of the declaration and who, therefore, broke with M. Sergii.[3]

The very fertile area of the Volga Basin is subject to periodic droughts, sometimes lasting several years in a row. The previous local famine caused by this factor was in 1891. Thereafter special stockpiles of grain were kept in the area to prevent a repitition of the 1891 tragedy. All these grain reserves were used up by the armed bands in the Civil War era, and the droughts of 1920–22 resulted in a famine of unprecedented proportions. It was Patriarch Tikhon who issued an appeal on behalf of the Russian Orthodox Church 'To the Peoples of the World and to the Orthodox Man' to help the hungry. This was followed by his similar appeal to the major heads of various religions outside Russia in August 1921. The Church formed a Famine Relief Committee, but a few months later the government ordered this committee closed, the money collected to be handed over to the appropriate government agency. The government insisted that the Church hand over to it all her valuables (chalices made of precious metals, precious stones and metals used in decorating icons, mitres, etc.). In response, the Patriarch appealed to his parishes on 19 February 1922 to surrender all objects of value except those used directly in sacraments. Nine days later the government responded by ordering the confiscation by state agents of all church treasures *including* those used in sacraments. The Patriarch issued another encyclical on the same day, urging believers to be very generous in their donations, but not to give up the objects used in the sacraments. The government jumped at this as the pretext for attacking the Church. It was obviously and deliberately heading for a direct confrontation, for which the Patriarch and many local bishops suggested that, in order to compensate for the sacramental objects, their monetary equivalent should be donated instead, this was refused, as was the Patriarch's request that Church representatives be included in the government commissions inspecting, confiscating and accounting for the confiscated valuables.[4] Consequently, by mid-1922 there had been 1414 bloody clashes between the faithful and the Soviet armed detachments protecting the confiscating commissions, and fifty-five trials of 231 group cases.[5]

One of the bloodiest clashes was in the old textile-industrial town of Shuia, not far from Moscow. According to a report in the Soviet newspaper *Izvestia* on Wednesday, 15 March, the day scheduled for the confiscation operation in the city cathedral:

> large groups of people began to assemble in the church square; many women and students. When the mounted police appeared they were met by threatening shouts and by hurling of rocks and firewood at them. Someone began to ring the tocsin-bell on the belfry. The bell rang for an hour and a half, bringing huge masses of people to the square.
>
> An infantry half-company and two armoured cars with machine-guns, brought to the square, were met by a hail of rocks and pistol-shots ... The army responded by a volley which killed four and critically wounded ten persons.[6]

The Soviet press of the time was full of similar reports about other churches and towns across the whole breadth of Russia.[7] The letter attributed to Lenin, which we quoted in vol. 1, Chapter 2, plainly shows that the perseverence with which the Soviet Government was pursuing this campaign of confiscations at all costs, had not been motivated by philanthropic considerations.

Since the writing of this letter, Lenin's opinion that it would be wiser not to arrest the Patriarch for the time being must have drastically changed, for arrested he was on 10 May. Two days later a group of rebel-priests in collusion with the GPU took over the offices of the Moscow Patriarchate and set themselves up with an interdicted bishop at the head as the Higher Church Administration. This in essence is the Renovationist *putsch*. The Renovationists declared their full loyalty to the Soviet Government, proclaimed Marxism a social projection of Christianity and actively supported the campaign of church-valuables confiscations, and their leaders began to act as witnesses for the prosecution at the trials of Orthodox clergy and laypersons, especially in connection with the church-valuables issue.[8] So we see that the persecutions in connection with the valuables and with the Renovationist issue are interrelated.

As from March 1922 *Pravda* and other Soviet newspapers began to publish floods of ugly reports (usually anonymous) against bishops, other clergymen and lay churchmen. These mostly led to arrests and trials. The same issue of *Izvestia* which reported on the Shuia incident, also published a list of 'Enemies of the People' from among the clergy, accompanied by anonymous reports on their alleged anti-Soviet activities. The list was headed by Patriarch Tikhon, and included the names of twenty-seven other bishops inside Soviet Russia, all the émigré bishops, the whole clergy of the cities of Rostov-on-Don and Arkhangelsk, all the participants of the Clergy Conference of Siberia, and all the monks of the Saviour Monastery in the Iaroslavl Diocese. This is a good illustration of the sweeping character of the campaign and the accusations.

The first widely publicized Moscow trial of 54 churchmen in connection with the church valuables was concluded on 10 May, resulting in twelve executions (mostly clergymen) and twenty-seven different prison sentences. The total number of churchmen prosecuted by Soviet courts in connection with the valuables issue between May and December 1922, according to the data assembled by Valentinov from the Soviet press, was 708. He also cites at least four cases with undisclosed numbers of defendants, namely, trials of groups of the clergy of Kharkov, Novocherkassk, Irkutsk, and of a whole monastic community in the Chernigov Province.[9] Another source gives the figure of 732 defendents in connection with church valuables in the first half of 1922 alone.[10] Of these, three cases involve Roman Catholic clergy, and one, eleven Jews including a rabbi. In the case of the Orthodox defendants, at least 35 persons (23 of them clergy) were condemned to death (some death sentences were commuted to long terms of imprisonment). In contrast, the six Roman Catholic clergymen received only prison sentences of three to five years, and of the eleven Jewish defendants, the rabbi was sentenced to three years in prison, four were conditionally released, and the others received terms shorter than three years. Of Valentinov's known 708 Orthodox cases (May to December 1922) only 121 were set free after the trials. The severity of sentences meted out to the Orthodox, contrasted with the relative mildness of sentences given to the Catholics and the Jews, once again shows that at that time the regime continued to see the Orthodox Church as its main enemy.

The most notorious of the trials was that of Metropolitan Veniamin of Petrograd with a group of leading Petrograd clergy and theologians. Its notoriety comes from the fact that the main victim was innocent from the point of view of the Soviet-Marxist class theory in all its aspects. The Metropolitan came from the humble family of a rural priest in northern Russia. As a vicar-bishop in Petrograd Diocese he continued to behave like a parish priest, visiting the poorest workers' dwellings, performing the rites of baptism, marriage, funeral; was ready to respond to any call at any time. His residence was always full of poor and humble folk in need of help, charity, or advice; and the bishop was always attentive, loving, generous and caring. The flock responded to this by democratically electing him their metropolitan in 1917, soon after the February Revolution. This appears to have been the first free election of a diocesan bishop by the laity and clergy since the seventeenth century. His sermons were very simple and were loved by the common people. In short, he did not fit at all into the stereotype of a prince of the Church, a representative of the ruling and exploiting classes and of the tsarist ruling circles. But a leading churchman who had such a charismatic appeal and following among the working masses was too much of an ideological embarrassment for the new masters. His fate must have been decided upon by them irrespective of how he would react to the valuables issue.

The Petrograd section of the State Famine Relief Commission (*pomgol*) was at first apparently not aware of the political calculations of the Kremlin and treated the issue quite genuinely as aiming simply at saving the hungry from starvation. Therefore, when on 6 March 1922 the Metropolitan in person presented his plan to the Commission, they accepted it entirely; and the meeting ended with the Metropolitan rising, giving his benediction to the commission and saying with tears in his eyes that he would personally take the precious ornaments from the most revered icons and hand them over to the commission 'to aid the starving brothers'. His policy, accepted by the commission, consisted of the following conditions: that the Church was prepared to donate all her possessions to aid the starving; that it was necessary that the act be a voluntary donation of the Church, otherwise the peace and order of the Church people could not be guaranteed; that for the sake of preservation of the same peace it was imperative that representatives of the Church participate in controlling the further disposal of the church treasurers; that no force be applied for otherwise he could not guarantee peace; moreover, as a bishop he would be forced in the latter case to condemn the actions of the state.

During the following two days Petrograd newspapers reported the agreement in approving terms. But then Moscow must have informed the Petrograd Soviet of its real aims in the campaign. Suddenly the Metropolitan was told by the latter that the clergy could not participate in the commission and that all confiscations would be done by Soviet commissars administratively. Meanwhile, twelve Petrograd initiators of the Renovationist schism published a letter in the *Petrograd Pravda* on 24 March condemning all clergy loyal to the Patriarch as counter-revolutionary. The Metropolitan was so eager to prevent bloodshed by any means in the course of the confiscations that, using the leading schismatics as intermediaries, he reached a new accord with the Leningrad Soviet, according to which the believers could keep the precious objects used in the Sacraments as long as they collected the equivalent value in currency.

Peace was restored until the arrest of the Patriarch and the seizure of his chancellery by the same Petrograd priests who led the group which had signed the above letter. Veniamin refused to recognize the validity of the coup and excommunicated its perpetrators (priests Vvedensky, Belkov, Krasnitsky). The Soviet press responded by wild attacks on the Metropolitan, threatening him with the 'sword of the proletariat' which would 'fall on the Metropolitan's neck'. Then he was presented with an ultimatum from the Leningrad government: either the excommunicated priests be restored or the Metropolitan and those close to him would be arrested, charged in connection with the church-valuables issue, and would pay with their lives. So much for the separation of state and religion.

The Metropolitan did not budge and a few days later he was arrested. The trial began on 10 June. The defence lawyer was Ya. S. Gurovich, a Jew whom the Metropolitan had personally asked to be his barrister. It was an open trial in a hall with room for up to 3000 people, and during this trial it was always packed.

Everybody rose when the Metropolitan was brought in. The Metropolitan extended his benediction to all. At the trial he continued to stand firm on the issue of the church valuables. The chief witness for the prosecution was one of the Renovationist leaders, the Priest Krasnitsky. Gurovich ruined Krasnitsky's attack on the Metropolitan as a reactionary and counter-revolutionary by recalling that before the revolution Krasnitsky had been an active member of and a chaplain to the *pogromist* Union of Russian People, that he had published wild antisemitic 'treatises' and, until November 1917, militantly anti-bolshevik articles. Another Renovationist priest, Boiarsky, to the unpleasant surprise of the prosecution, presented an impassioned plea on behalf of the Metropolitan, praising him as an excellent human being and sincere Christian. Vvedensky, the Renovationist leader originally scheduled to be the chief prosecution witness, at the time was in hospital with a deep gash in his skull caused by a rock hurled at him by the angry Orthodox city folk.

Gurovich in his defence speech, lasting nearly six hours, rejected the indictment point by point. He stressed that the Metropolitan had done everything to preserve peace in the city and had achieved this despite the unco-operative behaviour of the Soviets. He pointed out that the Leningrad city soviet had accepted his terms; and that precisely because the prosecution had no case against the Metropolitan, it was constantly trying to divert the debates to historical and émigré issues unrelated to the case. The prosecution even dared to reproach 'the Russian Orthodox clergy for the Beilis case'.[11] But Gurovich responded:

> It is common knowledge that the Russian clergy is ... innocent of the infamous Beilis case, its best representatives fought against that bloody slander levelled at the Jews. The tsarist justice officials searched in vain for a convenient 'expert' from the ranks of the Orthodox clergy for a long time. No one agreed; and the prosecution had to settle on a notorious Lithuanian Roman Catholic priest, Pranaitis, dug out for this purpose from somewhere in Siberia ...
>
> I am fortunate that in this historic and profoundly

sorrowful moment for the Russian clergy I, a Jew, can testify to the whole world the deep gratitude of, I believe, the whole Jewish people to the Russian Orthodox clergy for their attitude to the Beilis case at the time.

Sobs of some defendants and members of the public forced Gurovich to make a pause. Then he went on to characterize the Metropolitan as a true and saintly Christian. He concluded this passage by telling the prosecution: 'You can kill the Metropolitan, but it is not in your power to deprive him of his courage and of his noble thoughts and deeds.' Then he analyzed, in contrast, the ignoble acts of the Renovationists and warned the Soviets that they were not a reliable ally: the people might follow a wealthy and successful Saul who turns into the persecuted Paul, but it will not follow the reverse transformation, especially when this is accompanied by acts leading to the arrest and death of their former brethren. He rightly prophesied the imminent failure of the renovationists. The lawyer warned the Bolsheviks that history would condemn them for murdering the innocent bishop, and moreover: 'The faith grows and gains its strength from the blood of its martyrs.'

The end of his speech was drowned in the massive applause of the whole public, including the large contingent of communists brought in as a support for the prosecution.

In his final plea Veniamin stressed that in 1917 he was elected metropolitan by a true people's judgement, not because of any particular talents but because they loved him:

> I have worked ... for the people, bringing peace and pacifying the masses. I've always been loyal to the state authorities and shunned politics. Of course, I reject all accusations. And now ... I am calmly awaiting the verdict ... well remembering the words of the Apostle: ... if you suffer because you are a Christian, don't be ashamed of it but thank God'
>
> [Peter iv, 15–16].

Another of the accused in the same group, Archimandrite Sergii, also condemned to death, described in his plea the essentials of the ascetic life of a monk, pointing out how little there was that connected him to the life of this world, and he ended by saying: 'Can it be that the court thinks that the break of this last thread may frighten me? Do your deed. I am sorry for you and I pray for you.'

Ten persons, including the Metropolitan, were condemned to death. Six sentences were later commuted to long imprisonments; fifty-nine other defendants (plus the six with commuted death sentences) received prison sentences of various lengths, and twenty-two were freed.[12]

No sooner had the wave of trials and executions in connection with resistance to the confiscation of church valuables subsided, than the press began to accuse the clergy and the church people of hiding away and even stealing (from themselves – D.P.) church valuables. A series of arrests and trials with heavy sentences on these grounds followed. At least two bishops, numerous priests, and in many cases all members of parish councils, were arrested and sentenced to several years of imprisonment; eight years being the longest imprisonment meted out in connection with these accusations, according to Valentinov.[13] But this campaign was cut short by the failure to conceal the massive black-market operations of Soviet officials involved in the church-valuables operation. Soon private shops in Constantinople, Lvov (Poland), Riga (Latvia), Kharbin (China) and other major cities close to the Soviet borders began a lively trade in precious Russian church artifacts. In Kharkov alone 'several billion roubles' worth' of church valuables had thus been stolen; and the Soviet press was forced to admit that the criminals caught included train attendants in railway carriages reserved for foreign diplomats and other Soviet petty officials, who apparently purchased these treasures from unnamed and untried higher Soviet officials. There was not a single person associated with the Church involved in these affairs. In another case a local communist party organization sold a precious ancient shroud on the black market to replenish its currency reserve. The case was reported in *Pravda* beause it had caused a local believers' protest riot.[14] This shows how justified was the Patriarch's original insistence that the confiscation commissions include church representatives, and also his suspicions that charity and concern for the starving were not first priorities in Lenin's campaign.

All in all, an unknown number of laymen and 8100 members of the clergy were murdered in connection with the church-valuables issue, of which 2691 were married priests, 1962 monks and male novices, 3447 nuns and female novices.[15]

The other pretext for persecutions was claims of miracles and mass religious rituals honouring these miracles. For instance, an icon was found in a Tula belfry. For some reason the local church people considered this find miraculous, and a special service was celebrated in front of it. Consequently, the local bishop, Yuvenalii, was sentenced to ten years' imprisonment; the dean of the church where the icon had been found, Fr. Uspensky, his church warden and numerous other laymen were sentenced to five years' imprisonment each.[16] Obviously, dissemination of information on miracles was seen by the regime as a vile and very effective propaganda for religion, but since religious propaganda could not be criminally prosecuted until 1929, claims of miracles in the atmosphere of direct confrontation between the State and the Church must have been treated as acts hostile to the Soviet regime. Believers traditionally tend to view miracles as signs from God to strengthen them and their faith in the most trying situations. Thus, the regime could interpret these manifestations as attempts to strengthen the believers in their struggle in defence of the Church valuables, and against the desecration of the churches by the state commissions.

The struggle against claims of miracles must be seen in the same context as the campaign to compulsorily open up Saints' relics, confiscate them from the Church and place into state museums (as we discuss in Chapter 5). Obviously, the position of the state was that if religion could not be liquidated, at least it ought to be 'demysticized'.[17] This campaign also met considerable resistance from the believers and caused many clashes and arrests.[18]

The distinction between direct prosecutions and propaganda aimed at presenting the believers as contemptible syphylitics (see Chapter 2), semi-humans, as it were, is very unclear, because developing such attitudes toward the believers leads to all forms of their mistreatment. A teacher who loses his or her job because of religious convictions is a victim of persecution. And it was with the call for an antireligious school to replace an areligious one, from 1926 on, that teachers had to begin to conceal their faith and to abstain from visiting churches in order to keep their jobs.[19] Similarly, the introduction of the continuous work week in 1929 (four working days followed by a day off) and the banning of days off on church feast days, deprived people of the possibility of going to church on a regular basis and brought job discrimination and punishment in cases of truancy. This amounts to religious persecution.

Finally, in line with Lenin's words that the communist state should be much more tolerant towards amoral and even criminal priests than towards those of high moral standing, authority and popularity, the regime removed, imprisoned, and even shot the most popular clergymen wherever it could. Many examples have already been cited from the Civil War era and from the fraudulent trials of the 1920s; but in all of the latter there were formal accusations, however flimsy, unconvincing and fraudulent. In the provinces, however, away from the limelight of the major cities and the eyes of foreign observers, a systematic campaign was led throughout the decade to liquidate the most popular monks, to shut down the most popular and morally authoritative monasteries. One of the first of these to go was the Optina Monastery to which almost every Russian literary figure of note had made pilgrimages. The monastery, transformed into an agricultural commune in 1922, was forced to close in the following year, converted into a state museum and a national monument. Many of the monks were allowed to remain as employees of the institution; but in the same year the most popular of them, the widely loved elder Nektarii, was arrested. Even earlier, in 1919, a saintly thirty-year-old monk-priest Nikon had spent some time in prison. Their only crime was that they were monks, and popular. In 1928 the museum was closed by the state and before 1930 all the surviving monks of that monastery were either dispersed and in hiding across the country, or in prisons and concentration camps. All seven churches of the nearby town of Kozelsk, where some of the monks had served since the closure of the monastery and the eventual expulsion of the monastic museum employees, were shut by 1929, depriving the whole local population not only of their former elders but of church services as well.[20]

Obviously this is persecution. Clearly, not for a moment was there ever any real separation of Church and State in the Soviet Union. The totalitarian system, trying to cultivate a new materialistic faith in the people, could not tolerate a dynamic faith in the Supernatural, capable of inspiring and leading millions of people. The faith had to be weakened, neutralized, turned into the private affair of an isolated individual, made as invisible as possible, if it could not be destroyed altogether. A schism in the Church was one of the new hopes of the regime. The details of the schism of the Renovationists or of the Living Church are described in my *Russian Orthodox Church under the Soviet Regime*.

As was seen in the case of Metropolitan Veniamin, the regime obliged by arresting, administratively exiling (without trial) and even shooting those bishops and priests who continued overtly to declare their loyalty to the imprisoned Patriarch and those who categorically refused to submit to the 'Renovators'. It is estimated that, in addition to the 1922 church-valuables trials, 165 priests were executed after 1923, i.e. after the church-valuables issue had subsided.[21] By early 1925 there were at least sixty-five bishops in prisons or administrative exile in distant areas, not counting those who had repeatedly been detained for short periods and then released. The arrests continued. Some returned from exile in 1925, while another twenty bishops were arrested in that year, including Metropolitan Peter (Poliansky), who became the locum-tenens of the patriarchal throne after Patriarch Tikhon's death in April of that year. Peter and many other bishops faithful to him were arrested towards the end of 1925, clearly for their refusal to come to terms with the Renovationists, and accept them as a self-contained part within a reconsolidated Orthodox Church. Now the regime wanted a reunification: the Renovationists had failed to attract the laity, so they ceased to be of interest to the Soviets as a separate entity; but because of their readiness to co-operate with the authorities and their close connections with the GPU, they would have been very useful as activists within the regular Orthodox Church.[22] Metropolitan Peter's intransigence in relation to the Renovationists, as well as that of many other bishops, including Archbishop Illarion (Troitsky) of Krutitsy, cost them their lives: they died in exile – Metropolitan Peter in the Arctic in 1937, Illarion in a prison transit hospital in Leningrad in 1929.[23] Illarion, as well as Peter's locum-tenens, Metropolitan Sergii, were among the twelve bishops arrested in 1926. Now the regime was aiming at forcing the Church hierarchy to bend even lower in a declaration of loyalty to the Soviets than Patriarch Tikhon had done in 1919, in 1923, and again in his last testament in 1925. The Patriarch had emphasized the freedom of the Church in the situation of the separation of Church and State and the duty of her flock to be loyal to the Soviet state in all civic matters. He had likewise declared civic loyalty of the Church to the Soviet state, in as much as this loyalty did not contradict a Christian's primary loyalty to God.[24]

At this time bishops secretly undertook the election of a new patriarch by means of a ballot by correspondence via trusted messengers, travelling from one bishop to another. The arrests of 1926–7 are mainly the state's retaliation for this secret undertaking, discovered through the arrest and execution of two laymen, I. A. Kuvshinov and his son, who were acting as such messengers. Lists and names of the voting bishops were found at the time of their arrest, which apparently had also led to the arrest of the third messenger, the Monk Tavrion (1898–1978) who subsequently spent a total of twenty-seven years in prisons, camps and exile.[25] Consequently the number of arrested bishops rose to 117 by April 1927 according to one source, and to over 150 by the middle of that year, according to another.

Metropolitan Sergii was released in 1927 and signed a declaration at last worded in terms acceptable to the state, not only promising loyalty, but alleging that the Soviets had never persecuted the Church and even thanking them for the 'care' they had shown her. But at just that time several bishops were imprisoned for their loyalty to Sergii.[26] On 14 June 1927:

> three bishops and ten young promising priests were taken in Petrograd. Some students in the Pastors' School [underground Orthodox or legal Protestant?] were also seized ... For the first time Finnish Protestants were disturbed, twenty ... being arrested.
>
> In Odessa ... a number of priests of the Catholic Church were taken ... [plus] three Orthodox priests were arrested [in fact] ... it was rumoured fourteen had been taken.
>
> In Moscow the priest, deacon and reader of the Holy Ghost church were arrested.[27]

The contemporary report, which has no claim to omniscience, goes on enumerating individual arrests, situations of exiled bishops, etc., but apparently its author was still unaware of the contents of Metropolitan Sergii's Declaration of Loyalty and reactions to it. In fact, it caused such an upheaval that schisms on the right developed; they were conservative church movements refusing to accept Sergii's policy. Consequently, most of the bishops arrested in 1928–32 were those in revolt against Sergii (while those who had been arrested earlier for following Sergii continued to serve their sentence). The detained churchmen in those years were often cynically questioned by the GPU during the interrogations: 'what was their attitude to "our" Metropolitan Sergii, heading the Soviet Church?' According to internal secret statistics, 20 per cent of all the inmates of the dreaded Solovki camps in 1928–9, or about 10 000 of the 1930 estimates of 50 000 total Solovki inmates, were imprisoned in some connection with the affairs of the Orthodox Church.[28] Between 1928 and 1931 at least thirty-six additional bishops had been imprisoned and exiled, the total number of bishops in prison and exile surpassing 150 by the end of 1930.[29] The number of bishops breaking with Sergii on account of the above declaration was no less than thirty-seven.[30]

In the Ukraine the clergy faithful to the Patriarchal Church began suffering mass reprisals as early as 1919–21, owing to Soviet support for a Ukrainian nationalistic church movement, the so-called Autocephalists (also known as Lypkivskyites), which broke away from the Patriarch. Having achieved this three-way split in the Ukraine (the Patriarchals, the Renovationists, and the Autocephalists), this effectively weakened the Church as an institution in general, and seeing that the vast majority of the population in the Ukraine continued to cling to the Patriarchal jurisdiction,[31] the Soviets lost interest in the Autocephalists and began their selective persecution in 1924. In addition, in the second half of the 1920s the regime began its first manoeuvres to curb and eventually destroy local nationalist movements, including the Autocephalist Church which was an enclave of the most extreme Ukrainian ecclesiastical nationalists. A wholesale persecution began: its leader was imprisoned in 1926 and, after a number of reversals, the Church was forced to declare its self-liquidation at its last council in 1930. Practically all its self-appointed bishops, most clerical and lay activists, were incarcerated, many were executed.[32]

1929-41

The separation of the pre-1929 period from the post-1929 one is somewhat artificial. A scrutiny of the few available biographies of priests and lay believers persecuted for their faith reveals that many of them had begun their prison odyssey in the 1920s, continuing in the 1930s, 1940s, 1950s, and even in the early 1960s in the few cases of those who lived long enough.[33] Yet 1929 is a watershed of sorts.

To begin with, it was the year of the first Soviet comprehensive antireligious legislation, which deprived the Church of all rights except that of fulfilling rituals within church walls. All pretence at a struggle between religion and atheism on equal terms was shed once and for all: from now on only atheists had the unlimited right to propagate their ideas, the right of information and propaganda. The Church was not allowed even to run study groups for religious adutls, organize picnics or cultural circles, organize special services for individual groups of believers, such as schoolchildren, youth, women or mothers.

But in addition to the main laws, other instructions and regulations – mostly of 1928–30, all of them having the force of law – progressively straightened the situation of the Churches, and in particular of the clergy and their families, making arbitrary persecutions against them ever easier, particularly after the issuing of a number of discriminatory financial, land use and housing regulations.

The Soviet constitutions of 1918 and 1924 declared the clergy of all ranks and religions (including monks, nuns and novices) and their dependents 'the non-labouring elements', to be deprived of the right to elect or be elected to any Soviet organs of government or administration, popularly known as *lishentsy*. Additional instructions stipulated that members of rural clergy could be granted land plots for private cultivation, but in each case only with the special permission of the county government. Such permission could be granted only as a 'last priority' after all the land use needs of the 'toiling elements' had been satisfied, and only if no one in the given rural community requested the land for their use. Should such a request arise, the administration had the right to take the plot away from the clergyman. The clergy had no priority of claim over any part of the land that had belonged to the Church prior to the revolution.

As to co-operatives and collective farms, the 'non-toiling elements' were deprived of the right to join them by a 1928 piece of legislation. In other words, whatever land the rural clergy may have used for cultivation prior to the collectivization, they would lose it now. As well-to-do farmers (Kulaks and 'sub-Kulaks') were liquidated in the course of collectivization the village clergy lost its subsistence, as the wealthier peasants alone could pay the monstrous taxes levied by the state on the clergy as 'private entrepreneurs'. But even before the collectivization, no rules or criteria regulated or limited the rights of the county government to refuse a plot of land to a clergyman. This meant that there was no limit for arbitrary decisions and discrimination against the clergy either during or before the collectivization.

As has already been said, the 'income' tax the clergy had to pay was on a par with that of private entrepreneurs, which could be as high as 81 per cent of income, but there were no clear criteria on how personal income was to be assessed; thus a broad avenue was opened for financial persecution. As for the rural clergy, the 1929 regulations stipulated that they pay the full tax on any land use, plus 100 per cent of the tax on income received for their clerical functions, plus a special tax paid by those deprived of the right to elect or be elected. In addition, all church communities had to pay an annual tax on the leased church building in the amount of 0.5 per cent of the 'market' value of the building, arbitrarily assessed by the State Insurance Office (*Gosstrakh*) which enjoyed complete monopoly.[34]

A number of Draconian measures were brought into force in 1929 regarding housing for clergy. Needless to say, all residences that had belonged to the Church before the revolution were nationalized by the 23 January 1918 decree. In 1929 it was decreed that clergy occupying any part of such housing in the rural areas would henceforth pay 10 per cent of their 'commmercial' value in rental payment per annum; while 'the toiling elements' living in the same had to pay only 1 per cent of the value in rent if it was a stone house and 2 per cent if it was made of wood. As far as the urban clergy was concerned, a decree of 8 April 1929 stipulated that none of the clergy whose total annual income surpassed 3000 roubles could continue to reside in any nationalized or municipalized buildings, and that they had to be evicted by that date. No such housing could be leased to any clergy (even earning less than the above sum) after that date, nor would they be allowed to reside there in apartments rented by 'toiling' individuals. The eviction 'is to be carried out administratively without any provision for replacement living space'. Henceforth priests could reside only in rented living space in private houses, of which after the collectivization almost nothing but semi-rural cottages remained. Moreover, in the climate of enhanced religious persecution not many laymen dared to offer such housing to members of the clergy. This measure forced many priests to 'unfrock', conceal their former vocation and take on civilian jobs.

The clergy and conscientious objectors had to pay a special tax for not serving in the active forces, but still had to serve (whenever called up) in the auxiliary force mobilized as labour detachments for felling trees, mining and doing other jobs over a certain period of years. The size of the military non-service tax (the clergy could not serve in the army even voluntarily, because this privilege was reserved only for full citizens with full voting rights) was equal to 50 per cent of the income tax on an annual income of under 3000 r., and to 75 per cent of the income tax over the said annual income size, but was not to exceed a total of 20 per cent of one's income. But if the clergyman was already paying over 80 per cent of his arbitrarily assessed income in income tax, then together with the military non-service tax this would amount to more than his income, not counting the other taxes and the rent.

A stipulation was included in this decree stating that avoidance or delays in paying this military tax should be regarded as regular crime and punishable by imprisonment.

Finally, an instruction of 5 August 1929 deprived the clergy of any social security rights. Up to then church councils could insure their clergy for medical care and even for pension by paying the required sums. From the date of this decree all such sums paid would be kept by the state, but no insurance or pensions provided for the clergy, even to those already in retirement. Henceforth the clergy could be served by doctors only privately who could charge as much as they wanted.[35]

1929 was the year of the beginning of forced mass collectivization of agriculure and of destruction of all private enterprise by a combination of absurdly exorbitant taxes and imprisonments, even executions for 'deliberate' avoidance of taxes, which were often classified as deliberate wrecking activities aimed against Soviet industrialization and the Five Year Plan. The Church and the clergy, categorized as private enterprise (although forbidden by the legislation to set and collect membership dues), were treated likewise.

> Collectivization often began by closing of the village church and the deportation of the village priest as a kulak. During this period a priest could be seen mounting the pulpit in his underclothes – all that he had left.

Priests' wives nominally divorced their husbands in order to get jobs to support their families and to get their children into schools; while 'priests began to line up in rags in front of the churches begging for alms'.[36]

The Soviet press and the LMG resolutions of 1929 and early 1930 are full of such slogans as: 'let us deal a crushing blow to religion!'; 'we must achieve liquidation of the Church and complete liquidation of religious superstitions!'[37] And, of course, liquidation in the Che-Ka jargon meant nothing less than execution. Indeed, Oleshchuk wrote towards the end of the last pre-war decade about the necessity of the final liquidation of the clergy (compare with Hitler's final solution of the Jewish question).[38] The intensity of the attack of 1929–30 can be illustrated by the example of known individual regions of the country. Thus, in the central Russian region of Bezhetsk 100 of the surviving 308 churches were shut in that year, as compared with twelve closed between 1918 and 1929. In the Tula diocese 200 out of 760 churches were closed during the same year. The LMG press is also full of boastful reports and photographs of demolished, dynamited churches or (more often) of their adaptation for secular use. Priests were treated as *kulaks*, and failing to pay their taxes in kind were exiled *en masse* to Siberia and to prisons. All this was only temporarily halted by Stalin's devious 'Dizziness from Success' article of 15 March 1930, calling for a slow-down in collectivization and 'condemning' the use of force.[39] The protests of Western Christians and Western states against the wild persecutions, and mass public prayers in Britain, Rome and other places on

Persecutions, 1921–41 65

behalf of the persecuted Russian believers, contributed greatly to this temporary halt in the antireligious holocaust. Stalin could not afford total alienation of the West: he needed its credits and machines for his industrialization.

The terror of the 1930s was conducted in a climate of maximum secrecy after the bad publicity of the 1929–30 campaign. Hence, even to this day, detailed and systematic information on terror of that decade in general and on that in relation to the Church in particular is lacking. All we have is multiple individual stories retold by witnesses and survivors. And that is what this chapter, of necessity, will have to consist of.

But let us first reconstruct the trends of persecutions. Following the round-up of the anti-Sergiite bishops, their churches were being closed *en masse* and the parish priests of these churches generally followed their bishops to exile and prison. The last officially functioning anti-Sergiite church in Moscow was closed in 1933; the last one in Leningrad, in 1936.[40] Once these churches were closed, they were usually either wrecked or turned to secular use. As, following Sergii's 1927 Declaration of Loyalty, a majority of parishes both in Moscow and Leningrad and up to 90 per cent of the parishes in those dioceses which were headed by anti-Sergiite bishops went into opposition, the destruction of the anti-Sergiite churches must have diminished the number of functioning churches by a very high proportion; although a large number of these schismatics on the right had made peace with Sergii by 1930, when he officially claimed the loyalty of 163 bishops and 30 000 parishes.[41]

1932 was the year of a near-complete destruction of the remaining overtly functioning monasteries. In the words of Levitin, a well-known Russian religious author and a witness of the time described, 'on 18 February 1932 all monks disappeared behind the bars of concentration camps'. His data, however, is based on Leningrad alone, where 318 monks and nuns were put behind bars on that day. In addition, the Leningrad transit prisons were bursting at the seams after that date with monks and nuns from the Leningrad province. (There is evidence that at least in the Ukraine some vestiges of semi-overt monasticism survived until 1935 and even 1937.) It was following the liquidation of monasticism that the 1929–30 wave of destruction of the rural churches reached the cities.

Levitin enumerates some twenty-two Leningrad churches alone closed during the week following 18 February 1932. More churches were closed during the subsequent months. Then there was another relative lull for over two years before the new and total assault of 1934–9 would begin.[42]

In Moscow alone over 400 churches and monasteries were dynamited. Of the total of over 600 religious communities of all faiths in pre-revolutionary Moscow, only fifteen orthodox and perhaps five or six communities of other faiths survived in 1939.[43] Even the Soviet general press presented occasionally revealing statistics on the destruction of churches, For example:[44]

City or city and district	Before rev.	1934–7
Belgorod and district	47 churches and 3 monasteries	4 churches (1936)
Novgorod (city)	42 churches and 3 monasteries	15 churches (1934)
Kuibyshev (former Samara) and its diocese	2200 churches, mosques and other temples	325 (1937)

But the above table brings us only to the end of 1936; two years of continuing and escalating liquidation of the Church were still to come. No religions were spared, not even the Renovationists, who were of no more use to the Soviets. The attack on them began in 1934 when, according to Levitin who was then an active Renovationist, the appearance of religiously dedicated youth in its ranks, including young priests, promised a possible transformation of Renovationism into something more than just an obedient GPU tool.[45]

The official Soviet 1941 figure of over 8000 religious communities of all faiths, including 4222 Orthodox, included the recently annexed territories of Moldavia, eastern Poland, the Baltic republics and parts of Western Karelia, where the number of Orthodox churches was well over 3000 and that of Roman Catholic, Protestant and Jewish religious centres must have been even higher. Levitin and many other Soviet citizens estimate that there were only around a hundred Orthodox churches still officially functioning in 1939 on the autochthonous Soviet territory. Indeed, in Leningrad, of 401 Orthodox churches functioning in 1918 only four Patriarchal and one

Renovationist parishes were still open in 1939, a little over 1 per cent of the original; extrapolating this proportion nationally one would achieve an estimate of some 500 churches for the whole Union. But Moscow and Leningrad were the cities most frequented by foreigners. Hence a more 'relaxed' policy towards the Church should have prevailed in these cities than in the rest of the country. Thus, the actual total may have been quite close to Levitin's estimate.[46]

The human toll of this holocaust must have been at least as great. Regelson has the following statistics on the known arrests of bishops from 1932 on: one in 1932, nine in 1933, six in 1934, fourteen in 1935, twenty in 1936, fifty in 1937; eighty-six bishops of the 163 boasted by Metropolitan Sergii in 1930 were behind bars seven years later (ignoring the thirty-six bishops arrested in 1928–31, since they were mostly anti-Sergiites). Twenty-nine bishops had died during the same period, twenty-seven were 'retired', which in most cases meant that the given bishop was banned from functioning as a bishop by the Soviets. This adds fifty-six bishops to the progressive 'evaporation' of the original figure of 163; but during the same years twenty-four new bishops were consecrated; therefore there should have been forty-five diocesan bishops still functioning after 1937. In fact, an Act of 1 January 1937, confirming Metropolitan Sergii as the sole legitimate locum-tenens mentioned fifty-one diocesan bishops. This precedes the arrest of fifty bishops in the course of 1937. By 1939 only four persons still occupied the posts of diocesan bishops in Sergii's whole hierarchy.[47] Levitin adds to this that to protect themselves from the effect of frequent arrests of bishops, throughout the 1920s a multitude of persons were consecrated, some secretly, as 'reserve' bishops. The practice was to have at least two to three bishops in each diocese, so that a vicar bishop could always take the place of an arrested diocesan one. Consequently, he believes that there was a total of at least 290 bishops alive in the main Orthodox Church (including those in prisons) by the early 1930s; while the Renovationists, who consecrated married priests as bishops quite indiscriminately (partly as a way of attracting priests from the Patriarchal Church) had 400 bishops before 1935.

In 1941 each of these Churches had about ten bishops at large, some diocesan, others in semi-retirement serving as regular parish priests. Thus he estimates that 280 Patriarchal and 390 Renovationist bishops were either shot or died in prisons in the 1930s and 1940s.[48] Probably the figure was a little lower, owing to the rate of natural attrition (partly accounted for by Regelson above) and to the fact that about a score of old bishops did reappear in the 1940s and early 1950s and joined the ranks of the Patriarchal hierarchy, some of them former Renovationists who had to be reconsecrated. In any case, the toll of bishop-martyrs of both factions must have been close to 600 in those dreadful years.

The toll of the parish clergy was proportionally similar. There is no way at the present time to give an exact estimate. But here we can again extrapolate the Leiningrad figure, where of a hundred priests still serving the Orthodox Church in 1935, only seven survived to 1940; and of fifty Renovationist priests in 1935, only eight survived to 1941. Again, if anything, the Leningrad rate of clerical survival must have been above the average for the country as a whole, for the reasons mentioned above. At the end of the 1920s the Renovationist Church had over 10 000 parish priests and the Patriarchal Church over 30 000. At the above 10 per cent combined survival rate, therefore, no less than 35 000 priests must have been imprisoned or executed in the 1930s, not counting new ordinations and the toll of natural death and retirement in the same decade. Again, a few thousand priests were released after the Stalin–Sergii concordat of 1943. Even then, there must have been at least some 25 000 to 30 000 martyred priests in the 1930s and 1940s. This makes a Western estimate of over 42 000 Orthodox clergy martyred by communism in Russia[49] an understatement if we add the Civil War and the 1920s toll plus the physical liquidation of at least twenty thousand monastics.

How could so much brutality go on? – a lot of it publicly (destruction of churches, burning of icons, throwing out of priests into the streets with their families), in which many young Komsomol and LMG enthusiasts participated. In Vasili Grossman's novel, *Forever Flowing*, a disillusioned and repentant former collective farm enthusiast says that in order to make the annihilation of *kulaks* acceptable to the other peasants, the propaganda had to single them out from the rest of the peasantry and brain-wash the non-*kulak* children and youth, if not the mature peasantry, to see the *kulaks*, the *nepmen* and other terrorized elements as subhumans, as vermin of sorts. One may be sorry for the drowning of superfluous kittens but one accepts this as a necessity; as for the destruction of rats and their litter, one would not even think twice. And the propaganda said that the bourgeoisie, the *kulaks*, were worse than rats.[50] Well, as the posters in Chapter 2 illustrate, the clergy, indeed the Deity as well, were treated precisely in this way. A manual of readings for schoolchildren, likewise, tries to evoke nothing but contempt, a sense of fastidiousness towards the believers in its readers, when pilgrims are depicted as a combination of morons, repulsive-looking alcoholics, syphilitics, plain cheaters and greedy money-grubbing clergy.[51] At the end of the story there remains no sympathy or empathy of the reader towards the believer: he or she is just a harmful parasite, spreading ignorance, filth, disease; the sooner that vermin is liquidated, the better. Yaroslavsky, the chief supervisor of all antireligious activities and publications of the time surely could not have been serious when he referred to the condemnation of the use of force against religion or to close churches declared by the Eight Party Congress. Posing as a moderate thinker, in another textbook Yaroslavsky protests that religion is not merely 'an invention of the priests': 'the roots of religion are much deeper and they must be brought to the surface'.[52]

He admits direct religious persecution only in the past, which he calls 'a period of storm and thrust with the antireligious Komsomol carnivals, mass closure of churches . . .', which he justifies for the 1920s as having been 'to some extent a response to the clergy's counter-revolutionary activities during the Civil War and to the resistance of some clergy to the confiscation of church valuables'.[53] But all this ended in 1922, while, as we have seen above, the real mass church closures began in 1929, and the antireligious hate propaganda intensified from that year on, now under the pretext of the clergy's wrecking activities against industrialization, as the posters in Chapter 2 also illustrate.

As for the drastic reduction of the number of functioning temples, the official propaganda claimed that it corresponded to the decline of religiosity in the population, and that the closures were in accordance with the will of the toilers. But here is a story from the Soviet press from a slightly earlier period. A church was closed in 1923 in a factory settlement not far from

Moscow, allegedly according to the decision of a workers' meeting. But four years later a young priest collected over 2000 signatures under a petition to allow the building of a new church, the original one having presumably been wrecked. The signatories, the same workers and their families who had allegedly voted to liquidate the parish, now prove so energetic in their demands that permission is eventually granted.[54] Although the Soviet author maintains that the signatures were obtained by fraud, this can hardly explain the perseverence of the group. The true explanation could only be that either the church had been shut arbitrarily against the will of the people, or that over the short span of four years of Soviet experience masses of non-believers returned to the faith. Most likely the truth of the matter was that with the growing disillusionment with socialism and materialism people were strengthened in their faith and were now more ready to fight for it than in the early 1920s. In the latter case, the tough legislation of 1929 and the intensified persecutions which accompanied and followed it can only be seen as a hysterically defensive action of a bankrupt ideology.

Be that as it may, the atheistic press of our own day will occassionally admit that there were persecutions in the 1930s. Yankova, for instance, admits pre-war persecutions as a means to refute the popular opinion that the reopening of the churches at the end of the Second World War and immediately following it was caused by a massive religious revival during the war. No, says Yankova, 'the opening of the churches is not only a sign of some revival of religiousness ... but also a manifestation of the fact that at the end of the 1920s and throughout the 1930s churches ... were shut in many places without the approval of the believers'. Furthermore, she admits that of the approximately 950 churches in the Riazan' diocese before the revolution only nine or ten remained by the end of the 1930s, while as a result of believers' petitions after the war some sixty churches were reopened, reaching a total of sixty-nine.[55] This renders the proportion of functioning Orthodox churches by 1940 as less than 1 per cent of the pre-revolutionary number. If we assume that Riazan' was a typical case, and there is no reason to do otherwise, then it brings us back to the earlier estimate of under 500 churches functioning by 1939, much less than the 1934–6 figures would suggest.

Yaroslavsky's own estimate of believers as numbering over

50 per cent of the total population must have been on the low side, because throughout the existence of the LMG he and his League were boasting of their great successes in making headway against religion; and as has been shown before, in the atheistic euphoria of the late 1920s their estimate of the religious sector of the population was under 20 per cent.[56] But even taking Yaroslavsky's 1938 estimate at its face value we see that 1 per cent of the former number of churches was serving 50 per cent of the population. This alone is a clear recognition of direct persecutions in the 1930s, and on a colossal scale.

But shutting the churches and liquidating the clergy were not the only means of direct persecution. The atheist press greeted the continuous work week (*nepreryvka*) as a mortal blow to religion, depriving the believers of regular Eucharist. Cartoons depicted groups of priests in rags in front of empty churches with signs: 'Preachers' Employment Office'. A Christmas cartoon depicts an angel asking St Joseph whether to blow his horn announcing Christmas. Joseph: 'No use, brother ... there is no Christmas; the continuous work week has killed it'.[57]

But had it? The Soviet press itself answered this question in the negative: *Bezbozhnik* for 1937–8 published cartoons on the 'roaming priests' who wander from village to village, surreptitiously performing religious services in believers' homes. They are often disguised as wandering repairmen, offering to sharpen knives or do other odd jobs, or they have to conceal their real vocation from the authorities and the informers.[58] The notorious Oleshchuk, complaining that young people continued to be attracted to religion and were even converting, whether to the Evangelical sects or to Orthodoxy, tells about priests hiring themselves out *free of charge* (so, the clergy is not that greedy after all) to youth parties as games organizers, musicians, choir directors, readers of secular Russian literature, drama-circles directors, thus bringing the rural young into the sphere of religious influence.[59]

The admission that being caught as a church member – whether clerical or lay – was very dangerous in those days, is contained in the following passage written in typically Aesopian language, full of contradictions:

> There are many regions where churches have been closed on toilers' requests ... either because of the absence of a church

The slogan on the flag reads: 'I am going over to the continuous workweek'.

in the district or out of shyness (ashamed to observe religious rituals overtly) many believers do not address themselves... to the local priest.

Adapting themselves to the new conditions leaders of religious organizations... perform many rituals in absentia.

The story gives details on how marriage ceremonies are performed over the wedding rings sent to a distant priest by the absentee bride and groom. Funeral services are performed over an empty coffin into which the corpse is later laid and buried in a secular ceremony.[60]

According to official statements there have never been any persecutions for faith in the Soviet Union, only for anti-Soviet acts. But the most convincing evidence to the contrary is that the majority of bishops and priests were never brought to trial except in connection with the confiscation of church valuables. Most of them, in the 1920s at any rate, were simply administratively banished to labour camps or into internal exile for three years, which was the maximum legal duration for administrative exile in Soviet law of the time until the creation of the NKVD in 1934, which received the right of giving administrative exile for up to four years. After serving this term bishops and priests mostly returned to their dioceses or parishes. Those whose term ran out around 1930 were often later transported under surveillance to an isolated village in the far north or north-east, never to return. Such was the fate of Metropolitan Peter and many others. The already quoted Fr. Polsky cites numerous similar individual cases of bishops and priests, for instance, the case of Bishop Victor (Ostrogradsky) of Glazov. He served his first term of administrative exile in 1922–5. In 1928, following his protest against Metropolitan Sergii's Declaration of Loyalty, he was sent to a concentration camp at Mai-Guba. Three years later he was sent to an isolated settlement in the Province of Arkhangelsk, and there disappeared after 1933.

Bishop Alexander (Petrovsky) was consecrated in 1932 and appointed by Metropolitan Sergii to Kharkov. In 1939 he was suddenly arrested, never officially charged; but he soon died in prison, naturally or unnaturally – no one knows. Then the authorities decided to close the last functioning church in the city. Therefore during the 1941 Lent, the parish was ordered to pay a tax of 125 000 roubles, when the average *annual* wage was about 4000. The money was collected and submitted on time, yet the church was administratively shut just before Easter. The Passions were celebrated in the square in front of the church – over 8000 people participated, forming a close circle around numerous priests dressed in civilian clothes who quietly pronounced the prayers, picked up by the impromptu choir of thousands of people: 'Glory to Thy passion, O Lord!' The same was repeated for the Easter Resurrection service, with an even bigger crowd....[61]

Thus the laity struggled to keep their martyred bishop's church alive.

A blatant case of prosecution for mere popularity was that of the priest and, later, bishop, Arkadii Ostal'sky, accused in 1922 of inciting the masses against the state. When all witnesses refuted the charge, the prosecutor retorted that their defence was the best indictment against the priest, because it showed his great popularity, while 'the ideas which he so passionately preached ... contradicted the ideas of the Soviets, therefore such persons ... are very harmful to the Soviet State'. Fr. Arkadii was sentenced to death, then commuted to ten years' hard labour. On his return from the camp he was consecrated bishop. Exiled to the Solovki camps around 1931, he returned three years later, went into hiding, was caught and sent to a concentration camp again. Released shortly before the Second World War, he informed his friends that the camp administration had promised him safety and job security if he would agree to stay in the area of the camps and give up the priesthood. He refused. A short while later he was rearrested and disappeared.

Metropolitan Konstantin (D'iakov) of Kiev was arrested in 1937 and shot in prison without trial twelve days later.

Metropolitan Pimen (Pegov) of Kharkov was hated by the communists because he had managed to nip the Renovationist schisms in the bud in that city. He was arrested on a trumped-up charge of contacts with foreign diplomats. He died in prison in 1933.

Bishop Maxim (Ruberovsky) returned from prison in 1935 to the city of Zhitomir, to where by 1937 almost all priests from the Soviet part of Volhynia were expelled, a total of about 200. In August, all of them, including the bishop, were arrested and shot in the early part of winter without trial. Posthumously, the

Soviet press accused them of subversive acts against the state.

Antonii, Archbishop of Arkhangelsk, was arrested in 1932. The authorities tried to force him to 'confess' that he was an enemy of the Soviet state, but he categorically refused. In a written questionnaire on his attitude to the Soviet Government he responded that he 'prayed daily that God forgive the Soviet Government its sins and that it stop shedding blood'. In prison he was tortured by being given salty food without adequate drink, and by shortage of oxygen in a dirty and overcrowded damp cell without ventilation, until he succumbed to dysentery and died.

Metropolitan Serafim (Meshcheriakov) of Belorussia was hated by the Soviets for having returned to the Orthodox Church with much public penance after having been a very active leader in the Renovationist schism. Soon after the penance he was arrested in 1924 and exiled to Solovki. Shortly after his return he was re-arrested and shot without trial in Rostov-on-Don along with 122 other priests and monks.

Metropolitan Nikolai of Rostov-on-Don was exiled without trial to the Hungry Steppe in Kazakhstan, where he and other exiled priests built huts for themselves out of clay mixed with some local grass; this grass was also their staple food. In 1934 he was allowed to return to Rostov and to re-occupy his post. Rearrested in 1938, he was condemned to death, but miraculously survived the firing squad. Next morning believers picked up his unconscious body from a mass open grave and secretly nursed him. He then served as Metropolitan of Rostov under the German occupation and was evacuated to Romania. His subsequent fate is unknown.

Bishop Onufrii (Gagaliuk) of Elisavetgrad was first arrested in 1924, obviously without cause, because he had simply been deported in a prison train from his see. A year later he was already again the ruling bishop of Elisavetgrad. But after two more years he was arrested once again and exiled to Krasnoiarsk in Siberia. On return from the Siberian administrative exile, he occupied two more episcopal sees, only to be rearrested in the mid-1930s and deported beyond the Urals where, according to rumours, he was shot in 1938.

Bishop Illarion (Belsky) was exiled to Solovki at least from 1929 to 1935 in retaliation for his stubborn resistance to Metropolitan Sergii. He was arrested again in 1938, apparently for his refusal to recognize the ecclesiastical authority of Sergii, and shot.

Bishop Varfolomei (Remov) was shot in 1936 for the 'crime' of having secretly organized and run for several years an unofficial graduate theological academy when none were permitted by the state. He was denounced by his own pupil Alexii, a future bishop (not to be confused with Patriarch Alexii).[62]

Whereas the anti-Sergiites were arrested and even shot for their insubordination to Metropolitan Sergii (a strange 'crime' in a country where the Church and State are alleged to be separated from each other), it would be wrong to think that the position of the clergy loyal to Sergii was any more secure. A case in point is the fate of two remarkable clergymen and close friends: Bishop Maxim (Zhizhilenko) who had broken with Sergii after the Declaration, and Fr. Roman Medved' who remained loyal to Sergii. The former was arrested in 1929, the latter in 1931. The bishop was executed in 1931; Fr. Roman was released from a concentration camp in 1936 because of ruined health, and died within one year. Bishop Maxim had worked as a Moscow transit prison medical doctor-surgeon for twenty-five years before his consecration as bishop in 1928. His medical and humanitarian fame spread far beyond the walls of his prison hospital. He ate prison food, slept on bare boards and used to give away his salary to prisoners.

He returned many a criminal to Christ. Under the Soviets he was secretly ordained priest while continuing to serve as prison doctor. Thus he could officiate religiously to prisoners seeking pastoral help, and hear their confessions. The Soviets could not forgive him two 'treasons': one, that such an outstanding and popular Soviet medical officer 'deserted' them for the Church; two, that he chose the most militantly anti-Sergiite faction, that of M. Joseph. Neither could they tolerate his charisma as a bishop: in less than one year as bishop of Serpukhov all eighteen parishes in that town and almost all churches in the nearby towns and villages (all in the vicinity of Moscow) went over to him from Sergii's jurisdiction. Finally, in response to the official Church policy since 1923 that prayers be said for the Soviet Government at the liturgy, Bp. Maxim was said to have been the author of a special 'prayer for the Church' (known also as 'A Prayer for Bolsheviks'), pronounced in his and many other churches both under Sergii and in those in opposition. It called on Jesus to keep His word that the gates of Hell would not overcome the Church and that He 'grant those in power wisdom and fear of God, so that their hearts become merciful and peaceful towards the Church'.

In one description, Bp. Maxim 'was a confessor of apocalyptic mind'. In contrast, his friend who remained a stalwart and powerful defender of Sergii's line, was described as a man 'of spiritual sobriety and calm'. Yet, both perished at the hands of the GPU, because they shared a common 'crime': a magnetic personality, immense pastoral charisma, devotion and charity which drew people to the Church. Despite the liquidation of Fr. Roman an unofficial church brotherhood set up by him in the 1920s exists to the present day.[63]

Another illustration of the similar fate of several of the most outstanding and charismatic priests, each of whom took different attitudes to M. Sergii's line, deserves to be mentioned. The most famous of these were Frs. Paul Florensky and Valentin Sventsitsky. Florensky was one of Orthodoxy's greatest twentieth-century theologians. At the same time he was a professor of electrical engineering at the Moscow Pedagogical Institute, one of the top counsellors in the Soviet Central Office for the Electrification of the USSR, a musicologist and an art historian. In all these fields he held official posts, delivered lectures and published widely even under the Soviets, while continuing to serve as a priest and refusing to take off his cassock and pectoral cross even when lecturing at the university. This brought him one arrest after another, beginning in 1925, and concluding with his terminal incarceration in 1933 (although even in the camps he was given a laboratory). In his last years he was apparently doing research for the Soviet armed forces. He died in a concentration camp in the far north in 1943. Throughout these years he never broke his allegiance to M. Sergii and the official Church.[64]

Fr. Sventsitsky was a journalist, a religious author and thinker of Christian-socialist leanings before the revolution. Some of his writings had brought him trouble with the tsarist police and he was forced to live abroad for a number of years. Immediately after the Bolshevik *coup d'état* he sought ordination in the Patriarchal Orthodox Church and became its great defender against the Renovationists, which brought his first arrest and exile as early as 1922. He became one of the most influential priests in Moscow, forming parish brotherhoods of moral rebirth. In 1927 he broke with M. Sergii. In 1928 he was exiled to Siberia, where he would die three years later; but before his death he repented to M. Sergii, asking to be reaccepted into the Orthodox Church, as he had understood that schism was the worst sin in the Church: 'every schism is separation from the True Church'. He died as a member of Sergii's Church after having written a passionate appeal to his Moscow parishioners to return to Sergii's fold and begging them to forgive him for having led them in a wrong and sinful direction.[65]

Among the most outstandingly influential priests could be also named Alexander Zhurakovsky of Kiev and Sergii Mechev of Moscow. Fr. Zhurakovsky joined the opposition to Sergii after the death of his diocesan bishop, who had remained loyal to Sergii but with whom Zhurakovsky could not break because of personal attachment (*sic*). Fr. Zhurakovsky was arrested in 1930 and sentenced to ten years' hard labour; suffering from TB he had been close to breaking-point in his health by 1939 when he received another ten years without seeing freedom even for a day. At the end of that year he died in a distant northern camp. Fr. Sergii Mechev occupied a position in between: he recognized the authority of M. Sergii but refused to utter public prayers for the Soviet Government. His arrests began in 1922, long before the anti-Sergii split. In 1929 he was administratively exiled for three years, but released only in 1933. The following year he was sentenced to fifteen years in a concentration camp in the Ukraine. When the Germans attacked in 1941 the Soviets shot him along with all prisoners with terms exceeding ten years.[66] The only thing that these pastors had in common was their charisma, wide respect, devotion and love of the faithful, and unique qualities as pastors and spiritual leaders. This was their common 'crime', not the issue of their attitude to Sergii's loyalty to the Soviets.

Among the few bishops who had survived the tortures of long imprisonments and returned to their archpastoral duties after the concordat of the Church hierarchy with Stalin, were: Manuil (Lemeshevsky) formerly of Leningrad, the surgeon-bishop Luka (Voino-Yasenetsky), a founder of the Tashkent University and its first professor of medicine, and Afanasii

(Sakharov) a vicar-bishop of the Vladimir Archdiocese. The former two had been loyal to M. Sergii throughout; Afanasii opposed Sergii's form of the declaration of loyalty (it denied the Church was ever persecuted by the Soviets and thereby betrayed the martyrs), was one of the most respected leaders of the underground Church through the early 1940s, but returned to the Patriarchal Church on the election of Alexii in 1945, and called upon all the 'undergrounders' to follow his example.

Bishop, later Metropolitan, Manuil became a thorn in the flesh of the Soviet regime for his very successful struggle against the Renovationists, which he had begun as early as 1922 when the Patriarch was in prison and hardly anyone dared to pronounce his name publicly. It was then, when all but two or three parishes in Petrograd were held by the Renovationists, that he was responsible for a mass return of parish after parish in his diocese to the Patriarchal Church. In 1923 he was arrested and after almost a year in jail was exiled for three years. On his return in 1927 he was not allowed to reside in Leningrad. Appointed Bishop of Serpukhov, although loyal to M. Sergii, he soon found the moral compromises called for by Sergii's new political line too frustrating. In 1929 he retired, probably finding it morally unbearable to be in the opposing camps with Bp. Maxim (Zhizhilenko) in the same city, and later even worse after Maxim had been arrested. Nevertheless, in 1933 he was taken out of his retirement and once again administratively exiled for three years to Siberia. His subsequent respite was short: in 1940 he was rearrested, formally charged with spreading religious propaganda among the young, and sentenced to ten years' hard labour. Released in 1945 and appointed Archbishop of Orenburg he achieved such success in reviving religious life there that in 1948 he was imprisoned once again. Released in 1955, he served as Archbishop of Cheboksary and Metropolitan of Kuibyshev. He died a natural death in 1968 at the age of 83, leaving a considerable volume of scholarly papers behind him, including a multi-volume 'Who's Who' of Russian twentieth-century bishops.[67]

In December 1945 at a solemn ceremony honouring the surgeon professor-archbishop Luka Voino-Yasenetsky with a medal for the service he had rendered to Soviet war medicine,

Luka's response to the Soviet officials was as follows:

> I have always taught and am willing to continue to pass my knowledge on to other doctors. I have returned to life hundreds, perhaps thousands of the wounded; and certainly would have helped many more had *you* not grabbed me and, without any guilt on my part, thrown me around from prisons to exile and back for eleven years. So many years have been lost and so many people have not been cured by no fault of mine whatsoever.

His first imprisonment occurred in Tashkent in 1923 when the Renovationists felt they could not compete with this highly prestigious young bishop-doctor, chief surgeon and professor of medicine at the University which he had helped to establish, and a brilliant sermoniser. His 'crime' was that he remained faithful to the Patriarch; but officially he was accused of treasonous ties with foreign agents in the Caucasus and Central Asia simultaneously (*sic*), and exiled to a distant north-Siberian town, Eniseisk, for three years. His freedom had been short: 1927 to 1930, when he was rearrested and without any trial exiled to Arkhangelsk for another three years. His third and physically harshest imprisonment came in 1937. He was tortured for two years (many times badly beaten, interrogated for weeks without cease – the so-called 'conveyor interrogation' – and went on hunger strikes) in vain NKVD attempts to have him sign false confessions. Having failed in that, the NKVD simply deported him to northern Siberia. With the beginning of the war his unique expertise in treating infected wounds was suddenly remembered. Without removing from him the status of exilee, he was brought to Krasnoiarsk and made chief surgeon for infected wounds at the main military hospital. In 1946 the new and enlarged edition of his book on infected wounds won him a Stalin Prize for medicine while he was the Archbishop of Tambov. He donated the prize to war orphans.[68]

One of the most fantastic biographies is that of Bishop Afansaii, fantastic in terms of the total duration of incarcerations and in terms of his survival. As he noted in his own curriculum vitae, at the time of release from his last imprisonment in 1954 he had been a bishop for thirty-three years. Of these he had spent: 'thirty-three months performing episcopal functions; thirty-two months at large without any occupation; seventy-six months in exile; 254 months in prisons and slave labour camps'.

His first prolonged incarceration occurred in 1922 when he was arrested jointly with M. Sergii (the future Patriarch) and two other bishops in connection with the church valuables, and sentenced to one year of imprisonment. Five more arrests and short periods in prisons, exile and hard labour followed during the subsequent five years. Once he was simply told that he would be left alone if he agreed to retire or leave his diocesan city of Vladimir. He refused to abandon his flock voluntarily. Again arrested in April 1927, he spent some time in the same cell with M. Sergii, but by June of that year Sergii was released to issue the Declaration of Loyalty, while Afansii with a number of other bishops soon received three years' hard labour in Solovki for belonging to Sergii's group of bishops. He suffered seven more imprisonment and exile terms, mostly without formal indictments, between 1930 and 1946. From this last incarceration, which included very hard manual labour and which formally ended in 1951, he was in fact not released until 1954. He writes that he survived all this thanks to the memory of his faithful believers who had continued to send him generous parcels during all these years; their love not fading away but intensifying during the length of separation: 'If in the first two years and four months of imprisonment I had received seventy-two parcels, during 1954 alone, I received 200 parcels.' The much-loved bishop was born in 1887, died in 1962.[69]

The numbers of laymen, parish priests, monks and nuns martyred by the Soviets in the 1930s and 1940s for their faith were just too great, and the proportion of the known cases to that of the unknown too small, to be discussed in this study. Even the most detailed study on the subject, namely that of Fr. Polsky, further exacerbates this disproportion. He lists over 190 priests, over 160 monks and nuns, but less than a dozen laymen for that period. Moreover, it is more difficult to distinguish the 'reasons' for a layman's incarceration and even execution: whether the person was imprisoned for his or her faith or for an act treated by the state as anti-Soviet behaviour. For instance, in 1929 two Russian émigrés came to Leningrad from the West with forged identities to help a certain Countess Z-n to escape, also with forged papers brought by them. The mission was successful, but the naive woman, on arrival in a West Eurpean capital, informed the press of all the details of her sensational escape. Consequently, forty of her former friends and acquaintances were arrested in 1930. Six of them, including her parish priest, Fr. Mikhail Chel'tsov, were executed. Now, the priest's 'crime' was that he performed a Te Deum on behalf of the success of her escape. Obviously, he was executed for performing his pastoral duty, for the Church could not see a sin in the desire of her spiritual daughter to change her place of residence, and the priest's duty was to pray for the health and God's protection for any member of his flock. But the five laymen were executed for actively helping the woman to escape; they were considered to have engaged in anti-state activities in terms of the Soviet law, however hideous this might sound from the point of view of the law codes of democratic states.[70]

But even this case is an exception. Most of the other murders or murderous incarcerations of clergy cited in Polsky's book are not even indirectly related to 'anti-state activities'. Following are some particularly notorious examples.

There was a highly revered convent in the vicinity of Kazan' which the authorities had closed in the late 1920s and forced the nuns to resettle privately in the area, but they allowed the main cathedral of the convent to reopen once a year (its patron saint's day?), on 14 February, when the former nuns, monks and masses of lay pilgrims would converge on the church for that unique service. During such a service in 1933 huge armed GPU detachments surrounded the church and arrested everyone coming out of it. Two months later ten monks, nuns and lay persons were executed, and most other pilgrims received concentration camp terms of five to ten years in duration. Their 'crime' was: participation in an unregistered church service. The community was not in M. Sergii's jurisdiction.[71]

A group of geologists, surveying in the Siberian Taiga in the summer of 1933, had camped for a night in the vicinity of a concentration camp when they suddenly saw a group of prisoners being led by camp guards and lined up before a freshly dug ditch. When the guards saw the geologists they told them that these were priests, 'an element alien to the Soviet Power'. This was the only rationalization for their execution.

The geologists were told to remove themselves to the nearby tents. From the tents they heard how, before every individual execution, the victim was told that were he to deny God's existence this would be his last chance to survive. In every case, without exception, the answer was: 'God exists'. A pistol-shot followed. This procedure was repeated sixty times until the whole operation was over.[72]

Fr. Antonii Elsner-Foiransky-Gogol, a distant relative of the famous Russian writer, Nikolai Gogol, was a priest in Smolensk, with only a three-year absence (1922–5) owing to imprisonment and exile. In 1935 his church was closed and he moved to a nearby village. In 1937 only two churches in Smolensk remained open. One of them lacked a priest, so the parishioners begged Fr. Antonii to become their priest. He agreed. At first he was registered with the Soviets as superintendent of the church receiving the right to live in the vacant superintendent's cottage. Then the parishioner began to petition for the right to reopen the church officially for services and to register Fr. Antonii as their priest. Several thousand people signed the petitions, but the local NKVD refused and warned the priest that he would suffer consequences. The petitions reached the central government in Moscow and received a positive reply. Thousands of people congratulated Fr. Antonii and began to decorate the church for the first service to take place on 21 July 1937. But the night before the first service the priest was arrested. On 1 August the prison authorities refused to accept a parcel for him from the priest's wife. Fr. Antonii was shot.[73]

Early in 1934 three Orthodox priests and two lay believers were taken out of their special regime Kolyma camp to the local OGPU administration. Each of them was asked to renounce his faith in Jesus. Instead, all of them re-confirmed their faith, although they were warned: 'If you don't deny your Christ, [death] awaits you.' Without any formal charges they were then taken to a freshly dug grave, and four were shot. One of the three priests, however, also without any explanation, was told to bury the dead and was spared.[74]

Towards the end of the 1930s there remained only one church open for services in Kharkov. The authorities refused to grant registration to any priest to serve there. One such registered priest living in the city was Fr. Gavriil. He could not control himself when Easter Night (1936?) arrived. He went to the church and began to serve the Resurrection Vigil. This was his last service. No one saw him again.[75]

In the diocesan city of Poltava all the remaining clergy were swept up by the NKVD during the night of 26–27 February 1938. Their relatives were soon informed that all of them, without exception, were sentenced to 'ten years without the right to correspond' – a euphemism for the death sentence.[76]

The previously described Archbishop Luka and Bp. Maxim (Zhizhilenko) were not the only medical doctor-priests among the GPU/NKVD/KGB victims. The Elder Sampson was born in 1898 to Count Sivers d'Espera and an English mother and baptized in the Anglican Church. When fourteen years old he chose to convert from Anglicanism to Orthodoxy. After gaining a degree in medicine he went on to receive a theological education, and in 1918 joined a monastic brotherhood near Petrograd. In the same year he was arrested and taken to a mass execution in which he was only wounded and covered up by other bodies. From this heap he was rescued by fellow-monks. In 1929 he was arrested again, by this time a tonsured monk-priest. Released in 1934, he was rearrested two years later, and sentenced to ten years in prison. All these years he served as a prison doctor. The authorities refused to release him when his time was up in 1946 because they needed his medical services. This was in Central Asia. He decided to escape. His wanderings without food and water through the hot Central Asian deserts, avoidance of arrests and subsequent years of pastoral work without any legal papers in Stalin's Soviet Union appear miraculous indeed. To the hundreds of his spiritual children Elder Sampson, who died in 1979, was a saint who in all his sufferings never ceased to repeat: 'How lucky we are to be Orthodox! How wealthy!'[77]

Bishop Stefan (Nikitin) was also a medical doctor and this helped him to survive his imprisonment working as a concentration camp doctor. He retells a miracle that he experienced at the hands of a crippled holy woman. In the camp he was too merciful to the overworked and underfed prisoners and periodically allowed them to stay in the hospital to recuperate. This became known to the higher-ups and he was informed that a new trial was probably awaiting him, with a possible maximum sentence of fifteen years for wrecking the Soviet industrial effort by taking workers from their jobs. His nurse who informed him of the danger, advised him to ask a certain Matrionushka in the Volga city of Penza to pray for him. 'But I would get my 15 years before my letter reached her,' said Bishop Stefan. The nurse retorted that all he had to do was to shout three times: 'Matrionushka, help me in my predicament!' She will hear from thousands of miles away. Indeed, he did not get the extra fifteen years, and on his release several weeks later chose Penza as his post-prison residence, in order to meet the woman. On the train he was told by people from the area of Penza that once he left the railway station and asked any passer-by he would be directed to Matrionushka. This is precisely what happened. When he reached Matrionushka's habitation, he found the door open. There was a practically empty room with a table in the middle. On the table stood a long box and nobody was to be seen. He asked, 'May I come in?', and suddenly heard a voice from the box, 'Come in Serezhen'ka' – the voice was addressing him by his pre-monastic secular name. He looked into the box and there was a blind woman with short stumps instead of arms and legs. 'How do you know my name?' he asked after greeting her. 'How could I not have known? Haven't you called for me? And I prayed for you to the Lord.' The two became friends, but not for long: she predicted that she would die in prison, and indeed, 'Soon Matrionushka was arrested, transported to a Moscow prison, and died there.'[78]

As for the 'villains' and 'parasites' who were being liquidated for 'wrecking' and 'subverting' the USSR, like Ivan Churikov and his associates (see Chapter 2), such allegations became quite plentiful in the Soviet media, particularly after 1929. As mentioned in Chapter 2, antireligious textbooks of those years, not to mention *Bezbozhnik* and other periodicals, were full of allegations of clergy appealing to the population to sabotage the Five Year Plan.

In 1929, according to the Soviet press, 'an important spy organization in the Baptist community', in the pay and service of the Polish intelligence service, was uncovered in the Ukraine. Allegedly the organization, headed by a certain Baptist leader Shevchuk, had a hundred secret agents serving the Polish intelligence as spies. In return, the Poles provided them with literature which they distributed in the Baptist communities. The literature, allegedly, was 'not only religious but also counter-revolutionary'. The report loses all credibility and sense of proportion when it adds that the Baptists were selling Soviet military secrets to the Poles, which they had allegedly obtained from fellow Baptists serving in the Red Army. Obviously, in the conditions of particular suspicion towards religious believers and the search for any excuse to prosecute them, no religious leader in his right mind would engage in espionage, and no informed foreign intelligence (which the neighbouring Polish intelligence service was) would have assigned such chores to a religious leader. The motive for this clearly fraudulent report was that at that time a majority faction of the Baptist Church had decided to allow its members to serve in the armed forces, depriving the Soviet propaganda of the possibility of attacking 'the sectarians' as irresponsible pacifists who would parasitically enjoy the security provided them by the patriots ready to shed their blood for their fellow-men, while cowardly and selfishly refusing to do the same. So a new platform for attack and persecution had to be found: and this was that the Baptists had changed their policy and agreed to serve in the Red Army in order to subvert it and spy on it.[79]

In 1930 there were at least three fraudulent show trials of three fictitious anti-Soviet organizations, allegedly associated with the Church. One was that of a so-called Union for the Liberation of the Ukraine, under the pretext of which the Autocephalist Ukrainian Church was finally quashed and numerous leading Ukrainian nationalist lay intellectuals and clergy executed or given long imprisonment terms. The second trial was of an alleged liberation organization in Leningrad, under the pretext of which many former students of the Leningrad Theological Institute, closed by the authorities in 1925, were incarcerated. The third was that of the alleged 'Industrial Party' (liquidation of the top bourgeois engineers and technical scientists) which the Soviet media presented as a spy-ring financed by the Western powers and the Vatican and co-operating with the Russian émigré clergy.[80]

To justify or rationalize the mass arrests and liquidation of the clergy and the faithful, a 'criminal record' had to be produced showing a historical propensity to immorality, treachery and crime of all kinds, political, economic, or regular criminal behaviour, in religious leaders of all times. We read that Fr. Georgii Gapon, the leader of the first St Petersburg trade-union organization who had led the Bloody Sunday March in January 1905 (and at the time was praised even by Lenin), was a Japanese spy. Patriarch Tikhon is claimed to have been 'connected with English and other capitalist agencies, participated in the activities of the British agent Lockhart...'. The list continues: 'A Leningrad Orthodox priest organized a subversive band out of a *dvadtsatka* [the group of twenty believers, responsible to the government for a church].' No names are given, but one of its members allegedly managed to penetrate a defence industry factory where the GPU caught him red-handed. A Leningrad dentist is alleged to have used her office as an espionage headquarters connected with an underground counter-revolutionary religious organization financed from abroad. Allegedly a number of sectarian, Lutheran and Roman-Catholic dignitaries were likewise uncovered as foreign spies in 1929–30.

As the story unfolds it becomes totally phantasmagoric. It is alleged that a Leningrad priest openly appealed in his sermons for co-operation with the Trotskyites and Zinovievites in their struggle against the Soviets, and therefore against Stalin. Apparently Trotsky's record as one of the most energetic and militant atheists does not embarrass the author, who goes on to accuse Nikolai Bukharin, 'the damned enemy of the people' of having deliberately promoted a line of physical and extremist attack on the Church through *Koms. pr.* in 1929 in order to demoralize the godless front and strengthen the defensive position of the believers.[81]

Another report claims that a Riazan bishop was arrested with a priest and a deacon for stealing 130 kg of silver.[82]

Then we hear that a bishop Dometian (Gorokhov) was tried for black-marketing and for writing anti-Bolshevik leaflets. Black-marketing was the easiest possible label to stick on any churchman, particularly after the abolition of the NEP: the sale of a cross or icon to a believer could be categorized as illegal private enterprise, as these were neither produced nor sold by the state. As to the leaflets, even according to the Soviet report their distribution had occurred in 1928, while the trial and sentence of execution occurred in 1932, although there is no suggestion that the bishop was in any way hiding. The death sentence was commuted to eight years' imprisonment, which for him as for most other clergymen with similar sentences in the 1930s resulted simply in a protracted death sentence.[83] Conspicuously, in the sordid year of 1937 a story appears in *Izvestia* about a certain Bishop D., who may have been the same Dometian, but changing the mode of his 'crime' now precluded the possibility of quoting his full name. This bishop was allegedly recruiting young people as assistants and disguising himself as 'a famous professor Ch'. He paid three young people and trained them to copy and distribute manuscripts for him (early *samizdat?* – D.P.), but in fact 'was training cadres for espionage and terrorism on instructions from a foreign intelligence service'.[84] Such a loaded 'crime' in that year carried a certain death sentence with it.

Wherever possible, VD and lechery were attributed to a clergyman, especially a well-known and highly educated one, for how else but by a moral decline and dishonesty can the adherence of an intellectual to religion be explained when the line is that religion is the domain of the uncouth exploited by hypocritical swindlers? And thus the arrested and soon-to-disappear Renovationist M. Serafim (Ruzhentsov) was alleged to have led a counter-revolutionary espionage network of monks and priests, who used altars for orgies and raped fourteen-year-old girls, infecting them with venereal disease. The Paris-based émigré Metropolitan Evlogii was alleged to have commanded a Leningrad terrorist band led by an archpriest. The Kazan Archbishop Venedict (Plotnikov), executed in 1938, was alleged to have headed a church band of subversive terrorists and spies.[85]

A bishop A. of Ivanovo is reported to have formed a military industrial espionage group under the guise of a choir of young girls. Ivanovo is a centre of the textile industry, so what sort of military secrets were there available to those girls? The purpose of this sort of propaganda, apparently, was not even to convince the reader of its plausibility, but to drive a lesson home: don't associate with the clergy, don't join church choirs if you want to avoid imprisonment and charges punishable by death.

Characteristically this series of fantasies ends with Stalin's call 'to bring to completion the liquidation of the reactionary clergy in our country'.[86]

The ubiquitous Oleshchuk attacked the Church and the clergy for 'misinterpreting' the new Soviet constitution's article

146 allowing social and public organizations to put forward their candidates for elections to the soviets, including the Church as a public organization. He cites the supreme procurator Andrei Vyshinsky's statement that the only public organizations that may forward candidates for election to the soviets are those 'whose aim is active participation in the socialist construction and in the national defence'. The Church falls under neither of the categories, according to Oleschuk, because, first, she is anti-socialist, and second because Christianity teaches to turn the other cheek, to love the enemy, wherefore a Christian cannot be a good soldier and a true defender of the socialist homeland. To strengthen his argument Oleshchuk told of the unmasking in 1936 of the supreme Moslem Mufti of Ufa as a Japanese and German agent who had turned the whole Moslem Spiritual Administration of Ufa into a giant spy ring. A little to the west

> a whole network of Orthodox priests [who were] subversive agents was recently liquidated in Gorky. It was headed by Feofan Tuliakov, the Metropolitan of Gorky, Bishop Purlevsky of Sergach, Bishop Korobov of Vetluga ... The aim ... was subversion of collective farms and factories, destruction of transportation, collection of secret information for espionage, creation of terrorist bands.

The practical achievement of this subversive group is alleged to have been the burning of twelve houses of collective farmers: a rather illogical act for secret spies aimed at destroying the Soviet State. But the level of credibility of Oleshchuk's writings (and along with him of the whole Soviet 'science' of atheism, for he was one of its leaders both in the 1930s and again in the 1950s and 1960s) is brought to naught when he adds to the above fantasies: 'The Trotskyite–Bukharinite bandits ... have been strengthening and supporting the reactionary clergy.' Trotsky, of course, was one of the most violent enemies of the Church in the 1920s. What is behind this conglomeration of fantasies is the cold fact of mass executions of the clergy under the guise of sabotage.[87]

To be known as a believer in the late 1930s, to be associated with the Church, was like being infected with the plague. It was dangerous to life to be seen having any contacts with her, as even a fleeting visit to a functioning church could mean the loss of employment, and irreparable damage to a career; it could lead to expulsion from an educational establishment and even to arrest.[88] *Samizdat* recounts cases of wild persecutions for the mere wearing of a pectoral cross *under* a shirt or blouse.[89]

In the 1930s people were arrested for such things as having an icon in the home, inviting a priest to perform a private religious rite or service at home owing to the closure of all churches in the district. Priests who were caught performing such functions were inevitably incarcerated, often disappearing forever in NKVD dungeons.

The available unofficial lists of clergy and laity imprisoned or executed for nothing but their faith and for its overt witness however incomplete and scant, make one shudder. Their main 'crime' was their personal charisma, stature, and spiritual authority, which were undermining the effect of antireligious propaganda.[90]

4 An 'Interlude': From 1941 to Stalin's Death

Massive persecutions were halted or at least made much less conspicuous after the annexation of the western territories by the USSR between September 1939 and summer 1940. Rather than offend the nearly twenty million newly acquired Christians by a frontal attack on the Churches and by the negation of the Lord's Day through the five-day-week calendar introduced in 1929–30, the regular seven-day week with Sunday as the official day of rest was reintroduced in 1940. This was followed by the closure of all antireligious periodicals by the end of 1941, soon after the German attack, officially 'on account of paper shortage'.[1] This process of Church–State *rapprochement* continued through the war, motivated by Stalin's realization of the need for the Church to arouse a sense of patriotic sacrifice in the nation (which the Communist Party was powerless to do), as well as by the much more positively tolerant attitude of the German occupiers to the religious desires of Soviet citizens. It culminated in the 4 September 1944 meeting of the three senior hierarchs of the Russian Orthodox Church with Stalin, and in the subsequent election of one of them, Sergii, as the Patriarch of All Russia less than a week later. It was thereafter that thousands of churches could reopen and many of the surviving priests and bishops returned from the camps and prisons.

But even during this most liberal era for the Church, direct and indirect persecutions did not entirely cease. To begin with, numerous bishops and priests imprisoned for refusing to recognize the conditions of Sergii's 1927 loyalty pledge, remained in their places of exile and imprisonment, unless they agreed to renounce their position and pledge loyalty to Sergii.[2] But even making peace with the Moscow Patriarchate could not bring them freedom automatically. A case in point is Bishop Afanasii (Sakharov), the leader of one of the major groups of 'non-commemorators' (those who had refused to commemorate M. Sergii as the head of the Russian Church).

He recognized the validity of M. Alexii's election to the patriarchal throne, and jointly with other priests sent a congratulatory address to Patriarch Alexii from their prison camp. Bishop Afanasii likewise sent a circular letter to the catacomb groups under his jurisdiction asking them to come out of their underground and to join the official patriarchal Church. Most of them did so, thus putting an effective end to the Catacomb Church as a cohesive and widespread institution. Nevertheless, neither he nor his like-minded imprisoned priests were released until their terms, based on framed-up charges, were served fully, or until after Stalin's death. The numerous biographies of Bishop Afanasii (see also Chapter 3), for instance, amply demonstrate that he had been persecuted solely for his pastoral and ecclesiastical work. He never meddled in politics, unless an ecclesiastical disagreement with Metropolitan Sergii's post-1927 policies can be considered a political offence against the Soviet state.[3] According to a KGB defector, in the Perm area of North-West Urals alone there were still ten bishops imprisoned in 1945 in the prison camps, of whom only one was later released.[4]

Soon after the Soviets regained the territories which had been under the German occupation, many priests and bishops were arrested and sent to Soviet prisons and camps for very long terms, allegedly for serving the enemy, although most of the clergy-victims of the NKVD had remained loyal to the Moscow Church in the face of Nazi persecutions. Their only crime was that they had taken the opportunity of greater religious freedom under the Germans and helped to rebuild religious life under the occupation. The details of only a handful of such cases are available to this author.

Fr. Nikolai Trubetskoi (1907–78), a Riga priest and a graduate of the Paris St Sergius Orthodox Theological Academy, served the Moscow Patriarchate loyally both under the Soviet (1940–41) and Nazi (1941–4) occupations of Latvia. In 1944, when the Germans were retreating, he secretly escaped from a German evacuation boat and hid from the Germans in a Latvian peasant's house, awaiting Soviet troops, only to be arrested by the NKVD and sentenced to ten years' hard labour 'for collaboration with the enemy'. His real 'crime' was his zealous pastorate and his very successful missionary work in the German-occupied area of Russia south of Leningrad, where:

> We opened and re-consecrated closed churches, carried out mass-baptisms. It's hard to imagine how, after years of Soviet domination, people hungered after the Word of God. We married and buried people; we had literally no time for sleep. I think that if such a mission were sent today to the Urals, Siberia or even the Ukraine, we'd see the same result.[5]

He said this shortly before his death in 1978.

But waves of arrests are rarely limited to only one area or a single category of 'crime' in the Soviet Union, particularly in Stalin's time when the general rule was preventive rather than punitive terror. And so the mass arrests of clergy and lay religious activists in the formerly enemy-occupied territories had its echo also in the parts never occupied by the enemy. In April 1946, for instance, there was a wave of such arrests in the area of Moscow. A number of priests who had belonged to the Bp. Afanasii group of 'non-commemorators' and who had recently returned to the official Church, were sentenced to long terms of hard labour. Mass arrests were made and long prison terms were handed out to the sizeable group of their spiritual children, among them the lay theolgian and religious philosopher, S.I. Fudel. The latter, as well as all the priests of that so-called Sakharov Group (after Bp. Afanasii Sakharov), had already served earlier prison terms. Almost none of them would see freedom again until after the death of Stalin. Vexed by their failure to catch the senior spiritual father of the group, Fr. Seraphim (Batiukov), who had died in 1942, the MGB dug out his body from the grave and disposed of it elsewhere, probably to prevent future pilgrimages to the site, as Fr. Seraphim was believed to be a saint by his followers.[6]

Stalin was prepared to tolerate a controlled Church, but not active priests, promoting her expansion. Such was the case of the 'Sakharovites' (see Chapter 3 for details). In 1945 Bp. Manuil was appointed head of the Orenburg Diocese in southern Urals.

> In the three years of his administration Bishop Manuil managed to reopen several dozen parishes . . . He raised a

great wave of religious zeal in the Orenburg Diocese... Like no one else, the late hierarch knew how to revitalize parish life, how to attract talented people, how to turn lukewarm people into enthusiasts with a burning faith, how to start fires in ice-cold hearts.

Consequently, he was arrested in 1947 and sentenced to another term of eight years' hard labour. Manuil had never been under any German occupation.[7]

But to return to the fates of those bishops who suffered for the crime of not neglecting their archpastoral duties while under the Nazi occupation, cases in point are those of the late Iosif (Chernov) and Archb. Veniamin (Novitsky). M. Iosif (1893–1975), Bishop of Taganrog before the Second World War, had spent a total of nine years in Soviet prisons and camps by the time of the German occupation of the city. Under the Nazis he remained steadfastly loyal to M. Sergii of Moscow, publicly commemorating his name during church services, suffering threats and arrests from the Germans as well. Yet he was very active at reviving church life in the occupied territory. This earned him another eleven years' hard labour in Eastern Siberia until his final release in 1955. He died as the Metropolitan of Alma-Ata and Kazakhstan.[8]

Archb. Veniamin (1900–1976) was born and lived in the territory belonging to Poland from 1921 to 1939. In 1941, just before the German attack, he was consecrated bishop under the Moscow Patriarchate, to which he remained faithful under the Germans as well – although the occupying forces were not happy with that position – and while the Ukrainian Banderist nationalist partisans directly endangered the lives of such clerics and killed quite a few of them, including their head metropolitan.[9] Yet soon after the return of the Soviet troops, Bishop Veniamin of Poltava was arrested and spent the following twelve years in the horrid Kolyma death camps, never physically recovering from that experience, eventually losing all his hair as a consequence of the camps and prisons.[10]

The arrests of such individuals as the then student of theology, and now priest Dimitri Dudko, for unpublished religious poems,[11] and of groups of Moscow University students running a private religio-philosophic study group in the late 1940s, should serve as another illustration that even during this, Stalin's religious thaw, arms against religious life, if not officially against the established Church, were never laid down. The above study group was inspired and formed around 1946–7, partly by Ilia Shmain a 16–17-year-old youth

The Pope in his full regalia.

Sticking out of his pocket: 'Decree on the excommunication of communists and their sympathizers'.
The pope has been awarded the title of American policeman *honoris causa*. Robert Barret, the chief of the Washington, D.C. police, presented to him the golden crest of the policeman. (*Krokodil*, no. 26, 20 September 1949)

at the time, and a Moscow University student of philology from 1948. The circle arose from Shmain's conclusion that dialectical materialism, or any materialistic philosophy for that matter, was inadequate to explain fundamental existential questions. The group began to meet regularly to discuss art, philosophy, and religion. Although beginning with a mixture of Hinduism, Yogi, and various other occult ideas with abstract and all-inclusive concepts of Godhead, the youths were discussing, among other issues, the question of undergoing baptism and joining the Church at the time of their arrest. Politically they were still totally loyal to the Soviet system, although rejecting Marxism as a philosophy but not as a social doctrine. On 16 January 1949 they were arrested and soon sentenced to terms of eight to ten years' hard labour in accordance with Art. 58 – agitation and organization. The charge: 'the submission of the teachings of Marxism–Leninism to hostile criticism at illegal meetings'.[12]

In terms of propaganda there was a new differentiation in attacks on religion, reversing the trend of the early 1920s. Stalin was building up his Iron Curtain. Eager to isolate his empire and its citizens from the non-communist world and from religious centres beyond the physical control of his security organs, he launched a systematic smear-and-hate propaganda campaign against the Vatican. Caricatures of Pope Pius XII and other Roman Catholic bishops depicted them as warmongers, and supporters of police brutalities. The cartoon on p. 95 is typical of this propaganda. This was accompanied by the liquidation of the Uniate Church (the Roman Catholic Church of the Eastern Rite) in the Ukraine, Czechoslovakia, Poland and Romania and their enforced merging with the Orthodox Church. Although theoretically those who did not want to join the Orthodox Church had the option to become Roman Catholics of the Western Rite, absence of functioning temples of this rite, except in the larger cities, incarceration of the Uniate clergy refusing to join the Orthodox Church, and the popular dedication to the Byzantine ritual and church traditions by the masses of the population, would practically preclude such a choice.[13]

Attitudes to the Orthodox and the Protestants in the post-war era were more tolerant, at least up to the time of Khrushchev's new attack of 1958–64. Nevertheless, at least from 1946, the Soviet press began to criticize a passive and areligious attitude toward religion, particularly in youth organizations (the Komsomol and the Pioneers) and at school, demanding activization of antireligious propaganda and education on all levels. In practical terms, local plenipotentiaries of the Council for the Affairs of the Russian Orthodox Church wasted no effort in making it more difficult for bishops and the clergy to protect the recently reopened churches from closure (this probably applied to other religions, too). For instance, in 1949 they managed to shut three out of the fifty-five churches in the diocese of Crimea, probably in an effort to scale down the prestige and achievements of its famous martyr-bishop and surgeon Luka (see Chapter 3). In order to facilitate the closure of churches a regulation was imposed, according to which a church could be closed if it had not been served by a priest on a regular basis for over six months.[14] But only the regime was to blame for the terrible post-war clergy shortage. The reasons for this were several. They included the mass liquidations in the 1930s, and the fact that the mass reopenings of churches in the 1940s were not matched by a proportional reopening of seminaries, prevented both by the Germans (whose policy was to limit the education of the Slavs to the first two primary school grades) and by the Soviets. In addition there was the great loss from the mass arrests after the war of the majority of those clergy who had served as pastors in the territories occupied by the enemy. They comprised the absolute majority of priesthood in the Soviet Union, for most of the churches had been reopened in the occupied territories.

Thus the persecution of the most dedicated and religiously active believers and pastors never ended under the Soviets. The use of administrative decrees and political articles of the criminal code were but a thin disguise for religious persecutions against those who saw dissemination of their faith as their primary Christian duty, be they laymen or pastors.

5 Renewal of the Incendiary Propaganda, 1958-85

'Should theologians explain the Universe even from the scientific [materialistic] point of view but in the name of religion and even God Himself ... we shall not stop our fight against religion [because] religion will never cease to be a reactionary social force, an opiate for the people ...'
(Evgraf Duluman, Kiriushko and Yarotsky, *Nauchno-tekhnicheskaia revolutsiia* ...)

UNDER KHRUSHCHEV

Khrushchev's brutal antireligious attacks and persecutions went by almost unnoticed in the West, partly because the predominantly agnostic Western media wanted to see a liberal in Khrushchev and did not care much about religion, but partly also because the features of antireligious campaigns prominent in the 1920s and 1930s were almost absent now. True, a special antireligious mass propaganda journal did appear in 1959. But this *Science and Religion* (*NiR*), although aggressive and vulgar at times, as the following blasphemous illustrations demonstrate, was not comparable to the viciousness of *Bezbozhnik* or *Bezbozhnik u stanka*. The methods and excuses applied in the mass closure of churches and other forms of persecutions will be discussed in the next chapter. Plenty of unofficial and semi-official reports were available in the West about these brutalities and terror. Many of them even found their way to the Western media, yet the outside world paid little attention to these 'unconfirmed' reports. These were several reasons why this onslaught drew so little world public attention at the time.

First, even given the habitual Soviet custom of rewriting history, the regime simply could not obliterate from people's memories the patriotic behaviour of the Church in the Second

World War, the political loyalty of the Church tested by the war, and the post-war obedient and supportive behaviour of Church leaders in all sorts of Soviet-directed or Soviet-inspired peace campaigns. Therefore, the new wave of antireligious propaganda avoided attacking the Church leadership and even from time to time had to stress the loyalty and political reliability of the Church establishment. It limited its attacks to individual religious activists and clergymen, and avoided naming any names. Such roundabout attacks had only a limited effect on the general public, and consequently even in the Soviet Union those not directly involved in Church life in those years were not well informed about antireligious activity.

Second, the repeated public denials of persecution and suppression of churches by the Church hierarchy at international peace and theological conferences and in press conferences abroad blunted the Western public's awareness and responsiveness to the problem.

Third, the Soviet media campaign against religion, although quantitatively quite large, was not as vicious in tone as that of the pre-war years. No plans were openly announced to liquidate the Church in the immediate future. No promises were made that the word 'God' would soon disappear from the Russian vocabulary, as had been done in the 1930s.

And finally, although highly placed officials such as Leonid Il'ichev, the CPSU Central Committee Ideological Department head, instigated contempt and hate against believers by calling them 'political rascals and opportunists . . . [who] cheat, dissemble, hiding their hostility towards our political system under a mask of religion',[1] the masses of organized and often genuinely enthusiastic 'militant godless' were not there anymore to pick up such commanding 'war cries' from the top.

Nor did the new antireligious attack, apparently, arouse any enthusiasm in the Soviet artistic community, in contrast to the pre-war years, when such talented avant-gardists as Moor painted flashy, provocative and often talented antireligious cartoons in *Bezbozhnik*, *Krokodil* and other periodicals, as well as propaganda posters. Now *NiR* was more often forced to employ the talents of foreign antireligious artists, for instance those of the French communist cartoonist Maurice Henry, as the blasphemous illustrations on page 100, quite insulting to religious feelings, show.

The Last Supper: Jesus playing card tricks

Soothsayer : 'One of the three will be famous'.

Porter

Are you unemployed? Well, pray to God, this will be your work.

Nir (*Nauka i religiia*, i.e. Science and Religion) no. 11, 1968, pp. 96-7.

The enhancement of the antireligious attack after 1958 became just another lifeless routine of the centrally planned system. As Powell, one of the best authorities on Soviet antireligious propaganda, says:

> Although each newspaper is supposed to have a plan governing the content and frequency of anti-religious articles, few papers go about the task so systematically. Many of the atheistic articles printed in the Soviet press are sent out by the press bureau of *Pravda* or are prepared by TASS or some other news agency ... A number of papers feature regular columns devoted to religion and atheism; they are given such names as 'The Atheist Corner' or 'The Militant Atheist'. Most editors, however, confine their anti-religious efforts to publishing articles prepared by TASS or to reprinting items from other newspapers.[2]

Powell further remarks that even when the official policy is to criticize religion without insulting the feelings of believers, this 'official policy ... is violated in practice, so often ... as to cast doubt on the authenticity of the policy'.[3] The attacks were even more unrestrained when prodded by the CPSU Central Committee. And indeed, articles inciting contempt and hatred for the believers appeared in ever-growing numbers in the specialized atheistic and general Soviet press between 1959 and 1964 in particular, under such derogatory titles as: 'The Howls of the Obscurantists', 'The Vultures', 'The Wolfish Fangs of "God's Harmless Creatures"', 'Swindlers in the guise of Holy Fathers', 'A Theologian-Fomenter', 'Hysteria on the March'. Believers were called 'toadstools', 'swindlers', 'a horde', 'anti-Soviet subhumans' (*liudishki*), 'wicked enemy of all that lives', 'the rot'. A secret monk becomes 'a milksop'. A theologian of a banned Orthodox branch, the so-called True Orthodox Christians, becomes a 'malignant'.[4] Levitin-Krasnov, who dared to speak up for the Church at the height of Khrushchev's persecutions in his multiple *samizdat* tracts, was called a 'Smerdiakov', the despicable Karamazov's bastard in *Brothers Karamazov*. The man paid for his writings in defence of religion under Soviet conditions, by losing his job as a high-school teacher and with two prolonged imprisonments in 1949–56 and again in 1969–72. Yet *NiR* calls him a 'hypocrite' *par excellence*. His 'hypocrisy' expressed itself, allegedly, in his daring to teach Russian literature at school while using one pseudonym to publish theological articles in *ZhMP* and another for his *samizdat* apologetic essays 'full of spite and arrogance'. Similarly as in the 1920s, one of the first manifestations of Khrushchev's antireligious attack was a campaign for the removal of practising believers from the teaching profession. It was in 1959 that Levitin-Krasnov lost his job as a schoolteacher. In the same year reports appeared 'unmasking' secret believers among students of faculties of education. In one reported case a Christian student was asked how she would teach in the affirmatively atheistic school. She replied: 'I'll give all answers in accordance with Marxism [stating that this is the Marxist position]. What are my personal convictions is no one's business.' The article calls for a more aggressively atheistic curriculum at pedagogical institutes, particularly since other students, when questioned, said they were atheists, but would not be able 'to gain a victory in a discussion with believers'.

The attacks were slanderous in tone and often fraudulent in content. An example is the case of Levitin, whose father was a lawyer, a Jewish convert to Christianity, of modest means and whose mother came from a family of Russian schoolteachers. *NiR* made him out to be a scion of a wealthy Russian aristocratic family who had never forgiven the Soviet regime for depriving them of their estates. This was said to be the motivation for his allegedly anti-Soviet tracts. In fact, however, Levitin considered himself a Christian Marxist (moving somewhat away from it only in the last few years in Switzerland to where he was expelled in 1974). As to his pseudonyms, he used them in order not to embarrass his school colleagues and pupils. There is no other option for a Soviet teacher who believes in God when the state does not permit confessional schools nor allow believers to teach in state schools. It is the state in this case which imposed the need for its citizens to dissemble. Yet the Soviet press always accuses the believers of duplicity and hypocrisy, blaming their behaviour on religious teachings.[5]

Again, as in the 1920s, the general attack on religion slanders the clergy and believing laity as lechers, drunks and parasites who refuse to do socially useful work.[6] Hate-and-contempt propaganda goes hand-in-hand with arrests of clergy, discussed in the following chapter. The arrest, trial, and sentencing of Archbishop Iov of Kazan' in 1960 and of Archbishop

Andrei of Chernigov is accompanied by slanderous articles against them, written in accordance, apparently, with a pre-set pattern. Both bishops had lived under the German occupation, so both had to be accused of anti-Soviet activities. In the case of Archbishop Andrei his imprisonment soon after the completion of theological studies under Stalin is reported as bona fide evidence of his criminal anti-Soviet activities, although the article appeared less than one year after the 22nd Party Congress with its condemnation of Stalin's crimes and promise to fully expose the invalidity of the criminal prosecutions of his time. Both bishops are depicted as greedy lechers (one homosexual, the other heterosexual), hated by their flocks for their high living, conspicuous luxury, and the misappropriation of diocesan funds. 'Careful' calculations are presented of their incomes, with one careless oversight: the fact that the clergy and their employees had to pay up to 81 per cent income tax on their salaries is nowhere mentioned. There are other deliberate oversights in the reports, casting serious doubts on their reliability. Regarding Iov, it is stated in one place that he had been consecrated bishop immediately after the war by Metropolitan Alexii (Gromadsky) of Kiev, who in fact had been killed by Ukrainian nationalistic partisans in 1943. The lechery, luxury, pilfering, and accusations of materialistic greed are a constantly repeated cliché in all such writings, including those by ex-priests giving their reasons for deserting the vocation. Such 'confessions' often end with appeals to former colleagues who still remain priests, to 'stop fooling [and abusing] the credulity of the believers. When will you stop enriching yourselves by abusing the ignorance of the believers?' The conclusion is that the clergy are deceitful.[7] Even the former professor of theology, Alexander Osipov, who broke with the Church in December 1959, warned against such oversimplifications. He warned that religion is much more dangerous than the oversimplified image which such primitive propaganda suggests. 'Sometimes it even attracts educated people, intellectuals.' He protested against the tolerant attitudes of children towards their believing parents or grandparents; referred to religion as 'dope, opium', which has a long experience of 'well thought out and skillful struggle for human souls'. He stressed the flexibility and adaptability of the Church which it would be wrong to see as 'a simple and senile institution'. He approvingly referred to Il'ichev's Central Committee Plenum speech of June 1963 which had stated that 'religion is the chief enemy of the *Weltanschauung* [Marxism] inside the country'. Osipov contrasted the dynamism of religion with the prevalence of bureaucratic routine and ignorance in the atheistic camp: ignorant lecturers in atheism confuse Jehovah's Witnesses with Old Believers; *NiR* published cartoons of Evangelical Baptists praying before a row of icons; much of the propaganda is reduced to 'priest-baiting', while believers and clergy are often quite erroneously depicted as either 'demoralized weaklings or as some vicious criminals from a detective story'. Although logically all the above should lead to the conclusion that any means should be used to kill and destroy such an evil as religion, Osipov suddenly warned against insulting the believer's feelings. But then, enumerating literary works and films with an antireligious thrust, he mentions a film *The Confession*, produced by the Odessa Studio, which 'in vain depicts all seminarians as semi-idiots and rascals ... Nevertheless this film is also beneficial.' In other words, again, just as in that debate of the late 1920s between *Bezbozhnik* and *Bezbozhnik u stanka*, lies, slander, and incitement against religion are permissible as long as they serve the atheist cause. Osipov laments that 'the old guard of atheists, Yaroslavsky's colleagues, is dying away', that is the people who had been responsible for the most brutal physical annihilation of clergy and believing laity, the people who had barbarously destroyed thousands of churches and icons of unique artistic value. Thus, Osipov contradicts his preceding call for more sophistication in the struggle against, what he terms (similarly to Yaroslavsky) the most powerful internal enemy of the Soviet State. But then, for purely practical reasons, Osipov advises that *NiR* should be reserved mostly for educational material for the atheists, because the journal was not read by lay believers, as a rule. To reach the latter, the real attacks, the antireligious propaganda and agitation material, ought to appear in the general mass media: cinema, television, theatre, and the mass press.[8]

Osipov may have been wrong: according to other information, *NiR* is often subscribed to by believers, who make clippings of all its quotations from the Scriptures, diverse theological writings or saints' *vitae*, in lieu of unavailable religious literature. Probably that was one of the reasons why his advice was not heeded and *NiR* has continued to publish material of antireligious propaganda and agitation along with 'educational material'.

Such antireligious agitation was often synchronized with antireligious decrees and their implementation. Thus, a decree of 1961 categorically reconfirmed the ban on group pilgrimages to 'the so-called "Holy places"'. This was a blow to one of the most ancient traditions of Russian piety. Pilgrimages are traditionally made to monasteries or churches, or sites where according to a local oral tradition some miracle had once occurred. In all instances they are made in particular on the appropriate patron saint's feast-day. Now that these pilgrimages were banned, a campaign of character assassination began in the media against pilgrims and monasteries.

The monasteries were slandered also in order to rationalize the mass forced closure of most of them during the same years. One of the crudest Soviet 'religiologists', Trubnikova, published an article at the end of 1962 slandering one of the most nationally revered shrines, the Pochaev Lavra, as a nest of fat, greedy, lustful loafers, allegedly raping young female pilgrims and robbing people of their money.[9] This was at the height of the persecution of the Pochaev monks and pilgrims, which was often accompanied by their physical abuse by the police (see Chapter 6). Another author issued a brochure, *Truth about the Pskov Monastery of the Caves* (circulation 200 000 copies), misrepresenting the whole history of the monastery, presenting it as a nest of national traitors from the Middle Ages to the Second World War. In fact it had been a formidable fortress defending Russia's western frontiers first from the Teutonic and Livonian knights, and in the sixteenth and seventeenth centuries from the Lithuanians and the Poles. The Soviet author even accused the monastery of disloyalty for its condemnation of Ivan the Terrible's reign of terror.[10]

Soon assorted articles began to attack pilgrims and pilgrimages as charlatanism, clerical swindles to extract donations, distraction of people from socially useful work, especially on the farms. Among these one of the most vicious was Trubnikova's 'Hysteria on the March', an ugly caricature of the traditional centuries-old pilgrimage to an allegedly miraculous spring in a Kirov Diocese village, Velikoretskoe, on one of the feast days of St Nicholas. He is supposed to have appeared to some believers there hundreds of years ago, and in his memory a church honouring St Nicholas stands by that spring. Trubnikova participated in the pilgrimage disguised as a humble pilgrim, spying on the genuine ones and depicting them as alcoholics, hysterical women falling into trances, hypocrites and swindlers who simulate trances or disguise healthy persons as invalids, who after a dip in the spring shed their crutches and pretend to have received a sudden cure. The author shows no compassion to these thousands of humble believers, each going to the holy place with hopes of physical cure or in search of help in a family crisis. For Trubnikova they are 'a savage horde'. The story ends with alleged robberies among the pilgrims, wild sexual orgies in cemetery woods, and a drunken murder. A voluntary police aide rescues the author in the middle of the night by warning her not to join a band of the unofficial 'True Orthodox' pilgrims:

> Where are you going? ... They'd easily break you there before you could say knife ... These 'true Orthodox' wouldn't hesitate for a moment to gun you down. They have no shortage of anti-Soviet subhumans.

In conclusion she makes an appeal to prevent all pilgrimages in the country and to ban them categorically, comparing them to locusts or worms who 'are crawling ... through forests, ... crawling before the very eyes of the Soviet public'.[11]

Trubnikova depicts the believers as an uncouth lot. She loses her credibility when she confuses the Slavonic term for 'dying' with the modern Russian word for 'introduction' (*predstavitsia* and *prestavitsia*); and again when in a story on secret monastic communities of the Old Believers she asserts that one of the causes of the seventeenth-century Russian Church Schism was Patriarch Nikon's attempt to abolish the annual chronology.[12]

In Trubnikova's writings we see the revival of the old Marxist-Leninist identification of religion with alcohol, crime, mental abnormality, and disease. Trubnikova was not an exception among antireligious Soviet authors in this respect (neither would she have been an exception today). Countless articles appeared claiming that the rites of all religious faiths disseminated disease. The Judaic and Moslem rite of circumcision was cited as a frequent source of gangrene, often leading to fatalities. Particularly long discourses have reappeared on the alleged spread of infectious diseases through the Orthodox tradition of mass veneration (kissing) of icons, crucifixes, and relics; on the Orthodox communion in two forms (the body and the blood) from a single common chalice; and on the general Christian rite of baptism. It is alleged that the Orthodox and Baptist-Evangelical rite of full immersion during baptism, particularly in winter months, often leads to colds, influenzas, and even pneumonias, particularly in infants, sometimes with a fatal conclusion. In particular it is stressed that, owing to overcrowding, sometimes twenty or thirty infants are baptized using the same font and the same water, thus helping to spread contagious diseases. What the authors pass over in silence is the cause of such overcrowding: namely, Soviet closure of churches, refusal to open or build additional churches and baptistries, closure of seminaries, and strict limitations on the numbers of seminarians and annual ordinations. Nor is there a word anywhere on the notoriously unhygienic conditions in Soviet secular communal bath houses, swimming pools and hospitals.[13]

It is not objectivity and truth that the authors are after. Their purpose is to build up an image of believers, commonly called for the purpose 'religious fanatics', disseminators of epidemics, social pests, or criminals, in order to justify their persecution to the public and to get approval for the destruction of pilgrimage centres, churches and monasteries. Whether the propaganda is effective enough in achieving this aim depends on the attitude of the public to it. Il'ichev's concern over the tenacity of the Church and her ability to attract new believers,[14] seems to indicate the reverse. But since this contradicts the Marxist doctrine of the inevitability of the withering-away of religion under socialism, the process of adult conversion had to be presented as a sort of rape, figuratively speaking. In a story on the 'True Orthodox Christian Wanderers', an illegal Old Believer sect, a monastic priest is depicted as a wartime deserter from the army. In his wanderings through the woods, hiding from the law during the war, he comes across a band of sectarians who agree to hide him, assuring him that life could be lived without working. Their *samizdat* book of spiritual life 'breathes hatred toward everything human, or worldly, and to things Soviet in particular!'. This deserter-turned-priest, Mina, 'has a bony predatory nose'. His disciple, who had deserted a college to join the sect, is 'a pimply ninny'. To dispel the impression that college students seek out God on their own, this is how this 'ninny's' conversion is described. In the Siberian city of Novokuznetsk, Fr. Mina meets this 'ninny in spectacles' who in the course of their conversation 'expressed some doubt: "who knows, maybe there is something in the sky up there . . ." This is just what the sectarians were waiting for.' Soon Mina persuaded him, and the two were on their way to a Taiga *Skete*. On the way, in the middle of the night Mina decided to baptize the new convert: 'Grasping his trembling, sweating hand in a mortal grip, Fr. Mina dragged the convert to water.' Mina ordered him to destroy all his papers, including the passport, but not the money, which he took for himself, calling him a madman when the youth wanted to destroy the money as well. And a few lines later Mina and all his co-religionists are characterized as 'a malicious enemy of all living things'.

It is a detective story of sorts; a series of mysterious disappearances of young people, students, married men and young women are being investigated. After several years of fruitless searches a kidnapping network of sectarians is allegedly unmasked and all their victims 'rescued' and brought back into the secular world from their secret Siberian *sketes* and underground theological schools. All the leaders are depicted as criminals, swindlers, loafers using religion to extract money from foolish religious simpletons. Their young converts are 'ninnies', 'infantile semi-idiots'. The state sends the former to prison, but rescues their foolish disciples, returning them to fruitful productive life.[15]

Once again the persecution of clergy and active laity was being justified by this kind of story, the readership was being conditioned to accept such acts of the state as inevitable and positive. But according to the propagandists of atheism's own admissions, not many were convinced.[16]

AFTER KHRUSHCHEV

NiR reflected the general concensus after Khrushchev's fall that the persecutions and brutal propaganda of hate-and-contempt did not pay, when they published an editorial letter to one of its former contributors, A. Ia. Trubnikova. Three editorial authors, B. Mar'iamov, G. Ul'ianov and Shamaro criticized Trubnikova for the very things of which their own journal had been guilty.

First, Trubnikova was criticized for not trying to understand the cause of the persistence of religious belief and its ability to attract contemporary Soviet people. The implication is that the persistence of religious belief cannot be reduced to 'survivals of the past' alone.

Second, she was criticized for the reduction of the whole religious phenomenon to a giant swindle of credulous fools, along the line of eighteenth-century French materialistic thinkers (sic); and worse: 'representing monasteries and pilgrims in such a way as if there were no faith in God at all'.

Third, she was accused of simplified misrepresentation of religious societies, especially of the 'true Orthodox Christian Wanderers' as a 'secret anti-Soviet organization ... of opportunists, parasites, haters of all and everything in the Soviet Union ... living [literally] underground ... created by *kulaks* for counter-revolutionary underground subversive work'.

Finally, it was wrong and counterproductive, the editors wrote, to represent believers as mentally handicapped sub-humans and enemies, against whom any means may be used, who are worthy only of 'unmasking' and contempt.

Such representation, they write, does not explain why masses of people believe, why there are pilgrims, why people join monasteries and dedicate themselves to God. 'You insult not only the human dignity of believers, but also their genuine religious convictions' ... when describing them by rude pejorative terms, and falsely depicting pilgrimages and life in monasteries as drunken orgies and lechery.[17]

Although the post-Khrushchev *Science and Religion* displayed a less militant and nihilistic tone, it has not consistently avoided the 'sins' of which it so pointedly accused Trubnikova. It often adopts the tone of a dialogue with believers. But believers' letters are rarely printed in full; even meaningful excerpts are an exception. At best, only those excerpts are cited which are necessary for a response. More often only false, imaginary, believers' assertions are printed, followed by a disproving tirade. For example, in reply to the question that surely God must exist since millions of people believe in Him and they cannot all be wrong, there follows a lengthy explanation that there have been many cases in history when popular beliefs were proved wrong: for instance, the belief that the Earth is flat. Throughout history there have been millions more heathens than monotheists, but this does not prove that paganism is true. Finally the author cites the unproved Marxist hypothesis that early primitive man did not believe in any god, as if this were an established fact, and primitive man a superior model to be followed by modern man, ignoring his whole intellectual and cultural evolution.[18]

The former theologian Osipov, in a polemical work on the 'sad' fate of woman in Christianity and her liberation under Marxism, written in response to the reproaches of some of his female readers that there is a true 'iron curtain' in the Soviet Union against the believers because their writings are never published in full side-by-side with atheistic attacks on them, justified this by stating that no theological publications would publish articles by atheists. Thereby he asserts Marxism to be a counter-Church, and atheism a counter-theology, particularly when he expresses the fear that by publishing the writings of believers a Soviet periodical would destroy its purpose, would disseminate religious propaganda, especially since many of these writings 'border on anti-Sovietism'. He then suggested that his religious opponents should resort to the religious press of the Soviet Union, as if he did not know that it was limited to one small monthly and two even smaller bi-monthlies with a total circulation of around 50 000 for the whole Soviet Union, and that more than two-thirds of its content was filled by official information and the obligatory 'struggle for peace' section, imposed on these publications by the state.[19]

To get around this dearth of religious literature, believers resort to all forms of *samizdat* (do-it-yourself press), one of the most popular forms of which are the so-called 'holy letters' – a text from the Scriptures, prayers or writings by some Church Fathers, handwritten, with an instruction to make nine copies and to forward them to other addresses, or else God would punish the receiver. Many of them, apparently, contain excerpts from St John's Revelations. *NiR*, attacking the letters and the letter writers, does not cite a single one of them, but creates situations to show how 'malicious', selfish and inhuman are such writers. In every situation the journal cites, the letter arrives in the middle of a family tragedy, when the receivers are incapacitated by a grave illness or some other cause, making it impossible to fulfil the instruction to duplicate the letter. Being superstitious, the recipients go through agony and often are forced to ask a schoolchild to rewrite the letter, thus traumatizing the poor soul with 'religious propaganda'. In the same vein, imports of religious literature from the West are condemned as anti-Soviet subversion (see below). The same is true for the Jehovah Witnesses and their literature. Agreeing with Osipov, the journal hypocritically exclaims: 'A *Weltanschauung* ought to be disseminated only as a free influence, without any compulsion. It ought to be accepted voluntarily, not under threat.'[20] Unfortunately the Soviet system of education and media monopoly offers no such options.

It is quite obvious that no genuine discussion, or dialogue, can take place when one side possesses a monopoly of the media; one side can lie, and the other may not expose the lies.[21] Moreover, if equal opportunity were granted to both sides, there would be no employment for the huge army of mediocre atheistic lecturers, writers and propagandists, about whose low level of erudition and inability to convincingly argue with a believer the Soviet media complains constantly. As will be shown below, the volume and quality of more serious critical studies of theology, church history, and believers has markedly increased since the mid-1960s, although it is still biased and one-sided. But the majority of Soviet religiologists are simply incapable of such work.[22] Primitive attacks using an accumulation of half a century of clichés and name-calling are much easier. Moreover, there is a danger from the Marxist point of view that once you begin a serious critique of religion you admit its respectability, which is the last thing the Ideological Commission of the CPSU Central Committee could tolerate.[23]

In this dilemma *NiR* attempted to play the role of a friend and kind counsellor of the reader. Their main argument was that man turns to religion as a result of some misfortune in life, loneliness, lack of compassion from one's colleagues, heartless attitudes of government offices and the like. The journal regularly publishes articles showing kind, compassionate, spiritually rich and generous atheists.[24] As a counterforce, they depict believers in a negative, disparaging way. Believers continue to be shown as fanatics, intolerant and heartless people, breaking up marriages when one of the partners is a non-believer. In such cases believing parents disregard the happiness or grief of their daughter or son, they counterfeit miracles, provoke anti-Soviet and anti-socialist frenzy; even as the teachings of Christianity, allegedly, deprive man of courage, human pride, freedom, by preaching humility.[25] Since the late 1970s religious believers may have become more intolerant, but the reason may be, as one of Osipov's correspondents, a 58-year-old female, pointed out in 1964, that when in her youth the majority of the population were brought up as systematic Christians, there was much less drinking and debauchery and much less religious extremism. She blames the Soviet intolerance towards the believers for the rise of the believers' intolerance towards the atheists. Osipov's retort is weak and unconvincing on the latter count, while he passes over in silence the point on alcoholism altogether.[26]

The other important subject that the Soviet antireligious publications have to cope with is the rise of interest in national culture and history, including iconography and religious art in general, especially in those aspects of art and culture which could be least rationalized in terms of materialism. The Soviet press admits that fascination with religious art brings many young intellectuals to church (as the caricature below illustrates). The Soviet media go out of their way to argue that culture and religion are things totally apart, and that religion simply bastardized art and culture. They argue that religious artist had no way to express his talents other than through religious symbols, by means of which, allegedly, even such great iconographers as the monk Andrei Rublev or Theophanes the Greek were expressing humanistic, secular concepts.

In contrast to its former policy, *NiR* now dedicates many pages to colour photographs of icons, Italian religious art, churches and monasteries, interpreting them now as secular art. The language may be more civilized than some of the citations above, but the essence of this attack on religion remains the same: that religion is a parasite on all aspects of human progress, whether art, architecture, literature, history, or whatever.

At the same time the journal consistently attacks museum guides, in churches and monasteries converted into museums,

Renewal of the Incendiary Propaganda 113

Can you imagine: it all began with an innocent collection of religious art.
(*Krokodil*, no. 4, February 1983, p. 6)

for giving only architectural and artistic information to the public, and for adding an uncritical theological dimension – for example, explaining the theology of icons, their role and function in the Orthodox Church, explaining the theological symbolism of church services, the purpose of monastic life and, even, uncritically citing from saints' *vitae*. According to *NiR*, the guides should explain 'the class character' of the Church, monasteries, and religion. They should give a secular explanation of religious art and should dwell on the history of the usage of monasteries as prisons for heretics as feudal land holders.[27]

In contrast to Khrushchev's era, the press avoids insulting attacks on the Church establishment, but continues to hurl insults on the active evangelizing individual priests and laymen (as exemplified in the above 1966 attack on Levitin-Krasnov) and on banned sects and religions – for example, the underground Ukrainian Uniates (Eastern Right Roman Catholics), Jehovah Witnesses, the unofficial Baptists. One of the leaders of unofficial Baptists, while in exile in Siberia, far from his wife and family, allegedly had a love affair with another woman. This was immediately heralded by the atheist press, without, however, explaining the circumstances or why he was in Siberia to start with. This plain case of character assassination is meant to show the underground Baptists as lechers, and lechers cannot be Christian martyrs.[28]

Soviet antireligious media's attention has been growing towards another extremist religious outgrowth of Soviet religious intolerance, the so-called *Pokutnyky*, an eschatological sect of the banned West Ukrainian Uniates, which appeared in the mid-1950s. The *Pokutnyky* activists are accused of counterfeiting 'signs from God', such as putting a 'holy mountain' and a stream on fire by secretly pouring petrol, inventing an apparition of the Virgin predicting the immediate end of the world, and terrorizing disenchanted former members of the sect by setting their houses on fire. To convince people that the Virgin did indeed appear to believers, a photo has been distributed by the *Pokutnyky*, where, the journal alleges, the image of the Virgin is simply stuck on with glue and paper to the original picture of people praying at the foot of the 'Holy Mountain', and then multiplied by photocopying.[29]

Thus, once again, religion, swindle, terrorism, intolerance – are all interrelated. But the Soviet state, which causes religious persecution, terrorism and intolerance of even moderate religious faiths such as the Eastern Roman Catholic Rite, is never identified in connection with religious swindles.

By the same token, despite the above letter to Trubnikova,

the journal continues to describe Old Believer sects as an antisocial and even criminal institution. A story on a suicidal movement in one such sect, written by Shamaro, who had nine years earlier accused Trubnikova of falsely blackening and distorting the world of the religious believer, is guilty of serious distortions. This sect of *Skrytniki* (concealers), led by a Khristofor Zyrianov in the woods of northern Russia, allegedly had engaged in mass suicides from the mid-1920s to 1936. What does not tally in this story is that although it is believed that Soviet authorities had begun to suspect as early as the late 1920s that Zyrianov had been murdering his charges, in 1932 he was sentenced only to a few years of internal exile, and not until 1936 was real justice done. The total human toll was more than sixty members of the sect killed. In view of the standards of punishments applied to even innocent believers in the 1920s and 1930s, it is incredible that Soviet 'justice' would have tolerated the sect and its suspected murders for some eight years. Apparently, the self-immolations were these religious extremists' response to the persecutions of the 1930s, but Shamaro deliberately extends this period into the mid-1920s to divert guilt from the Soviet regime. Moreover, to confuse the issue further, he calls the sect sometimes by its proper name, and sometimes as 'The True Orthodox',[30] who in reality are simply a branch of the regular Orthodox Church which has refused to recognize the legitimacy of the accommodation of the official Orthodox Church with the Soviet State.

The Old Believer sect of the 'True Orthodox Wanderers' is confused with the 'True Orthodox' and some clergy in the official Orthodox Church, in a novel supposedly based on true facts, published in instalments in *NiR*. The plot concerns the 'vile' entrapment of a young Moscow Komsomol girl. First, she is brought under the influence of a regular Moscow Orthodox priest, who then sends her off with a pious woman go-between, to a Siberian underground *skete*. There secret elders train her and other girls for future missionary work and prepare her for secret monastic vows. Severe fasting, hatred of the surrounding world, despotic exploitation of the young charges, banning of all books but the Scriptures and some sectarian tracts, living in dug-out cellars without seeing the sun, absence of smiles or friendly words, rudeness – such is the depiction of that world of fanatical sectarians, from whose net the girl is eventually rescued by a group of Sherlock Holmes-like and heroic Komsomol friends of the girl . . .[31]

The confusion of the world of the sectarians with the regular Orthodox is probably deliberate, in order to throw a shadow of suspicion on the latter as well, as if to warn the 'true Soviet patriot' never to trust any believer. Take the case of Fathers Nikolai Eshliman (died in 1985) and Gleb Yakunin, who had received world-wide fame owing to their brave 1965 memoranda to the Soviet Government and to the Patriarch Alexii protesting the persecution and the forced closures of the churches and the inactivity of the Patriarchate and its bishops in defending the Church.[32] The atheist press got busy morally assassinating Yakunin. Allegedly he decided to become a priest for purely pecuniary reasons. It is natural that in view of the paucity of religious publications in the USSR an evangelizing and missionary-oriented priest will try to acquire them from wherever they may be available, usually from the West. The Soviet regime treats this as a crime. So, Yakunin, Eshliman and other active clergy and laity began to be branded as connected with the criminal world, black-marketeers, and even with Western intelligence services, who by secretly sending batches of religious and theological literature into the Soviet Union were engaging in ideological subversion.[33] Many articles, brochures and books paint a picture of close ties between religious dissenters and foreign intelligence services and with such anti-communist Russian émigré organizations as NTS.[34] Descriptions of confiscations by Soviet customs officers of caches of 'subversive' religious literature, stress their acceptance by wide circles of religious believers. Religious ideology is hostile to the Marxist-Leninist ideology, runs such logic; therefore religious believers are not sensitive to the threat of the ideological enemy of the Marxist Soviet Union; they even tend to feel an affinity to Western Christians. But the Vatican and most other Western Christian establishments co-operate with the CIA in order to infiltrate the USSR ideologically. Orthodox priests broadcast messages to Russian Orthodox Christians via the Voice of America and other 'subversive' services. In short, even if a Soviet Christian is a loyal citizen in his regular behaviour, he is considered to be the weakest link in the Soviet defence line; he cannot be relied on and is a potential enemy of the Soviet State.[35]

For a long time the Soviet press refused to admit the growth of religious sentiment among young generations of Soviet intellectuals. They brushed the evidence aside as either an empty fad or an intellectual swindle as in the Trubnikova 'report'. It is probably the flood of readers' letters, some of which mention with concern the growing frequency of young intellectuals turning to the Church,[36] which caused the appearance in the 1970s of a special irregular publication, *The World of Man*, issued by *The Young Guard* (*Molodaia gvardiia*), the Komsomol literary monthly. The miscellany shows Nazis as religious mystics, albeit trying to revive pagan cults, but still religious and therefore irrational. Hence beware of the religious mentality: it is akin to Nazism. The journal responds to the growing interest in Russia's pre-Marxist culture by claiming that Alexander Pushkin was an atheist, on the flimsy evidence of his 1824 letter in which he admits his intellectual interest in atheistic literature. An essay on Gogol, in contrast, demonstrates the destructive effect of religion on that author. Such writings are admittedly a response to letters from young Soviet Komsomols to the publication who state that they see no harm in their Komsomol friends getting married in church. 'We think it's wrong to turn away from our old traditions', they write. And the miscellany retorts: 'Penetrating daily life relations the religious ideology influences the views and emotions of our youth.'[37] Unable to conceal the revival of interest in religion among Soviet youth, the propaganda blames it on Western ideological subversion, Western broadcasts and Western religious organizations which smuggle religious literature and bibles into the Soviet Union. As usual, Soviet propagandists dress it all up as CIA and other Western intelligence services operations, repeatedly quoting the late General Secretary K. U. Chernenko's words at the June 1983 CPSU Central Committee Plenum:

> The multiple ideological centres of imperialism are trying not only to support but also to cultivate religiosity, giving it an anti-Soviet nationalist orientation.[38]

NiR likewise tries to respond to the phenomenon of the conversion to Christianity of Soviet youth. One such response was in the form of a story of one Sasha Karpov, who had taken monastic vows a very short while before. The obvious aim of the story is to show that those young educated Soviets who turn to religion are hypocrites looking for fame and distinction or originality in society, without possessing any qualities that would give them equivalent prestige in ordinary Soviet life. In the course of the narrative, a few vague sentences reveal other practising Orthodox intellectuals, without once explaining this phenomenon satisfactorily, replacing any such explanation with a few contemptuous and negative comments.

Sasha's mother is described as a biology teacher at a rural school: a cold woman with no warmth for or interest in her children. Her divorced husband was an alcoholic and did not care for his children. On her retirement from schoolteaching this woman, who 'for thirty whole years taught biology . . . and Darwin's theories', suddenly retired to a village where there was a functioning Orthodox church and became a pious parishioner, telling her surprised children: 'Probably I have always been a believer, but have kept this to myself.' There is no explanation that had she not kept it to herself, she would long ago have lost her teaching job; instead, it is left to the reader to conclude that she has been a hypocrite and a heartless woman all along.

Her Sasha is left on his own. He wants to prove that he has a great talent. He tries his hand at singing, writing poetry (and eventually singing it to his own tunes), studying at an institute of education to become a teacher. But his endeavours prove mediocre, and the latter career frightens him with the prospect of hard work and an inconspicuous, very modest life in a faraway village. Then he tries to distinguish himself as a singing hippy, and comes across a priest, who hires him as a church reader and singer. Six months later he breaks with the priest, but not before getting from him a list of addresses of his acquaintances in Moscow. Eventually he drops in on one of them. There he finds a couple of young physicists (husband and wife), whose apartment is full of icons and Russian artifacts. They adore Sasha as a rural talent and seeker of truth. He soon adapts to their religious habits by not entering the apartment without crossing himself facing the icons, praying before meals, and so forth. Eventually he decides to join a monastery, after he is told that with his voice and musical talent his monastic duty will most likely be choral singing. It is never explained in the story why his uncle, who 'occupies a very responsible post in a government department' and therefore is undoubtedly a party member, not only does not seem to object to Sasha's choice to become a religious hermit at first and a monk in a monastery later, but even equips him for the trip, buying warm winter clothing, supplying him with food. The author stresses that now when Sasha visits his friends and relatives in Moscow he deliberately wears his cassock in order to shock everybody, and to impress them. Her unequivocal comment on Sasha as a person and on his choice of life is: 'Everything can be turned into fraud in life, poetry, intellectual curiosity, religious frenzy.'[39]

In addition to such stories, *NiR* periodically publishes episodes from Russian history in which churchmen can be depicted as negative and even criminal characters, in order to remind its readers once again that Christian morals are deficient, that the Church is a greedy parasitic institution breeding alcoholism, fraud, crime and misanthropy not only in the past but also in the present.[40]

The official line, constantly repeated by *NiR*, may be that believers' feelings ought not to be insulted, their beliefs should be respected.[41] Yet the hate-and-contempt posture towards religion is always present. For instance, stories about the traumatic difficulties that believing children experience in Soviet schools appear quite often in the Soviet press. But the blame is always placed on the believer, not on the school. In a novel, a schoolboy attempts suicide rather than live with the 'shameful' label of a 'religious believer'. Yet the author blames the priest, the religious family of the boy and the family's friends, but not the fanatically atheistic schoolteacher who is the real cause of the conflict. Another author argues that because of the conflict between the atheistic school and the faith of religious children, the latter are usually less successful in their academic pursuits than the non-believing students. Surely it is the intolerance and aggressive ideological commitment of the Soviet school to atheism which force the believer to be constantly under stress and to conceal his real views, thereby traumatizing his whole spiritual development. Instead, the author blames the religious family and its upbringing for precipitating the conflict and thus being guilty for the child's poor showing at school. This implies that religious students all over the world are poor scholars by definition.[42]

The professional atheistic establishment is well entrenched and well paid. It is not in their interest to show believers in a positive light or as a constructive element in society.[43] Therefore the religious believer will always be judged the guilty party, regardless of the circumstances.

6 Persecutions under Khrushchev

Most of us in the West were totally unprepared for that fourth antireligious holocaust in the first fifty Soviet years, and we should hardly be blamed, for it appears that the attack was an unexpected shock for the believers inside the Soviet Union as well. Few of them, if any, seem to have remembered the first signs of the gathering clouds: the two 1954 Central Committee resolutions, mentioned in Volume 1 of this study. This is understandable in view of the fact that in actual practice the period between 1953 and 1957 appeared to have been the most peaceful and even somewhat promising for the Church: student numbers in seminaries were growing, after the near-freeze of Stalin's last three years. Reports again began to appear on rebuilding and repairing of churches and even on some new church construction. Also, new bishops of the younger generation began to be consecrated.

Yet the resolutions were there, and Khrushchev and his ideological officials periodically reminded the population that a decisive struggle against religion was in the offing, which would not be limited just to propaganda.[1] This was not the result of any external (or CP leadership) pressure on Khrushchev,[2] but fulfilment of his longstanding atheist convictions. Therefore, the idea of building the communist society which he began to promise for the immediate future was accompanied by his personal antireligious zeal. It was under Khrushchev as the First Moscow City Party Secretary that in the year 1932 alone more than 200 Orthodox churches were dynamited in that city, including a large number of medieval architectural and artistic treasures. 'Having gained national power, Khrushchev carried over into our times the methods which he had practised in his youth'.[3] The CPSU CC Committee resolution of 10 November 1954, 'On Errors in the Conducting of Propaganda of Scientific Atheism', made it quite clear that Khrushchev personally was the initiator of the July resolution when the November resolution said: 'Some speakers allow themselves to insult the clergy and the believers

... unfoundedly misrepresenting [them] ... as politically untrustworthy', for it was Khrushchev who in a public address soon after the July resolution attacked the Church, its clergy and believers precisely in those terms.[4] Likewise, the aggressively antireligious campaign promised in the July document began to be implemented only in 1959, after Khrushchev's complete consolidation of power following the purge of the 'Anti-Party' group of 1957 and the consolidation of the premiership and party leadership posts in Khrushchev's hands alone in March 1959. Moreover, the successful launching of the first manned satellite by the Soviet Union in September 1959 may likewise have been a contributing factor, not only in the sense that Khrushchev felt more firmly in the saddle and conscious of the prestige he had earned when under his leadership the USSR had overtaken the USA in the most advanced form of competition, but also because his primitive mind may have been sincerely impressed by the fact that the cosmonauts had not seen God in the heavens. This did become one of the most frequently used arguments of the Soviet antireligious propaganda for years to come.[5] Technically, 1959 coincided with the Extraordinary 21st Party Congress, and the launching of the Seven Year Plan as the beginning of a twenty-year programme of constructing communism, which was to include the annihilation of religion, for communisim could neither be constructed nor live side-by-side with a flourishing Church.[6]

THE CLOSURE OF THE CHURCHES

There is by now a considerable amount of information and documentation available to illustrate the processes of closure of churches. One of the best-documented cases is that of the Kirov Diocese in the north-eastern part of European Russia, thanks to the late Boris Talantov, a mathematics teacher of Kirov who had lost his job because of his faith. He was one of the first Soviet citizens to begin to sound the alarm when the authorities started to close churches in his diocese, by sending his reports first to Soviet newspapers and to the central government in Moscow. When this proved futile he began to use *samizdat* channels to alert the West, for which he eventually paid with his life, dying in imprisonment in 1971. In a 1967 report he described the persecutions in his diocese in the following terms:

> the antireligious campaign of 1959–64 was aimed primarily at the mass liquidation of churches and religious associations. This was being fulfilled by the Council on the Affairs of the ROC [CROCA, later Council for Religious Affairs, CRA] and its local plenipotentiaries supported by local governments.
>
> ... the following was the most usual procedure. The provincial CROCA plenipotentiary would at his own discretion de-register the priest serving the church earmarked for liquidation, or would move him to another parish. Then during the six to eleven subsequent months he would refuse to issue a registration permit to any clergy candidates suggested by the parishioners, either stating that he owed no explanations to them for his actions or plainly and cynically admitting 'I shall not register anyone.'
>
> In the years 1960 to 1963 twenty-one of the original eighty priests of the diocese were thus de-registered, and not a single new priest was permitted registration in their stead.
>
> While the church remained without a priest the local government organs used all forms of intimidation to force a few members to quit the 'religious association' ('twenty'), thereafter it was declared that the local religious association ceased to exist. Simultaneously the Provincial Executive Committee declared the church closed and the building handed over to the local collective farm or town soviet for other uses. Contrary to the existing laws, the religious association in question was not informed of this decision, which was instead directly transmitted to CROCA in Moscow. Subsequently, the latter would de-register the religious association in spite of its protests.

Talantov remarks that such cases could not be excused by any lack of information: believers sent many written complaints to CROCA in Moscow, as well as delegations, presenting physical evidence that the religious association in question still existed, that the collective farm in question did not need the church building for a club or whatnot. In no case was the written text of the resolutions on de-registration of a religious society shown to its members or petitioners. The text was kept in secret because, apparently, it was in accordance with some secret instructions which contradicted the formal laws but which in fact regulate Soviet life much more often than the published laws.

> The liquidation itself of the house of prayer ... would take place under the protection of the *militia*, often in the middle of the night. Believers were not allowed into the church. The contents were confiscated without any inventory.

Talantov's description of liquidation of individual churches in the diocese shows the senseless barbarism of the operations: icons were broken up and burned, service books and Scriptures destroyed, the Communion wine consumed by the raiders. This, he writes, occurred in all cases in the Kirov Diocese without exception. In some cases, in addition, the very church building would be wrecked (or burned, if it was made of wood) – for example, the beautiful church of Zosima and Savvatii in the village of Korshik, which was recognized as the best and most precious example of eighteenth-century Russian architecture and art in the Kirov Province. It had been under state protection and continued to function even under Stalin. Despite the fact that the petitioners on behalf of this church, closed early in 1960, had been assured by a CROCA official in Moscow in the same year that as an architectural monument the church would be returned to the believers and restored to its original use, it remained shut. In 1963 its interior was totally destroyed, and the domes cut off in the process of transforming it into a collective farm club – which was unlikely, adds Talantov: 'this renovation would cost more than building a new club'.

By these methods the number of functioning Orthodox churches in the Kirov Diocese was reduced from 75 in 1959 to 35 by the end of 1964; that is for a territory three times the size of Holland and with a population of over two million. Before the revolution there were over 500 churches in the diocese. At least by the time of the completion of this report, remarks Talantov, not a single one of the churches was restored to the believers, despite hundreds of group protests, oral and written, addressed to the central Soviet Government, to the CROCA headquarters, to the Patriarchate, to major Soviet newspapers, and to all sorts of local authorities. Some delegations consisted of several hundred people at a time (five hundred in one case), and petitions signed by similar numbers. None of the closed churches were insolvent or in ill-repair. The shouts, insults, beatings, and other forms of intimidation to which the most active petitioners were subjected by local authorities resulted in several deaths, some physical injuries (at least one for life) and nervous breakdowns. None of the guilty officials was ever punished.[7]

And this is how such violent liquidation of churches is presented in the official press:

> Conversations went around the village: Will the church remain, or won't it? ... The church had no business to be standing next door to the school. Moreover, in summer there was usually a pioneer camp in the school. Finally, before the war ... there was a cafe there, with a snack bar in the chapel. The church at Yastrebino was opened by the Germans during the occupation. So, 'it's an echo of the war', ran the argument in the village ... But the weightiest argument which had an effect even on believers,*[1] was this: the children ...
>
> They all argued about religion, but finally arrived at the same conclusion – a club ... You could argue about a church, but not about a club ...
>
> ... By now in surrounding villages they were already gathering signatures beneath an application to the village soviet requesting the closure of the church.[8]

The procedure is the very reverse of that described by Talantov. But there are two characteristic features of the campaign mentioned in this passage. One is the fact that the church was reopened under the German occupation. The Soviet law invalidating all acts passed by the enemy on the Soviet soil was applied in these very years to close most of the churches and monasteries reopened during the war on enemy-occupied territory, although none of them was actually opened

---

* This is an example of the typical logical *non sequitur* of Soviet atheistic propaganda. Why should a believer object to the church's presence in the vicinity of a school? On the contrary, parents would be happy that it would constantly remind the children of the Church's existence and hopefully attract them.

by the enemy. It is under this thin pretext that at least '210 religious congregations of various denominations' were shut down in the Odessa diocese;[9] the total number of Orthodox churches in Belorussia was reduced from some 1200 to less than 400.[10] The Dnepropetrovsk diocese was reduced from 180 to 40 parishes;[11] the diocese of Crimea was eventually reduced to some 15 churches. But Kirov, of course, never was under German occupation; hence not even semi-legitimate excuses of the above kind could have been advanced to 'legitimize' mass church liquidations. Nor could the nullification-of-enemy-acts law be applied to the republic of Latvia, where only 75 of the original 500 Roman Catholic churches remained open after 1964, or to the formerly Polish province of Volhynia where 180 parishes were liquidated in those eventual years: in both places the churches had been there and had functioned before the German occupation.[12]

The other argument in the same passage is that the church was adjacent to the village school. Apparently masses of churches could be and were closed under this pretext, because the majority of pre-revolutionary rural schools were actually parish schools. Obviously most of them were built next to the church. There were many primary schools run by the church in urban areas as well. And we know of at least one case, already, in the 1970s, when a church in Zhitomir was closed and dynamited on the pretext of being situated too close to a school and thus serving as a 'corrupting influence' on children.[13]

Even the Soviet press itself admitted on occasion that the campaign was guilty of unnecessary barbarism. It printed, for instance, an early warning by a group of leading Soviet writers and artists protesting the senseless dynamiting of the Ufa Cathedral on 2 June 1956, 'a most valuable historical and architectural monument . . . destroyed, despite the protests of the Academy of Sciences and the Ministry of Culture of the USSR.' It was possible to publish the letter because it vindicated the Soviet Government of any responsibility for this particular barbarism, pointing out that the Ufa authorities had 'no special permission from the government, which is obligatory in every such case.'[14] However, the central government was perfectly aware of what was going on and took no measures to rectify the situation. Talantov's reports are not the only source of confirmation. Another, though somewhat indirect, confirmation comes from an article in the prestigious official journal of the Soviet Academy of Sciences, *Soviet Ethnography*, in the form of full approval of the post-1959 offensive against religions. There is not a word of warning against offending religious feelings. On the contrary, referring to the CPSU CC resolution of 9 January 1960 (which all believers in the Soviet Union interpreted as the first printed evidence of the official approval of the persecutions), 'On the Aims of Party Propaganda in the Contemporary Conditions', it says:

> The Party has never reconciled itself and never will, with ideological reaction of any kind ... The struggle against religion must not only be continued, but it ought to be enhanced by *all possible means*.[15] [italics mine, D.P.]

and this, of course, included all the brutalities and barbarisms just described, for otherwise they would have been subjected to criticism.

There is also indirect, but sufficiently convincing, confirmation in the official press that the closure of churches was just as unwarranted in the 1960s as in the 1930s by reason of religious decline. A brochure on the condition of the churches in the north Russian autonomous republic of Komi states that where there had been 150 churches before the revolution there were only three now; but then adds that besides these three officially registered there are over twenty unregistered Orthodox communities with unofficial priests. This is in addition to one or two 'catacomb' communities of the 'True Orthodox' (those who do not recognize the Moscow Patriarchate).[16] In other words, the three registered churches are insufficient for the number of believers in that republic; while the fact that the other twenty or so cannot gain official sanction for their existence is evidence of harassment by the Soviet state. A book on the Old Believers of the Trans-Baikal area admits that a survey has indicated that the proportion of religious believers in the city of Ulan-Ude constitutes nearly 20 per cent of the population, while that in the rural areas is between 32 and 36 per cent. The latter were represented by two villages, both populated by Old Believers, yet there is not a single officially functioning Old Believer church in the area. The higher proportion of 36 per cent in one village is explained by the fact that there had been an open Old Believer church there until recently, and even 'after its closure the priest, Simonov, continued to celebrate at his home'.[17] Obviously a church closed with 36 per cent of the population daring to declare their faith even after its closure, could only have been shut down by force.

During the same years the cowed official representatives of the Moscow Patriarchate continued to declare that in all but very exceptional cases the closures were caused by a decline in believers and resulted mostly in amalgamation of adjacent churches.[18] Talantov describes such alleged amalgamations in his diocese, of churches standing forty kilometres apart.[19]

While the leaders of the Moscow Patriarchate were forced to make these mendacious statements, writers belonging to the Soviet establishment, enjoying greater freedom of speech, came closer to the truth in the following admission:

> In some places educational work with believers was being replaced by crude administrative arbitrariness, causing among the believers only dissatisfaction and bitterness, used by foreign reactionary circles for anti-Soviet propaganda.[20]

DEMORALIZING THE REMAINING PARISHES

As several Soviet-Russian Orthodox authors point out, the attitudes and role of the CROCA-CRA and of its local plenipotentiaries changed in 1960 from that of at least allegedly impartial intermediaries between the Church and the State to that of dictatorial administrators over the Church, local dioceses and parishes, aiming at their destruction or at least demoralization.[21] This coincides with the retirement of M. Nikolai who had dared to protest against the new wave of persecutions in his sermons. Among other things, he had been the autor of the Patriarch Alexii's Kremlin speech at a Soviet peace conference in 1960, in which he openly admitted persecutions and warned the hostile Soviet establishment audience that whatever they did 'the gates of hell shall not overcome the Church'. The Patriarch praised the role of the Church as the spiritual leader of the nation throughout Russia's history, saving her several times in periods of the deepest national crises.[22] This was the high point of Church officialdom's resistance to the new holocaust, resulting in

Nikolai's forced retirement and mysterious death a few months later, and the Patriarchate's submission to the pressures, reflected in the behaviour of diocesan bishops as well, as described by Talantov and other writers. The result of this submission was the acceptance in 1961 of new Church bylaws, imposed by the Soviet regime through the CROCA, which deprived the bishop and the priest of any effective control over the parish, handing over all power to the lay parish executive council of three persons; this was followed by the penetration of the religious associations (the 'twenties') and the councils by Soviet agents.[23]

It was at this time that the CROCA plenipotentiaries virtually appropriated for themselves the function of appointing and removing priests by a relentless and arbitrary application of the registration and de-registration rights. In the Kirov diocese as well as in others this led to the removal of the most popular and spiritually most influential priests and the refusal to register clergy candidates chosen by the laity to replace the former priests.

> When the parishioners of the church where the priest had been de-registered appealed to their bishop to appoint another priest, the bishop instructed them to apply to the provincial plenipotentiary to register the parishioners' candidate. The plenipotentiary refused, giving no explanation. Returning to the bishop the petitioners were told he had no other candidate, was powerless against the plenipotentiary, and they would have to find another candidate themselves.

Cowed by the officials, the local bishop ordered the priests to fulfil all CROCA plenipotentiaries' orders, or risk losing their registration. Under the threat of de-registration the priests ceased to deliver topical and uplifting sermons, criticizing atheism and materialism, and limited themselves to abstract discussions of Christian ethics. How abstract this discussion had to be is shown by the fact that under the threat of losing their posts, priests were forced from 1960 to speak against the presence of beggars on church steps, and from 1963 even the militia (police) began to raid church porches and yards expelling them. These people were without any means of existence, and to deprive them of the fruits of Christian charity was the broadest possible interpretation of the 1929 laws banning all church charity. It was obviously another means of undermining the moral prestige both of the clergy and of the Church in general.[24]

In the conditions of great scarcity of functioning churches, many faithful come long distances to a service, sometimes too far to return the same day. Until 1960 it was normal practice to let these pilgrims stay overnight at the so-called night watchman's hut (small houses commonly built in Russia in the church yard). After 1960 the CROCA began to forbid the use of these huts for this purpose across the whole Soviet Union. Fearing reprisals, church councils began to expel pilgrims from them, although most stood empty. In the areas where the church councils nevertheless surreptitiously allowed the pilgrims in, the militia would arrive at night (even in the middle of winter) and expel these, mostly old, people into the cold. Thus they made it almost impossible for people from afar to go to church,[25] thereby artificially reducing church attendance. This measure must have been particularly effective in the sparsely populated rural areas of the north, north-east, and the east, where in this way the church's attendance and income could be greatly reduced, thus helping the plenipotentiary to close it under the pretext of poor attendance and insolvency. It ought to be kept in mind that no religious organization in the USSR is allowed to levy any membership dues or to canvas private residences for donations to the church. The only legal income is from voluntary donations of believers and pilgrims on the territory of the temple or monastery.

In the Kirov Diocese from the end of 1959 priests began to receive oral orders from the plenipotentiaries forbidding them under the threat of de-registration, to administer confessions, communions, baptisms, extreme unctions and other private religious services at private homes, even to those terminally ill, without the express permission to do so in each individual case granted by the local soviet on request from the priest. Two years later the clergy of the Moscow Archdiocese were even forced to sign an unpublished pledge with similar stipulations. The text of the pledge and the priests' signatures remained in the hands of the CROCA without any copy given to the priest.[26] This measure, besides being an act of blatant persecution and infringement on the alleged Church—State separation, was once again meant to strike at the social and moral prestige of the priest. He was made to appear a lazy selfish person who would let a sick person die without spiritually attending to him, since not a single priest could produce a document to vindicate himself from such suspicions. Talantov, in fact, cites a case in point. When a delegation of Kirov believers went to Moscow in 1963 to complain to the CROCA headquarters about this regulation, an official responded: 'Don't you believe this. Your priests are simply lying to you. No special government permission of any kind is required to administer communion or unction at private homes.'[27]

The Soviet press made many admissions at the end of the 1950s and early in the 1960s of the growth of religiosity among the young.[28] Undoubtedly this was at least partly caused by their disillusionment with the official doctrines, particularly after Khrushchev's condemnation of Stalin and his inability to substantiate in practice his claims that there was a truly attractive alternative model of Marxism-Leninism. Failing in this, the only other alternative open to the regime to prevent the increase of young churchgoers was to use coercion. Their opening salvo banning the attendance of children and youths at church services was apparently aimed at the Baptist Chuch, as early as 1960. The probable reasons for starting with the Baptists are several. Being a Church of adult baptism, in contrast to the Orthodox Church, the children were not full members; hence the Soviets must have thought the Baptist Church might accept this pressure more readily than the Orthodox. Second, as a fundamentalist religion, without the complex symbolic ritualism and involved theology of the Orthodox Church, the Evangelicals and Baptists were most accessible to the theologically illiterate but religiously searching Soviet youth than the Orthodox and thus were attracting *proportionally* more young people than the Orthodox.

Be that as it may, in 1960 the central leadership of the All-Union Church of Evangelical Christian-Baptists (AUCECB) issued a *Letter of Instructions* which, among other things, stipulated that: sermons should cease to sound like appeals; 'an effort must be made to reduce the baptism of young people between the ages of 18 and 30 to the minimum'; 'Children . . . should not be allowed to attend services.' Much to the surprise of the Soviet authorities, two years later this caused the most significant split in the Russian Baptist Church in its history, lasting to the day of present writing. Henceforth this other branch of the Baptists, known at first as the *Initsiativniki* or Action Group, but later adopting the name of Council of Churches of the Evangelical Christians and Baptists (CCECB), has become an institutionally persecuted Church in the Soviet Union, with hundreds of its members constantly lingering on in Soviet concentration or labour camps and prisons,[29] while in contrast, the AUCECB enjoys more privileges than the Orthodox Church, including the right of regular national councils with relatively genuine elections and candidates nominated from the floor.[30]

The Baptist rebellion caused the civil authorities to use more circumvention in imposing similar changes on the Orthodox Church. First of all, it appears to have been only in 1962 that a circular was addressed by the state to the Orthodox Church instructing the priests not to conduct church services in the presence of children and youths; although in some localities instructions to this effect were given to the Orthodox clergy as early as 1960 or 1961.[31] The text of the instruction was never shown to the clergy. Instead, the plenipotentiaries generally telephoned local priests, threatening to deprive them of their registration if they allowed children to be present at services or administered communion to them. In the Kirov Province measures to prevent children and youths under the age of twenty from attending the liturgy began to be applied as late as the summer of 1963.[32] The first and direct attempt in Kirov failed: women bringing children to church physically assaulted the policemen and their Komsomol aids encircling the churches and broke through, the policemen not daring to beat the women in public. It was after this failure that CROCA plenipotentiaries began to threaten the priests by telephone, instructing them to refuse to administer communion to or accept confessions from children and youths, even if present in the church. The threat of de-registration and lack of support or defence by the bishop worked.[33] Foreign diplomats remember how they had to show their foreign passport in those days to Komsomol patrols in front of most Moscow churches on Sundays and feast days if they wanted to take their children to church: the measures were applied unevenly and not uniformly, because numerous priests continued to administer the Holy Sacraments to children throughout those years, and even conduct special *Te Deums* for schoolchildren on the eve of the first school day in September.[34] But the punishment for this sort of 'crime' now became severe. In the Orenburg Diocese alone forty-six priests were in prison in 1960. Soviet press reported trials and prison or labour camp sentences meted out to various clergy, among them the dean of the most popular church in Leningrad (nicknamed *Kulich i paskha*), who was given six years' hard labour, and numerous priests from Moldavia, one from Dneprodzerzhinsk, and others.[35] Although the Soviet press did not reveal the cause of these arrests, in other instances attempts to attract youth and children to the church were cited as cause for imprisonment of priests, for example in the Kalinin Province and in the town of Likhoslavl.[36] The harassment of clergymen for working with youth continues to the present day.[37] Talantov tells of two young men in his diocese who applied to the Moscow seminary for theological studies to prepare for priesthood. Both were accepted, but when the local government discovered that both young men had given up their employment to prepare for the seminary entrance exams, they were arrested, tried as parasites evading work, and sentenced to three years' forestry work in the far north. The priest who had helped them to prepare for their studies and who had given them letters of reference was deprived of registration in 1961.[38] That the authorities were aiming simply at depriving the Church of the most popular and active priests is demonstrated by the case of a popular priest, T. G. Perestoronin, arbitrarily deprived of registration in 1961 in preparation for the arbitrary closure of the church he served in. The priest then moved to Kirov to work as a reader in the local church, leaving his wife and children in the parish house in the village of the closed church. The house was built especially for the priest by the parishioners with their own money and labour. But the local village boss decided to throw the woman out of the house in the middle of the winter of 1962. The court sided with the official, threatening the poor woman with deprivation of parental rights as a parasite. When the local schoolmistress hired the priest's wife as a charwoman to save her from prosecution, the village boss sacked her from the school. Brought to such an impasse, the priest ceased working for the Church and took a job as a plumber, whereupon all harassment ceased, and he received the right to return to his village and to live with his wife in his former house.[39]

Bishops who had tried to resist the closure of churches and monasteries were either forced to retire, like M. Nikolai and Archbishop Ermogen of Tashkent,[40] or were arrested. The very popular Veniamin (Novitsky, see above), Archbishop of Irkutsk, was a target of Soviet press attacks, and there was an attempt to indict him in 1961 in connection with the trial of a church warden or guard who had inadvertently killed a juvenile thief. The evidence apparently was too flimsy even for a Soviet court to indict him. Nevertheless, Veniamin was such a thorn in the CROCA-CRA eyes because of his great popularity, spiritual leadership and resistance to atheists, that eventually, under Brezhnev, he was removed to the much less conspicuous diocese of Chuvashia.[41] The Archbishop Venedikt died in prison in 1963, awaiting trial, arrested for resisting the closure of churches.[42] Two bishops were in fact sentenced: the very popular and energetic Iov (Kresovich), Archbishop of Kazan', who had vehemently fought against the closure of churches, was sentenced to three years' hard labour allegedly for tax evasion; Archbishop Andrei (Sukhenko) of Chernigov, who had already served a term of imprisonment under Stalin, was sentenced in 1961 to eight years' hard labour for having resisted the closure of a monastery in his diocese. M. Nikolai, in his last secret interview given to Archbishop Vasilii of Brussels, confirmed that all these charges were a fraud: the bishops were imprisoned for standing up for their Church. Soon after his release Iov was appointed Archbishop of Ufa. Had he been truly guilty of tax evasion and stealing from the diocesan treasury, the Church would not have reappointed him, nor would the state have tolerated the appointment. Andrei was likewise reappointed diocesan bishop soon after his release, but the camp had affected his mind and he eventually had to be retired to a monastery for mental health reasons.[43] Needless to say, not only the Chernigov monastery but even the cathedral of Chernigov was closed soon after Andrei's arrest. Similarly, as this author was informed by the late M. Nikodim (Rotov), although no churches could be closed in the Archdiocese of Tashkent while Ermogen was there, after his forced retirement the authorities came down with a vengeance closing perhaps more than they had originally planned.[44] This shows that unless there is a total unity of the nation with the Church and undivided popular support for her, as in Poland, thereby leaving no alternative for the communist regime except to negotiate with the Church as a partner and adversary and not as a powerless subordinate, steadfast resistance of a bishop or a priest will simply result in his retirement and replacement by a more compliant one. It is probably this lesson that was drawn in these years by the Patriarch and the rest of the bishops, hence their compliance and lack of support for the parishes struggling for survival – a reproach repeatedly levelled at the hierarchy by Talantov, Frs. Nikolai Eshliman (deceased in 1984) and Gleb Yakunin, and many other *samizdat* authors.[45]

It was in these years that five of the existing eight seminaries were closed by Soviet authorities, and even in the surviving seminaries the number of students was artificially reduced. According to M. Nikodim, there were only seventy students at the Leningrad schools of theology when he took over (in contrast to 396 students in 1953 and about 400 by the time of Nikodim's death in 1978).[46] As the above example of two student-candidates to the seminary from Kirov shows, this reduction of the student body was achieved by direct persecution of the candidates, as well as by preventing their registration at the seminaries by refusing to give them a residence permit in the area where the seminary was situated. Another ploy was to call up most of the students and candidates for military service. Having thus emptied most of the seminaries, the authorities then shut them down.[47]

All these means of direct and indirect persecution resulted in the reduction of functioning Orthodox churches from over 20 000 prior to 1960 to 6850 by 1972, and a simultaneous decrease in the numbers of registered Orthodox priests (those officially permitted to perform priestly duties) from over 30 000 to 6180.[48] Obviously this could not be explained by attrition and a reduced number of new ordinations alone; while the Soviet press boasted at the time that over 200 Orthodox priests resigned during the 1960s.[49]

MONASTERIES AND PILGRIMAGES

Another form of persecution was the reinforcement in 1961 of the 1929 law banning all group pilgrimages, although according to Talantov, in Kirov, at least, such a ban had been issued by the local government as early as 1960. It expressly forbade the believers to erect monuments to persons whom the believers revered as saints or to care for them or to visit their graves. Simultaneously the state began to destroy these grave-sites and monuments. The author describes sites considered holy not only locally but in Russia generally, situated in the Kirov Province, some of which have been the objects of national pilgrimages made up of scores of thousands on certain days of the year from as far back as the fourteenth and fifteenth centuries. In 1960 a beautiful eighteenth-century Transfiguration Chapel built on one of those sites with a traditional pool of water formed by a natural spring considered to have had healing powers, was closed. A year later it was blown up.[50] Pilgrimages to this site, nevertheless, continue to the present day, although the authorities have filled the pool and blocked off the spring.[51]

Apparently out of fear, the local bishop, the late Ioann of Kirov, supported the Soviet authorities. On 20 May 1964, he forbade pilgrimages in his diocese. When a group of Kirov Christians in 1966 complained to the Moscow Patriarchate that Bishop Ioann was acting against the interests of the Church and should be removed, they were told he could not be removed because the CRA categorically refused to allow his retirement, thus admitting that the Church was being ruled by CRA, not by the Patriarch and his Synod, who only reigned.[52]

The greatest centres of national pilgrimages have always been the monasteries and convents. And it was against them that the government turned most vehemently in the early 1960s, reducing the number of functioning monasteries and convents from 69 in 1959 to 17 by 1965 (there were over 1000 of them in 1914). This was a protracted and apparently well-planned campaign. First, all financial exemptions and tax privileges granted to the monastics in 1945 and 1946 were revoked by three different decrees of 1958. Up to 1958, monastic institutions were exempt from paying property and land taxes. The newly introduced land tax was to be 4000 old roubles (400 r. after the 1961 devaluation) from one hectare. The other exemptions which the monastics now lost had been the bachelor and childless-couple taxes. Moreover, a decree of 16 October 1958 plainly intended to devise ways and means of reducing the land lots controlled by the monastic institutions and the number of functioning monasteries.[53]

We are fortunate in having detailed information on what measures have in fact been used to force a monastery to close, in the example of the Pochaev Lavra, one of the most revered monasteries in Russia, which despite nearly twenty-five years of harassment and indirect persecutions, the authorities have as yet failed to close. One of the reasons for its survival has been the publicity the case has received owing to the number of its monks and lay supporters who have written dozens of detailed reports on these persecutions, sending them far and wide. The other important factor is the religious devotion and support for the monastery by the vast majority of the local population. These citizens often confronted the militia even physically, defending the monks, and wrote many appeals on their behalf to the Patriarch, to the Soviet Government, the UN and other places, giving the monks publicity through *samizdat* channels.[54]

The troubles began in 1959, when the local soviet tried to deprive the monastery of its livelihood by confiscating its ten hectares of agricultural fields, its fruit orchard, including the adjacent 'hothouse, drying room, gardener's cottage, storage and other anciliary premises. Then they took away an apiary containing over 100 beehives';[55] but the community continued to thrive thanks to the generosity of the pilgrims and local believers.[56] In 1961 the soviet confiscated the Bishop's Palace which had been used as a hostel for pilgrims. A year earlier it forbade any restoration work to be carried out on the premises, as well as any overnight visits of pilgrims anywhere on the monastic premises. To enforce this order the militia began to raid the monastery at night, throwing out pilgrims sleeping either in the yard or in the main cathedral which the monks now kept open for devotions twenty-four hours a day to allow the pilgrims to repose there during the night. At the same time, militia began raiding private houses in the vicinity, hunting for pilgrims. The reports of numerous laymen as well as of the Spiritual Council of the Lavra confirm that in these raids many pilgrims were not only insulted verbally but also beaten so severely as to result in several fatalities. The Spiritual Council report also enumerates four monasteries which were closed by the soviets in 1959, their monks having found protection at the Pochaev Lavra, residing in the Bishop's Palace until its confiscation the following year and expulsion of these monks by the militia.[57]

A year later, in 1962, the secular authorities began their attack on the resident monks directly, reducing their number by the end of the year from 146 to 36.[58] Besides the report of the Spiritual Council summing up the harassment and persecutions over a seven-year period (1959–66), there are a number of earlier personal letters written by the persecuted monks, addressed either to the Spiritual Council, the Patriarch, or to soviet authorities. They report the deprivations of residence permits and subsequent brutal militia expulsions of monks, some of whom had resided there since before the war, when the territory of the monastery belonged to the Polish state. Here are some excerpts from the letter of one of such victims, Fr. Ilarii:

> I have been living in the Lavra since 1942. In March 1962 I received a summons to the local militia station . . . and was told that it would soon be closed and I must return to the place of my birth.
> I refused.
> Henceforth I was being summoned daily, sometimes twice daily . . . [along with] ten or fifteen other monks each time . . . Sometimes they would act kindly, saying . . . [that] the government has decided to discontinue all monasteries, 'We don't want to throw you out in the street, and have to decide whom to assign to an old folks home, whom to his relatives, and who could find secular jobs for themselves.' I refused their kindness. Then . . . they began to attack and threaten me: '. . . in the 1930s we used to shoot those of your kind without much ado; now we are talking to you, but if you will not do as you're told, we'll apply other means'.
> After that they began to make raids on the Lavra, . . . check the passports, take them away in many cases and then deprive these monks of residence rights.
> Once I was celebrating an *akathist* to the Virgin Mary in the church; enters the dean, Fr. Vladislav, and orders: 'Unvest yourself immediately, the militia wants you at 11.'

He describes how the militia called in senior monastic council members, trying to force them to expel him from the monastery. The Council refused. But the militia continued to torment him by daily summonses accompanied by threats, shouts and insults, ruining his health. Then on 1 September the militia came by truck to the monastery, grabbed him in the kitchen where he was working and took him to his cell where he found fifteen militiamen waiting. They took his passport and ordered him to leave the monastery in five minutes. He refused. The militia grabbed his belongings and pulled him up by force to the truck. Along with him another monk, Fr. Alipii, was thrown onto the truck. Both were given back their passports with stamps cancelling their residence permits in the area. Driven for 300 km in the open truck in the rain, Fr. Ilarii was thrown out in the middle of the street in his native village.[59]

Late in 1964, roughly at the time of Khrushchev's fall from power, the persecutions of the Pochaev monks temporarily stopped. According to an insider's report, the respite followed several events that could be interpreted mystically:

> the daughter of one of the chief persecutors of the pilgrims burned to death in strange circumstances. Her charred bones were brought for burial to the Pochaev Monastery, but her father moved from Pochaev ...
> He was replaced by a military officer who, worse than his predecessor, began to persecute not only the pilgrims but the monks as well. Then he suddenly committed suicide, and peace was restored in the Lavra.[60]

But this peace proved to be short-lived. By 1966 Fr. Ilarii was being persecuted again, for he had secretly returned to the Lavra and had been given back his cell by the Father-Superior.[61] This indicates that the monastery authorities did not agree with the actions of the soviet. The most conclusive evidence of this is the previously cited report-complaint of the monastic Spiritual Council of 1966, addressed to Podgornyi, then the chairman of the USSR Supreme Soviet Presidium.

The report gives some details about the expulsion of fifty-nine monks (adding in most cases 'and others'), making a mockery of the statement in a state-published brochure, *The Pochaev Museum of Atheism*, that sixty-nine monks had left the monastery voluntarily.[62] In addition to the methods described in Fr. Ilarii's letter, the following means of expulsion are also listed in the document:

(1) 'A commission set up under the Pochaev District Military

Board ... found certain monks [three are listed, 'and others'] mentally ill, although they were completely healthy.' They were forcefully incarcerated in a mental hospital and 'treated' in such a way that a perfectly healthy 35-year-old monk Golovanov died within a few months at the hospital.

(2) Another commission diagnosed six healthy monks as carriers of 'infectious diseases' and they were sent off by force to another hospital.

(3) On 13 March 1962 another medical commission was set up, but now monks simply refused to appear before it, wherefore sixteen refusers were simply expelled from the monastery when the militia cancelled their resisdence permits.

(4) Another thirteen young monks were conscripted into the army, but sent to fell trees in the north instead. Of these, three were in very poor health, one being almost totally blind, yet 'the doctors passed them "fit" for military service'. In fact, they were discharged at the nearest military assembly point, and meanwhile their Pochaev residence permits were cancelled.

(5) A novice night-watchman came to the rescue of women pilgrims who were being brutally beaten by the militia one night in the monastery yard. The militia in response beat him savagely, while the KGB, after the incident, confiscated his passport and expelled him from the monastery.

(6) On 20 November 1964, four monks were attacked in their cells, beaten up by the police and sentenced to various terms in prison on false charges. One of the arrested monks, being too old for prison, was placed in a mental institution. Subjected to injections, his body swelled up and he became an invalid for the rest of his life. His relatives were allowed to take him from the hospital only after he signed a promise not to return to Pochaev.

The tortures continued after Khrushchev's fall at least until 1966, and were renewed some fifteen years later; this will be discussed in the next chapter. In the course of 1965, 'many monks died prematurely ... Yevgenii died after torture outside the monastery, as did Andrei and a number of others. Some who survived lost their good health.' Some arrests and sentences still continued in 1966: one monk was sentenced to two years' hard labour after he had reported the militia's brutal beatings of pilgrims in July 1965 for spending the night at a nearby cemetery.

Also at that time the dispersed monks were returned to the monastery, including those having completed their army and prison sentences. One of them, a perfectly healthy 25-year-old novice, Grigori Unka, did not return, however: he 'died suddenly' in prison. When his parents opened the coffin they saw a body 'black and blue from bruises, the clothes were torn and pierced right through the side. He . . . had been tortured to death.'

Among the regular monastic pilgrims there was a 33-year-old woman, Marfa Gzhevskaia, who in her youth had sworn an oath of virginity, and lived in a private home in Pochaev, worshipping daily at the monastic churches. On 12 June 1964, the militia raided the house where Marfa lived, found her in the attic and threw her from there out into the yard; thence they 'dragged her . . . into the garden. There they defiled her virgin body, pulled her out on to the road half-dead and left her there.' The following day she was found there by neighbours who took her to a hospital, where she died:

> On police instructions, however, the doctors diagnosed that Marfa died from acute lung trouble . . . covering up the crime . . . In Pochaev they similarly killed Lydia Tokmakova . . . The police lay in wait at the public lavatories and picked up those who needed to go out at night, dragging them to [their] headquarters . . . girls were raped, money confiscated, and people beaten until they lost consciousness . . . they robbed and raped Maria [Morozova], an aged nun . . . The same happened to Maria Gerasimchuk and Yustina Korolenko.

Several times petitioners on behalf of the monastery, both monastics and laity, went to Moscow to seek justice. The Patriarch expressed his condolences but was powerless to do much more than that; although he did intercede with CROCA on Pochaev's behalf 'saying that the monks were within their rights to return there'. At the CROCA headquarters one of its deputy heads, Plekhanov, shouted at the monks, accusing them of slandering the Soviet Government. At the Supreme Procuracy, a senior official Taran cynically advised them to cease their complaints, for the USSR was moving toward communism, 'when there would be no monasteries, and so there were no grounds for their complaints'. In reprisal for their complaints all three monks were, on their return from Moscow, expelled from the Pochaev Monastery by the local soviet.

Another delegation of several monks apparently reached the public official who was their interlocutor:

> speaking on behalf of the Party Central Committee, [he said] that the latter approved of all methods of combating religion ... he added: 'In my opinion all believers are psychologically abnormal people and it is entirely natural for them to be sent into mental hospitals ... it is our aim to liquidate religion as quickly as possible; for the time being we partially tolerate it for political reasons, but when a favourable political opportunity arises we shall not only close down your monastery but all churches and monasteries.'[63]

As we know (see chapter 5), at that very time the Soviet press was carrying on a massive contempt-and-hate propaganda against monaticism, full of libel against the contemporary monks as well as the history of the institution.

PARENTS AND CHILDREN

When the authorities saw that no pressure to keep children away from church services could succeed, because of the resistance of parents, and because the Patriarch apparently refused to co-operate with the Soviet authorities on this matter, instructing parents and priests 'to administer communion to children and let them attend church service',[64] they tried other methods. Parents of children who openly demonstrated their faith at school, or who refused for religious reasons to join the pioneers (communist scouts) or to wear the pioneer kerchiefs, began to be prosecuted by the courts or the administration. After these prosecutions, many parents, both Orthodox and sectarian, were deprived of parental rights and their children were forcibly sent to closed boarding schools. One of the first such cases reported in the Soviet press took place in 1962, when a forester in the Pskov Province, by the name of Sokhraniaev, was tried for allegedly forcing his two children to observe fasting days, to attend church regularly and to act as readers of Scriptures there. He and his equally religious wife were deprived of parental rights and the children sent off to a boarding school. In the following year, a group of leaders and active members of the Pentecostal Sect were tried in the Kharkov Province and similarly deprived of parental rights.[65] But one of the most moving accounts is that of Feodosia Varavva, at first in Minsk and later in L'vov. A doctor's aide by profession, she had volunteered for active military service on 30 June 1941, and worked in the front-line hospitals to the last days of the war. Nevertheless, after the war, because of her religious faith she was forced to work as an orderly and junior nurse in the most infectious sections of hospitals. Nor was the family ever given decent living quarters; they lived with two children in a single room, a sort of corridor 19 m long by less than 1 m in width, without any conveniences, plus a tiny kitchen without a window. Her husband, who had also served in the army for twenty-eight years, retired as an invalid. In the course of her petitions for a more decent apartment, a communist neighbour reported that she was a religious believer, had icons in the room and took her children to church. After that the local communist office advised her husband, a CP member, to divorce her and take the children with him; then he would be given a flat. The husband refused. Then the activists began to advise Mrs Varavva to give up her faith, whereafter she would be granted both a good job and a nice flat. She refused, and all doors were shut to her. Her problems began in 1959 when her six-year-old son asked to be allowed to serve as a bishop's acolyte. One day the school headmaster saw her children going to church. He began to pester her to let her son join the pioneers. She refused, on the grounds that this was an antireligious organization; if he joined the pioneers he would be lying. The headmaster threatened her with a court trial, but she finally found an apartment in L'vov and moved there. The teachers, in the meanwhile, both in Minsk and in L'vov, were instigating the children against their mother.

When the Soviets began to expel children from church services and to forbid the priests to administer the Sacraments to them in 1961, Varavva went as far as the chief CROCA plenipotentiary for the Belorussian Republic. Arguing that she had the constitutional right to educate her children as Christians, she forced him to give oral instructions over the phone to the Minsk cathedral clergy to administer the

Sacraments to her children in the sanctuary, so that others would not see. But Varavva continued to fight on principle, for other children were still denied the Sacraments. Eventually, the Soviet press began to write about the Varavva case, reporting on parent–teacher meetings carrying resolutions to deprive Varavva of her parental rights. This was in 1964. After Khrushchev's fall the fury subsided, but at least one article on the case was again published in 1965. It depicted the mother as an intolerant, aggressive woman, attacking the school and the teachers, and the latter as victims of her persecutions. The son is presented as an atheist forced by the mother to go to church against his will.[66]

But there are many *samizdat* documents of the time, especially on the Pentecostals and the opposition Baptists – both unofficial sects – reporting forced separation of children from their parents, both under Khrushchev and since his fall.[67]

In the supercharged atmosphere of hate propaganda against the banned sects, the Pentecostals were accused of causing their members serious mental and physical stress by their practice of severe fasting and by inducing a state of ecstasy and trance during their religious services. Clergymen of the sect have periodically been tried and sentenced to hard labour. A case in point was trial of a Pentecostal presbyter, Kondrakov, in the Donets Basin mining area. He was accused of having caused reactive psychosis in his parishioners. 'Fulfilling the will of the people, the court sentenced Kondrakov to eight years of deprivation of freedom.'[68] Indiscriminate persecution of the Pentecostals and the banned faction of the Baptists continues to the present day, as the following chapter will show.

7 Persecutions after Khrushchev

Although the post-Khrushchev period saw some easing off in government oppression of religion as far as the average uneducated elderly believer is concerned, a selective persecution of certain religious targets not only continued to persist or to be heard of periodically, but has even been on the rise, particularly since the second half of the 1970s. The persecutions took on a more sophisticated and sinister character, well reflecting the style and methods of the man in charge of terror in the USSR in the 1970s: the late Yurii Andropov, the head of the Soviet state in 1982–3. Although attempts had already been made in Khrushchev's time to tie the struggle against religion to a return from Stalin's arbitrary rule to socialist legality,[1] the crudeness and brutality of the persecutions reflected the crude and primitive impulsiveness of Khrushchev's personality more than anything else. We have seen how the persecutors resorted to oral threats and orders and were guided in their actions by secret instructions.

As mentioned in Volume 1 of this study, soon after Khrushchev's fall Soviet religiologists concluded that the persecutions had done more harm than good to the cause of atheism, first by embittering the believers against the Soviet state, and second, by pushing religious groups underground in the areas where churches had been closed. Obviously an underground church, not open to easy supervision and control, was more dangerous than an overt one. Also, their oppression of the church had only served to draw the sympathy of the surrounding non-religious public towards the believers and increase interest in their faith.[2] But this self-criticism did not result in any radical reversal of state policies. There was no large-scale reopening of the closed and destroyed churches; none of the closed seminaries or monasteries was reopened.

However modest the church reopenings in the very first years after Khrushchev's fall, the process was soon reversed again, with new individual closures of churches, mostly in the distant provinces, and consistent rejections of believers' pleas to reopen old churches or to open new ones.³ Only in the very late 1970s and the 1980s did the pendulum again, it seems, begin to shift positively to the churches. The Orthodox Church built or reopened at least forty churches in the six years between 1977 and 1983, while the official Baptists were allowed to register 170 new communities between 1974 and 1978.⁴

The reader now may ask: why then have a chapter on church persecution in these years? The following will answer this question.

THE CLOSING OF CHURCHES

The Orthodox

We have already mentioned the closing of the Zhitomir church of the Epiphany, despite the vehement appeals and protests from the believers, addressed to CRA, the UN, and to Soviet newspapers. This happened in 1975. In 1966, on the night of 15 November, a church of the Holy Trinity was blown up in Leningrad. When the unsuspecting believers came to their church the following morning, they found a pile of rubble instead.⁵ One of the most malicious closures occurred in 1968 in the rural town of Kolyvan' in the vicinity of Novosibirsk. The city of Novosibirsk was built at the end of the nineteenth century, so early-nineteenth-century buildings constitute a historical antiquity in that region. The beautiful large church of Alexander Nevsky in Kolyvan' is the oldest architectural monument in the whole province; and indeed the local CRA plenipotentiary, Nikolaev, boasted since 1962 that he would turn the church into a museum. First, the local fire-fighters' service requested that a special water reservoir should be built next to the church to protect it from fire. The church council duly complied, but as soon as the reservoir was dug, the local militia declared the work illegal and took all building materials away from the church council. However, allegedly because of breaking the fire-fighters' regulations (absence of the reservoir), the church doors were sealed and entry banned to believers. Six years later Nikolaev organized a barbarous attack on the church with the help of the wreckers' brigade. The icon screen was smashed to bits, all the interior fixtures including the floors were stolen, and the domes were dismantled. Beams and other wooden parts of the structure were sold to the population for a pittance. In the course of the 'reconstruction' a falling beam killed an eight-year-old girl.

The faithful continued church services, now without a priest, in the watchman's house in the church yard. At first, the authorities harassed the believers, raiding the house, keeping the organizers under arrest for several hours at a time. Eventually Nikolaev gave in, granting the faithful a twenty-square-metre basement in an old wooden house, the upper floor of which is occupied by non-believers. The place is a fire and health hazard, especially since it is always overcrowded, with close to two hundred communicants each feast-day. There are no hydrants in the vicinity, yet no commission is concerned about this. Meanwhile, the desecrated and disfigured church of St Alexander Nevsky stands completely unused, unattended and neglected.[6]

In the town of Rechitsa in Belorussia a church was closed in 1979 in a sadistically mocking fashion. The house of prayer was too small for the numbers. The faithful had asked for and were granted permission to reconstruct and enlarge the building. As soon as all the work (at the faithfuls' expense) was completed, the house was declared a fire hazard and closed. The building is guarded day and night by militia to prevent its occupation by the faithful who gather for communal prayers by the church's gate.[7]

An eighteenth-century church in the village of Mshany in the L'vov diocese was closed in March 1978 and turned into a grain storage. A year later, believers gathered around the church trying physically to prevent the laying into the church of a new supply of grain. The militia was called in to disperse the crowd. One woman was sent to jail for fifteen days for 'hooliganism'. None of the complaints and appeals signed by over 200 people and addressed to the Patriarch as well as to the civilian authorities have brought any results.[8]

These probably represent only a small proportion of the actual church closures in the last decade and a half. We have more reports on believers' attempts, mostly unsuccessful, to reopen churches closed under Khrushchev or before.

There have been at least three such unsuccessful attempts in the Volhynia Diocese, which had lost over 180 churches under Khrushchev. One was a church in the village of Znosychy near Rovno. Not without the local government efforts the church had been deprived of a priest for several years, during which the faithful took loving care of it and gathered there regularly for prayers. From 1977 the authorities began their attempts to wreck the church. When the population had prevented this, the authorities laid grain into the church. The following day the village went on strike: the adults did not show up for field work, the children stayed out of school. The authorities were forced to remove the grain. Finally, on 25 April 1979, the whole population of Znosychy was assigned work in an adjacent village, while their children were kept locked up at school. During this time the church was wrecked and the site bulldozed. The operation was carried out under the personal command of the chief district attorney. The faithful of this and of neighbouring villages began to gather at the site of the former church for prayers: 'Sometimes up to twelve pilgrims spent the night in each Znosychy house.' The authorities put up patrols and barriers on all roads leading to the village, preventing anybody from visiting it. The faithful began to decorate pine trees around the church and pray under them. The village authorities cut down all the trees. But the villagers continue to gather regularly at the site of the former church for communal prayers.[9]

In at least two other Rovno Province villages the population has been trying to reopen their churches closed in the early 1960s. In one case, in 1973, when the population was busy with the harvest in the fields, the authorities dismantled the domes and stored grain in the church. When the population protested furiously the grain was eventually removed, but the church remained closed. In 1978, finally, after years of complaints a commission arrived in the village, but the village soviet chairman pointed out only two Orthodox Christians to the commission, claiming that believers were a tiny minority in the village population. Although the crowd gathered outside to protest, the commission members got into their car, paying no attention to the protesters, and left. In the other case, the church had actually been badly ruined in the early 1960s, but from 1973 the faithful were appealing to all quarters for permission to rebuild it at their own expense. All their efforts were in vain. The officials told them to travel to a neighbouring town for services, although the church in question had served four villages with at least 100 practising Orthodox Christians in each. Finally, in the autumn of 1978 a CRA representative came and said they would soon have their church back. In the meantime the village soviet told the villagers to append their signatures to a pledge not to let their pigs roam the village streets. After the villagers had signed the paper without reading it, it turned out that they had signed a statement that no one needed a church in the village. After that the district authorities refused to accept any more pleas from the Christians of the village.[10] Thus tricks, lies, and abuse of peasants' credulity from the typical arsenal of the state's struggle against religion.

By the time of this writing there are several dozen reports of unsuccessful attempts literally across the whole Soviet Union to open or reopen churches. In the city of Chernigov with a population of 200 000 where, after the closure of the cathedral in 1973, only a small wooden church remained, the faithful have been pleading for a second church ever since 1963. They still have not got it.[11] In the city of Gorky the population has now surpassed 1 500 000, yet it has only three small Orthodox churches, where before the revolution there had been over forty Orthodox churches for a population of some 110 000. The pleas to reopen some of the closed and unused churches in the city for worship began in 1967 with a petition to the provincial CRA plenipotentiary, A. P. Volkov, signed by over 1500 believers. Receiving no satisfaction, the petitioners forwarded similar appeals to the Supreme Soviet, the CPSU Central Committee, *Pravda* and the Moscow Patriarchate in the following year, as well as a petition, signed by 36 industrial workers, to Eugene Blake, the then WCC General Secretary. The latter also described the subsequent harassment at work and professional demotions to which the petitions' signers were subjected once they had categorically refused to recant and remove their signatures. Eventually the number of signatories rose to 2000. The CRA officials told them to break up into groups of twenty according to city districts. This they soon did, forming at first five and later six such 'twenties', each in a different city district, petitioning for the reopening of a church in each. At the time of this writing they have not succeeded in gaining even one of the six churches asked for.[12] Indeed, the 1975 revisions and amendments of the 1929 Laws on Religious Associations, on the one hand grant supreme auhtority in the matter of closing and opening a church to the CRA, but on the other hand do not even obligate it to any definite time-limits in which to respond to appeals and petitions of the kind. In contrast, the 1929 regulations stipulated the time limits and also left the responsibility for the opening and closing of churches with the local soviets. The believers, therefore, could then appeal to higher authorities, whereas now there is no one to appeal to beyond the CRA, which is both the first and last court of appeal.

The struggle to open a church in the town of Naro Fominsk in the Moscow Province began in 1968 with an address to the city soviet signed by twenty-four residents, asking to be registered as the town's religious association of 'twenty'. Two months later, in December, the city soviet received a letter of support of the 'twenty', signed by 693 persons. The last church in the town was shut in the early 1930s and the nearest open church was twenty kilometres away. As the responsible secretary of the city soviet refused to accept the petition, the signatories addressed an appeal to the city attorney. When this failed to draw any response an appeal was addressed to the Moscow provincial attorney on 3 February 1969. The attorney passed all the paperwork over to the CRA with a recommendation to look into the matter. When the CRA replied to the believers in the negative, the believers addressed a collective letter to the local newspaper criticizing the Narofominsk city soviet executive committee, pointing out that its incompetence should be kept in mind during the forthcoming city elections. The same day the petitioners received a written reply from the executive committee that, as they had been informed earlier, their plea could not be satisfied. And so it dragged on from one office to another. Meanwhile the number of signatories rose by 1970 to 1443. In February 1971 an article appeared in the local newspaper which said that the believers' petition could not be satisfied because the former church building was about to be transformed into a museum, and that in fact there were not that many practising Christians in the city. The article was defamatory and self-contradictory. It said: 'this is a dirty business initiated by evil people' aiming at 'heating up religious fanaticism and to gain a cushy job in the new church'. What sort of religious fanaticism was this, and how could anyone hope for a cushy job if the number of religious believers in the area was as insignificant as the paper claimed? Moreover, the plaintiff on behalf of the signatories was Dr Boris Zuckerman (now in Israel), a professor of nuclear physics, a man of considerable means by Soviet standards, whose summer house, just like that of the cellist Mstislav Rostropovich, was situated in the vicinity of the town. On 26 April 1971, there was a session of the local court devoted to the subject. The signatories demanded the following: first that they either be granted one of the existing closed town churches, or be permitted to build a new one or to rent a house – since the closest church was twenty kilometres away, the suggestion that the believers ought to be satisfied with that one was unreasonable; second, that the newspaper print a denial of its original claim that the signatures were fraudulent. The court rejected both pleas. An appeal hearing of 8 May 1971 at a higher court brought no satisfaction either. The court stated that 240 people whose names appeared among the signatories did not reside at the indicated addresses. The court, however, refused to cite the names of such people and said nothing about the remaining 1200 signatories.[13]

Many more cases of such frustrated appeals to open churches could be cited,[14] and probably many, many more are not even known to us. But the above is a typical example of how much bureaucracy (and expense) is involved in each application for a church and how slim are the believers' chances of success. Of course, the Orthodox are not the only ones whose pleas are rejected by the authorities.

The Old Believers

The Old Believers, who had split from the state Church in the seventeenth century, and who in some respects have shown more independence than the post-1927 Orthodox Church, have at least as much difficulty in preserving their functioning churches. We have already cited the case of the Trans-Baikal Province in Eastern Siberia where, despite the presence of several Old Believer villages, not a single officially open Old Believer temple remains. A 1969 Old Believer *samizdat* document enumerates a number of difficulties encountered by the

Church and her members, including the probable KGB murder of a young healthy priest after his refusal to work for the KGB. He had been serving a community of Old Believer repatriates from Turkey. It also tells of petitions submitted to the state authorities to have Old Believer churches open in such cities and towns as Alma-Ata, Barnaul, Vitebsk, Leningrad, Dzhambul, Frunze, Beltsy and others.[15] Had they been successful, the same authors would probably have informed us in the same way as they managed to give publicity to the above document.

The Roman Catholics

The Roman Catholic Church in the USSR is concentrated in Lithuania and southern Latvia, with a sizeable sprinkling of Roman Catholic communities in Moldavia, in the western regions of Belorussia and the Ukraine; some Armenian Catholic minorities are found in the Caucasus. The Catholics of the western regions and Moldavia came finally under Soviet control only at the end of the Second World War. For them the Khrushchev onslaught was the first massive attack on the Church as an institution – hence, proportionally, the particularly heavy toll suffered by that Church (comparable with the toll of the Orthodox churches in the same areas). One illustration has already been mentioned: the decrease of Roman Catholic churches in Latvia from 500 to 75. In Lithuania the decline was expressed in the forced reduction of the number of seminaries from three to one, and of the clergy from 1500 to 735 (or 708 according to another source) serving 628 churches. Judging by these figures, the number of churches in pre-war Lithuania must have been at least double the current figure.

Attempts are being periodically undertaken systematically to persecute the Lithuanian Roman Catholic Church. Priests are being harassed and imprisoned for preparing for First Communion, that is by giving them basic catechetical knowledge. This is interpreted by the state as organized religious instruction to minors, banned since 1918. But the task of the regime is more difficult in Lithuania. Because there is almost as strong a national identification of the Lithuanians with the Roman Catholic Church as that of the Poles, the persecutions are more difficult to pursue and they receive much wider publicity and cause much more massive protests than in Russia. For instance, 1344 Lithuanians signed a protest letter to the Soviet Government over the sentencing of Prosperas Bubnis, a priest, to one year's labour in 1971 for giving religious instruction to children. And further, in January 1972, 17 054 Lithuanian Catholics signed a memorandum to Brezhnev, protesting against religious persecutions, the exile of two Lithuanian bishops, Steponavichus and Sladkiavichus, the imprisonment of the priests Bubnis and Zdebskis, the sacking of a teacher for her religious views, and the wrecking of Catholic churches in the country, among other things.[16]

A report of the Roman Catholics of Lithuania simply says: 'very many churches were closed and destroyed, the building of new churches is not permitted; the church of St Kazimir has been turned into a museum of atheism, the Vilnius Cathedral, into an art gallery, the church of Resurrection in Kaunas, into a radio-making factory, the Jesuit Cathedral of Kaunas, into a sports hall'.[17] One of the worst episodes is that of the Klaipeda Cathedral. The city had been badly damaged by the war. After many years of petitioning the believers were allowed to build a cathedral. Collections were made across the whole country, and in 1961 a spacious cathedral was erected in the city. But then the authorities began to invent bureaucratic excuses to prevent its religious use, eventually closing and confiscating it from the believers. Needless to say, the money and labour of the faithful were wasted and not rewarded in any way. The battle and petitions of the believers to have the church reopened have continued without result into the 1980s, although a total of 148 149 signatures were collected making up a book of 1589 pages forwarded to Brezhnev.[18] This case is comparable to the Kirov Province, where at least two of the churches closed and destroyed in the early 1960s had been built by the faithful themselves with their money and labour after the war,[19] and this could not be shown in any way to have been the work of the 'exploiters', of the 'tsarist reactionaries' to keep down 'the dark masses'. But as with the Orthodox, the regime in Lithuania has not shown any signs of reversing Khrushchev's acts against religion. For instance, in the village of Zhaleyi a church was closed in 1963. But then, apparently to try to put to an end the believers' struggle for its reopening, in 1977 the church was converted into a flour mill. But the local miller refused to work in the church. Consequently, the mill is in operation only four hours a week. Petitions signed by 149 Zhaleyi residents and 114 residents of a neighbouring village to open the church have been so far in vain.[20] The situation is much worse in those areas where the Roman Catholics constitute a small minority. Thus most Roman Catholic churches in western Belorussia were closed in the 1960s (a little over 10 per cent of Belorussia's population is technically Roman Catholic). In Moldavia, where the Roman Catholics constitute a mere 15 000 in a population of 3 000 000, all their churches were closed except for a small cemetery chapel in Kishinev, the capital. Being a multi-national group, Russian is their only *lingua franca*; yet their only priest, Fr. Zaval'niuk, was forbidden around 1977 to use Russian in his sermons or services. He was allowed to use only German or Polish, technically the languages of most of the Catholics, depriving the Catholics of a sense of communal unity and the church of potential converts. Next, the priest was forbidden to visit the provincial communities. In the biggest of them, Rashkovo, the population decided to enlarge their temple, as it was insufficient to house all the pilgrims who came on the rare occasions of pastoral visits. But on 25 December 1977, the church was wrecked by a detachment of militia and a wrecking brigade brought in from outside. On the eve of this, the whole population was ordered to hand in their hunting rifles. Early on 25 December, the group of religious activists who had guarded their church from destruction day and night, were arrested in their beds, thrown into a car and driven away for the duration of the day, while all schoolchildren were kept at school under lock and key. Meanwhile the wrecking was carried out.[21] These were the familiar methods also used in the Rovno Province village of Zhosychy described earlier.

The 'Unregistered' Ones

This category includes both those religious groups whom the Soviet Government refuses to legalize or register such as the breakaway independent or Initiativist Baptists, the Pentecostals and those who refuse to be registered, that is to be controlled by an atheistic state, such as the Jehovah Witnesses and the authentic Russian Jehovists. It also includes other groups, such as the Buddhists, who for some reason are allowed to exist as ethnic religions of such Soviet nationalities as the Buriats or the Kalmuks, but forbidden to spread to other nationalities. Although in a 1983 trial of a group of Jehovah Witnesses it was stated that they were free to register and become a legal Soviet religious community, in view of the constant Soviet propaganda associating the group with its 'subversive' Brooklyn, USA headquarters it is doubtful the regime would ever agree to register the group. It is these 'unregistered' groups that are subjected to particularly systematic persecutions. The amount of space in the Soviet press dedicated to attacking the Jehovah Witnesses and the Jehovists in the course of 1983–5 indicates the vitality and probable growth of the movement. At least fifteen of their activists had been brought to trial in the course of 1984, of whom at least seven received prison sentences. The Soviet press, which for a long time had criticized the masses of religious chain letters circulating in the USSR, at last in 1985 named their source: the Jehovists, a sect founded by a Russian artillery Captain, N. S. Il'insky, some 150 years ago. It is very similar to the Jehovah Witnesses but even more radical in condemning all state power as the kingdom of Satan. Apparently such radical-eschatological sects find a fertile soil in the intolerant world of Marxism as a radical expression of total disillusionment with this artificially imposed secular faith.[22]

The Buddhists were subjected to a new wave of attack once some Russian and other Soviet-European intellectuals began to be converted to it. In 1972 one of the USSR's leading Buddhist and Tibetan scholars, Bidia Dandaron, was arrested, tried and sentenced to five years' hard labour. His crime was that he was a secret Buddhist monk, lama and teacher, and that under his influence a number of Soviet scholars of Buddhism and Tibet converted to Buddhism and became his disciples. Formally, other than purely religious excuses had to be found. And the local Buriat press began a campaign, even before the actual trial was to start, accusing Dandaron of organizing drunken orgies under the guise of religious meetings, of bribe-taking, cultivating adoration of himself and 'corrupting' the youth. Along with him twelve of his nearest academic associates and religious followers (Russians, Lithuanians, Estonians and others) were arrested. At the trial it was proved that Dandaron had not touched alcohol for over three years, that none of the converts to Buddhism was brought to the religion through him, that there were no orgies, and that the teaching which the press misspelled as 'Dandarism' in fact was 'Tantrism', a Tibetan religious philosophy (the press and originally the court accused Dandaron of forming his own subversive teaching named 'Dandarism'). During the trial the judge made such statements as: 'If it were in my power I would send all religious believers to Kolyma.' When the defence pointed out that Dandaron could not be tried as a recidivist, because after spending nearly twenty years in prisons and camps under Stalin (from age 24 to 43) he was fully rehabilitated, the judge replied: 'Under Khrushchev they used to rehabilitate both the innocent and the guilty ones.' Most of the accusations had to be annulled as unsubstantiated. Nevertheless, Dandaron was sentenced to five years' hard labour. Four of his disciples, active research scholars and teachers, were sent off to forensic psychiatric institutions; the remaining eight 'simply' lost their jobs.[23] In 1981 or early 1982 the Soviet press reported the disbanding of Krishna groups in Krasonoiarsk (Siberia) and Moscow and the sentencing of their chief, a Yoga teacher E. Tretiakov, to a prison term for 'parasitism'. 'Involvement in the Krishna movement', pontificated a Soviet newspaper, 'invariably leads to law-breaking, because the propagandizing of social passivity leads to parasitism.'[24] The more probable reason, however, for such attempts to destroy the oriental cult in the bud is that for most Soviet intellectuals who convert to Christianity the Yoga classes, Buddhism and Hinduism have been first stepping-stones from materialism to spirituality.[25]

The Pentecostals, the breakaway Baptists (ECB or CC ECB), and the breakaway, so-called 'True and Free', Seventh-Day Adventists (AUCTFSDA), are in many cases denied legitimization by the authorities, but often the groups themselves refuse to register their communities, which renders them illegal in terms of the Soviet law, and thus facilitates their persecution. They wish to retain their spiritual freedom, arguing that the prerogatives of the CRA are so broad that they deprive the registered communities of the possibility of living a full spiritual life as a Christian community. To illustrate the legitimacy of this position, of the over-700 priests of the legal

Lithuanian Roman Catholic Church, 554 signed a statement in 1977 refusing to accept the new laws on religious associations, because they infringed on the internal liberty of the Church and contravened the canon law by depriving the priest of the control of his parish.

The state has reacted rather cautiously to this act, as it represents the vast majority of the Lithuanian clergy and undoubtedly has the support of most of the believers. Several priests from among the signatories were arrested and sentenced, but there had been no blanket attack on the signatories as a body.[26] The regime could hardly have done much more in Russia than in Lithuania had the vast majority of the Russian Orthodox clergy been as steadfast as their Lithuanian-Catholic confrères in opposing the 1961 bylaws and the 1975 revisions; but the spine of the Orthodox Church had been broken in the 1920s and 1930s by persecutions of a magnitude unknown by the Lithuanians or by anyone who had not experienced the pre-war Soviet persecutions.

The Uniates

The Uniates were outlawed in the USSR in 1946–9 following the congresses annulling the Uniate Churches of Galicia and the Carpathian Ukraine, forcing both to join the Orthodox Church. Seven bishops and some 2000 priests who refused to do so were exiled to concentration camps and prisons. Yet the Uniate or Catholic Church of the Eastern Rite exists underground to this day, even experiencing a certain renewal in the 1960s and 1970s, particularly since she is associated with the Ukrainian nationalist identity and her renewal is so potent in the extreme western part of the Ukraine, where the Uniate church had been the major religious body since the early seventeenth century. Because this church is illegal, it is persecuted mercilessly by the Soviets, and all the places of worship are being constantly raided and brutally smashed.[27]

The 'True and Free' Adventists

The 'True and Free' Adventists as they call themselves, broke away from the official Church of Seventh Day Adventists in 1924, at their Fifth Congress in Moscow, when the leadership and the majority of the delegates declared Lenin's socialism a blessing and Lenin a God-chosen leader, proclaiming their full support of and dedication to the Marxist-Leninist social system. The break between the two groups became final at the sixth Congress in 1928 which declared it the duty of each Adventist to serve in the Soviet Red Army and to bear arms. This contradicted the conscientious objectionist creed of the sect. Henceforward the TFSDA became the object of non-stop persecutions. Its leader, the late V. A. Shelkov, eighty-four years old in 1979, had served three sentences (one being a commuted death sentence) totalling twenty-three years, prior to his fourth sentence of five years in 1979 (which he did not survive). He proved a phenomenal organizer of an underground life of the sect. Despite raids, discoveries, and long spells in prison, the sect managed to keep several printing presses for publishing and distributing bibles and other religious tracts. In a wave of massive arrests of Adventists in 1978–9 the KGB was apparently trying to locate, without success, their latest printing press, 'The True Witness'. In the course of this raid there were over 200 searches made across the country, from Riga to Tashkent. Thirty-nine persons were eventually tried and received various terms of imprisonment – some for conscientious objection, although the victims asked to be enlisted into the army construction battalions, objecting only to bearing arms.

Despite all their severity, the authorities could not close any Adventist temples, because, in contrast to the legal Adventists, they have no temples, but gather on Saturdays for communal prayers at the private quarters of some of their members.

The only crimes of this peaceful and pacifist religious movement are their refusal to register with the state of its terms, the printing of literature underground because they cannot print it legally, and conscientious objection. Yet it is endlessly and severely harassed, as demonstrated in the description of the search of Shelkov's daughter's flat in Tashkent, where the old man lived and was arrested at the end of the search.

The search began on 14 March 1978, and lasted continuously for four days. The twenty searchers, led by a city attorney, were fully armed. They also had walkie-talkies, mine detectors, floodlights, cameras, axes, crowbars and spades. In the course of the search, floors and ceilings were cut open, walls and chimneys ripped; blankets, mattresses and pillows unstitched; two-metre deep holes dug out across the yard. Indeed, two hiding places were found underground, containing suitcases full of religious literature, tapes with sermons and psalms, *samizdat* human rights documents, and underground religious bulletins. Many tapes contained Western radio broadcasts, presumably of a religious character.[28] Guns and mine detectors were the only weapons of this supposedly ideological regime against the written and spoken word.

The Evangelical Christian Baptists

The Evangelical Christian Baptists (the split-away faction) are not against registration of their communities in principle, but they will accept it only on their own terms, which are: recognition of the ECB as a separate body independent from AUCECB; official permission for periodic congresses of the ECB; the right for free and genuine elections of the ruling Council of Churches of the ECB, and an end to persecution of its members; and inner freedom for the spiritual life of the ECB communities without petty interference by the CRA and its plenipotentiaries.[29]

This inner spiritual freedom was obviously meant to include the right to unhampered baptism of willing adults and to the teaching of religion to willing children of Baptist parents, which the Soviet regime categorically denies to them. *Samizdat* documents, in fact, are full of reports on imprisonments for teaching religion to children.[30] For instance, Eugene Pushkov, a former Cheliabinsk Symphony Orchestra violinist who had given up that post to devote himself fully to the ECB church work, was sentenced to three years' hard labour in 1980 for organizing Baptist youth musical-choral church groups and for serving as an ECB pastor in the Ukrainian town of Khartsysk. Forty-three years of age at the time of his release in 1983, he was asked by the KGB to co-operate with them — that is, to be a KGB informer. '"I cannot compromise", was his reply. After only twenty-five days with his wife and eight children, he was rearrested. . . . Pushkov appealed his new sentence of four years. Authorities responded by doubling it.'[31]

To legitimize the persecutions, two new decrees were issued

by the RSFSR Supreme Soviet on 18 March 1966 (nos 219 and 220). The first one stipulates a fifty-rouble fine for: refusal to register a religious community; organizing religious meetings of youth or children; any literary or other circles under the auspices of a religious community and organization of religious conferences, processions, and the like. The second decree stipulates a prison sentence of up to three years for persons repeating the above activities after having already been fined according to the former decree.[32]

Article 142 of the RSFSR Criminal Code and its equivalents in the other Soviet republics concerning the infringements of the laws on the separation of Church and State, actually forbids all religious activities except 'the performance of the cult' within the church walls. It was on the basis of this article together with the above decrees that by mid-1967 202 ECB members had been tried, and over 190 were actually sentenced to terms of eighteen months to ten years of various categories of imprisonment.[33] The total number of ECB prisoners in the concentration (labour) camps has been growing at the following rate:

Years	Prisoners
Late 1979	87
Late 1981	120
Late 1982	165
Late 1984	over 200[34]

One of the most common causes of harassment has been connected with the establishment of a house of prayer and the problem of its registration. For instance, in the course of 1975 alone the Moscow ECB community members had to pay a total of 4000 roubles in fines for holding religious services without a registration permit, despite the fact that 'we have applied to the appropriate authorities for registration many times'. In every case the CRA's responses were nebulous and evasive, but the KGB officials were more direct in their conversations with some members of the community, saying: 'you shall not receive registration as long as you remain under the Council of Churches [the ECB ruling body]'.[35] There are many reports of brutal and barbarous bulldozing and other forms of destruction of these unregistered houses of prayer, including those of Vladivostok, Dzhambul, Perm', and others. In Chernovtsy (western Ukraine) a huge tent was raised by the ECB believers, but one morning the militia appeared. It stopped all traffic in the area and cordoned off the tent, forbidding people in adjacent houses to walk out, stating that there were land-mines in the tent. Then three bus loads of college students arrived and the destruction of the tent-church began. In five hours 1200 members of the local ECB community lost their place of worship. Thereafter believers began to gather in the same place for open-air worship, subjecting themselves to regular fines for group prayers outside church walls. As in closures of Orthodox churches the malicious sadism of local officials was evident. For instance, 'the local government in the city of Issyk, Alma-Ata Province, had suggested to the local ECB minister in 1974 that a permanent house of worship be built, which the community happily did. In 1976 the authorities suddenly began to order the believers to wreck their temple. The believers refused.' Subsequently the building was taken away from them and sealed. The minister was imprisoned for breaking the laws on religious cults. 'The city government requests that the community apply for registration.'[36] But, as the above Moscow case shows, no applications for registration of the independent ECB communities are ever granted.

At the same time, the Soviet press as usual engaged in character asassination. One of the most irritating facts for the Soviets had been the existence of ECB underground printing presses. A Soviet newspaper spoke of the release from prison in 1977 of 'an influential leader of this sect', P. Rumachik, and connected his name with the ECB publishing enterprise: and then a few lines lower spoke about a 1980 KGB uncovering of 'several clandestine print shops, one of which was in Dnepropetrovsk Province'. The affair was being linked again to Rumachik and George Vins, the formerly imprisoned ECB Council Secretary, expelled to the USA in 1979 (straight from a prison camp). Rumachik was sentenced to another five years' hard labour, but this was not enough. It had to be shown that the religious connection was also politically subversive. It was alleged that messages from Vins, illegally transmitted via 'tourists' from the USA, contained instructions to 'protest the USSR legislation on religious cults'. Obviously, the newspaper thought this was not subversive enough, and linked the whole affair to Dimitry Miniakov (born 1922), an ECB pastor in Estonia. To justify his arrest a 1978 report in an Estonian newspaper was cited, according to which Miniakov had been taken prisoner by the Germans in 1941 and subsequently actively collaborated with the enemy administrators. The article exclaimed: 'Is there any need for more proof that the ECB Council activity has little in common with religion?'[37]

This might have satisfied a Billy Graham, who upon his two visits to the USSR declared there was religious freedom there; but not an informed reader, who will have noticed that all three sentences meted out to Miniakov have been for his church-related activities. At the time of this writing his health has rapidly deteriorated to the extent that he is unable to write letters in his own hand anymore.[38]

The Pentecostals

The Pentecostals, or, as they call themselves, Christians of the Evangelical Faith, are that remnant of the sect who had not merged with the Baptists in 1945 within the All-Union Council of Evangelical Christians and Baptists formed in 1944. But apparently after the events of 1961–2 more Pentecostals left the amalgamated Church (without joining the independent ECB); for it is in the 1960s and 1970s that the Pentecostals became particularly vocal and prominent. In contrast to the AUCECB, the Soviet state does not recognize the independent Pentecostals, therefore they have no legal central organization of any kind, although in some areas Pentecostal communities have been granted registration by the local CRA. About 50 per cent of Pentecostal communities are thus registered, mainly in Odessa, Kiev, Rovno and numerous west Ukrainian villages. The Pentecostals of Central Asia, Siberia and the Far East refuse to register their communities because:

> In practice registration includes a virtual ban on the religious education of children, on youth and women's prayer meetings, on preaching, missionary work and charity, in addition to the practice of the most important religious rites.[39]

These objections to registration show that the nature of persecutions of the Pentecostals are the same as those of the independent Baptists: fines and arrests for prayer meetings at private homes or unregistered temples.[40] In addition, Pentecostals refuse to bear arms or to give the military oath, but agree to serve in engineering or medical corps. In this they fall into the same category as the Adventists and the Jehovah Witnesses, and are similarly severely punished.[41]

Numbers of unregistered communities are constantly harassed. Their houses are searched and all religious literature, including bibles, confiscated. Fines, threats, and arrests are common. 'In 1971 a firehose was used to disperse the faithful in Chernogorsk, after which the house where the believers had met for prayers was bulldozed.'[42]

Because of a high proportion of members of German background in the sect, some of its groups, particularly in Siberia and the Far East, have been trying for many years to emigrate (some to Israel, confusing it with the Biblical Israel), and thus have in addition been persecuted for such attempts. As recently as April 1985 leaders of a Far-Eastern Pentecostal community were brought to trial for staging hunger strikes and protest demonstrations in an attempt to emigrate to West Germany. Their pastor, Vicktor Valter, was sentenced to five years in a labour camp.

PERSECUTIONS OF CLERGY AND LAITY

According to a 1983 count, over 300 clergy, laity and monastics of all religions were in prisons, labour camps or psycho-prisons solely for practising their faith.[43] According to more recent evidence, the actual number, particularly in psycho-prisons, is considerably larger and has grown further since 1983.[44] But far greater numbers of religious believers are subjected to administrative harassment and persecutions from day to day, the concrete examples of which reach us only sporadically. However, they are sufficient to draw a general picture of the situation. Grounds for such persecutions are well laid out in the internal secret CRA reports to the CPSU Central Committee, some of which have become available to us in the last few years. Among the 'crimes' of the clergy, contravening the Soviet law on religions, and therefore requiring punishment, are the following.

First, is acts of charity. One archbishop was reported to be secretly subsidizing repair works in the poorer parishes in his diocese which are unable to fully fund such expenses on their own. Individual church wardens, priests, and parish councils-were denounced for issuing support money for the poorest parishioners at the expense of decreasing the practically obligatory Peace Fund contributions. In other parishes, peasants whose houses had been destroyed by fire received financial aid from their church. Finally, a widespread illegal charity includes public dinners for as many as 300 parishioners at a time, mostly moneyless pilgrims from distant villages and towns without a functioning church. According to recent *samizdat* reports, monasteries (in particular, the Pochaev Lavra and the Kiev Ascension Convent) have lately been subjected to harassments again, precisely for feeding such pilgrims.[45]

Second, continuing group pilgrimages to venerated holy places, is also a 'crime'. 'Such pilgrimages are usually organized by lay believers, either fanatics or opportunists looking for income', alleges a 1968 CRA report. Surely these are less risky ways for opportunists to make money than by organizing pilgrimages which have been subjected to very brutal attacks by the militia and the Komsomol voluntary aids with much physical injury to the participants.[46]

Third, in the same category is group worship in private residences and performance of such rites as baptism, church marriages and funerals, either in private homes or at the church, but without reporting these in the church register. Naturally the clergy and parish councillors try to protect the believers involved from subsequent harassment at work or school, because the registry books are regularly inspected by the soviets and thus become available to the KGB. But the CRA official pretends that the real reason for non-registration is to earn additional private income from the unrecorded believers' donations. We know that this is not the case, from personal interviews of several neophytes, who had deliberately searched for such priests who would not register their baptism, in order to avoid later repercussions at work.[47] But the most reliable confirmation comes from the former Bishop of Poltava (Eastern Ukraine), Feodosii, in his 1977 letter to Brezhnev, where he stated that most adults desiring to join the Church went to the retired priests for baptism, because the latter could do this without entering the names of the newly baptized into the registry. According to Feodosii, the provincial CRA official, objected to this, demanding that instead the clergy report to him about every adult baptismal candidate, thus delaying the baptism for a few weeks, during which, the Bishop added, the CRA agents would create such problems for the candidate at his place of work or study that he might change his mind. Naturally, the Bishop refused to oblige.[48]

Furov, the CRA vice-chairman, includes in his report (of 1975?) a table of the steady decline of Orthodox clergy in the USSR, from 8252 in 1961 to 5994 in 1974, as irrefutable evidence of a dying Church. To begin with, there are a number of logical and arithmetical errors in the table. The year 1961 happened to be the third year of Khrushchev's physical attack on the Church, during which masses of priests were simply deregistered, prematurely forced into retirement, imprisoned, exiled, had to look for secular jobs in order to survive, or (the most heroic of them) simply went into the underground, becoming so-called wandering priests, never again appearing on any of the CRA registers. Thus, had Furov begun with the year 1958 instead of 1961 his decline of registered priests would have been even more spectacular: from over 30 000 to 5994 in 1974. Then he says that 'in the last three years', 1972–5, the rate of absolute annual decline of clergy through death and retirement has decreased from 190 to 66; but the absolute figures he cites for a total of these years break up into 146 new ordinations per annum and 179 deaths and retirements; this makes the absolute decline exactly one half of his figure of 66! Moreover, in another place in the same secret report to the CPSU CC he says:

> The CRA plenipotentiaries, as in past years, have been taking measures in co-operation with the local soviets to prevent the enrolment of fanatics, extremists, and physically abnormal persons in the seminaries.

We know that these categories mean in the Soviet context, particularly the category of 'psychotics'. And then, among the examples of persons prevented from enrolling at the Moscow theological seminary, Furov cites a graduate (born in 1930) of the highly prestigious Institute of International Relations, to which only students with politically impeccable biographies are admitted, usually sons and daughters of highly placed personalities from the Soviet establishment. In priest's robes this man would have been a serious embarrassment to the establishment and its official values. Another rejectee was an engineer, born in 1946, who had been guilty of anti-Soviet views. Still another was a young village soviet deputy.

Then Furov promises to close the gaps in the CRA control over the seminaries and seminarians, in accordance with an apparently unprinted CRA resolution of 29 July 1974, 'On the State of Supervision over the Activities of the Theological Educational Establishments of the Russian Orthodox Church':

- to give constant and never declining attention to the supervision and influence in the selection and distribution of the administrative and teaching cadres . . . to the study of their moods and to measures aimed at decreasing their religious zeal;
- to take all the necessary measures to preclude the attempts of fanatical persons to penetrate the seminaries, either as teachers or as students;
- to continue the review of the teaching manuals through the Patriarchate's Education Committee and seminary rectors with the aim of adopting new manuals . . . which would take into consideration the need to elevate the sense of citizenship among the teachers and the taught;
- . . . to enhance the mass political education of the teachers and the taught, as well as individual forms of work with them aimed at the development of profound patriotic convictions.[49]

In other words, the aim is to replace the spiritual pastors with lukewarm church bureaucrats, 'performers of the cult' in the official Soviet jargon; and any bishop or priest who does not fit into this category is subjected to harassment amounting to persecution in one form or another.

Besides screening the would-be seminarians, we have seen with what ease the most dedicated and ecclesiastically active clerics are deprived of the right to function legally as priests. A careful scrutiny of *samizdat* would reveal dozens of such names, amounting to only a small fraction of the real figure. A case in point is Vladimir Rusak, a deacon of the Russian Orthodox Church and a graduate of the Moscow Theological Academy, who had worked for several years on the board of editors of the

Journal of Moscow Patriarchate. In 1980 he completed a manuscript on the history of the Russian Church under the Soviets, calling it *A Witness of Prosecution*. When he confessed this fact to his immediate superior, Archbishop Pitirim, the editor-in-chief of the *Journal*, the latter begged him to destroy the manuscript. When the deacon refused, he was simply dismissed from his work and later sent to serve in a church in the Belorussian city of Vitebsk under Metropolitan Filaret of Belorussia, at that time the head of the Church's Department of External Relations and of its parishes in Western Europe. On 28 March 1982, he delivered a sermon at a Lenten Passion service on the passions of Christ and the suffering of the Church in this world. He said that a Church suffering, a Church persecuted, is spiritually stronger, closer to God, than a Church triumphant in this world. In this context he condemned the Constantinian legacy of national and state Churches, and praised the Bolshevik Revolution for having once again raised the sword against the Church, thus purifying her of all but the dedicated ones. Then he elaborated on the persecutions under Lenin, Stalin and Khrushchev, and criticized the official policy of the contemporary Russian Orthodox Church (ROC for short) of disowning the new martyrs, owing to whom in fact the contemporary Church had survived all the attack and persecutions. He did not call for any disobedience to the state. On the contrary, he said that now the believers were more secure than at most times since 1917. He simply encouraged them not to lose heart when their lives are less comfortable than those of the atheists or when their children are expelled from the universities for their faith. This is normal, he said: you should not expect both an easy life in this world and a reward in Heaven.

This was to be Deacon Vladimir's last church sermon. His registration was immediately revoked and he was sent to a monastery. The ruling bishop, Filaret, told Vladimir Rusak he could not do anything for him however much he wanted to help, for 'anonymous forces stand behind him'. In other words, M. Filaret the head of the Moscow Patriarchate parishes in free West European countries at the time, and the ROC chairman of Ecclesiastical Foreign Relations is controlled by the KGB. Filaret advised him to look for a secular job, for after such a sermon he stood no chance of gaining any position in the

Church whatsoever, under the present regime.⁵⁰ This was, at least, a form of criticism of the Soviet state which no totalitarian regime would tolerate.

On the other hand, Archbishop Feodosii of Poltava, in his 1977 letter to Brezhnev, recounts completely unprovoked forms of reduction of the numbers of clergy by the CRA. In 1960–64, until its closure, Feodosii had served as the faculty secretary of the Volhynia Seminary in Lutsk. The provincial CROCA plenipotentiary had tried all means possible to have advance access to the list of seminary applicants.

> Having finally gained this access he reported these names to certain addresses [local KGB officials]; whereupon the candidates would not receive release from work or from the lists of military recruiting points, in other words he did everything to prevent their arrival at the seminary. The few individuals who nevertheless miraculously managed to come to the seminary were then refused local residence permits on the plenipotentiary's instructions. And thus, in 1964, the Volhynian seminary was shut down under the pretext of lack of students.

The Bishop compares the Volhynian precedent with the contemporary behaviour of the Ukrainian CRA plenipotentiaries: there is practically a ban on new clerical ordinations in the Ukraine, he writes. In 1975 the Poltava plenipotentiary, I. A. Nechytailo, requested the Bishop to ordain as few priests as possible.

Finally, Nechytailo forbade the Bishop to ordain any home-educated candidates. Since the seminaries do not provide enough priests, adds the Bishop, this means by 1980 twenty churches in the diocese will be left without priests through the process of natural attrition.⁵¹ That is how the CRA achieves the decline in the numbers of clergy boasted in the CRA's vice-chairman Furov's report, referred to before.

In fact Furov proudly states that in 1974 only 30 per cent of Ukraine's seminary candidates were accepted.⁵² The information from a reliable Church source is that in 1981, when the total number of seminary students was almost double that of the early 1970s, still only 20 per cent of the applicants were accepted in the seminaries, owing to lack of space.⁵³ Given the fact that an unsuccessful application to a seminary, as has been

Persecutions after Khrushchev 169

demonstrated above, results in all sorts of harassment and persecutions for the applicant and at least constitutes a considerable blow to his future career in secular life[54] (which is evidence that the applicants are moved by a strong religious motivation and devotion), it is obvious that had there been no CRA screening and had all the able and sincere candidates been accepted, the numbers of clergy would easily have tripled or quadrupled.

Returning to the account of Church–State relations in Archbishop Feodosii's report, we read that Nechytalio asked him to close a few churches by amalgamating them with others (although during Khrushchev's persecutions the number of churches in the diocese was reduced from 340 to 52); to which the Bishop replied that his function was to open churches, not to close them, and added that each parish is of greater importance to him than his own life, hence he would fight for them with all his might. The result of this was the plenipotentiary's report to Moscow that 'no mutual understanding exists between him and the Bishop'. This meant, said the Bishop, that he would soon be either retired to a monastery or transferred to a distant and more humble diocese. His words proved prophetic: although the Church had rewarded him for his zeal by elevating him to the title of Archbishop less than a year after the writing of this letter, in 1979 he was transferred to the north-Russian diocese of Vologda with only 17 open churches.

The Archbishop (bishop at the time) lists a wide array of direct and indirect persecutions practised by the CRA methodically and almost daily. A parish priest fell ill on a Saturday night, so the Bishop sent one of his cathedral priests to replace him for that Sunday only. Nechytailo, the plenipotentiary, attacked the Bishop for acting without his, Nechytailo's, permission, and temporarily deprived the filling-in priest of his registration, warning him that the next time he would be deprived of it permanently. In several villages (they are all listed by name in the report) old rural cottages were used as prayer houses. Their roofs were leaking and their size was too small for the thousands of believers, the proportion being one church serving up to 26 villages. In order to replace these huts by brick structures somewhat larger than the original huts and with a taller ceiling for breathing comfort, the faithful had to send delegates with petitions as far as Moscow. In one particular case, having gained oral permission to go ahead as early as 1971, they started raising the brick walls, then one night the site was raided and wrecked by the komsomols and militia. The believers had to wait another two years before the permission was finally granted. The Bishop was accused by Nechytailo of breaking the law, because he supported such petitions by words of encouragement and at least in one case by writing a petition of his own.

Another form of persecution, discreetly aiming at the reduction of functioning churches, is the Peace Fund and the Fund for the Restoration of Historical Monuments, to which each church has been obliged to make regular 'voluntary' contributions since 1968. Bishop Feodosii cites the escalation of these contributions by the Poltava Diocese under direct pressure from the CRA, from 36 210 roubles in 1968 to 161 328 roubles in 1976, while the total contribution of the diocesan parishes to the diocesan centre was only 124 296 roubles. At first, he writes, the churches of the diocese were donating 5 per cent of their income to these funds, then 10, 15 and 20 per cent of their total income, which in many cases would result in a net annual deficit. And he cites one rural parish whose total annual income is 3500 roubles, of which the priest gets 1500 per annum and other church assistants are paid 746; current repairs take 200 roubles; 'donations' to the state funds take another 1050 at the above rate; leaving only four roubles to pay the land rent, insurance premiums, the clergy pension fund, etc. With such contributions to the fund the parish will simply have to close down. Nor can the Church reduce her pension fund, since most of the eventual clergy pensions are no higher than thirty-five roubles per month.

Cases of persecution of clerics for their dedication and selfless service could be cited almost endlessly, from the life of contemporary Orthodox as well as Lithuanian Catholic, sectarian and other Churches.

A young Kiev priest, Vasili Boiko, lost his position as the choir director at the Virgin Mary Protection church in Kiev for having organized a youth choir, consisting mostly of recent converts or returned prodigals to the Church. The choir was disbanded by the Soviets and he was sent as a reader to a provincial church.[55]

A young Kiev engineer, Zdriliuk, turned to God, joined the

Orthodox Church, and after passing the necessary theological examinations privately, was ordained priest at thirty years of age by Filaret, the Metropolitan of Kiev. Three years later the republican plenipotentiary de-registered him after a police search revealed large quantities of *religious* literature at his home. Some books and brochures, including prayer books and the like, were found in great quantity. This, and the fact that the priest was distributing prayer books to believers, was supposed to be proof of his 'criminal activities', in a country which claims to have religious freedom.[56]

The story of Fr. Dimitry Dudko is well known. While a priest in a Moscow church he gained considerable popularity as a preacher and catechist, preparing hundreds of adults for baptism. To satisfy a growing spiritual thirst he began to hold question-and-answer sessions instead of regular sermons at his church. This made him very popular with the people, but highly unpopular with the authorities. Under their pressure the ecclesiastical administration was forced to remove him in 1973 to the rural parish of Kabanovo, eighty kilometres from Moscow; the area is out-of-bounds to the foreigners who had also frequented his church in Moscow. But soon people were coming to the rural parish in no less numbers than in Moscow. In December 1975 the local soviet forced the church council to dismiss Fr. Dimitri from this parish as well; thereafter he was transferred to another rural parish in the vicinity of Moscow. It was there that he began to realize his dream of creating a well-knit church community as the basis of the amorphous parish. He began to publish a mimeographed bulletin, the first of its kind since the 1920s. In his sermons and writings he attacked state atheism in no uncertain terms, blaming it for moral decline and rising alcoholism. In January 1980 he was arrested, and less than six months later, broken and humiliated by his jailors, he appeared on the state TV with a self-condemnatory speech of apology, confusing the interests of the USSR with those of the Russian nation, declaring himself a patriot and condemning all his former contacts with foreigners. As a result of this spectacle he lost all his former followers and his prestige as a pastor and a spiritual leader. Now that he was harmless, the regime could magnanimously forgive him and allow him to return to his pastoral duties.[57]

In the Furov report a popular priest, Fr. Vasilii Romaniuk of the Ukrainian village of Kosmach in the Carpathians, was criticized for organizing illegal carol-singing youth groups, and visiting the homes of the believers at Christmas-time. The CRA official claimed that the aim of the priest was to earn extra money through donations.[58] But the fact is that four years later the same priest was given two years in jail, five years in an especially strict labour camp, plus three years of enforced internal exile, technically for appending his signature on behalf of a certain Ukrainian nationalist, the prisoner Valentyn Moroz.[59] In fact the KGB must have been looking for an excuse to get rid of the priest for many years. First, at the age of nineteen, in 1944, having committed no crime whatsoever, he was sentenced to ten years' hard labour in Siberia. On his rehabilitation and return to his native land in 1959 he attended brief pastoral courses and was ordained deacon. But the local CROCA plenipotentiary refused to allow his ordination to the priesthood. Only upon that official's death in 1964 could he become a priest, an enthusiastic one at that, winning the love and respect of the believers and the hatred of the atheists. The latter's harassment continued. In the eight years of his parish work he was forced to change six parishes, ending up with another ten-year prison term in 1972 merely for expressing his criticism of the imprisonment of someone whom he thought to be innocent. This was obviously an excuse to eject another zealous pastor.[60]

The Fr. Romaniuk story is not an isolated case of persecution for religious zeal and dedication. A 31-year-old enthusiastic priest, Fr. Pavel Adelgeim was arrested in December 1969 in the Uzbek city of Kagan where he had served as the rector of the only local Orthodox church. The charges against him as reported in the main Uzbek Russian language paper at the time were confusing and contradictory. On the one hand, he was accused of having used his charismatic qualities and prestige in the community to attract children and teenagers to the church, and teaching them the catechism. It is stated that he was very successful. On the other hand, he was presented as a sadist who enjoyed beating his wife and the very young girls whom he was attracting to the church. However, the trial transcript and his lawyer's and Adelgeim's appeals to the republican supreme court, show that he had never personally beaten the girl in question. The girl had given false evidence on the instruction of the matron of the hostel where she wanted to live. She was told she would surely get a room if she agreed to report that a priest had beaten her. The real reason for his incarceration was his writings criticizing the legal status of religion in the USSR, calling Marxism 'an empty shell', and having contact with Fathers Eshliman and Yakunin, the authors of the 1965 memoranda to the Patriarch and the Soviet Government on the persecution of the Church. In fact, Yakunin's apartment in Moscow was searched while Adelgeim was under pre-trial investigation. According to his defence lawyer, Lev Yudovich, the whole trial was a complete fraud, the purpose being to get rid of a popular priest who was making religion too popular.[61] The priest was sentenced to three years' hard labour. He lost a leg in the camp. Returned to priestly duties, he became the second priest in the Uzbek town of Fergana, where new trouble awaited him in 1974. The parish had just expelled the former rector of the parish for dishonest financial operations, inappropriate observation of religious rituals, and other misdemeanours. But the unscrupulous priest suited the atheists, and the local CRA plenipotentiary wanted to bring him back. As the parishioners refused to oblige, the plenipotentiary retaliated by depriving Fr. Adelgeim of registration and replaced him by another, unpopular and greedy, priest.[62]

Most of this information was gained from the unofficial Moscow Christian Committee for the Defence of Believers' Rights (MCCDBR) set up in 1976 by Fr. Gleb Yakunin, an Orthodox priest. The committee meticulously assembled all cases it had found of abuse of believers' rights by local administrators. At first it reported these cases to central Soviet authorities. When this had no effect, it began to pass this information to Western journalists and the Church bodies in the Free World. In 1979 Yakunin was charged with anti-Soviet agitation and propaganda (Art. 70) and sentenced to five years in a strict regime labour camp followed by five years of internal exile. His and his Committee's only crime was that they spoke up for the alleged legal rights of believers of all faiths.[63] The priest and former Soviet historian, Fr. Vasilii Fonchenkov, who, along with another priest, Nikolai Gainov, took over from Yakunin, lost his teaching position at the Moscow theological academy and was soon transferred to a rural parish outside Moscow, deliberately making his work on the committee impossible. Thereafter the Committee worked incognito and supplied the world with information on persecutions anonymously, except for the document it submitted to the Vancouver WCC General Assembly of 1983, in which it emphasized the escalation of persecutions in the last few years. The Committee closely co-operates with the Legal Defence Group of the All-Union Church of the Free Seventh Day Adventists and the Lithuanian Catholic Committee for the Defence of Believers' Rights.[64]

Another MCCDBR memorandum reported on the three-and-a-half-year sentence meted out in 1983 to a very popular and dedicated Siberian priest, Fr. Alexandr Pivovarov, for distributing religious literature free of charge to his parishioners and others seeking theological education. He acquired this literature from clandestine Moscow Orthodox-Christian printers who had shortly before been arrested and sentenced. He was sentenced in accordance with articles 154 (Black-marketing) and 162 (Engagement in a trade forbidden by special laws or decrees) of the RSFSR Criminal Code, although it was proved in the court that he had never charged for the literature. His real 'crime' was his charisma, his ability to draw searching people to the Church, and the fact that in the adverse conditions of the Soviet Union he had succeeded in legally building a church in the Siberian city of Novokuznetsk.[65]

Indeed, such a treatment of popular and charismatic priests is fully in line with Lenin's infamous words that an immoral priest, guilty of seducing under-aged girls, is more desirable for the Communist Party than a sincere, intelligent and enthusiastic one who commands universal respect.[66]

Such, among others, was the case of a remarkable priest-monk from the Ukraine, Fr. Pavel (Lysak). Born in 1941, he had graduated from the Moscow (graduate) Theological Academy at the Trinity St Sergius Monastery where he was tonsured monk in 1970, only to be expelled by order of the secular authorities in 1975. They also deprived him of residence rights in the Moscow Province, where most of his spiritual children lived. A visitor may live in a city without a residence permit for up to three days at a time, and Fr. Pavel was making use of this regulation, often visiting Moscow to see his spiritual children, among whom there were numerous young people whose relatives remained staunch atheists. It was these atheistic relatives who helped the KGB to concoct a court case against him by sending in slanderous reports on him. Other false reports were obtained by extortion: arrests of neighbours in the apartment where Fr. Pavel stayed during his visits to Moscow, and threats of administrative imprisonment if they did not agree to make defamatory reports on him. The KGB made two raids on the Moscow apartment where Fr. Pavel had been visiting. Then they forced his landlady in the provincial city of Kimry, where he was officially registered, to sign a paper that he had indeed been absent from his apartment; whereafter they changed the dates so that the absence became five days instead of three. On 4 December 1984 he was sentenced to ten months at a labour camp for transgressing passport regulations.[67] But, as will be shown below, short imprisonments have lately been prolonged by re-trials in the labour camps themselves, shortly before the first term is due, and the prisoners sentenced to longer terms on fabricated charges, far away from the unpleasant publicity given to trials in the central cities. Such a fate will likely await this widely loved and righteous spiritual father, either before the term is due or soon after, in an isolated faraway place where he may be forced to reside by reason of semi-legally imposed passport and residence limitations.

This case is another illustration of the intensification of state attacks against the monasteries, the pilgrims and the monastics. But the most appalling case is reported to have occurred in the summer of 1983 in the Caucasian mountains sixty kilometres from the Abkhasian city of Sukhumi, where an unofficial monastic community was discovered by the authorities and dispersed. Eighteen monks, however, managed to hide in a narrow cave, whereupon barrels of an incendiary mixture were brought to the mouth of the cave, set ablaze, and the eighteen monks were burned to death.[68] Harassment of legal monasteries, their inhabitants, and particularly their pilgrims increased considerably in the early 1980s. In October 1981 there was a police raid on the Holy Virgin Protection Convent in Kiev on the day of the convent's patronal feast day, when there are masses of pilgrims to whom the nuns serve a fraternal meal after the liturgy. It is for these meals that the convent and its abbess, Margarita, are continuously harassed and subjected to administrative fines. Pilgrims are forbidden to remain overnight in the convent, so police patrols make periodic night searches and raids looking for hidden guests.[69]

But it is the Pochaev Lavra that continues to be subjected to the most violent persecution. Since the 1960–65 pogrom, the number of resident monks surpassed fifty by the end of 1976 (there had been 149 in 1960 and some 35 in 1965). It could have been several times as high, for on average two or three applications are received every day; but in the course of the whole year of 1976 the Soviets agreed to grant residence permits only to three novices. In 1979, the Monastery Spiritual Council addressed the Soviet Government as well as the ecclesiastical authorities with petitions to return the monastic hostel and fruit orchard to the monastery and to permit it to accept novices, at least to train them for monastic life on Mount Athos (in Greece). The hostel has been turned into a museum of atheism and a polyclinic; and the orchard, taken over by the state, is rapidly deteriorating, its precious fruit trees cut down. The response of the authorities was more searches, expulsions of pilgrims found overnight inside the church, and the expulsion of ten novices. But worse was to come. During Lent in 1981, after the expulsion of the highly revered spiritual father Amvrosii, his library, which included numerous religious writings published abroad or circulating in *samizdat*, became the object of special investigation by the KGB. A number of monks were arrested and manhandled. One of them, Archimandrite Alimpi, was obviously beaten to death since he had been in perfect health and less than fifty years of age; another, Pitirim, became mentally ill as the result of the beatings. Four monks were expelled from the monastery in connection with the Amvrosii affair. It may be of interest to note that Fr. Amvrosii was born in 1937 in Siberia. He had served in the armed forces and worked as a miner. A full-fledged Soviet product, he enrolled at the Moscow Seminary in 1966, later going into graduate studies at the Academy. His sermons and spiritual guidance attracted pilgrims from across the whole Soviet Union to the Holy Trinity St Sergius Lavra near Moscow. The authorities did not like this, and in 1976 he was transferred to the more peripheral Pochaev Lavra, where his sermons soon attracted the wrath of the local KGB. After much harassment and expulsion from the monastery he went into hiding, probably in the mountains of Caucasus.[70] Hence, it is possible that the brutal dissolution of this unofficial monastic community and the murders may have been part of the search for Amvrosii.

Why such a persistent harassment in particular of the Pochaev monastery? Because of its particular spiritual prestige and attraction for the growing numbers of faith-starved Soviet youth and intelligentsia and for the religious population in general. Until the pogrom of the early 1960s there had been many highly revered monasteries and convents in the Soviet Union. Their reduction by the Soviets from over seventy to seventeen left only two particularly holy places of that kind for the Russians: the Pskov Monastery of the Caves, and the Pochaev Lavra. The KGB, however, succeeded in subjugating the Pskov Monastery after the death of its popular abbot Alipii (Voronov). Under the CRA pressure, an unworthy KGB informer, Gavriil, was appointed abbot in 1978. Soon the Patriarch's office was flooded by complaints from monks and lay pilgrims, received in writing and by personal delegations. Gavriil was throwing out pilgrims, harassing the most revered monks for giving counsel or hearing confessions, forbidding group prayers, etc. The Patriarch yielded and issued a decree removing Gavriil from the post. But then, Furov of the CRA took a trip to the monastery. Something happened and the patriarch's order was rescinded. Gavriil continues to be the abbot there, reducing the spiritual importance of the monastery to the population at large almost to nil. As of February 1984, under pressure from the thirty Pskov-Caves monks who had escaped from there and were living illegally in Moscow, the Patriarch issued a second order sacking Gavriil, but the order so far remains unfulfilled and at the time of this writing Gavriil remains the abbot, and enjoys CRA protection.[71] As one pilgrim complains: at Pochaev there are three sermons each day; at Pskov now only one a week.[72] In 1983, reports of manhandling and really violent beatings of monks and pilgrims by Gavriil and his assistants have reached the West.[73] Thus, at the present time, among the male monasteries Pochaev remains, according to reports of pilgrims, the only truly spiritual centre among all the officially functioning male monastic communities of the country; hence the attacks on it.[74]

As the case of Fr. Pavel (Lysak) shows, even the very central Trinity St Sergius Lavra in Zagorsk (seventy kilometres from

Moscow), a showplace for foreign tourists and one of the patriarch's official residences, is not free from harassment and surreptitious persecutions. According to a reliable report, between 1975 and 1980, literally from under the nose of Patriarch Pimen, some forty of the most charismatic monks were expelled from it. Their only crime was their popularity among the pilgrims, as spiritual advisers and father-confessors. There is an unwritten rule that 'if there is a long queue of pilgrims for confession to a certain monastic priest, his days in the lavra are numbered'.[75]

In other cases, particularly in places far from the eyes of foreign correspondents, unwanted priests (as well as laymen) simply die in mysterious circumstances. Thus, on 17 December 1978, a popular Orthodox priest Fr. Nikolai Ivasiuk, in the Turkmen city of Chardzhou, was found sadistically murdered in his home. His hair was torn out, his eyes plucked out; the body bore marks of cigarette and iron burns, as well as knife wounds and carvings. The previous night believers saw a car pull up to the house with six uniformed militiamen leaving the car and entering the house. Needless to say, the murderers were never found.[76] In Vilnius, Lithuania, a very popular Catholic priest, Bronius Lauriniavichius, a member of the Lithuanian Helsinki-Watch Group was killed by a truck. Witnesses saw how four men pushed the priest off the pavement onto the throughfare when the truck was approaching. Less than a year later, a lay dissident secular activist, Valeri Smolkin, was advised by the KGB to emigrate or else his fate could be similar to that of Lauriniavichius – that is, they admitted it was a KGB murder.[77]

Psychiatric abuse in relation to religious believers, especially to those born and fully educated under the Soviet regime, is easily rationalized in terms of the Marxist doctrine of materialistic and environmental determinism. The infamous Professor Snezhnevsky applied it to psychiatry. According to this doctrine, any person whose ideas and behaviour deviate from the norms and values of the society in which he or she has been brought up suffers from a psychotic schizoid unadaptability to society.[78] Obviously this theory could most conveniently be applied to a Soviet young person, particularly with a higher education, who became a religious believer at a mature age, especially if he or she came from an atheistic family. It is not inconceivable that there are many Soviet doctors and other petty officials who, having been brought up on the Marxist categories of thought, sincerely believe that Christian neophytes with higher education, having gone through actively atheistic and materialistic education from the kindergarten to university, are indeed psychotic.

Although, as will be shown, such 'diagnoses' are often applied to lay believers, they are particularly useful in dealing with such religious eccentrics as monks and nuns or those rare people with full higher education among the sectarian preachers – where the usual levels of education are low. The sects are therefore written off by Soviet propaganda as something dark and backward.

Monks and nuns who are particularly popular among the pilgrims and yet whose behaviour makes it extremely difficult to charge them criminally even under Soviet conditions, are thus removed from the scene.

In recent years two cases have been revealed: that of the priest Iosif Mikhailov of Ufa, held in the dread Kazan' psycho-prison since 1972, and of Valeria (Makeev), a nun, held at the same place since 1978. The latter was first accused of black-marketing: she lived by making and embroidering various religious articles, which she sold to believers inside the churches. Having failed to build up a case against her, the authorities apparently did not want to look foolish and yet were too eager to remove her from public life to leave her alone. The obliging 'chartered' psychiatrists pronounced her mad. At the time of the last report, in 1981, both church and people were still in custody.[79]

Even more inconvenient to the regime are young Christian intellectuals with higher secular education, and those well-educated young priests who attract young Soviet intellectuals searching for religion. A case in point was Fr. Lev Konin, thrown into psycho-prison several times before his expulsion to the West in 1979. He had contacts with Leningrad students, and attended and spoke at an unofficial religio-philosophic seminar of young Soviet intellectuals in Leningrad.[80] A former student of history and literature, Yurii Belov, imprisoned at the Sychevcka psycho-prison, was told in 1974 by a representative of the central Moscow Serbsky Institute of Forensic Medicine: 'In our view religious convictions are a form of pathology, hence our use of drugs.'[81] A 33-year-old doctor, Olga Skrebets, with a Ph.D in medical sciences, was hospitalized in Kiev in 1971 and diagnosed as 'an early stage of schizophrenia' after she had withdrawn from the CPSU for religious reasons.[82]

The sectarians in Russia – Baptists, Pentecostals and Adventists – are mostly working-class people and peasants with very little education. Therefore, an educated sectarian, who is a zealous activist and missionary, becomes particularly undesirable to the state when he becomes prominent both in the sect and outside it. How can such a person be silenced if he does not break the law? The state declares him a psychotic and places him behind the bars of a psycho-prison. Such was the fate of a 44-year-old Baptist, Alexander Yankovich, who had engaged in unofficial writing and duplicating religious literature from 1957 to 1976, when he was finally caught and declared insane. Such was also the fate of Evgenii Martynov, a Pentecostal and a civil engineer, thirty-five years old at the time of his incarceration in the Cherniakhovski psycho-prison in 1978.[83] The ordeal of an Orthodox layman, Vasilii Shipilov, began in 1939 when, as a seventeen-year-old student at an underground seminary, he was sentenced to ten years' hard labour. Released in 1949 he roamed the length and breadth of Siberia 'preaching the word of God and telling people about the cruelties of Stalin's regime'. He was soon rearrested and declared insane. Except for short intervals, he has been in psycho-prisons since 1950, and in 1979 was still at the Krasnoiarsk regional psychiatric hospital in Siberia, where 'the orderlies ... are constantly beating him ... mocking his religion and the rituals'.[84] The Christian Committee for the Defence of Believers' Rights, reporting the psychiatric incarceration of Sergei Galliamov, a young Bashkir intellectual who had recently joined the Orthodox Church, stated in 1979 that about ten young intellectual Christian converts had been similarly treated in Bashkiria. The 'crime' of the twenty-year-old history student Galliamov was not only that he was baptized at eighteen, but that he spent the summer of 1978 as a pilgrim to the few remaining monasteries, associating with the monastic elders. He was diagnosed 'a psychopath of mixed type' and was immediately subjected to large doses of neuroleptics, causing nausea, high fever and heart attacks. He was released on probation less than two months after the arrest. The doctor warned him to keep away from his former friends and not to visit monasteries anymore, or else 'psychopathy can easily evolve into schizophrenia'. His name remained on the Ufa psychiatric register; this means he could be re-hospitalized by force at any time during the rest of his life.[85]

One of the most blatant cases of psychiatric treatment for religion was that administered in 1976 to a 25-year-old Moscow intellectual, Alexander Argentov, a neophyte Orthodox Christian from an atheistic family. He was a founding member of the Moscow-based religio-philosophic seminar founded in 1974 and headed by Alexander Ogorodnikov, a graduate student of cinematography, who was expelled from the institute, along with several other students, for trying to produce a film which aimed at reflecting the unofficial religious life of the contemporary Soviet youth. Ogorodnikov's religio-philosophic seminar declared itself a continuation of the religio-philosophic societies of Moscow and Lenigrad, dispersed by the Soviets in the 1920s. The harassment of the seminar began in earnest in 1976 after it had shown considerable vitality and signs of growth, having established subsections in such cities as Ufa (Bashkiria), Leningrad, L'vov (Ukraine), Minsk and Grodno (Belorussia).[86] The arrest of Argentov (and Fedotov, who was also locked up in a forensic institution for some time) was a terrorist act to threaten the seminar members with what was in store for them. Argentov was grabbed in a military draft recruitment centre, where he had been summoned to appear. From there he was delivered by force to a psychiatric dispensary, where the psychiatrist on duty told him plainly, 'We shall knock that religion out of you.' He was then delivered, again by force, to a psychiatric hospital. A pectoral cross was torn off his neck, and powerful neuroleptics were administered to him by force for the two months he was kept in the hospital. His early release was probably caused by the wide publicity given to the case at the time by the protests of the unofficial Christian Committee, the seminar members, and Argentov's parents. They were addressed to the Soviet Government, to the Patriarch and to the World Council of Churches.[87]

As these arrests indicate, persecution of religiously active laymen, especially young intellectuals, has also been on the increase at least since the second half of the 1970s, rising markedly in the early 1980s. This, no doubt, has been a defensive counteraction of atheism against the rising tide of conversions, religious renewal and searches among the above groups of the population in particular. The Moscow and Leningrad religio-philosophic seminars have already been mentioned. Their persecutions did not stop with the detention of Argentov and Fedotov in psycho-prisons. Simultaneously or soon after, the chairman of the Moscow Seminar Alexander Ogorodnikov, was forced to resign his janitor's job after it had been found that he had used his janitor's hut for seminar meetings. All his subsequent attempts to find a job were frustrated by the authorities, thus making him vulnerable to prosecution for parasitism. Indeed, in 1979 Ogorodnikov was sentenced to one year's hard labour for parasitism. At the end of the term, however, taking advantage of the fact that he was still a prisoner and the trial could take place without outside witnesses, he was re-tried, this time accused of anti-Soviet propaganda while in prison, and given a hideous sentence of six years' hard labour in a strict regime camp to be followed by five years of internal exile. The purpose was, of course, to cut him off effectively from reviving the seminar anywhere for eleven years, and in Moscow forever: a strict regime sentence usually deprives the victim of the opportunity of living in the capital cities.

The Ogorodnikov Seminar's popularity and success obviously infuriated the Soviets. Its active membership surpassed forty by 1979. It expanded its activities to several other cities, including Kazan', Odessa, and Smolensk, in addition to the ones mentioned above. In February 1979 there was a joint conference of the Leningrad and Moscow seminars. A Leningrad literary historian and learned librarian of considerable talents, Vladimir Poresh, became the seminar's representative there and the *de facto* deputy chairman of the Ogorodnikov seminar. Tat'iana Shchipkova, a professor of French and Latin at the Smolensk Pedagogical Institute, became its representative in that city. As she was a very popular teacher, she naturally attracted some students to the seminar; then followed the development of a local religio-philosophic discussion group under her leadership. The regime at first reacted, even before Ogorodnikov's arrest, with various forms of unofficial harassment, including a severe anonymous beating of one of its members. After this there were numerous KGB warnings to its individual members, raids and temporary arrests of the whole membership of the seminar during its meetings, and expulsions from jobs. In June 1978 Shchipkova lost her teaching position, and several students at the same institute who had attended the seminar, including her son and daughter-in-law, were expelled. By the end of August 1978 Shchipkova was deprived of her doctoral degree on political grounds; and in January 1980 the 49-year-old former professor was sentenced to three years' hard labour 'for malicious hooliganism': during one of the police raids of the seminar sessions she had slapped a Komsomol police aid on the face while he was twisting her arm. Two other members of the seminar, Sergei Ermolaev and Igor' Poliakov, were sentenced respectively to four and three-and-a-half years' hard labour in September 1979, allegedly for shouting anti-Soviet slogans. In April 1980 two members of the seminar, Viktor Popkov and Vladimir Burtsev, were sentenced to eighteen months' hard labour each, allegedly for counterfeiting documents. A few days later, Vladimir Poresh, the leader of the seminar after Ogorodnikov's arrest, was sentenced to five years' hard labour in strict regime camps followed by three years of internal exile. Just before the completion of his term Poresh was given an additional three years' labour camp term in October 1983.[88] this effectively put an end to the activities of the seminar to the best of our knowledge, at least for a time. In addition, two other active members, the already-mentioned Fedotov and Alexander Kuz'kin, were forcibly placed in forensic institutions.[89] The methods applied to the seminar members and the pretexts for their imprisonment are excellent illustrations of how religious believers are, and have been since 1918, persecuted and incarcerated under fraudulent criminal charges, allowing the Soviet Government and the cowed official Russian Church leaders to maintain that there are no imprisonments in the Soviet Union for one's religious faith.

Underground printing presses of the Free Adventists have already been mentioned. The unofficial Evangelical Christian Baptists have also been running underground presses publishing bibles and other religious literature – all under a single title, the 'Khristianin Publishers' – despite the fact that at least one such press was discovered by the KGB in the vicinity of Riga in October 1974, liquidated, and its workers sentenced to long terms of hard labour. None the less, as of February 1983 the Council of Relatives of the Imprisoned Christian-Baptists stated that its underground publishing house 'The Christian' continues its work, having published nearly half a million Gospels in ten years, despite the mounting persecutions of Church members: of its estimated 100 000 baptized membership (only adult baptisms), fifty persons were imprisoned in 1981 and seventy-three in 1982. A total of 165 members of the Church were in prison and camps by the end of 1982, more than 50 per cent of the total of prisoners-for-faith estimated by the Moscow Christian Committee, as reported above.[90]

The Orthodox Church appears to have come closest to establishing her printing base in the early 1980s. In April 1982 five young Orthodox Christians were arrested in Moscow accused of having illegally possessed a xeroxing machine and printing thousands of religious books and brochures, particularly prayer books, and selling them at a profit to Christian laymen as well as to Orthodox priests for distribution among the faithful. V. Burdiug, the main defendant, was apparently running quite a professional enterprise. Although it was proved in the court that the prices for the literature were set only to cover the costs and provide minimum survival levels for its staff of five to eight typists, printers and binders, and distributors, the case was a convenient one to try the defendants for black-market operations, and the chief defendant, in addition, for pilfering state property: the court conveniently requalified a broken xerox machine written off for scrap (which apparently the defendant subsequently repaired) into a fully functioning office machine belonging to the state. To demoralize the defendants as well as to lower the prestige of Christians, false rumours were circulated during the period of *in camera* investigation that all the defendants co-operated in giving evidence against each other. In fact only one of them, Sidorov, who had been a psychiatric patient after a suicide attempt, broke down fully under investigation. Another, a chauffeur who used to deliver the raw materials for the printers and the finished goods to the customers, believed his interrogator's lie that all the others had broken down, and began to co-operate with the investigation, retracting his evidence at the trial and asking the others for forgiveness. The remaining four or five (Burdiug, Nikolai Blokhin, two brothers, Sergei and Vladimir Budarov, and Krokhin) held fast. Burdiug took all the blame for the others, trying to help his colleagues. In December 1982 Burdiug was sentenced to four years' hard labour, the others to three years each. Searches for literature printed by the group were carried out (with a considerable catch) in the houses of many believers and of some priests, involving about a dozen families, including a nun, a priest, a Christian poet, and (*horrible dictu!*) a graduate student of CPSU history, Grigori Zaichenko. Technically speaking, under Soviet law, this was black-market operation. But had the Soviet state allowed the church to function normally, no need for undercover operations would have existed. The evidence in the court presented by witnesses and by the lawyer showed that the motives of the defendants were religious – to serve their Church as best they could – not to make money.[91]

One of the most blatant illustrations of suppression of religion, and persecution of those who try to promote religious enlightenment, was the arrest in 1982 of the 53-year-old writer and journalist, Mrs Zoia Krakhmal'nikova, formerly a successful member of the Soviet Union of Writers who upon her adult conversion began to apply her talents and professional skills to the promotion of Russian Orthodoxy. She began to publish *samizdat* typewritten collections of the wisdom and teachings of the Church. Some seven such collections under the name of *Hope: Christian Readings* had appeared and were in circulation by the time of her arrest. They contained excerpts from writings of Church Fathers as well as of modern Orthodox theologians, articles by neophytes on what brought them to Christianity, excerpts from the lives of popular saints, and unpublished religious and theological writings of Russian priests, bishops and theologians of the post-revolutionary era. The only political element in these collections was that the latter writings were normally accompanied by short biographical notes on their authors, which usually revealed their martyrdom for faith at the hands of the Soviets. Contrary to Soviet law, Krakhmal'nokova was never warned that her activities were considered hostile or that a case was being prepared against her. She was simply arrested on 4 August 1982 without any warning, tried on 1 April 1983 after a long spell of *in camera* investigation, and sentenced to one year in prison to be followed by five years of internal exile under surveillance. This meant that she would be totally isolated from normal life and from the possibility of serving the Church until the age of sixty.[92]

A new phenomenon appeared in the early 1980s: religious rock music, even religious rock opera – of course, unofficially. A certain Evangelical Baptist in his thirties, Valerii Barinov, organized a Christian rock music group, 'The Trumpet Call', around 1982. In January 1983 he and his friend Sergei Timokhin addressed a petition to the USSR Supreme Soviet requesting permission for the group to give legal religious concerts. The response was a campaign of character assassination in the Soviet press. In March 1984 the two friends were detained in the north-western Arctic port of Murmansk, accused of trying to escape across the border to Norway. Although both of them vehemently denied the charges at the trial in November, Barinov was sentenced to two and a half years' hard labour for attempting to leave the USSR illegally. Both prior to the sentence and after it, Barinov declared a hunger strike, requesting either release as an innocent or emigration papers for his family and himself. He was forced-fed, had a heart attack probably as a result of brutal forced feeding, and his health is in a precarious state. Barinov was released on schedule in September 1986.[93]

Among proposed future activities discussed by the defunct Ogorodnikov seminar was the organizing of Christian youth camps. As far as the unofficial Baptists are concerned such camps have been an annual reality for many years, especially for children of imprisoned Baptists, who are deprived of regular parental Christian education.[94] But throughout the 1970s and 1980s the state continued its practice of using all means to deprive children of the influence of and education by their Christian parents. As mentioned in Chapter 6, cases have been reported, especially by the unofficial Baptists and Pentecostals, of deprivation of parental rights for religious parents, removal of their children from them and their placement in special boarding schools.[95] Like so many other barbarous acts, these were rationalized in the Brezhnev era under the new 1969 Family Code and in the Brezhnev Constitution. Both documents oblige Soviet parents to bring up their progeny as good communists. But the CP membership stipulates that each communist must be an unrelenting fighter against religious 'obscurantism', so the requirement to educate one's children as communists means an obligation to educate them as atheists. Thus, what in Khrushchev's time was actually illegal or had no basis in law, and could be explained as an arbitrary act by a local official and be corrected through courts and a lot of unpleasant publicity, has now become a legitimate and legal action in accordance 'with due process of law'.[96]

In the late 1960s most of the human rights movement in the Soviet Union developed under the slogan of defence of Soviet legality, demanding that Soviet officials respect their own laws and observe them. The use of written laws to persecute religion shows that written laws are no protection for the individual in a totalitarian state. The real 'law' is the secret internal instruction, the text of which remains unknown to the public.

Epilogue

As far as religion and antireligious Soviet policies are concerned Gorbachev's second year in power has been rather inconclusive. On the positive side was the new law permitting teenagers to assist at church services (as acolytes, psalmists and choir singers, presumably – in the past there have been multiple cases of persecution of young people for such activities) and children to be present at them. The law, as mentioned in vol. 1 of this study, also granted for the first time a legal person status to the lay religious associations, permitting them now to buy, build and own church property, including the temples. This status has not been extended to the hierarchical side of the Chucrh (to the clergy, that is). But besides the January 1986 issue of the *Journal of the Moscow Patriarchate* the law has not appeared in any Soviet official law books, not even in the *Supreme Soviet Herald*. Moreover, life in the Soviet Union is governed not so much by published laws, as by unpublished secret instructions on how to interpret and apply (or ignore) the law. At the time of writing (February 1987) not a single case of a church passing into an ownership possession of a religious society has been heard of. High level internal Church sources, on the other hand, have confidentially stated that since the Gorbachev's coming to power there has been neither improvement, nor deterioration in the real position of the Church, but that Christians ought to be ready to expect the worst.

Although a few prisoners of conscience, inlcuding the Russian Orthodox poet Ratushinskaia and the Baptist Miniakov, have been released, others continue their terms in just as terrible prison and camp conditions as before, still others, including numerous Baptists-Initiativists, Pentecostals, Krishnaites, and Orthodox, have been arrested or re-arrested and sentenced in the course of 1986. According to the latest data of the Italian *Russia cristiana* Institute, 123 persons have been sentenced under Gorbachev for their religion-related activities, leaving the total number of religious prisoners roughly unchanged.

The degree of interference into the internal life of the Church by the Soviet state, which is a form of indirect but very effective persecution, has not changed either. Roman Catholic bishops of Lithuania had been denied the right to visit the Vatican in 1986, and the Pope has failed to receive permission to visit Lithuania in 1987 – the 600th anniversary of the signing of the treaty of royal union between Lithuania and Poland which included a clause of conversion of Lithuania to Roman Catholicism. (Up to that point most of Lithuania's princely and aristocratic families had been Orthodox, while the masses remained largely heathen.)

The state prevented the Orthodox Church from appointing Metropolitan Filaret of Minsk to the see of Leningrad, vacated by the death of Metropolitan Antonii (Mel'nikov) in 1986. Filaret (Vakhromeev) is a very popular and somewhat outspoken pastor, not favoured by the regime, which prefers the much more compliant Alexii (Ridiger). It was the latter who had to be appointed to Leningrad under the regime's pressure. Similarly, according to internal Church sources, the Church's choice for the next Patriarch, should the current ailing Pimen die, is the above Filaret; but the regime opposes his candidature. Its choice is Metropolitan Sergii of Odessa, too compliant even for the contemporary leaders of the Moscow Patriarchate to stomach. The fears are that the regime may force the Synod to accept Sergii.

There has been no visible change in the profile or volume of the antireligious publications in contrast to the general Soviet literary and cultural scene. The Gorbachev censorship relaxation in the sphere of arts and his admission of a catastrophic moral decline of the Soviet society have resulted in a flood of literary works, plays, films and sociological articles stressing a direct link between Christianity and national morals, Christianity and the family; and conversely, seeing the moral decline and falling apart of the family as a consequence of atheism.[1]

This has met categorical reprimands from the Party ideological establishment. The counter-attack was begun by the veteran of the antireligious establishment, Kryvelev, in *Komsomol'skaia pravda* (30 July 1986), who condemns contemporary Soviet writers, particularly Astafiev, Aitmatov and Bykov, for 'flirting with a god' (Lenin's phrase) and reminds them that for a communist morals are a product of class struggle, not a legacy of the Church. Similar attacks followed in other newspapers, particularly in the central *Pravda* (28 September 1986), where a policy line editorial took Soviet literary figures to task for confusing morals and religion and thus departing from the 'scientific' interpretation of the world. The article reminded them of the new Communist Party Programme adopted at the Twenty-seventh Party Congress in the Spring of 1986, which had called on the intensification of 'scientific-atheistic upbringing', but then stressed the importance of 'the creation and broad dissemination of new Soviet rituals'. In other words, the Programme suggests overcoming the faith in a Supernatural by a religious mythologisation of communism and its temporal leadership.

But the call to intensify antireligious struggle and to divorce ethics and morals from Christianity (or any other religious teachings for that matter) did not stop on the level of newspaper editorials, albeit as important as *Pravda*'s. L. N. Ligachev, the CPSU Central Committee's Second Secretary, i.e. the man in charge of all ideological policies, without mentioning names, picked up the attack on those men of arts and other Soviet authors who 'encountering breaches in socialist morals begin to call for a more tolerant attitudes to religion, want to return to a religious morality'. He virtually repeats all the theses of Kryvelev and of the above *Pravda* editorial in his address to the All-Union Conference of the Heads of Chairs of Social Sciences at the higher learning centres of the USSR (*Pravda*, 2 October 1986), and calls for a more intensive, effective and decisive struggle against religion and all its influences. In a milder form this call was repeated by Gorbachev in a speech in Tashkent (*Pravda Vostoka*, 25 November 1986).

What is unusual is a dualism incompatible with the principles and practices of totalitarianism. On the one hand all forms of religious apologia are condemned from the highest possible party platforms, on the other, following an appeal to this effect at the June 1986 Soviet Writers' Union Congress, a Soviet Culture Fund was formed under the chairmanship of D. S. Likhachev in November 1986. The aim of the Fund is to protect and finance restoration of historical monuments and the education of the nation in the spirit of love and respect of the national history and culture. The Fund seems to have a more official backing and greater prerogatives than the republican associations for the protection of historical and cultural monuments (VOOPIK in the Russian Republic). Needless to say, the main objectives of restoration and protection will be churches and monasteries, and religious art; and the masses will supposedly be educated to appreciate them in their proper context, although exhibited as and in museums. But most interesting is the combination of personnel in the Fund's administrative board. The chairman is Professor Dimitri Likhachev, a practising Christian, actively defending Christian culture and even the positive role of the churches in the moral upbringing of the nation in many of his latest writings and speeches. Other members include Gorbachev's wife and Archbishop (Metropolitan at the time of this writing) Pitirim, the chairman of the Moscow Patriarchate's Publications' Committee and editor-in-chief of the *Journal of the Moscow Patriarchate*.[2] This is the first case under the Soviet regime that a representative of the Church participates in such an official secular body (not counting peace committees which exist for foreign propaganda purposes alone).

Moreover, some of the attacks on religion did not remain unanswered in the Soviet press. A Belorussian philosopher and, *horrible dictu*, the antireligious *Znanie* Society lecturer, Pylilo, criticised Kryvelev, flatly stating that the morality of many people is of Christian origin and that 'the time has come to reject the practice of unfounded denunciation of the whole heritage of religion and its morality'. *Kom. pravda* counter-attacked and stated that Pylilo should be ousted from the *Znanie* Society.[3] But two months later it published two articles: one by the occasionally controversial poet Yevtushenko, the other by a militant atheist, philosopher Kaltakhchian. Yevtushenko takes Kryvelev to task, hinting that he belongs to that army of Soviet semi-intellectuals who lack real culture owing to the one-sided Soviet education depriving whole generations of the Christian cultural heritage. He laments the lack of Bibles for free sale in contrast with the *Qoran*, which has been officially published. Atheism, writes Yevtushenko, 'ought to be one of the expressions of our society, along with belief in God'. Needless to say, Kaltakhchian defends the Leninist programme of militant atheism in the same issue of the Communist youth newspaper.[4]

The year ended just as inconclusively. The December issue of the journal which most often publishes Russian nationalists, *Our Contemporary*, came out with two articles on the tragic demographic and family situation in the Soviet Union, linking it to a national moral catastrophe as well as Soviet socio-economic conditions. The authors of the more explicit of the two articles conclude that the traditional family was held together by:

> firstly, certain economic relations strengthening the stability of the family;
> secondly, Christian ethics morally strengthening the stability of the family;
> thridly, public opinion which used to be . . . 'rather severe, unrelenting' in its requirement to live according to Christian morals.[5]

But an authorative article in *Pravda* about a month later, indicates that the Party continues to be bent on a programme of unrelenting militant atheism, will not accept the concept of an organic connection between religion and culture and religion and ethics.[6]

Does this mean a further intensification of antireligious propaganda and persecutions, which in the Soviet context, as the volume has demonstrated, is inseparable from concerted antireligious campaigns? Or in need to gain support of the non-party masses and, particularly, of the non-party intelligentsia for his economic reform mainly opposed by the party establishment, will Gorbachev continue to tolerate the current 'dialogue' in the media? In the latter case the general 'climate' in which the believers live and function is bound to become milder.

Appendix 1

The following four documents were written by Metropolitan Sergii, Junior, of Vilnius (Lithuania) and Exarch of Latvia of the Moscow Patriarchate during the German occupation of the Baltic territories. M. Sergii, a Soviet citizen and one of the only four surviving ruling bishops of the Russian Patriarchal Church on the Soviet territory, was appointed Exarch for the Baltic republics on their occupation by the Soviets in 1940. In 1941 he went into hiding as the Germans were advancing, instead of retreating with the Soviet troops.

The first document was apparently one of M. Sergii's memoranda to the Germans on the real situation of the Church in the USSR, especially of the late 1930s, explaining and justifying the enforced loyalty of M. Sergii, Senior, and his Church administration to the Soviets, and thus justifying his own continuing loyalty to the Moscow Patriarchate even under the Germans.

The second document shows his continuing apologia for his superior in Moscow, even after the latter's anti-German propaganda statement. It is an article in the Riga (?) diocesan journal of October 1942.

The third document, of 14 May 1943, is the Exarch's article which was apparently printed in a German language newspaper, *Neue Ordnung*, published in Croatia, according to a German caption in long hand above the text.

The fourth document is the Exarch's most detailed analysis and account of the history and life of the Church in the USSR before the war, giving details on the legal position of the clergy and of the Church *per se*, or rather, lack thereof. This report, written apparently for the Germans in January 1944, could with only minor alterations be a description of the position of the Church in our own days (especially after 1961), as a thoughtful reader will undoubtedly conclude. Note that there is in that document, in contrast to Document 1, a note of doubt regarding the wisdom of the 1927 Declaration of Loyalty, or at least a legitimization for such doubts. Four months after this last document had been written the Exarch was brutally murdered when his car was attacked by an armed band dressed in German uniforms. The Exarch and all his companions were machine-gunned. The Germans declared the murderers were Soviet partisans. The official Soviet version is that he was murdered by the Germans. The latest *samizdat* evidence indicates that the murderers were Soviet agents indeed (Pospielovsky, *Russian Church*, vol. I, 232).

METROPOLITAN SERGII OF VILNIUS, EXARCH OF LATVIA AND ESTONIA, UNPUBLISHED REPORT (TO THE GERMANS) ON THE CHURCH UNDER THE SOVIET REGIME

From the beginning of the Bolshevik Revolution, the Soviet authorities declared a struggle against all types of religious convictions, based upon the principle that religion is the opium of the people, as is, in general, any idealistic *Weltanschauung*.

The main blow was directed against Orthodoxy. Although the Decree even spoke of the freedom of the performance of the 'religious cult', the authorities pursued the church activists with the utmost cruelty, covering up their persecutions of the Church and believers by the struggle with counter-revolution and its political opposition. Of course, no one doubted the simple truth, that every member of the Church, and most of all her servants, were persecuted before all else for their faith and adherence to Orthodoxy.

Such a condition existed already in 1923, that the Head of the Russian Orthodox Church, His Holiness Patriarch Tikhon, was forced to acknowledge – as was the entire Church – his guilt before the Bolsheviks for 'anti-Soviet' activity. Having made public his confession through the press, the Patriarch expressed regret over the former position of the Church, and with his return from house-arrest he promised to change his political course, refusing not only active, but even passive interference with the Soviet government.

What conditions called forth such a step by the Head of the Orthodox Church with its flock of many millions?

The Bolsheviks, having siezed power by means of ruthless violence, and by shedding a sea of blood of the Russian people, above all encountered the Church's censure. Only the Church openly dared to declare the truth to them to their face. The ruling circles and the intellegentsia either perished honourably in the struggle with the usurpers, or were forced to flee abroad. The voice of the Church remained solitary because the Russian people, worn out by terror, could offer no real support. Hope remained alive for the first five to ten years for assistance from the European states; but even this receded further and further with each passing year, remaining only a distant and perhaps insubstantial dream for the Russian people. Thus, on one side there remained a small group of cruel usurpers – atheists – who were never troubled by their methods of terror, and on the other 130 000 000 believing Russian people. Meanwhile, life took its course, but each side understood the necessity of some legal form, defining the position of the Church. This position was especially strengthened after the recognition of the Soviet Government by the European states. The Bolsheviks had to demonstrate their 'tolerant' relationship to Church life.

If, in 1923, Patriarch Tikhon found it necessary to make a sacrifice of personal humiliation for the sake of the Church, then at the moment of the accession to the direction of the Church by Metropolitan Sergii of Nizhni-Novgorod, one of the locum-tenens of the Patriarch, there arose with full clarity the necessity of the stabilization of the Church administration. It is necessary not to forget that the Bolsheviks, for reasons outlined above, had already taken their own peculiar steps at 'legalising' the Church. Through the agents of the Cheka they found a group of bishops and priests who announced the deposition of the Patriarch, named themselves the 'Living Church' or 'Renovationists', and who were already prepared to seize the Church administration in their own hands. They even advanced the political correctness of the Bolsheviks, and started on the path of open collaboration with the organs of the Cheka. But this 'rebellion' against ecclesiastical truth

Appendix 1

suffered a great defeat – the people did not follow them, and since the vile intentions of the Bolsheviks became well known, the latter were forced to change their tactics.

They even understood that the persecution of believers and the Church was repeating the glorious historical page of the Christian martyrs of the past and only strengthening the Orthodox consciousness of the Russian people.

Metropolitan Sergii, who had ascended to the direction of the Church administration, was a man of high culture and a wide diplomatic mind, a doctor of the historical sciences and of canon law. Having grasped the mood of the episcopacy, the clergy, and believers, he fulfilled Patriarch Tikhon's undertaking of the legislation of the Central Patriarchal Administration of the Russian Church. In his declaration, founded on the true religious duties of the Church, the Metropolitan announced both a refusal of the utilization of his religious convictions for political goals, and the total loyalty of the Church to the Soviet system. It must be said bluntly, that the Soviet Government was deeply interested in establishing quiet amidst the émigré circles and demanded appeals to these circles, which were under the jurisdiction of the Moscow Patriarchate. The Metropolitan – the locum-tenens of the Patriarch – agreed to this, because these anti-Soviet statements on the part of the émigré church activists did not have any practical meaning, but especially painfully reflected on the Church in Russia. Every anti-Soviet statement made in exile drew forth great sacrifices from among the episcopacy, the clergy, and even from the ranks of the believing intellectuals.

Briefly put, by the efforts of the Head of the Church an external agreement with the Soviet government was reached – a certain legal status of the central Church authority – though inwardly they undoubtedly remained enemies. This was clear to both sides, and Metropolitan Sergii and his co-workers did not delude themselves with the hope of the transformation of Bolshevik cruelty into any kind of mercy.

HOW DID THIS BENEFIT THE BOLSHEVIKS?

1. Having agreed to the existence of a central Church authority, they had the possibility of controlling the actions of this ecclesiastical authority.

2. To gain the general approval of the Western governments there now existed the 'facade' of a free Church within Soviet conditions.

HOW DID THIS BENEFIT THE CHURCH?

There was the possibility of a united leadership, bearing in mind the existence of ecclesiastical schisms and the atmosphere of an extreme disintegration of church discipline. The suffering Russian people knew the cost of this sacrifice, but they understood that for the preservation of Church order and life this sacrifice was necessary. These very people reached a fundamental conclusion: to unite the church masses around the genuine source of Orthodoxy.

This step by the Head of the Russian Church drew forth the false conviction among the leaders of Western and exiled believing circles that for the price of the betrayal of ecclesiastical freedom, personal well-being was purchased.

Life itself refuted this false view. All church activists recognized the necessity of unity with Metropolitan Sergii and they all sincerely supported his undertaking, but their destiny did not escape the cruel punishing hand of the Cheka.

There also arose the conviction that the Moscow Patriarchate was not free in its ecclesiastical actions. On account of their foreign-political position and protecting the consciousness of the 'free' religious liberties of their Soviet citizens, the Bolsheviks decided never to interfere crudely in the decisions of the internal administration of ecclesiastical life. And was it really necessary for them to resort to using the Moscow Patriarchate? If the animation of ecclesiastical life in this or that place was disagreable to them, if it was necessary to paralyze any undertaking of the Patriarchate, then the Bolsheviks resorted to their favourite method of administrative violence – the exiling of the bishop and clergymen, the closing of churches, and so forth. It should also be noted that they manifested great interest in the decisions of the Patriarchate concerning foreign questions, and then only expressed their wishes in personal conversations with the patriarchal locum-tenens. These conversations were always confidential, and were known of by hardly anyone in the Church. We knew of the Bolsheviks' personal interest to place us – for the most part the episcopacy – under their control. In that case they recommended someone from among secular people to be placed in the capacity of a secretary, a servant, a cell-attendant. Usually, we easily perceived such an appearance of 'concern' and considered it for the better to have around oneself a notorious agent, instead of a secret one who would suddenly succeed in entering into one's confidence.

The Bolsheviks realized their fundamental control over ecclesiastical life through the so-called 'Commission concerning the cults'. The Central Commission was created under the Presidium of the Supreme Soviet, and it further descended into a network of corresponding local commissions. The composition of the Central Commission and of the local ones remained secret, but they were undoubtedly ruled by the GPU–NKVD. The Commission chose the so-called 'instructor concerning the cults', i.e. a well-known lecturer who entered into the life of every community. Apart from the central ecclesiastical organ – the Patriarchate – he demanded from every unit the necessary information. Directly, they handed over to him lists of believers, forms with the names of those who had signed agreements for the use of a church and property, or concerning the composition of the clergy, and so forth. The instructor entered into certain ties with separate persons of the community, not only checking out the life of the community through them, but also the actions of the central church authority, very often discovering in her decrees objectionable sides. The Patriarchate presented information concerning the composition of its members, workers, and the status of its dioceses to the Commission under the Moscow soviet.

From the above, the Patriarchate itself, as the central ecclesiastical establishment, existed, as far as the Bolsheviks were concerned, only as a prop for the sake of credulous foreigners.

The Patriarchal locum-tenens, we – the episcopacy and his closest helpers –

reconciled ourselves with this humiliation and disgrace for the sake of the relative preservation of the Church for the Russian people and in the hope of future deliverance from the atheistic yoke. I repeat, the position itself of the Moscow Patriarchate did not protect her members from Bolshevik persecutions at all. Many of her members suffered, many had yet to suffer, but their hour had not yet arrived, by the will of God. Metropolitan Sergii personally compared our position with chickens in the kitchen garden of a cook. The day would come when even from the small garden the next victim would be snatched. All were doomed, but the cruel cook did not lead all to the chopping block immediately.

My accompanying service record will testify that I kept myself all of this time enclosed within the life of the Church, never abandoning her for a piece of bread or any personal benefit. Being the closest bishop to the Patriarchal locum-tenens, I consciously supported his heroic feat of service to the Russian Orthodox Church, and was convinced and remain convinced of the correctness of his position concerning the external state of the Church in the horrible conditions of the Soviet atheistic terror. As regards my direction of the Exarchate in the Baltic territories, evidence of it exists among the organs of the local Latvian clergy. During my three-month-long stay in Riga under Soviet control I did not have any kind of relations with the civil authorities, for the statute itself dealing with ecclesiastical communities was not introduced here by the Bolsheviks.

Sergii, Metropolitan of Lithuania
Exarch for Latvia and Estonia

20 August 1941
City of Riga

THE EXARCH-METROPOLITAN SERGII'S REPLY TO THE DECLARATION OF THE METROPOLITAN OF MOSCOW

We have been informed that London radio has recently broadcast the new political declaration of the Metropolitan of Moscow. In this declaration it was supposedly said that the Germans, upon seizing certain territory, are destroying the Orthodox Church and its sacred things and are persecuting the Orthodox people. Based upon this, the Metropolitan of Moscow supposedly drew the conclusion that Orthodoxy, and Christianity in general throughout the world, could only be saved by the victory of Bolshevik military might.

In answer to this appalling declaration, we consider it to be our duty to say the following:

During the entire time of their rule the Bolsheviks have subjected the Orthodox Church, and in general every religion, to the cruellest of persecutions. We know this by first-hand experience, for in the course of many years spent in the Soviet Union serving the Church, we were subjected repeatedly, as were others, to painful humiliations, imprisonments, and every sort of brutality, open or secret. The destructiveness of the Bolshevik persecution of the Church is irrefutably witnessed to by hundreds of thousands of executed, tortured, incarcerated, and exiled persons – true sufferers for their faith. The world has yet to see anything comparable to the Bolshevik's destructive rage against everything that is holy. All churches have been plundered by the Bolsheviks, and almost all have been profaned and closed, while many have been altogether destroyed. The Bolsheviks have closed all the monasteries and church schools without exception, they have destroyed the ecclesiastical press, and they have completely eliminated all preaching. The teaching of the Law of God has been forbidden in all schools, and children are now growing up knowing nothing about Christ, His teaching, and His Church. And what is worse – in the last years the majority of children have not even been baptised. We can hardly be surprised, then, that under the evil rule of Bolshevism all that is holy is being uprooted from the soul, the people are being depersonalised and growing wild, and the soul of the people is dying in convulsions. The Bolsheviks are systematically exterminating Christianity. And this is natural. Communist doctrine demands this.

The Bolsheviks cannot renounce their militant atheism and fierce hatred toward the Church. To do this, they would be forced to renounce communism and cease to be Bolsheviks. This is also impossible, as impossible as it is for ice to become hot and not melt. But the Bolsheviks are capable of any kind of sham. When it comes to lying and hypocrisy, they are unsurpassable. This is their true element. In the course of only a quarter of a century, they have managed to deceive Russia and the entire world. If it would prove to be politically advantageous for them, then they would even pretend to be the defenders of Christianity.

As the instrument of their lie, the Bolsheviks have now chosen the Metropolitan of Moscow. They forced him to write appeals which would be to the liking of the Archbishop of Canterbury. We have no dealings with the latter, but we know the Metropolitan of Moscow. May God be merciful to him. We are co-suffering with him, because we see that the Bolsheviks are forcing him to publicly contradict his personal convictions. And having known him for a long time, we can clearly imagine what horrible moral torments the Bolsheviks are using to force him to utter these false words. For he knows of no others that are worse – that without the Church Russia is a corpse, and that under the Bolsheviks the Church is in a grave, from which she can arise and in truth will arise together with her people only after and in consequence of the final destruction of Bolshevik power. And he so clearly understands that to desire the victory of the Bolshevik army means to desire the death not only of Russia, to call for the annihilation not only of the Russian Church, but that this ultimately means to court disaster for all of Europe, and for the entire Christian world. For the victory of the Bolsheviks would be tantamount to the general destruction of Christianity. But God will not permit this victory. The Bolsheviks are doomed.

The Metropolitan of Moscow cannot but know that his public declarations are casting the relationship between the Germans and the Orthodox Church in a false light. We will not speak about this question in all of its breadth, but will limit ourselves to what is happening in our ecclesiatical jurisdiction.

In this district there are, first and foremost, the dioceses of Lithuania, Latvia, and Estonia, united in the Exarchate which was entrusted by the patriarchal locum-tenens to our ecclesiastical care. Further, in our district there now exists vast Russian territory which adjoins the countries just mentioned, limited to the east by a linear front which extends from the environs of Leningrad and the shores of Ladoga to Il'men and farther to the southeast. In this territory there are several million Russian Orthodox people, amongst which there are only about a hundred priests, but not one bishop. Such are the fruits of Bolshevik rule. We considered it our duty to bring this territory under our archpastoral protection for a while, in order slowly to begin the restoration of church life, and for this goal we sent there missionaries from our Exarchate. These were clergymen whom the Bolsheviks did not succeed in liquidating during the short time of their rule in the Baltic countries. And so we are loudly testifying that within our ecclesiastical jurisdiction the German authorities have not only not begun to struggle against the Orthodox Church, but have, on the contrary, granted her free development. In every possible way, they also have helped to lighten our difficult task of liberating Russian territory from the Bolsheviks.

The German authorities are in no way violating the canonical order of our district which, as before, forms part of the Russian Orthodox Church and freely maintains prayerful communion with the locum-tenens of the Patriarchal throne. During a battle, of course, churches, side by side with other buildings as well, could suffer – this is inevitable. But the allegation that the Germans destroyed or profaned our churches with premeditation is simply slanderous. In Novgorod, it was Soviet – and not German – artillery that was exploding around the St Sophia Cathedral. And this was deliberate, allowing shell after shell to explode in this ancient holy site of ours during a lull in the battle. On the contrary, the Germans returned to us those churches confiscated by the Bolsheviks.

These churches had been transformed into warehouses, clubs, theatres – now they were again consecrated, and the word of God is resounding in them. The allegation that the Germans are in some manner oppressing the believing laity is also slanderous.

Sergii (Voskresensky)
Metropolitan of Vilnius
Exarch of Latvia

BOLSHEVISM MUST BE SMASHED

In the world there is much evil and sorrow, but there is nothing more frightening and pernicious than Bolshevism. Bolshevism rose up against God and trampled down man. Bolshevism not only destroys, but corrupts. It destroys all that is sacred and of value, by which the soul of man is alive. It transforms free persons into faceless slaves. It poisons them with its lie, and tortures them with its brutality. A country with Bolshevism is ruled by fear, hidden under the mask of a manipulated devotion and dictated enthusiasm. Fear for oneself and one's own, fear of poverty and hunger; fear of denunciation; and fear of the GPU and before each other. In a country under Bolshevism all are forced to dissemble and lie, in order to escape a swift reprisal. There people suffer not only because they are half-starving and going about in rags, exhausted by unendurable toil, not knowing any rest and nightly awaitng arrest; but they suffer all the more acutely and irrevocably because they feel themselves to be a people whose dignity has been trampled upon and who live with a contemptible fear rankling in their breasts. There they do not know the joy of free initiative, free labour, of free creativity; they do not have consolation in a free faith, in the freedom of the search for truth. In a country with Bolshevism everything is reckoned and determined from above, beginning with the doctrine of Marxism and ending with the daily schedule of compulsory work and further with the compulsory participation in public meetings of various sorts. There every person becomes the unwilling screw in the iron machine of communism. And how repulsively this machine works! Constructed with the aim of bringing order to everything, it leads everything into disorder. A schedule established to move the entire country forward in five years, brings destruction daily everywhere. Everyone fears responsibility, shifting it on to the next person and thus causing stagnation in all matters. Everyone hates their forced labour, shirking it, and trying only to become a little less tired from their hateful drudgery. This resulted in the breakdown of all programmes and in constant confusion. People felt their lives becoming meaningless, ugly, and lawless, filled with gloomy boredom and irrational fear. But they did not dare admit this. They were compelled to maintain the pretence of happiness. As slaves they were ordered to proclaim that they were the most free of all the peoples on earth, that there was nothing more joyful than their suffering lives, that they loved their hateful overlords, that Bolshevik savagery was the highest form of culture, and that the Bolshevik humiliation of human personality raises one's dignity.

But they hate it all! Oh, how they hate their executioners! They did not forget, nor did they forgive their humiliations and their sufferings. And really, could they forget and forgive? Never! Russia demands requital, awaiting the hour of retribution. For victory over Bolshevism we, the Russian people, are prepared for anything. And therefore Russia awaited the war, desired the war. In the war, she saw the sole possibility to smash Bolshevism, to enter into new open space, to a free life, and to begin anew the thread of her national history – that scared thread unravelled by the Bolshevik revolution. Our Church shared this desire, because only in the military destruction of Bolshevism did she see the path to her liberation. She was almost smothered by the persecutions heaped on her and survived, I am determined to say, by a miracle; a miracle of that simple, heartfelt, unlearned faith which the Russian people succeeded in preserving in their heart, despite all of the efforts of the Bolshevik pogrom-makers. If the Bolsheviks would now succeed in winning the war, then the Russian Church would be doomed to destruction. Driven into a corner by German arms, the Bolsheviks realised that they could not drive their slaves into battle only by machine-guns, or excite them only by the slogans of communism. In Russia, no one has believed in these slogans for a long time. And so the Bolsheviks began to speak of the defence of the Homeland and Faith, appealing to feelings of Russian patriotism and Orthodox religious sentiment. They were convinced of the strength of these feelings in the Russian people, and decided to exploit them. But they did not forgive the Russian people for these feelings. For whoever had these feelings rejected and hated both Bolshevik godlessness and the Communist International. The vitality of these feelings in the Russian people manifested the failure of Bolshevism, its cruel persecutions and crazed propaganda. In the event of its victory, Bolshevism will avenge this failure – it will disperse the Russian people throughout the world, destroy all the churches, and annihilate the Russian clergy to the last man. For Bolshevism cannot change or be regenerated. Its satanic nature is immutable and unchangeable. Only naive people, deceived by Bolshevism and completely misunderstanding its essence, could think otherwise. There are no such people in Russia. But unfortunately, one can meet such people abroad, where they have neither experienced Bolshevism, nor encountered it face to face.

The mendacity of Bolshevism surpasses all probability. There are people who cannot imagine such deceitfulness. And they accept the assurances of the Bolsheviks at face value. They think that, indeed, Bolshevism entered the war not for the sake of international revolution and the universal triumph of the Communist International, but for the Homeland, the Faith, and the freedom of the people – especially the Slavs; for the self-determination of national culture and the salvation of European civilisation and so forth – in a word, for everything that is dear to the opponents of Bolshevism and hateful to itself, for everything about which Bolshevik propaganda so importunately clamours, yet insightfully allowing for the fact that by the open propagation of internationalism, communism, and atheism it cannot presently attract to its side public opinion in either allied Bolshevik, hostile, or neutral countries. And so with unparalleled cynicism, Soviet propaganda is now shouting out the very slogans for which the Bolsheviks have shot a million people, and for which, in the event of their victory, they will yet shoot many more millions. 'Only let us win, and then we will settle all accounts' – this is the fundamental principle of the contemporary wartime propaganda of the Bolsheviks. And the world will suffer if it does not understand this and deceives itself!

The Bolsheviks are forcing the Church to be their accomplice in order to further promote this deception. They are forcing the Church to call for a war against the Bolsheviks' enemies, though they themselves are the cruelest of her persecutors. This persecution is so monstrous that some people are incapable of imagining its possibility and are therefore inclined to think that, indeed, the Church in the Soviet Union is now free and that on her own initiative and conviction is calling upon the believing people in Russia and beyond her borders to arise in the defence of godless Bolshevism. But surely everyone understands that this assumption is absolutely absurd, that it is impossible for any kind of Church to support atheism by its own will. Be assured that the voice of the Church resounding out of Russia now is counterfeit. It is not her voice at all. It is the voice of the Bolsheviks speaking in her name. They squeeze the throat of the Church for the words they need. But the Church cannot speak the words she desires to. Yet I hear these unsaid words. Here is what they say: 'Whoever believes in God – help us! Never believe the Bolsheviks about anything! We are in captivity, we are being tortured! They are forcing us to lie! Forgive us, for you have not experienced what we are experiencing! Do not nail the Church into a grave! Do not nail Russia into a grave! Destroy the Bolsheviks! May God reward you for this! If the Bolsheviks prevail, then we will both perish!'

Do not think that this authentic voice of the Church exists only in my imagination and that I am speaking about something of which I do not know. No, I know what is happening in the Soviet Union and I know that there the Church is suffering. I know also the mind of the Church, for I have come from there. Until 1941 – the time of my appointment to Riga – I lived in Moscow and intimately participated in the labours of the Patriarchate, carrying a common cross with my fellow brother-bishops. I know of the horror there to this very day, and everything of which I am speaking is grounded in my personal experience, accumulated at the altar, in a cell, in prison, and in many years of personal contact with archpastors, pastors, and the laity of Russia scattered throughout various cities and villages. I have the right to witness to the local life and expectations of the people and churchmen, and I am obliged to do this, so that by my silence I do not render indirect assistance to the diffusion of Bolshevik lies and the perpetuation of Bolshevik persecution.

And do not imagine that the words which I am speaking were prompted or dictated by someone from the side. No, I am now absolutely free – as free as is my three-million-membered flock in Lithuania, Latvia, Estonia, and the vast Russian province from Leningrad to Pskov and farther south. The German army brought them this freedom, having driven out the Bolsheviks. Now that, as before, we are in canonical dependence to the Mother Church in Russia, we are able to work in the vineyard of Christ unhindered. The Germans have returned what the Bolsheviks have deprived us of. They have returned to us the churches taken away by the Bolsheviks and we are now able to serve and preach in them with freedom; they have returned to us the right, abolished by the Bolsheviks, to teach the Law of God in secular schools, to establish our own schools for the preparation of pastors, and to publish an unlimited number of books and newspapers with religious content. And in truth, according to our strength, we use all of these rights of ours – we use them and thank God Who has granted us such freedom.

We do not want to lose this freedom. Freedom is as dear to us as the air we breathe, as life itself. Listen to what the believers in our Russian villages and cities are saying: 'We will bear anything – not only Bolshevism!' And again: 'There is no sacrifice that is too dear to us, if it leads to victory over Bolshevism!' You have not experienced Bolshevism. Perhaps it is not very easy for you to understand us. But we know that an ally of Bolshevism is an enemy of God and humanity. And whoever is able to participate in the struggle against Bolshevism, but does not because of one pretext or another, indirectly supports Bolshevism and – whether he likes it or not – he is helping those who are crucifying and tormenting the Church of Christ. Do not believe them or their agents, or those who assure you that we here are suffering from oppression and only dreaming of the return of the Bolsheviks. This is simply a shameless lie! We, all of us, are praying for victory over Bolshevism, for the liberation of the Church and Homeland from the communist yoke, for the gift of strength in this struggle with them, and for blessings upon those who enter into this struggle. And we believe that the Lord will have mercy upon the Russian people and upon those people who come to our assistance; we believe that Bolshevism will be destroyed, that humanity will be saved from it, and that the Church of God will arise to a new, free and joyful life.

Sergii
Metropolitan of Lithuania and Vilnius
Patriarchal Exarch of Latvia and Estonia

14 May 1943

THE CHURCH IN THE USSR BEFORE THE WAR

The self-appointed goal of the Bolsheviks was to obliterate Christianity. Renunciation of this task would have been tantamount to self-destruction for Bolshevism. Such a renunciation was inconceivable. This is clear to everyone who realizes the satanic essence of Bolshevism.

From what source were statements taken that Bolshevism had reconciled itself with Christianity and had even supposedly come forward as its defender? The Bolsheviks themselves set these rumours in motion, considering such a masquerade as beneficial for themselves due to the nature of the times. And even earlier, in the interests of their foreign propaganda, they feigned innocence concerning the persecution of the Church. The lie, together with brutality, was always their favourite weapon of political action.

Besides the lie and brutality, Bolshevism availed itself of no other means. Only by these means did it wage war against Christianity. With these tools it attempted to root out the Orthodox faith from the Russian soul. But the Russian soul did not betray its faith. And therefore, one can look to the Russian future with hope.

The Orthodox Church stood and stands on guard of the Russian soul. She herself was struck by some of the most terrible blows of Bolshevism. It subjected the Church to the worst possible brutality and entangled her with pernicious deception. But it enkindled in the Church the reciprocal strength of a confessing and suffering heroism. And this spiritual strength, the strength of righteousness is unconquerable. The flame of faith which was arising anew in the churches blazed up on the former ruins.

Bolshevism directed its blows against all aspects of ecclesiastical life. It drove away, exiled, and annihilated almost the entire clergy and those members of the laity who were distinguished by their work for the Church; it closed all the monasteries and almost all of the churches; it liquidated all educational and charitable institutions of the Church; expropriated ecclesiastical property; prohibited church publications; deprived believers of the right to conduct religious propaganda, i.e. the right to defend and spread their faith; and organized and conducted a violent atheistic propaganda.

Bolshevism expended special efforts to destroy the internal organization of the Church. To achieve this, it first reduced the organization of the Church to a position of illegality, and thus unrecognized by the State. The established Church, her canonical structure, her hierarchy, her organs, her membership in the Universal Church, and her subdivision into dioceses, deaneries, and parishes were all concepts unknown to the Soviet law. To allude to such concepts in their relationship with the Soviet State was both juridically inadmissible and practically useless.

Only the so-called 'groups of twenty', which were at the head of separate churches, legally existed in the Soviet Union and these groups of twenty laymen were in no way obliged to submit even to the Patriarchate. At least this is how conditions remained until the war. From that time, perhaps, there occurred some kind of 'decorative' changes in their relationship of which, however, I know nothing definite and of which, therefore, I am unable to say anything. I speak only of what I know by my own experience acquired in the pre-war years when I personally participated in the struggles of the Patriarchate.

But I do not doubt that if some kind of changes did occur in the position of the Church then, from the Bolshevik's perspective, this was only a new simulation or a new form of malicious deception by which they always shrouded their relationship to the Church. In actuality, the position of the Church could not have changed and, of course, would not change as long as the Bolsheviks ruled in Russia.

What is this 'group of twenty?' It is twenty laymen or laywomen who were personally responsible for directing, under extremely difficult conditions, a nationalized church temporarily leased to them by the State for the organization of public liturgical services. The realization of just such a procedure to open a church so that the religious rites could be served in it depended upon the local 'commission concerning the cults'. It was also dependent upon this commission as to whether or not a church was to be closed at any given moment and, circumventing the authority of the corresponding group of twenty, dismiss it from its direction. Equally as well, the commission could, without closing the church, turn it over from one group of twenty to another even if they did not belong to the same faith, or in specific cases, to the same – using the Soviet expression – 'religious orientation'.

The commission concerning the cults used this right extensively, as for example when they forcibly took churches away from believers of the 'Tikhonite orientation' and handed them over to supporters of the 'Renovationist orientation'.

The commissions were made up almost exclusively of party members active in the League of the Godless. The commission set itself the goal of stifling the religious life of the population, over which it was commissioned to direct a most severe supervision. In particular, the commission directed the registration of the entire local clergy. One must bear in mind, that according to Soviet law, the right to celebrate the religious rites was granted only to those priests who were registered in the corresponding commission of the cults. They could exercise this right in that church to which they had been assigned as a priestly celebrant by the commission – to celebrate the religious rites in other churches or outside of the churches was strictly forbidden to them.

To all intents and purposes the group of twenty is totally dependent upon the commission of the cults.

The composition of a group of twenty contained Soviet agents who reported to their superiors about everything in the church, including the

Appendix 1

behaviour of the clergy and believers. The slightest carelessness or impropriety in the implementation of those conditions in which a given church was turned over to the management of a group of twenty was sufficient to cause the church's closure, and the registered clergy, members of the twenty and others who had ties with the church, to be exiled.

The church had to be maintained in good condition by the group of twenty and could be closed if the authorities found that its appearance was not properly kept up. This always gave the authorities the possibility to close the church under the pretence that it was in danger of collapsing on the congregation – for appearance's sake this was done by means of an official act. Arbitrarily closing the churches under such false pretences, the Bolsheviks contended that this measure was in no way an act of struggle against religion, but rather one exclusively concerned with the safety of the believing congregation.

The use of a church for liturgical services was regarded, essentially, as a lucrative business undertaken by the group of twenty; as a 'milking' by it and the clergy of great profits from the population and its 'religious prejudices' or, to put it better, as a kind of shameful trade which the State tolerated as a temporary necessity. But, showing such condescension to this deep-rooted 'vice of religiosity', the State strove to render it harmless by extracting from the church or, more precisely, from the group of twenty, a huge tax which must have devoured the entire net income of their 'religious enterprises'. The rate of this tax was fixed altogether arbitrarily; however, a delay in its payment involved the closure of a church. This allowed the authorities, with the appearance of legality, deliberately to fix a back-breaking tax and, under the pretence of its non-payment, to close churches, again contending that this was being done not for the sake of the struggle against religion, but exclusively for the defence of the material interests of the believing population against exploitation by 'religious speculators'.

Such an excessive tax was exacted from the clergy. The income of the clergy was considered as unearned, as if to say, fraudulent. The tax had the goal of removing from the clergy this 'shameful' income, leaving them with a subsistence wage. On this foundation, the Bolsheviks contended that this taxation pressure placed on the clergy in no way served as a measure in the struggle against religion, but was only a necessary means of the social self-defence against the avarice of the 'priests'. A priest, not paying the tax by the appointed date, was excluded from the registration list and deprived of the right to celebrate the public liturgical services. Arbitrarily raising the rate of the tax, if possible of every clergyman, so that the believers could not help him, put him in a condition wherein with the appearance of legality the priest was removed from the cathedral. In the majority of cases the authorities in just such a manner rid themselves of the most popular and authoritative priests who refused to enter into their service, and yet were so cautious in their activities as to rule out a political indictment which could have even a shadow of verisimilitude.

However, political crimes were often charged against clergymen without the slightest foundations. An objectionable clergyman is simply accused of counter-revolutionary activities, although he has never committed any, or of hostile intentions, although he has never had any, and for this they judge him and then exile him or imprison him. Bear in mind, that even of this practice the Bolsheviks said again and again that in no way was it a measure in the struggle against religion, but only a weapon by which people of the revolution defended themselves against their political enemies. Actually, according to the letter of the law, celebrating the religious rites, as such, was still not a criminal offence – precisely speaking, there existed the notorious 'guarantee of the freedom of the cult' – and formally the priesthood was not punished for this, but for a host of other types of activity. In reality, the clergy were pursued precisely for their ecclesiastical activities, but, according to an edict of the Stalin constitution, the game being played out was that they were being pursued for crimes unconnected with these activities.

The celebration of religious rites, as we have mentioned, was allowed in no other than those churches specified for this. To serve in other places was to invite punishment. Secret religious rites therefore entailed a great risk. Stricken from the registration list a priest found himself unable to continue his service and deprived of the means of subsistence. To find other work was difficult for him, for he was considered socially discredited because of his membership in the clergy. This shame spread to his children. In order to find his daily bread and relieve the lot of his children, he was forced to cover up his past and, so as to find work, fill out the obligatory forms with false evidence. This again entailed a great risk, because his exposure inevitably meant a cruel reprisal for him.

The very appointment of a priest to a church formally depended upon the group of twenty, employing him for a determined fee. But, the decisive word actually belonged to the commission of the cults, which could, according to its judgement, refuse to register him. Not having secured the assent of the commission beforehand, it was not even worth presenting him for registration. Thus, the entire clergy was dependent upon the arbitrary will of the Bolsheviks, who allowed some to serve legally, but removed others, naturally preferring the worst over the better.

Under such conditions, a registered priest lived in the unceasing expectation of repressions. With trembling, day and night, he expected arrest, after which could follow exile or imprisonment. Fear in the face of arrest was so great, that people not possessing any remarkable strength of moral character were prepared to enter into any bargain with their conscience and to grovel before the Bolsheviks, if the latter would only leave them in peace. Therefore, among the surviving clergy registered by the Soviet authorities there remain relatively few truly steadfast unbroken persons, true to their lofty calling to the end.

The registered priest attached to a church committed himself to celebrate the liturgical services. Officially, this was his only role. He had no authority at all. He had no administrative rights. Everything was arranged and taken care of by the group of twenty, which had full authority to order the clergy about as they so desired. The twenty was not subjected to any kind of control from the side of the parishioners. It even imposed its will upon them. Therefore everything depended on the personal characteristics of the twenty's composition and on the skill of the parish dean to be on good terms with it. If the composition of the group of twenty was good, and if the parish dean possessed sufficient moral authority, then everything would proceed, more or less, beneficially. In such a case, the twenty would be transformed into a kind of parish council under the dean, who, contrary to the official-juridicial situation of things, would direct the parish and its life. On the other hand, when the twenty is composed of people of a minimal churchly stability and discipline, altogether self-willed and self-seeking – and such is the case often enough – then the life of the parish is extremely abnormal, completely free from the control of the clergy, and the latter have absolutely no authority or the possibility to direct it.

Under such conditions the commissions of the cults control the groups of twenty sufficiently enough so that according to its request, but disregarding the will of the parishioners, a renovationist priest instead of an Orthodox priest will be registered for a given church. In other words, the church will be taken from the Orthodox Church and handed over to the Renovationists, to those schismatics or, better to say, heretics, who have deviated far from pure Orthodoxy and, together with this, have obviously become agents of the Bolsheviks. We recall that Patriarch Tikhon forbade the Renovationist clergy to enter into pastoral service, and that they were defrocked. Equally, the group of twenty could, having reached an agreement with the commission of the cults, register in the ranks of the clergy for a church such a person who, though not belonging to the Renovationists, still did not have the canonical right to serve. For example, a clergyman who for some fault was banned from serving as a priest by episcopal authority; or who was defrocked; or even simply a self-styled priest who never even belonged to the ordained ministry. The commission of the cults, whose mission it was to struggle against Orthodoxy, would agree to register just such a person with great willingness, or incite and force the group of twenty to apply for his registration. Episcopal authority could not struggle against such a penetration of various imposters into the parish clergy.

Indeed, according to Soviet law the bishops in general had no real authority of any kind. In this regard, the illegal position of the Church reflected upon her life especially painfully. The lack of rights of the bishops meant that the Bolsheviks could absolutely ignore the episcopal structure of the Orthodox Church and in general recognize not the least juridicial authority for her canons.

On principle, the Bolsheviks considered the canons to be the organizational regulations of an illegal, or to put it strongly, of a forbidden association. The Church exists in the Soviet Union only as an illegal fact – for she has no acknowledged right to exist according to the State. Therefore, in official Soviet speech, even the very expression 'The Orthodox Church' is absent. From the point of view of Soviet laws, the Orthodox Church, as a legally organized whole, is non-existent, but is only an unco-ordinated, and so an unorganized, group of believers of the 'Tikhonite orientation', to which it is allowed, according to the observance of definite laws, to gather for liturgical services in the churches designated for this. Those priests who were registered in a corresponding church as 'servants of the cult' had the right to serve in it the desired rite – 'cultic acts' – and others had the right to be present at the fulfilment of these acts. They had no other rights. Only in this did the 'freedom of the cult' consist, as recognized by the Stalinist constitution.

From what was said above, one was certain that the so-called 'freedom of the cult' was hemmed in by conditions which made it completely illusory, guaranteeing nothing to practice, but being constantly and brutally violated. At this time it must be especially emphasised that the 'freedom of the cult' in no manner whatsoever meant freedom of belief or of religious conscience. In particular, 'freedom of the cult' did not grant the least right ot organize the life of a religious community on the basis of its religious profession, nor even the right that such communities in general could exist. The cult was torn away from its organic bond with religious life. It is difficult to imagine greater brutality against the religious conscience. In particular, for the Orthodox such a situation developed that here and there they could still legally celebrate the services according to their rite – however, before the war the assigned Orthodox churches already hardly remained – but with this they could not legally fulfil the demands of the faith concerning the canonical structure of the Church. They could only fulfil these demands in an illegal manner. In particular, this concerns the exercise of, and submission to, the ecclesiastical authority of the bishops.

Officially in the Soviet Union there simply are no bishops, and the very word 'bishop' is unknown to the jargon of Soviet laws. The Bolsheviks established only one expression, namely 'servants of the cult', for the designation of the various orders of the clergy of all the confessions of faith. All of the servants of the cult have equal rights, or to put it better, are equally without rights. In this situation there are essentially no differences between deacons, priests, and bishops. Each of them has the right to complete the 'cultic acts' in the church for which they have been registered – but possess absolutely no rights beyond this. Not one of them may issue any kind of orders. If a citizen who is by profession a servant of the cult – for example, a bishop – refers to the 'regulations' of one of the confessions – for example, the canons – and issues an order to other citizens who are perhaps servants of the same confession – priests, for example – then, according to the Bolsheviks he reveals himself to be a criminal for encroaching upon the freedom of these citizens and for violating the State monopoly by issuing such orders, and for attempting to establish organized associations forbidden by the State. For this they are subjected to criminal punishment. And if citizens are found who confess of similar orders issuing from the servant of the cult, then they too are subjected to repressions – for, on the one hand, revealing their participation in such an illegal association, and on the other for revealing socially 'retarded', and therefore dangerous, ideas. They are thus so damaged by 'religious prejudices' that they imagine themselves obliged to submit to certain orders, issuing not from the State authority but from the servants of the cult, to whom, on account of a harmful misunderstanding, they ascribe special properties, rights, and titles – especially to the bishops.

Bearing in mind the above, legally a bishop did not have any kind of flock and, in particular, any clergymen under his authority. He did not have the right to issue any sort of orders in his diocese. According to the law, the groups of twenty were completely independent of him and between them there were no ties of an organizational relationship. They voluntarily belonged to the 'Tikhonite orientation', but they had no right to draw any juridicial conclusions from this. The result of such a system must be one of a full paralysis of episcopal authority and absolute disorder in diocesan life. And indeed, as far as the Bolsheviks were concerned, actual dioceses only existed in the imagination of the believing people – the law did not know such organizations.

It goes without saying that believers cannot assent to such a situation. And therefore all dioceses continue to exist illegally. The Bolsheviks are forced to live with this fact. They know that among the servants of the cult several of them acknowledge the bishops, and that priests and members of the twenties appeal to them for orders, receive them, and then pretend that they received no such orders. They would then take the corresponding measures according to their personal discretion. In a number of cases, especially if no one from among the believers protests, the Bolsheviks close their eyes to everything. They close their eyes, for example, when a group of twenty submits a petition to register a certain priest, or to replace him by another and so forth, by receiving an episcopal blessing for this beforehand. But it is sufficient for a trouble-maker to make a denounciation, and the very same bishop and those obedient to his orders will suffer repressions for such actions. Therefore, the realisation of episcopal authority is virtually dependent upon two conditions – on the absolute good-willed readiness of believers to support their bishop and on the mutual trust between the bishop and them – a trust which allows both him and them not to fear denunciations.

However, such a trust could never be absolute. The actualisation of episcopal authority always remained a risk. In certain instances the bishop could take such a risk, in others he could not, finding the risk to be excessively great. Therefore, espiscopal authority is often forced to be inactive; it cannot show itself consistently and evenly, and manifests itself only under favourable circumstances. In connection with this, there is an absence of regularity in the clerical work of the diocese. In general, diocesan councils, departments, and chanceries do not exist – these are all hindered by the very illegality of the diocese. There is no flow of regular correspondence concerning diocesan matters. Everything is managed by the bishop himself, who prefers to do this orally, so as not to leave any written evidence. And for this oral management of business it is required that priests or members of the twenty come to the bishop from their places. In view of the fact that the dioceses are vast, but that citizens are constrained in their movement, these trips to the bishop have the character of being more or less accidental. One had to make use of every suitable opportunity which sometimes one was forced to wait a long time for. Under such conditions, the direction of the diocese was deprived of any regularity and was transformed into a kind of continuous improvisation.

In light of the conditions described, one need not be surprised that church discipline was shaken, but that it was not altogether destroyed. The main credit in this situation belongs to the very body of believeing people who demanded from their pastors purity of faith and valid liturgical services. The Living Church movement collapsed, before all else, on account of the opposition of believers, who poured out of the Renovationist's churches. And by this censure, which led to the emptying of these churches and the impoverishment of the clergy, the believers forced the clergy and the group of twenty to consider ecclesiastical discipline, even if in a small manner.

What is more, the passive opposition of the believers turned out to be a fact of such great significance, that even the Bolsheviks had to take account of it. Not wishing to annoy the believing mass excessively, the Bolsheviks were forced to reconcile themselves with the existence of Orthodoxy and with its victory over the Renovationists and to change their tactics in the struggle with the Church significantly. It became clear that it was impossible to take the Church by an open, lightning-like assault, but it was necessary to subject her by a slow, systematic siege. This even allowed the Church, although with great losses, to survive up to the present war, having preserved within herself a small measure of organisation – i.e. to gain time and patiently await those circumstances permitting her, for well-grounded reasons, to hope for the swift destruction of Bolshevism and, together with this, for the liberation, restoration, and revival of the Church.

Feasibly to delay and slow down the destruction of the Church undertaken by the Bolsheviks, was always the main task of the Patriarchate. It strove to protect the dogmatic purity and canonical integrity of Orthodoxy, to overcome schisms, to preserve the canonically valid succession of the supreme ecclesiastical authority, to maintain the canonically valid position of the Russian Church admist the other autocephalous Churches, and to lead, in such a manner, the Church to a better future when, following the destruction of Bolshevism, the Church will be able to rise to a new life. In order to work for the fulfilment of this task, it was incumbent upon the Patriarchate, before all else, to preserve its own existence which was threatened by a great danger.

Indeed, denying the existence of the Church as a legal organization, the Bolsheviks consistently had to deny the legal existence of the Patriarchate as well. From the time of the arrest of Patriarch Tikhon (1922) the Bolsheviks entered precisely upon this path, from which they were never deflected, both from after his liberation from arrest (1923), and right up to his very death (1925). But simultaneously Bolsheviks staged the establishment of something which was of benefit to themselves – the 'Living Church' – having legalized the supreme organ of its administration. The immediate task... [of the Bolsheviks] was the replacement or absorption of Orthodoxy by the Renovationists. For this goal they made a whole series of attempts to hand over into the hands of the Renovationists the administration of the Orthodox Church. Under Patriarch Tikhon not one of these attempts succeeded. The Patriarchate, although illegal, continued to exist, and the Bolsheviks found it expedient to take this fact into account. They acted so for two reasons: (i) abroad, they referred to the existence of the Patriarchate as evidence that, despite their atheism, they supposedly did not subject the Church to persecutions; (ii) they calculated that, nevertheless, it would turn out well for them to hand over the Patriarchate into the hands of their agents the Renovationists, thus destroying the Church from within.

After the death of Patriarch Tikhon, and under the locum-tenens Metropolitan Peter (1925), the Bolsheviks continued their attempts in this direction, but they did not achieve success. Metropolitan Peter was banished to Siberia by the Bolsheviks and shortly afterwards died in exile. But before his arrest he succeeded in appointing a successor to himself in the person of Metropolitan Sergii. The latter, having shown himself to be somewhat unyielding, was imprisoned (1926). But before his arrest he providently appointed a whole row of successors, who had to consecutively take upon themselves the responsibility of the leadership of the Church. However, the

Bolsheviks began to subject one after another of them to arrest, so that the Church lived without a leader and her business fell into total confusion. This was the period when the Patriarchate simply did not exist at all, but what did exist – and this legally – was the Renovationist administration, to which, however, the Orthodox Church did not submit herself.

This situation turned out to be awkward for the Bolsheviks themselves. On one side it compromised them abroad, hindering their success in propaganda there. On the other side the Bolsheviks were convinced of the weakness of Renovationism, of its unacceptability for stifling the majority of the Orthodox, of the impossibility of controlling the Orthodox Church with the help of the Renovationists. Therefore, the Bolsheviks decided to enter into a compromise with Metropolitan Sergii, who, from his side, also came to the conclusion that a compromise was necessary for the restoration of the canonical administration of the Church, and her liberation from the domination of the Renovationists. This compromise took place in 1927, and included Metropolitan Sergii's declaration that the loyalty of believers to the Soviet State was an obligation (Patriarch Tikhon had declared this earlier). The Bolsheviks registered the Patriarchate as a legal institution, abandoning all attempts to hand it over to the Renovationists. [This followed the] release of Metropolitan Sergii from prison, which granted him the possibility of fulfilling his responsibility as the Patriarchal locum-tenens.

Thus, the price of the political declaration of Metropolitan Sergii was paid for by the legalisation of the Patriarchate and the liberation of the Church from Renovationist domination. It was according to this model that further relationships between the Patriarchate and the Soviet State were built. When the Bolsheviks demanded certain political steps from Metropolitan Sergii, he accepted their demands only on the condition of this or that indulgence for the Church. I will relate an especially clear example. In 1930 Metropolitan Sergii was forced to grant an interview to foreign journalists, and according to the demands of the Bolsheviks he was to announce in this interview that the Church in the Soviet Union was completely free and not subjected to persecution. Metropolitan Sergii agreed to fulfil this demand of the Bolsheviks on the condition that Orthodox priests would not be subjected to the dispossession of the *kulaks*, such as was happening at that time, and this condition was actually fulfilled by the Bolsheviks. At the cost of this humiliating interview (during which agents of the GPU stood listening behind a wall), Metropolitan Sergii saved many village priests – at that time they still numbered around ten thousand – from destruction and death.

This example reveals that the Soviet authorities and the Patriarchate opposed each other as two hostile powers, forced – each for their reasons – to enter into a mutual compromise. But the Bolsheviks clearly carried more weight in the compromise. With time this has become ever more obvious. Having at first agreed to this compromise, and to certain concessions to the Church, the Bolsheviks subsequently deceived the Patriarchate, making these concessions illusory. Thus, no longer treating the rural clergy as dispossessed *kulkas*, and after an interval of time, the Bolsheviks simply began sending clergymen into exile in great numbers and closing churches under the pretence of certain legalities – most often for non-payment of a deliberately back-breaking tax. It must be said that the very legalization of the Patriarchate did not justify, in practice, those original expectations, since it was only the Patriarchate which became legalized.

This resulted in an absolutely paradoxical situation: the Patriarchate turned out to be the legal organ of an illegal organization. The Patriarchate was enabled to speak in the name of an unacknowledged Church and to legally issue orders which, however, were not juridically obligatory. The parish clergy and the groups of twenty preserved the full possibility to ignore the Patriarchate if they so chose. Neither the groups of twenty, nor the parish clergy of the individual churches, were formally subjected to the Patriarchate. They all remained under the exclusive authority of the corresponding local commissions of the cults, with which the patriarchate could not communicate.

What has been said applies equally well, to the episcopacy. A bishop, even though he belonged to the structure of the Patriarchate – including, evidently, the locum-tenens of the Patriarchal throne himself – was subjected, as was every 'servant of the cult', to be registered for a particular church, for which he had to apply to the corresponding commission of the cults. Therefore, without the agreement of the commission of the cults not a single bishop could be appointed, transferred, dismissed – not to mention the fact that every one of them could at any time be imprisoned and exiled. The bishops, including those of the inner structure of the Patriarchate, were held fast in the grip of the Bolsheviks.

Working in the Patriarchate, we compared our position with the position of chickens in a kitchen garden. The cook snatches his next victim from them – one today, another tomorrow, but not all immediately. We understood perfectly well that the Bolsheviks tolerated the existence of the Patriarchate only for the sake of its own advantage, primarily propagandistic, and that we were forced to be the almost powerless spectators of the continuous suffocation of the Church by the Bolsheviks. But, for the sake of the Church, we were all reconciled to our humiliating position, hoping in her ultimate invincibility and trying to preserve her until better times – until the downfall of Bolshevism.

In this, we were strengthened by the realization that the believing people, by willingly submitting to our authority, themselves helped us to maintain on a canonical foundation a certain minimal order in the Church, not allowing her to crumble. This submission to the direction of the Patriarchate could not be imputed to the believers as an illegal act because the Bolsheviks themselves legalized the Patriarchate. The Patriarchate remained the sole legalized organ of ecclesiastical administration, and therefore only the Patriarchate preserved the possibility to rightly order the life of the Church and hinder destruction by the Bolsheviks. We did not want this opportunity to escape us, because we saw in it a definite practical value, the repudiation of which, in our judgement, the Church should not have allowed.

Even now I think that we did not err in this regard. But all of our efforts, sufferings, and humiliations will turn out to be, of course, in vain, if godless Bolshevism does not fall. With its fall are tied all the hopes of the Orthodox Russian people. I believe that the Lord will not confound our hopes.

The Patriarchal Exarch – Metropolitan Sergii
A true copy of the original

Appendix 2

The following material consists of selected examples of trials and imprisonments for religious convictions in the USSR in the course of (approximately) the last five years. The illustrations were chosen from most of the existing religious faiths there, and the writer was careful to select only those cases where it was obvious that the victim was prosecuted for his or her active faith alone. The list is by no means complete, but only includes some characteristic examples of cases of blatant religious persecutions, illustrating what kind of religious activities are subjected to persecutions and under which pretexts.

List of abbreviations used throughout this section:

gen.	= general
ord.	= ordinary
str.	= strict
C.C.	= Criminal Code
ECB	= Evangelical Christian Baptist
r.	= roubles
VSASD	= All-Union Council of Seventh Day Adventists
yrs	= years
——,	= in place of surname same surname and direct relative of previous entry.

The following is a list of Articles referred to (summaries only, for full text refer to the Code) in the case histories.
Note that all Articles in the text refer to the Criminal Code of the RSFSR unless otherwise noted.

From the Criminal Code of the RSFSR:

   70   Anti-Soviet Agitation and Propaganda
        Agitation or propaganda, carried out for the purposes of undermining or weakening the Soviet government ... the spreading for the same purposes slanderous ideas, harmful to the Soviet governmental or social order, or the distribution or preparation or retainment for the same purposes of literature of harmful content.
  142   The Breaking of the Laws on the Separation of Church and State and Schools and Church.
  162   Involvement in Forbidden Production.
  188   Attempted Escape From Place of Imprisonment or From Under Guard.
  188–3 'Malicious' breaches of camp/prison discipline punishable by up to three years' additional imprisonment without release. Adopted on 1 October 1983.
  190–1 Distribution of Known False Ideas, Harmful to the Soviet Govermental or Social Order.

	Systematic distribution in oral form of ideas known to be false, harmful to the Soviet governmental or social order, or the preparation or distribution in written, printed or any other form of items of similar content.
206	Hooliganism ... purposeful actions, which vulgarly break the civic peace and which express an obvious disrespect to society.
209	Systematic Vagrancy or Begging.
214	Breaking the Safety Regulations Concerning Excavation Work.
227	Encroachment Upon a Person and a Citizen's Rights Under the Guise of Fulfilling Religious Practices The organization or leading of a group, whose actions carried out under the guise of performing religious acts, are aimed at bringing harm to health of citizens, or at inciting citizens to revoke their social participation or refuse to fulfil their civic obligations, or the recruitment into such a group of people who are not of legal age.

From the Criminal Code of the UkSSR:

62	Anti-Soviet Agitation and Propaganda (see Article 70 of the C.C. of the RSFSR).
138	The Breaking of the Laws on the Separation of Church and State and School and Church (equivalent to Article 142 C.C., RSFSR).
187	The Non-Reporting of Criminal Acts The non-reporting of clearly known preparations for or execution of criminal acts, which are covered by the following Articles ...
188	Resistance Against the Authorities or Representatives of Society who are Defending the Social Order.
209	Encroachment Upon a Person and a Citizen's Rights Under the Guise of Fulfilling Religious Practices (equivalent to Article 227 C.C., RSFSR).
214	Systematic Vagrancy or Begging (equivalent to Article 209 C.C., RSFSR).

From the Criminal Code of the LatSSR:

65	Anti-Soviet Agitation or Propaganda (Equivalent to Article 70 C.C., RSFSR).

ABRAMOV, Mikhail   Jewish   Moscow
15 July 1983 – arrested and sentenced to 15 days' imprisonment for gathering with Mark FEL'DMAN and Igor BRISKMAN for private prayers in their own homes.

AKHTEROV, Pavel A.   Pentecostal   Slavyansk   b. 1931
Author of religious texts, including *On the Path to Eternal Life* (published in

the West). Dec. 1981 sentenced to 7 yrs str. regime camp and 5 yrs exile under article 70, for writing and distributing his book *On the Path* . . .

ANDREI, Fr. (Anatolii SHUR) Orthodox previously a monk at the Pochaevskaia Lavra. Nov. 1982 arrested and sentenced to 1 yr str. regime camp under article 214. Released Nov. 1983. Rearrested Jan. 1984. The charge and sentence remain unknown.

ANTONOV, Ivan Ia., Presbyter, ECB Kirovograd, UkSSR
July 1981 completed a 2 yr sentence, having spent a total of 15 yrs in camps for religious reasons. Began receiving 'anonymous' death threats. May 1982 arrested again, sentenced to 5 yrs str. regime camp and 5 yrs. exile, with confiscation of property, under article 209–1 of the C.C. of the UkSSR. His son Pavel was also sentenced to 3 yrs gen. regime camp under article 138–2 of the C.C. of the UkSSR. He was arrested in Feb. of 1982. In May 1986 informed of new charges awaiting him before the 1987 release date.

ASATIAN, Fr. Ioakim Orthodox Shio-Mgvim, Georgia
7 Jan. 1982. He went to the Mamukelashvili museum/church in order to serve the Christmas mass for which he had official written permission. The museum's staff, however, beat up Fr. Ioakim and locked him in the temple. Had not passers-by heard his pleas for help and freed him, Fr. Ioakim would have most likely frozen to death.

BAHOLDIN, Semen F. VSASD Tashkent, UzSSr b. 1930
An ordinary worker, engaged all his life in manual labour. He was chosen by the authorities to be their witness against the head of the VSASD church – V. A. Shelkov. Semen was thus arrested on 15 April 1978. Despite threats, he refused to bear false witness against Shelkov; the authorities thus decided to make an example out of him. Before and after his conviction he spent many days in isolation, often without food or water. In Feb. of 1979 he was sentenced to 7 yrs str. regime camp and 3 yrs exile. Despite being in perfect health at the time of his arrest, in their desire to make an example out of Semen, the authorities quickly drove him to a state of exhaustion. When his wife visited him in March 1980, he was already so weak that he had to be carried. Witnesses told Semen's family that he was feeling well on November 10. He ate a full dinner at the prison hospital after which he suffered severe pain and died. Six days passed before camp officials informed relatives of the death. Semen's son and two sisters went to the camp to discover that he had already been buried; the doctors refused to give reasons for the death and refused to allow Semen's body to be moved to his native town. The official death certificate states that Semen died in Tashkent, and not in the camp (over 2000 km away).

BARATS, Vasilii M. Pentecostal Moscow
Editor of *Listy*, a Christian journal. Despite being an engineer he could not find work and was forced to accept a job as a guard at a garage. He kept this job for two months until the KGB forcibly took him to a psychiatric hospital for three days and had him fired. 3 June 1982, had his home searched, religious literature confiscated. 9 Aug. 1982, arrested while attempting to board an airplane. He was beaten at the airport and at the police station. Vasillii declared a hunger strike, which he maintained for thirteen days, demanding to know the reason for his arrest. It was not until Aug. 23 that

his wife was told where her husband was being held, yet still no pretext for the arrest was given. When his wife attempted to meet with Western correspondents she was also arrested. Vasilii is now serving a 5 yr camp sentence. His wife, Galina, is serving a 6 yr camp and 3 yr exile sentence.

BARINOV, Valerii A.   Baptist   Leningrad   b. 1944

17 Jan. 1983, officially requested permission to perform concerts of religious non-political music with his band 'Trubny Zov'. 24 Jan. 1983, temporarily arrested, ten letters and three cassettes were confiscated, no pretext given. Summer 1983, under governmental pressure, the official Baptist church kicked him out for wearing a cross with his jeans and for preaching to alcoholics, drug addicts, prostitutes and other undesirables. 11 Oct. 1983, picked up on the subway and forcibly interned in a psychiatric hospital. His wife was told by his doctor that although Valerii was not 'really ill', his views were so deviant from the 'norm of a Soviet man' that he must be treated. Other doctors told his wife that he was perfectly healthy but that his release was subject to the approval of a 'special commission'. After his case received wide Western publicity, Valerii was released on Dec. 20, but he refused to return as an outpatient for subsequent 'treatments'. In early March 1984, a visitor, claiming to be a fan from Murmansk, came to Valerii. He convinced him to come to Murmansk, which Valerii and his friend TIMIKHIN did on 3 March. Returning from Murmansk by train they were arrested and charged for supposedly attempting to leave the country illegally via Murmansk. Valerii was sentenced to 2½ yrs camp, despite the fact that the trial did not prove the charge, but rather focused on Valerii's activity in his Christian rock group, at the last performance of which, at the end of 1983, 80 people were arrested when police attempted to disband it. Released on schedule, 4 September 1986.

BATURIN, Nikolai G.   ECB   Shakhty, Rostov prov. RSFSR   b. 1927

Secretary of the ECB churches, arrested 5 Nov. 1979. Sentenced to 5 yrs camp, str. regime, under articles 138–2, 187–1, 209–2 of the UkSSR C.C., and 190–1 of the RSFSR C.C. During 1981 he was twice thrown into punishment cells for 15 days for praying and singing Christian hymns. The punishment cells are unheated, the prisoners are left without shoes or outer clothes. They are served one meagre meal a day – beginning only on the second day. After a term in the punishment cell the prisoner is usually too weak to stand, yet he is required to return immediately to work and fulfil his full quota. With one yr left on his sentence, Nikolai was rearrested in camp on 28 Sept. 1983. On 26 Jan. 1984, he was given an additional 3 yrs of str. regime camp. This was his 7th trial.

BIELAUSKIENE, Jadvyga   Lith. Catholic

May 1983, sentenced to 4 yrs str. regime camp and 3 yrs exile: for collecting signatures for a petition against the persecution of young believers; for her participation in the *Chronicle of the Lith. Cath. Ch.*; and for assisting in the religious education of children. Jadvyga had already spent 8 yrs in prisons. Released in October 1986 unconditionally. Exile term cancelled.

BUDZINS'KYI, Fr. Hryhorii,   Ukr. Catholic   b. 1900

Has spent many years in prisons and camps, and he continues to be harassed. On 24 Sept. 1981, he was fined 50 roubles; on 14 Jan. 1982, 10 r.; on 21 and 28 Jan. 1982, on 13 Jan., 17 Feb. and 5 May 1983, he was fined 50

r. each time. All of the fines were for performing an unauthorized religious service at his home. In Dec. 1983, 'thieves' broke into his home and robbed him of 270 r. The 'thieves' acted openly and without fear despite the fact that Fr. Hryhorii's home is subjected to 24 hr police surveillance.

BULAKH, Eduard   Pentecostal   b. 1941
He has a wife and three children, which, under Soviet law, automatically exempts him from military service. In Feb. 1981, Eduard was called up for a review. During the review the doctor ordered him to submit himself to a psychiatric hospital for 'evaluation'. Eduard, fearing imprisonment, refused to do so. On July 11 he was forcibly hospitalized but was released on the 22nd. On 9 Sept. 1981, he was sentenced to 1 yr of prison for 'evading military service' (refusing to submit himself to psychiatric evaluation). When his 1 yr term had officially ended, in Sept. of 1982, Eduard received an additional 2½ year term. Released in December 1984, nine months prior to the end of the term.

BURDIUG, Viktor   Orthodox   Moscow
April 6, 1982, arrested with Nikolai BLOKHIN, and Sergei and Vladimir BUDAROV. Viktor was sentenced to 4 yrs camp, with confiscation of all personal property, his three companions received terms of 3 yrs each. They were found guilty, under article 162, of printing and distributing very large quantities of Bibles, Psalm books, and prayer books.

DEMBITSKY, A. S.   VSASD   Riga
On 7 June 1980, 30 people gathered at the home of V. I. DURGUZHIENE for private workshop. The KGB arrived, without a warrant they searched the house, and took away nine males, who were all beaten. At the police station they were ordered to sign previously written confessions admitting 'their presence at an illegal gathering of unregistered believers, and promising never to repeat the offence'. The nine males refused, and demanded to write their own statements. This they were denied but 7 of them were released. Dembitskiy and G. E. Nikolaev continued to be held. Nikolaev was thrown into a cell with common criminals who were instructed to 'work him over'. When the lieutenant returned to find that Nikolaev had not been 'worked over' he informed the other criminals that they would not receive hot food, and then he proceeded to beat Nikolaev himself. Nikolaev and Dembitskiy were both sentenced to 15 days' imprisonment for singing 'anti-Soviet' hymns (Christian), for yelling 'anti-Soviet' slogans and for general 'hooliganism' at their worship service.

DRUK, V. F.   ECB   Nizhnii-Marineshty, Moldavia
Drafted into the army. 13 Aug. 1981, with two months left to his mandatory military service, he was stabbed in the heart by another soldier, under the orders of an officer. Druk was killed.

ESIP, Roman   Ukr. Cathol. priest   b. 1951
Sentenced in L'vov 28 Oct. 1981 to 5 yrs camp. gen. regime and 3 yrs exile, with confiscation of property, under articles 138−2 and 209−1 of the UkSSR C.C., for carrying out unauthorized religious services at people's homes, cemeteries and in churches.

FEDOTOV, Ivan   Pentecostal, Bishop   Maloiaroslavets, Kaluga prov.   b. 1929
1980 − released after 10 yr term. Not permitted to reside in Moscow with his mother, moved to Maloiaroslavets. 26 Nov. 1980, due to pressure from the

authorities he was fired from his job, despite the fact that he had nothing but positive references. The authorities informed him that if he could not find new employment he would be tried for parasitism. 27 Nov. 1980, fined 50 r. for refusing a policeman entry into a private home during a religious service. 21 April 1981, arrested. Searches conducted in connection with his arrest at the homes of 7 other believers as well as Fedotov's home revealed Bibles, religious literature and letters from abroad. Fedotov was entenced to 5 yrs str. regime camp and given a 1000 r. fine, under article 227. At the trial his crimes were revealed to be (i) that he headed a scet of Pentecostals whose membership included those who were not trade-union members (11 out of 129 parishioners), even though membership in trade unions is supposed to be 'voluntary' in the Soviet Union, (ii) that he had attracted others into the sect, and (iii) that he encouraged his parishioners to renege upon their civic duties (this was not proved). Released on 21 April 1986.

GALETSKY, Rostislav N.   VSASD, preacher   Tresviatskaia station, Voronezh prov.

1 July 1980, arrested. Sentenced to 5 yrs gen. regime camp under articles 190–1 and 227. During the trial he had all his notes confiscated, with which he was attempting to defend himself and expose the fabrication of the trial.

GRIGOROVICH, Stefani   Ukr. -Cath. priest   Mukachevo, Svaliavskoe distr.

Has already served 4 sentences. Fr. Stefanii and his daughter Katrusia returned their passports. Katrusia was dismissed from her 5th yr of medical school. 7 March 1984, they were both arrested and held for three days until they accepted their passports again. 18 March, 1984, Fr. Stefanii was rearrested.

IVANOV, Arkady   Christian   b. 1931

1 Sept. 1983 – declared 'dangerous to society' for teaching religion to children, holding prayer meetings, organizing a youth choir, and participating in worship services. Ivanov was confined to a psychiatric hospital. Released in Sept. 1985.

IVASHCHENKO, Yakov Efremovich   Pastor, ECB   Petrovsk, Kiev prov.   b. 1932

Member of G. Vins and Soviet Relatives of Prisoners organizations. Early in 1980 a series of searches resulted in the confiscation of religious literature. After these searches Ivashchenko went into hiding and was not arrested until 22 May 1981. On 19 August 1981 he was tried and sentenced to 4 yrs str. regime camp and 4 yrs exile under articles 138–1, 187–1 and 209–1 of the C.C. of the UkSSR. His son, Anatoly, is also an active religious youth leader and has also been sentenced to 2½ yr sentence.

KADUK, Vera Stepanovna   VSASD   Kalinin RSFSR   b. 1927

Arrested 16 July 1980, kept imprisoned until her trial in March of 1981. Sentenced to 2 yrs camp with confiscation of home and property under article 190–1.

KAKAVTSIV, Vasilli   Ukr. -Catholic, priest   L'vov   b. 1934

Sentenced to 5 yrs camp gen. regime and 3 yrs exile with confiscation of property under articles 138–2 and 209–1 of the C.C. of the UkSSR, for unauthorized performance of religious services at private homes, at cemeteries, and in churches.

KALIASHIN, Aleksei Aleksandrovich   ECB   Muron, Vladimir prov., RSFSR   b. 1955
Arrested 1 Sept. 1981, sentenced to 3 yrs camp gen. regime, under article 142–2. During his imprisonment Kaliashin refused to renounce his faith. When he was due to be released his family travelled to the camp to meet him. In Dec. 1984 sentenced to further 2½ yrs without release. 10 June 1985 married in camp.

KHOREV, Mikhail   ECB   b. 1931
Arrested in January of 1980 and sentenced to 5 yrs camp. The history of his imprisonment is one of constant harassment: he is ceaselessly subjected to night searches and gets woken up every hour; his visitation rights are often suspended; in 1981 he was thrown into a punishment cell for 10 days for reading the Bible. The prison authorities responded to his demands for a Bible by saying that, 'that is the same thing as giving vodka to a drunk'. Khorev is nearly totally blind and after his magnifying glass was removed from him he was unable to read or write. On 7 June 1984, he was given 15 days in a punishment cell for not greeting an officer – most likely due to his blindness. To these 15 days were first added 8 then another 9 days for 'spreading slanderous thoughts'. In July Khorev was sentenced to an additional two months of punishment – in total he spent over 100 days and nights in punishment cells during the summer of 1984. In late 1984 money was 'found' among his possessions – a violation of camp regulations. For this Khorev was sentenced to an additional 2 yrs str. regime camp on 28 January 1985, when his current term was supposed to have expired.

KHRAPOV, Nikolai   pastor, ECB   b. 1914
One of ten members of the Council of Churches of the ECB Church. Died 9 Nov. 1982, while serving a 3 yr str. regime camp sentence which he had begun in March of 1980. Over his lifetime, Khrapov was sentenced to a total of 50 yrs imprisonment.

KLIMUK, Pavel   Baptist
Christian poet, published in the Baptist *Herald of Truth*. Arrested in Jan. 1983 in L'vov and sentenced to 5 yrs camp under article 209–2 of the C.C. of the UkSSR. His trial was suspended six times to allow the prosecution to strengthen its case.

KOBRYN, Vasyl'   Ukr. Catholic   L'vov prov.   b. 1938
In 1983 he became the chairman of the Action Group for the Defence of the Rights of Believers and the Church in the Ukraine. On 22 June 1984 he was called out for a 'meeting' by the authorities. He was told to cease all his human rights activities 'for the last time', as any Catholic activity in the USSR is by its nature anti-Soviet. Kobryn was further told that the Action Group would be liquidated, and that 'all those who are with Rome are against us'. On 22 March 1985 he was sentenced to 3 yrs camp, gen. regime, under article 187–1 of the C.C. of the UkSSR.

KOLOPOVETS, Ivan   Dolgoe, Zakarpatia prov.
Member of a group which put on Christmas performances. On 6 Jan. (Christmas Eve according to the Old Calender) 1984 he was arrested while singing Christmas carols; other members of his group were beaten. Ivan was sentenced to 2 yrs health-hazardous forced labour.

KOZOREZOV, Aleksei Trofimovich ECB Voroshilovgrad, UkSSR b. 1933
Father of ten. Arrested 26 Dec. 1980, sentenced to 3 yrs camp, str. regime under articles 138–2 and 187–1 of the C.C. of the UkSSR. 20 Dec. 1983, as his term was almost completed, he was rearrested in camp and sentenced to an additional 1½ yrs on 12 March 1984, under article 187–1 of the C.C. of the UkSSR. This brought the total number of trials that Kozorezov has been subjected to to five. Upon completion of this last term, on 20 June 1985, he was released.

——, Aleksandra Timofeevna – wife of Aleksei b. 1936
Previously received a 3 yr suspended sentence. Chairman of the Soviet of Relatives of Evangelical Christian Baptists Prisoners. On 20 April 1982 she was attending a meeting of the Soviet of Relatives in Lozov, Khar'kov prov., UkSSr. The meeting was broken up by the authorities and seven people were arrested including Aleksandra. Upon her husband's release, in 1985, their house was searched and Aleksandra went underground so as to avoid arrest.

KRAHMAL'NIKOV, Zoia Orthodox b. 1929
Wife of F. G. SVETOV. Edited and compiled ten issues of the Christian journal *Nadezhda* (Hope). Although the authorities never expressed their opinions towards *Nadezhda* as being legal or illegal, nevertheless, on 3 Aug. 1982, Zoia was arrested. Searches at various private homes resulted in confiscation of Bibles, religious and philosophical books, her and her husband's archive of published and unpublished works, and two typewriters. In April 1983, Zoia was tried and then sentenced to 1 yr imprisonment and 5 yrs exile under article 190–1. She is serving her exile in Altai, where she lives in a small hut with no running water. She has to obtain her own wood for heating, grows vegetables. Dentists are unobtainable. Zoia is constantly 'visited' by the authorities, and although she was granted permission to travel to Moscow to seek medical attention, the permission was revoked shortly prior to her departure.

KRIUCHKOV, Gennady K. ECB pastor Tula
In 1965 he became the Chairman of the Soviet of Churches of ECB. Since 1970 Gennady has been living in hiding; as a result his family is subjected to constant persecution. The family, consisting of 15 members lived in a four-room (plus kitchen), one-bathroom house. In 1982 half the house was torn down by the authorities and Kriuchkov's wife is threatened with arrest as she attempts to rebuild the home.

KUZNETSOV. Nikolai Pentecostal Riazan' prov.
On 15 March 1981, Nikolai gathered with Nikolai KOSTIANOI, and Evgeniia NOZDRACHEVA at the home of PODOL'SKY in Riazhsk-Posadsky for private prayers. The police arrived and ordered the prayers stopped; they took down the names of those present and demanded that they all should proceed to the police station with them. The believers refused, as they had not been charged with any crime and had identified themselves. Ten more policemen arrived and dragged the three guests to the police station. Nozdracheva was fined 40 r. and Kuznetsov was given a 15-day sentence. To protest the breach of Soviet law and this insulting act

against believers, Kuznetsov declared a hunger-strike for the duration of his sentence. For this, his sentence was extended by another 15 days.

LAPAEVA, Anna Grigor'evna VSASD Solikamsk, Perm prov. RSFSR b. 1932

Anna was detained from 16 to 25 July 1980, in a psychiatric hospital in Perm. Upon her release, when she returned home, she discovered that her residence had been searched – the windows and doors had been broken, the kitchen floor was covered with dumped-out food, and everything in her home was turned over. A search warrant was never produced to Anna. After her release Anna fell gravely ill, but she was denied medical attention at all four hospitals to which she went. On 22, 25 and 19 July, Anna was called in for questioning and in August she was arrested. In November Anna was sentenced to 2 yrs camp, gen. regime.

LEPSHIN, Anna Sergeevna VSASD Kattakurgan, Samarkand prov. UzSSR

On 28 Feb. 1980, had her home searched during her absence. The search was witnessed by Anna's friend Nina I. VOROPAEVA, who was hit in the face, grabbed, and had her eyes poked. When 73-year-old Evdokiia KIREEVA, due to the excitement, became ill, the searchers prevented her relatives from administering her her medication.

LITVINENKO, Leonid Fedorovich Pentecostal

In prison camp, in the early spring of 1982, the camp guards demanded that he renounce his faith in God. He refused, and was beaten and had his ear torn off. He was left unconscious and his entire body was swollen. After regaining consciousness Leonid was refused hospitalization until he signed a statement promising not to reveal his attackers. When his wife visited him, his body was so swollen that his clothes had to be cut in order to fit over him.

LUDVIKS, Maris pastor, Latvian Evangelical Lutheran Church b. 1955

In May 1984, Maris was due to serve his first service after being ordained, when he was arrested. The exact charge remained unclear. The trial was set for 25 Dec. 1984, but was postponed indefinitely in order to 'call further witnesses'.

LYSENKO, Anatoli VSASD Novo-Pavlovka Sokuluksii distr. Frunze prov., KirgSSR b. 1951

Arrested on 14 Feb. 1980. While under investigation he was declared mentally unstable and confined to a secret psychiatric hospital.

——, Pavel L. – brother of Anatolü b. 1952

Arrested on 13 Feb. 1980 and, like his brother, also was sent to a psychiatric hospital. Pavel was also then tried and sentenced. In prison camp, for refusing to work on Saturdays on religious grounds, he is beaten, tortured, left outside in freezing temperatures, and thrown into punishment cells. On punishment rations of bread and water, he is required to fulfil his heavy manual work quotas.

MARINOVICH, Myroslav Orthodox

On 18 April 1982, in order to celebrate the Resurrection of Christ, fourteen prisoners gathered together in Permskii camp 36. Myroslav read a prayer, and then the gathering was broken up by the camp guards.

Myroslav, Viktor NEKIPELOV, and Mykola RUDENKO were each given 15 days in the punishment cell. Oles' SHEVCHENKO was deprived of his annual visit and also given 10 days' punishment.

MARKUS, Sergei Vladimirovich   Orthodox, Moscow   b. 1955
Worked in the Moscow Kolomenskoe museum of church architecture, where he organized a youth club 'Pod Shatrom' to which he lectured on Russia's cultural past. Markus also took his lectures to other cities and spoke at assorted gatherings. On 9 Jan. 1984 he was arrested. When his home was searched, all his icons, religious literature, all his family's pectoral crosses, and his Bible, were confiscated. In July 1984, he was tried and sentenced to 3 yrs camp, gen. regime, under article 190–1. At the trial it was revealed that Markus had expressed sympathy toward believers who were imprisoned in the USSR, and towards anti-Soviet actions in Poland, and that he had said that religious freedom in the USSR was minimal. Returned to Moscow in April 1986 after a public repentance over the TV system, condemning past anti-Soviet activities.

MIKULIANICH, M.   Jehovah's Witness   Grushevoe, Tiachevsk dist., Zakarpatia prov.
A search at his home revealed a Bible and religious journals including *Awake*. March 1984, he was tried and sentenced to 3 yrs camp, under article 209–1 of the C.C. of the UkSSR.

MINYAKOV, Dimitry V.   ECB, pastor   b. 1921
Unable to find employment since 1960. In 1965 Minyakov played an important role in the foundation of the Council of ECB Churches, and since then he has been one of its major leaders. Arrested on 21 Jan. 1981 and placed in solitary confinement. He was sentenced to 5 yrs camp without consideration of his state of poor physical health due to tuberculosis. During Minyakov's transport to the camp he was beaten up by the guards of the Irkutsk holding prison. Despite his poor health, he was forced to perform full work quotas throughout 1982–4; failure to meet quotas is punishable by being subjected to punishment cells. In Nov. 1984, Minyakov was finally transferred to a prison hospital for his tuberculosis. Weighing 116 lbs. he is now suspected of having lung cancer. Although Soviet law provides for the immediate release of critically ill prisoners, Minyakov remained unreleased.

MUZYKA, V. I.   ECB   Uman' Cherkassy prov.   b. 1963
Drafted in 1981, and when he was sent away from his home base he was promised that 'Alive, he would not return'. On 10 Jan. 1982, on his 52nd day of service, Muzyka was beaten to death by other soldiers.

NAPRIENKO, Veniamin   ECB, preacher   Moscow
On 18 June 1984, a farewell evening was organized for the American Council of Churches delegation at the official Moscow Baptist Church. Veniamin managed to get into the hall with his wife, Natalia, and together they held a banner in protest of the persecution of the unofficial ECB Church. The banners were torn from them, but Natalia was even able to hold a discussion with several American delegates on the persecution of the ECB Church. Three weeks later, on July 9, Veniamin was arrested and later sentenced to 2 yrs. In May 1985, Natalia was allowed a visit with Veniamin; she reported that he was not being given any of her letters and

that he had been tortured. After one beating, during which one rib was broken, Veniamin was forced to report immediately to work. Released on completion of his term in July 1986; but his and his family's harassment continues. Refused residence permit in Moscow. 15-day arrest for contravention of resid. regulations in July 1986.

OMASHVILI, Moisei   Orthod. priest   Saingilo, Azerbaidj, SSR
On 19 Dec. 1980, he was arrested, beaten and had his hair cut off for placing a candle in the closed church 'Malaia Alaverdy', the church of his forefathers. Despite the fact that there are no open churches in the area, and despite that fact that hundreds of believers have signed petitions to have this church opened, it remains closed.

PERCHATKIN, Boris   Pentecostal   Nakhodka, RSFSR
Arrested 18 Aug. 1980. Told that if he renounced his desire to emigrate and ceased all his religious activities he would receive a 100 r. fine. Perchatkin refused and was sentenced to 2 yrs camp, ord. regime, under article 190–1. On release went underground. Rearrested 21 Feb. 1983, sentenced to 18 months str. regime camps. Released on expiration of term, but placed under police surveillance. 36 years old in 1983.

PILIPCHENKO, Nikolai I.   VSASD   Vinnitsa, UkSSr
For his presence at a religious gathering in Vinnitsa on 29 Jan. 1981, he was fined 50 r.

PIVOVAROV, Fr Aleksandr   Orthodox   b. 1939
Secretary to the Archbishop of Novosibirsk. On 6 April 1962, a search at his home revealed that the priest had in his possession a Bible, prayer books, crosses, candles, and books of lives of saints. These were confiscated as well as some money and a typewriter. On 11 April 1983, Fr. Aleksandr was arrested. He was tried under articles 154– and 162–2 in the fall of 1983. The trial revealed that Fr. Aleksandr was active in assisting in the printing and distribution of religious books, and was connected with Viktor BURDDIUG and company (see BURDIUG). Fr. Aleksandr was sentenced to 3½ yrs camp, str. regime, with confiscation of property. Released in 1985, one year before the term's expiry.

PORESH, Vladimir   Orthodox, Leningrad   b. 1948
Edited the uncensored religious journal *Obshchina* and was also one of the founders of the Christian Youth Seminar, for which he performed the role of chairman at the Leningrad seminar of the 'Problems of religious rebirth in Russia'. Arrested 1 Aug. 1979. During his 9-month detainment while awaiting trial Poresh was not even permitted one visit with his wife. In April 1980, he was sentenced to 5 yrs camp. str. regime, and 3 yrs exile under article 70. In camp, Poresh had his Bible and prayer book removed; he responded by declaring a hunger strike. The authorities answered back by first suspending his right to receive packages, then his visitation rights, followed by a suspension of his correspondence rights, and finally by resorting to internment in the punishment cell. In Jan. 1982, as Poresh remained unbroken, the government tried a different tactic – he was returned to Leningrad, allowed to rest, and fed well. He was promised that if he admitted his guilt he would have his sentence lightened. Poresh remained unbroken, and new tactics were abandoned – he was now sent to the Chistopol' prison, known for its harshness. Only after a period of three

months was he permitted to write from his new prison, but his visitation rights remained suspended. His 5 yr prison term should have ended in August 1984, yet Vladimir was not released – instead he was sentenced to an additional 3 yrs imprisonment under article 188–8 for 'malicious disobedience of the orders of the administration of a corrective-labour institution'. Released in the spring of 1986 but banned from professional employment.

POTOCHNIAK, Anton   Catholic, priest   Stryi, UkSSR   b. 1912
Arrested Oct. 1983 while still recovering from a stomach operation. As a result, the operation had to be repeated in prison. He was sentenced to a 1 yr term in a str. regime camp; he had already served 28 yrs in the Soviet prison system. In the camp the warden refused to hospitalize Fr. Anton, saying he was a bad influence upon the other inmates. On 14 Dec. 1983, the warden, V. Povshenko, informed him that a new instruction had been received on how to treat Ukranian Catholics, and that from that point on he would have to fulfil the full work norm (Fr. Anton was 71 yrs old). Three days of these norms and he began suffering from internal bleeding. He was admitted into the prison hospital, but two days later, when higher camp officials discovered that he was there, he was immediately discharged from the hospital. On 29 May 1984, his health finally gave up and he died in prison.

PROTSENKO, Vladimir Antonovich   ECB   Kuz'molovo, Vsevolozhskii dist., Leningrad prov.   b. 1928
Held gatherings and services of the Leningrad ECB church at his home. Arrested 8 Dec 1981, and sentenced on 19 Feb 1982 to 3 yrs camp, gen. regime, with confiscation of home, under articles 190–1 and 227–2. Protsenko has six children, the youngest was born in 1969.

PSHONNAIA, Mariia P.   VSASD   Vinnitsky Hutor, Vinnitsa prov. UkSSR   b. 1940
On 28 Dec. 1980, believers had gathered at her home, police broke into the home, conducted a search and in the process beat up Mariia's sister, for allowing this gathering and for singing religious songs, Mariia was fined 50 r.

PUSHKOV, Evgenii N.   ECB   Hartsyzsk, Donetsk prov., UkSSR   b. 1941
Gifted violinist, pursued his beliefs as a musical minister. 1 May 1980, arrested at a peace gathering of youth and sentenced to 3 yrs camp. Released same day, only to be rearrested on 27 May 1983. Under articles 187–3, 188–1 and 209–1 of the C.C. of the UkSSR he was sentenced to 5 yrs str. regime camp, to be followed by 3 yrs exile. Pushkov has eight children, the youngest was born in 1981.

RAZDYMAKHO, Taisiia Andreeva   VSASD   Kattakurgan, Samarkand prov., UzSSR arrested in February 1980. On 28 Feb. her home was searched – the floors were ripped up and the yard was dug up; a Bible, a tape recorder, identification, a savings book and some religious literature were confiscated. There was nobody present during the search and when a fellow believer, Aleksei SPORYKHIN, rode by the house with his son on a motorcycle, and saw what was happening, he was grabbed and dragged into the yard. Aleksei, a second-class invalid, was hit and stepped on when he fell to the ground, and told to shut up when he attempted to call the neighbours for help. His son also had his mouth bloodied when he attempted to call for help. A warrant for the search has never been presented.

ROŽKALNS, Janis   Baptist   Riga, Latvian SSR
On 6 Jan. 1983, a search at his home revealed Bibles and religious literature. On 20 Jan., Janis declared his desire to emigrate to West Germany. On 13 April he was arrested. In Nov. 1983 he was tried and sentenced to 5 yrs camp. str. regime, and 3 yrs exile, under article 65 of the C.C. of the Latvian SSR – for anti-governmental behaviour. His state-appointed lawyer refused to discuss the case with him even once and Janis was prevented from cross-examining the witnesses. In transit Janis fell gravely ill, but a week passed before he was finally examined and diagnosed with advanced pneumonia. Nevertheless, he was not admitted into the prison hospital – the nurse informed him that the administration would not allow it. When he arrived at his camp, 37 – Perm', again a week passed before he received medical attention.

RUMACHIK, Petr Vasil'evich   ECB, presbyter   Dedovsk, Moscow prov.
b. 1931
Deputy and temporary chairman of the Council of ECB Churches. Also a past contributor to *Vestnik Istiny* and *Byulleten'*. Arrested 15 Aug 1980, found with various printing equipment, sentenced to 5 yrs camp, str. regime, under articles 162, 209–1 and 277–1. This was his fifth trial and he had already served 10 yrs in prison; he also suffers from very high blood pressure. After one year of imprisonment after this last trial, he has had his visitation rights suspended, he does not receive his mail and his letters to his family are either not delivered or delayed for long periods of time and heavily censored. Rearrested a week before the expiry of the sentence. On 7 Feb. 1986 sentenced to an additional 5 yr str. regime camp term in Chita (Siberia).

RYTIKOV, Pavel Timofeevich   ECB   Krasnodon, Voroshilovgrad prov., UkSSR   b. 1930
Arrested in 1979 and sentenced to 3 yrs camp for his participation in a Christian summer camp. Released in 1982, only to be rearrested on 2 April 1983 and sentenced to 2 yrs camp, str. regime, under article 214 of the C.C. of the UkSSR. Released in April 1985, upon completion of his sentence. On 1 June 1985, when police broke up a worship service, he was arrested with 8 others. After 15 days all were released except for Pavel, who was kept under arrest for another week. Upon his release he went underground to avoid arrest and a possible fourth trial. In Jan. 1986 rearrested. Sentenced in April to 1½ yrs str. regime camps for violation of administrative surveillance regs. Had ten children as of 1980.

SHAPOKA, L'onasa   Lith. Catholic, rector
On 10 Oct. 1980 his apartment was broken into and he was beaten for a period of over 4 hrs until he was killed.

SHELKOV, Vladimir Andreevich   VSASD   b. 1895
Chairman of the All-Soviet Church of the VSASD from 1949 to 1980. Was tried four times, the last time in 1979, for which he received a term of 5 yrs camp, str. regime, with confiscation of property and home. Died in the camps on 27 Jan. 1980; many consider that he was killed.

SHEVCHENKO, Oles'   Christian
Arrested 31 March 1980, and sentenced 24 Dec. 1980 to 5 yrs camp, str. regime, and 3 yrs exile, under article 62 of the C.C. of the UkSSR. Deprived of his annual visit and given 10 days punishment for his participation in an Easter celebration in April 1982 (see MARINOVICH). 10 March 1984, suffered a heart attack and lost consciousness. The guard refused to call for medical help as Oles' had already been visited by a nurse that morning. His hands turned blue, but his life was saved thanks to some liquid ammonia and glycerine tablets that another prisoner had. The next morning he was still unable to get up from his bed; for this he was punished with 15 days in the punishment cell – food only every second day.

SOLTYS, Fr. Ignatii   Ukr. Catholic
Was in prison for the following years: 1946–56, 1959–62, 1962–7, 1979–82. One month after his release in 1982 he was rearrested and sentenced to a further term of 5 yrs camp and 5 yrs exile, under article 209–2 of the C.C. of the UkSSR.

SUSHCHEVSKAIA, Ol'ga D.   Hari Krishna   Kiev
Tried late 1985/early 1986, sentenced to 3 yrs imprisonment under article 209–1 of the C.C. of the UkSSR. She was accused of organizing and leading a group whose actions 'are harmful to society'. As evidence, the government claimed that the condition of a 'mentally ill' Hari Krishna had deteriorated due to his repetition of the mantra. Konstantin GAVRILIUK, who was the Hari Krishna referred to, in his testimony denied that his condition had deteriorated, and further testified that he had been a member of the sect for a year and a half even prior to Ol'ga's conversion, therefore she should not be 'blamed'.

SVARINSKAS, Fr. Al'fonas   Catholic – Lithuanian
Member of the Catholic Committee for the Defence of Believers Rights. Arrested 25 Jan. 1983, sentenced 6 May 1983 to 7 yrs camp, str. regime, and 5 yrs exile, for 'anti-Soviet activities'.

SVETOV, F. G.   Orthodox   b. 1928
Husband of Zoia KRAHMAL'NIKOVA. Converted as an adult, has had a book of religious content published in the West (*Open Me the Doors*); suffers from asthma and a heart condition. Arrested on 23 Jan. 1985, in Moscow, on the day his daughter was giving birth, and shortly after being released from a hospital himself. Charged under article 190–1, sentenced in January 1986 to internal exile.

SVIDNITSKY, Fr. Iosif   Catholic   b. 1937
In mid-May 1985, in Novosibirsk, he was sentenced to 3 yrs imprisonment, for organizing a religious service.

TERELYA, Iosif   Catholic – Ukrainian
Founded and was the first chairman of the Action Group, in Sept. 1982, founded the Committee for the Defence of the Rights of Believers in the Ukraine; also believed to have compiled nine issues of the *Chronicle of the Catholic Church in the Ukraine* and the first issue of the *Ukrainian Catholic Herald*. Iosif had spent, up to 1982, 18 yrs in camps, prisons and psychiatric hospitals – over half of his life. After founding the Committee for the Defence of Believers Rights ... in Sept. 1982, he was arrested on 24 Dec. 1982 and sentenced to 1 yr camp, str. regime, for 'parasitism'. In

connection with the trial, searches were conducted at the homes of Iosif's relatives and friends; religious literature, books, and manuscripts were confiscated – supposedly to prove Iosif's 'parasitism'? He was duly released in Dec. 1983. On 16 Feb. 1984, the commander of the local militia paid a visit, late at night. In a drunken state he threatened to blow up Iosif's home, and displayed a package of dynamite that he had brought with him. On 8 Feb. 1985, Iosif was arrested again and charged with 'anti-Soviet activity'. In Aug. 1985 he was sentenced to 7 yrs camp and 5 yrs exile. Of 41 yrs of his life 18 have been spent in concentration camps.

TRIKUR, Mariya, Catholic
Mariya and her husband, Mikhail, have returned their passports – stating that they do not wish to have anything to do with a regime that persecutes Catholics for their faith. She has served three terms in prison, her husband has served five. Their children have been forcibly taken away from them and placed in boarding schools, where their pectoral crosses were confiscated form them. Both Mariya and her husband were arrested in Dec. 1982, and sentenced to 2 yrs imprisonment each. Both served part of their terms in psychiatric hospitals. In April 1984, Mariya was released from camp. On June 15, in the village of Dolgoe in Zakarpatia, she was attacked by a policeman in the middle of the day. Yu. Starosta dragged her through the village by her hair, to the police station, so as to have a 'chat'. He threatened her with rape and the destruction of her home.

VARRAVIN, Vitalii Fedorovich ECB Leningrad b. 1959
Arrested 19 Feb. 1982, and sentenced to 4 yrs camp, str. regime, under article 206. In 1984, in camp, he was beaten and spent 33 days in solitary confinement in one 2-month period. He was also threatened with a second term and with 'accidental death' for not 'reforming'.

VIL'CHINSKAIA, Galina V. ECB Brest, Belorussia b. 1958
Aug. 1979, she was arrested for leading Bible studies at a summer youth camp. She spent one year in prison, awaiting trial, before being sentenced to 3 yrs camp. After spending one year in the camp, performing 10 hours of heavy manual labour daily under conditions of poor nourishment and poor clothing, her hair began to fall out, she started loosing her teeth and her gums swelled up. After repeated threats of punishment if she did not 'keep quiet about God', she was beaten to a state of unconsciousness by four thugs, on 8 July 1982, who apparently acted upon orders of the camp commanders. Upon completion of her sentence in 1982, Galina was released. Police pressured her to act as a collaborator, threatening another term. She refused, and ten weeks later after her release police 'discovered' drugs in her suitcase at an airport security check. She received a 2 yr sentence. Upon completion of this sentence, when she arrived home in Nov. 1984, her parents were fined 50 r. for allowing a crowd of her friends to gather at their home to greet Galina.

YAKUNIN, Fr. Gleb Orthodox
Organized and founded the Christian Committee for the Defence of Believers Rights in the USSR in 1976. Arrested 1 Nov. 1979, and sentenced to 5 yrs camp and 5 yrs exile under article 70. In 1981 he had his Bible, prayer book and church calendar taken away from him in the prison camp (although Soviet law does not prohibit the possession of these in prison).

His Bible was returned to him only after an 80-day hunger strike. 1982 to 1984 were spent by Fr. Gleb in almost total isolation; his visitation and correspondence rights were suspended. In 1982 he was sentenced to 4 months' punishment cell for 'punishable behaviour, including the conducting of religious propaganda among youth'.

YANKOVICH, Aleksandr   Baptist   Moscow

April 1983 – given 72 hours by police to leave Moscow. He refused and was forcibly hospitalized in a psychiatric hospital. In May 1976 he had been arrested under article 190–1 and had spent the next 4 yrs forcibly interned in a psychiatric prison. He was released only in Sept. 1980

ZUEV, SERGEI V.   Hari Krishna   Moscow   b. 1953

Early 1984 sentenced to 2½ yrs imprisonment for his participation in the religious sect.

Notes and References

CHAPTER 1: THE EARLY PERSECUTIONS, 1917–21

1. For example, Nikolai Shchors and Vasili Chapaev were among such anarchistic Bolshevik leaders of semi-regular, semi-partisan forces, depicted very well in the figure of Strelnikov in Pasternak's *Doctor Zhivago*. As Pasternak mentions in the novel, most of them were quietly liquidated by Lenin towards the end of the Civil War when, like the SA in Hitler's Germany some fifteen years later, they ceased to be an asset, and became a dangerous liability to the new regime. See also: M. Zalygin, *Solenaia Pad'*, (M.: Voenizdat, 1981) *passim*; S. Golosovsky and G. Krul', *Na Manyche 'Sviashchennom'*; *Sektantskoe dvizhenie sredi molodezhy* (M.: Mol.gvard., 1931) p. 31.
2. For example, the address of the bishops imprisoned in Solovki to the Government of the USSR on the conditions of coexistence and co-operation between the Soviet State and the Orthodox Church (May 1927), Regelson, *Tragediia*, p. 422.
3. Chapaev appears to have in fact fallen in battle with the Whites, but Shchors is generally thought to have been one of the commanders killed on Lenin's or Trotsky's orders, although official Soviet sources say he was killed in battle, without saying which battle. See, *Sovetskaia istoricheskaia entsiklopediia* (M., 1976) vol. 16, pp. 388–9.
4. Regelson, *Tragediia*, p. 239; Protopresviter M. Polsky, *Novye mucheniki*, vol. 1, pp. 66–8. Polsky erroneously states that during the procession the faces of the imprisoned Tsar and his family were seen at the window of the house watching the procession. The bishop allegedly stopped and gave his benediction in the direction of that window. The point is that most of the family and the Tsar had been moved to Ekaterinburg the previous day. Soviet confirmation of the murder in: V. Arkhipenko. 'Zagovor Iliodora', *N.i rel.*, no. 9 (1968), p. 26; the excuse being his alleged 'counter-revolutionary activity'; for this reason the author justifies the murder.
5. Polsky, *Novye mucheniki*, vol. 1, pp. 77–81.
6. *Russkiie Vedomosti* (Moscow) 23 Jan./5 Feb. (1918). English translations in the N. Tsurikov Collection, *Hoover Institution Archives*, Folder B694.
7. Polsky, *Novye*, pp. 184–6.
8. Polsky, *Novye*, pp. 187–9.
9. A. A. Valentinov (ed.), *Chernaia kniga (Shturm nebes)* (no publication data, probably Paris, 1925) p. 43.
10. Ibid, pp. 50–1. Based on documents collected by allied missions attached to White Armies.
11. Polsky, *Novye mucheniki*, pp. 69–70. Regelson (*Tragediia*, p. 243) rejects Polsky's version that Andronik had been buried alive. Apparently it was another person, resembling Archb. Andronik, who had been killed in this manner. See also, M. Manuil, *Russkie . . . ierarkhi* vol. 1, pp. 256–8,

and vol. 2, pp. 85–8. Regelson's version is based on a report in the local diocesan journal of the time. He also cites notes for a sermon found in Andronik's papers which illustrate his premonitions of martyrdom:

1. I am happy to be put on trial in the name of Christ and for the Church...
2. Counter-revolution, politics – this is none of my business; for Russia... will not be saved by our squabbles and despair.
3. But the cause of the Church is sacred to me. Calling on everybody, I excommunicate, anathematize those who have risen against Jesus, who are attacking the Church...
4. Only over my dead body will you defile the sacred. This is my duty, wherefore I appeal to Christians to stand (for the Church) unto death.
5. Try me, but release the others. It is their duty to do as I say, as long as they are Christians. Otherwise anarchy, chaos... [will prevail].

Regelson, *Tragediia* 243 (from: *Tobol'skie eparkhial'nyia vedomosti*, no. 6, 1919, p. 96).
12. Polsky, *Novye mucheniki*, vol. 1, pp. 73–6.
13. Ibid, pp. 72 and 71; and Valentinov (on Nikodim), *Chernaia Kniga*, p. 36.
14. Valentinov, pp. 37, 42–3.
15. Polsky, pp. 11–24; Regelson, p. 231.
16. Polsky, pp. 81–3.
17. Valentinov, pp. 31–45.
18. Ibid, pp. 51–2.
19. Regelson, pp. 228–31.
20. Valentinov, pp. 26–7.
21. Regelson, p. 266.
22. Valentinov, p. 48.
23. Dennis J. Dunn, *The Catholic Church and the Soviet Government, 1919–1949* (N.Y.: Columbia Univ. Press; distributor: E. Europ. Monograph No. XXX, Keston Book No. 10) pp. 31–2.
24. Regelson, *Tragediia*, 226–7, 234.
25. Valentinov, p. 26.
26. Ibid, p. 42.
27. Ibid, p. 46.
28. Ibid, pp. 40–1.
29. Regelson, p. 255.
30. Ibid, p. 271. Also, N. F. Zybkovets, *Natsionalizatsiia monastyrskikh imushchestv v Sovetskoi Rossii (1917–1921)* (M.: Akademiia Nauk SSSR, 1975) pp. 110–11. He points out that the nationalization of monasteries continued on a rapid scale beyond 1921, and by 1922 722 monasteries were confiscated from the Church, leaving her theoretically with 531, but a large part of the latter was in the western territories annexed by Rumania, Poland, the Baltic states and Finland after 1918.
31. The most famous pre-revolutionary agrarian Christian communes were founded by a pious and philanthropic aristocrat, Nepluev, with the blessing of the Church. See: N. N. Nepluev, *Trudovye bratstva ... i khristianskoe gosudarstvo* (Leipzig, Germany: Beer & Hermann, 1893);

Kratkiia svedeniia o Pravoslavnom Kresto-vozdvizhenskom trudovom bratstve (Chernigov: tip. Gubernskogo pravleniia, 1905); N. N. *Nepluev, Podvizhnik zemli Russkoi* (Sergiev Posad: tip. Sv.-Tr. Sergievoi Lavry, 1908). Under the Soviets the Orthodox Church was denied the right to found such communes, even as the Evangelicals and Baptists were permitted to do so until the beginning of the mass collectivization by the state in 1929. Between then and 1933 all religious communes were disbanded by force. See: Putintsev, *Politicheskaia rol' i taktika sekt* (M., 1935) pp. 248–80; Ivan Prokhanov, *In the Cauldron of Russia, 1869–1933* (N.Y.: 1933) *passim*.
32. Regelson, p. 272.
33. Yaroslavsky's speech at the Second LMG Congress, *Razvernutym frontom* (M.: Bezbozhnik, 1929) p. 5; also Arkhipenko, n. 4 above.
34. Valentinov, p. 42.
35. Curtiss, *The Russian Church and the Soviet State*, 48–59.
36. Ibid, pp. 48–59.
37. Archb. Ioann (Shakhovskoi), *Vera i dostovernost'* (Paris, 1982) p. 27. The anonymous author of a *samizdat* manuscript on the life of a Volga priest, Fr. Sergii, also writes that the First World War caused a deterioration of relations between the people and the priests, blaming the latter's patriotism for the hardships of the war. A rumour was even circulating that priests held their savings in Germany, although 'why should they then have wanted the war', for which they were now being blamed? *Ostraia luka* (Ms., Keston College Samizdat Archives) p. 163.

As to the promised moderation towards the Church, one of the reasons for the premature closure of the 1917–18 *Sobor* was not only lack of funds but also the fact that the Soviet Government suddenly took away from the *Sobor* the building where most of its sessions were occurring. Regelson, *Tragediia*, p. 241. The era of War Communism concluded with the trials of the diocesan administration of Archangel (in Moscow) and of the Novgorod bishops (in Novgorod). The 'crime' of the former group was that they had sent a report on Bolshevik religious persecutions to the Archbishop of Canterbury; that of the latter, conducting 'counter-revolutionary propaganda' in the diocesan press. Archbishop Pavel of Arkhangelsk, and a priest and a lay secretary, were condemned to death. The absurdity of the punishment and of the 'crime' must have been evident even to the Soviets, for the death sentence was commuted to a mere five-year imprisonment. In Novgorod the trial concluded with a conditional five-year sentence meted out to Archbishop Arsenii of Novgorod and to his vicar-bishop Alexii (the future Patriarch). Regelson, pp. 271–2.
38. Prokhanov, *In the Cauldron*, pp. 175–7. He naively bought the official Soviet line, showed open hostility towards the canonical Orthodox Church, calling her 'reactionary', and much preferred the 'progressive' Renovationists, having even addressed their 'Second Sobor' of 1923 and having been presented by M. Antonin, the Renovationist leader of the time, with the huge Orthodox church of St Peter and Paul in Moscow for the use of the Evangelicals.
39. Bernhard Wilhelm, 'Moslems in the Soviet Union', *Aspects of Religion*, pp. 257–9.

CHAPTER 2: CONTEMPT AND HATE PROPAGANDA, 1919-39

1. *Revolutsiia i tserkov'*, monthly, Moscow 1919-24; circulation, around 5000 per issue. P. A. Krasikov, editor; M. V. Galkin (pseudonym: Gorev), deputy editor. The former was the head of the Department for Religious Affairs of the Soviet Commissariat of Justice and one of the chief Soviet theorists and propagandists of atheism. Gorev was a renegade Orthodox priest and a leading propagandist of atheism. The official purpose of the journal was to 'popularize the separation of Church and State among the toiling classes'.
2. *Nauka i religiia*, no. 1 (Moscow, 1922, circulation 50 000 copies).
3. *Bezbozhnik*, at first published thrice monthly, soon became a weekly newspaper: Moscow, 1922-41 (except from Jan. 1935 to March 1938, when it was not published). Emelian Yaroslavksy, ed. An illustrated journal by the same name was published from 1925 to 1941 monthly, except for 1926-32 when it was a fortnightly. Yaroslavsky was editor from 1925 to 1932 and F. Putintsev from 1933 on.
4. 'Musulmanskoe dukhovenstvo za sovetskuiu vlast', *RiTs*, no. 3-5 (1919) p. 59; reports on the resolution of the Moslem clergy congress of the Kazan' Province on full support for Soviet power and condemning counter-revolution.
5. For example, 'Vskrytie "moshchei" Tikhona Zadonskogo', 'Vskrytie... Sergiia Radonezhskogo', *RiTs*, respectively: no. 2 (1919) pp. 11-21; no. 6-8 (1919) pp. 56-60.
6. A. Volkov, 'Vskrytie moshshei Prepodobnogo Sergiia Radonezhskogo', *Nadezhda*, no. 5 (Russia: Samizdat) (reprint, Frankfurt/M.: Possev Verlag, 1981) pp. 272-89. The Vladimir story originates from the late learned Bishop-martyr Afanasii (Sakharov) who had spent over thirty years in prisons and internal exile for his faith. A monastic priest in Vladimir at the time, he was on duty during the opening of the relics of the local saints – Princes Gleb (12th c.) and George – the latter killed in a battle by the Tatars who had beheaded him by sword. Rather than allow the Soviets to do the act in the blasphemous way, Fr. Afanasii began an *akathist* service to Vladimir's saints, which led the arriving mobs to kneel, cross themselves and pray. When the relic shrines were opened, all the people present including the state authorities witnessed that the bodies of both saints lay untouched by decay; moreover, St Gleb's skin was as soft and elastic as when living, and St George's head had rejoined the body, and yet in such an irregular manner that the scar was seen and the two ends of the backbone did not fit. It was the state medical officer inspecting the bodies who later admitted his religious faith had been strengthened by the event. See, 'Krestnyi put' preosviashchennogo Afanasiia Sakharova', *VRSKhD*, no. 107 (1973) p. 178. The atheistic press, however, continued its 'unmasking' of 'fraudulent' relics for many years to come: e.g., P. Orlovets, 'Moshchi "sv." Evfrosinii', *Bezbozhnik*, no. 22 (November 1928) pp. 12-13.
7. See note 5 above; and 'Tserkovniki i ikh agenty pered narodnym

revolutsionnym sudom', *RiTs*, no. 9–12 (1920) p. 46. See also Dostoevsky's *Brothers Karamazov* episode with the decaying of the just-deceased saintly Fr. Zosima.
8. Bp. Leontii, *Political Controls over the Orthodox Church in the Soviet Union* (N.Y.: Columbia University, Butler Library, The Bakhmeteff Archives. Folder: Leontii, collection: Research Program on the USSR) pp. 11–4. Contrast M. M. Sheinman and Yaroslavsky (eds), *Antireligioznyi krest'ianskii uchebnik* (M. L.: Moskovskii rabochii, 1931) pp. 70–1; A. Zorich, '"Chudo" v Kalinovke', *My – bezbozhniki*, I. A. Flerov (ed.), (M.: Gos. antirel. izd., 1932) pp. 63–8.
9. Krasikov, 'Polozhenie tserkvi v Rossiiskoi Sovetskoi respublike', *RiTs.*, no. 1–3 (1923) p. 1.
10. 'Probuzhdaiushchaiasia derevnia', *RiTs*, no. 6–8 (1919) p. 61.
11. 'Ponemnogu osvobozhdaiutsia', *RiTs*, no. 6–8 (1919) p. 61.
12. *NiR*, no. 1 (1922) p. 1. Statements in support of confiscations by leading renovationists and their portraits are on pp. 41–51. Even in those early days the regime showed from time to time that its preference for one religion over another was only conditional and relative. *Krokodil*, the Soviet satirical journal (no. 31, 19 August 1923) makes a pun on the use of the term 'Living Church' by which the most numerous of the Renovationist factions called itself, and the 'Dead Church' of the Patriarch. It publishes a cartoon drawing of Patriarch Tikhon as a corpse with the caption 'Dead Church', and that of Bishop Antonin of the Renovationists as a half-corpse with the caption 'Half-Dead Church'.
13. Pospielovsky, *Russian Church* ..., vol. 1, ch. 3; and chapter 1 in this volume.
14. Priest Piotr Vinogradov, 'Komu anafema', 'Shuiskoe krovavoe delo'; B. Baranovsky, 'Moskovskie "ottsy" pered sudom' – all in *NiR* no. 1, pp. 36–8, 28, 29–33, respectively.
15. *NiR* no. 1 pp. 26–7.
16. *Razvernutym frontom. O zadachakh i metodakh antireligioznoi propagandy* (M.: akts. obshch. Bezbozhnik, 1929) p. 5; also my *Russian Church* ..., vol. 1, p. 39.
17. The absurdity of these assertions is more than obvious in the context of the poverty of the Russian clergy of the period in general, as a result of the colossal Soviet taxation on clergy which was not commensurate with their earnings whatsoever, and of the Renovationist rank-and-file clergy in particular because of the lack of support for the schism.
18. 'Sinagoga prispospobliaetsia', 'Obnovlentsy-obmanshchiki', 'Popy na vybor', 'Musul'manskie obnovlentsy i krest'iane' – all in *Bezbozhnik u stanka*, no. 7 (July 1927).
19. E.g.: In. Stukov, 'Udar po antisemitizmu – udar po religii i kontrrevolutsii', *Bezbust.*, no. 2 (1929) pp. 11–14.
20. The whole issue of *Bezbozh.* of 27 September 1925 is devoted to attacking Judaism and the contraposition of the Jewish proletariat and Jewish capitalists; the occasion being Yom Kipur. Also: *Koms. pr.*, no. 210 (Sept. 1929). I had a microfilm made only of the pages needed, but from mid-1929 the newspaper discontinued the printing of the date of the paper on each page, leaving only the cumulative number.

21. 'Pod flagom religii', *RiTs*, no. 6–8 (1919) pp. 94–6. See also, Pospielovsky, *Russian Church*, ch. 4.
22. 'Bezbozhnoe obozrenie', *Bezbust.*, no. 9 (1930) pp. 9–16; D. Gnezdilov, 'Rukovoditeli sektantskikh obshchin g. Saratova pered sudom obshchestvennosti', *Antireligioznik*, the monthly Scientific-Methodological Journal of the LMG Central Council, no. 1 (Jan. 1929) pp. 83–5.
23. 'Trudovoe sektantstvo', *RiTS*, no. 1–3 (1922) pp. 26–30.
24. *Bezbozhnik*, no. 1 (Jan. 1929) p. 15.
25. P. Zarin, 'Politicheskii maskarad tserkovnikov i sektantov', *Antirel.*, no. 10 (1931) pp. 9–16.
26. A. Rostovtsev, 'Kommuna "Bich"', *Bezbozh.*, no. 18 (October 1928) p. 5; Levitin, *Likhie*..., pp. 152–5.
27. For example, the following articles in the *Bezbozh.* magazine: Boitsov, 'Kulaki sektanty razvalivaiut kolkhoz' (no. 6, June 1933, p. 4) – adjacent to it is a caricature on the Virgin Mary's Assumption (whose feast is on 15 August) which allegedly wrecks the harvest gathering; Putintsev, 'Sektanty protiv kolkhoznogo urozhaia' (no. 7, 1933, pp. 6–7); P. Zarin, 'Religiozniki protiv podniatiia urozhainosti i kollektivizatsii sel'skogo khoziaistva' (no. 24, Dec. 1929, pp. 6–7); V. Shishakov, 'Religioznoe mrakobesie v bor'be s sotsialisticheskim pereustroistvom sel'skogo khoziaistva' (no. 19, October 1930, pp. 3–4); B. F-n, 'Tserkovniki protiv tret'ego bol'shevitskogo seva' (no. 5–6, March 1932, p. 17); N.G., 'Vreditel'skaia deiatel'nost' vraga za vremia uborki khleba' (no. 17–18, Sept. 1932, p. 20), etc.
28. A. Reinmarus, 'Sektantstvo v 1917 g.', *Antirel.*, no. 5 (May 1930) pp. 14–18.
29. Iv. Tregubov *et al.*, 'Sotsial'no-revolutsionnaia rol' sektantstva', and Putintsev's and editorial responses to it. *Bezbozhnik* newspaper, nos 49 (150) and 50 (151) (Dec. 1925); 'Sovremennoe sektantstvo', *Bezbozh.*, no. 11 (21 March 1926); Putintsev, 'Opyt uborki 1932 g. i zadachi bor'by s sektantstvom', *Bezbozh.*, no. 8 (1933) pp. 18–19; and his other articles in the same publication in 1933, including nos 1, 5, and especially 'Novaia taktika sekt' in no. 6, pp. 14–15; Oleshchuk, 'Otvet baptistu', *Bezbozh.*, no. 8 (Aug. 1934).
30. A. Arsharuni, 'Ideologiia sultangalievshchiny', *Antirel.*, no. 5 (May 1930) pp. 22–9.
31. See note 18 above; and Alexandre A. Benningsen and S. Enders Wimbush, *Muslim National Communism in the Soviet Union* (The University of Chicago Press, 1979) pp. 3–94.
32. Vl. Sarab'ianov, 'Piatiletkoi po religii', *Bezbozh.*, no. 21 (November 1929) p. 1.
33. See note 27 above. See also the *Bezbozh.* fortnightly, no. 3 (February 1932), where in several articles on page 19 and others, even former priests are attacked for working in the collective farm administration, while the latter are attacked for supplying a village priest with grain for food; context is: let the priests starve. See also no. 6 (June 1933) articles, 'Uborka urozhaia i bor'ba s religiei' and 'Chego stoiat prazdniki', pp. 2–3.

34. *Bezbust.*, no. 19 (1929) pp. 8–10. See also, V. Shishakov, 'Religiia i alkogolizm', *Bezbozh.*, no. 18 (Sept. 1929).
35. For example: M. Zhurakovskaia, 'Iz tserkvi – v sumasshedshii dom', *Bezbozh.*, no. 1 (1934) pp. 8–9; S. Mit-v, 'Religiia i prestupnost'', ibid, no. 9 (Sept. 1933) pp. 12–13.
36. Sidney Bloch and Peter Reddaway, *Russia's Political Hospitals* (London: Futura Publications, 1978) pp. 43–65, 220–57.
37. See Pospielovsky, *Russian Church*, ch. 12 and Chapter 7 of the current book, illustrating that this type of propaganda is a permanent feature of the Soviet ideological establishment.
38. M. Kostelovskaia (editor of *Bezbust.*), 'Ob oshibkakh v antireligioznoi propagande', *Pravda*, no. 20 (1925); E. Yaroslavsky, 'Ob oshibkakh tov. Kostelovskoi', *Bezbozh.*, no. 5 (1 Feb. 1925) pp. 2–3; Iv. Zyrianov, 'Ob antireligioznoi propagande', *Bezbozh.*, no. 46 (15 Nov. 1925); 'Stenogrammy Vtorogo plenuma TsSSVB', *Antirel.*, no. 5 (May 1930) pp. 116, 122, 126–7, etc. The last pre-congress attempt by the Moscow LMG to defend its positions against Yaroslavsky's line appeared in a *Koms. pr.* report (no. 128, 1929, early June, on the eve of the Second Congress) on the Moscow Provincial LMG Congress. It stressed that it contained 20 per cent of the All-Union membership of the organization (60 000 of 300 000) and that 60 per cent of the Moscow city and region LMG were CPSU members. It attacked the central LMG textbook for antireligious circles, for stating that Christianity was born as a religion of the urban proletariat and for having some good words on 'the toiling sectarian movement which began to fight for the Soviet power from the first days of the proletarian dictatorship'. The Moscow Congress resolved 'to take more active and decisive measures against the Orthodox and sectarian organizations' and to achieve 'a broad movement for the closure of churches'. See also Chapter 1 in this volume.
39. See note 33 above; or *Bezbust.*, no. 12 (December 1927) p. 3 – with blasphemous caricatures on the Nativity and other episodes of Christ's terrestrial life, and on Christian celebrations of the feasts. The verses under the 'Holy Family' cartoon are from *Gavriliada*, a blasphemous literary prank written by the teen-aged Pushkin.
40. *Krokodil* even calculated that over 40 000 Orthodox clergy consumed in food the equivalent of 9 per cent of peasants' state tax-in-kind (no. 7, 18 Feb. 1923); *Koms. pr.*, 1 Jan. 1929; and others.
41. See his 'Soiuz bezbozhnikov SSSR. O priemakh oskorbliaiushchikh religioznoe chuvstvo veruiushchikh', and 'Propaganda naiznanku', *Bezbozh.*, newspaper, respectively no. 25 (4 July 1926) and no. 27 (18 July 1926).
42. M. Kovalev, 'Boloto im. gospoda boga', and B. Kandidov, 'Khristos v zhivopisi – primer dlia rabov i pokrovitel' palachei', *Bezbozh.*, fortnightly, respectively no. 22 (November 1928) p. 17, and no. 17 (Sept. 1928) pp. 1–5. Kovalev confuses the ancient Assumption Cathedral in Vladimir with the nineteenth-century Kiev Cathedral of St Vladimir: he talks about the 'ugliness' of churches in the city of Vladimir, but the photograph in his article shows the interior of the Kiev cathedral with frescoes by the late nineteenth-century artist, Vasnetsov.

43. Photos with captions and comments in practically every issue of *Bezbozh.* in 1928 and 1929. For example, in 1928: no. 3, p. 17; 4, pp. 6–8. In 1929: 3, p. 6; 6, pp. 4–6; 6, p. 9; 9, pp. 10–11; 10, p. 10; etc.
44. On Loginov: n. 40 above. On schools and teachers: *Koms. pr.* 21 Febr. 1929, p. 3 etc. On Stalin: 'Poslednie resheniia partii i zadachi bezbozhnikov', *Bezbust.*, no. 2 (Feb. 1928) p. 2.
45. 'Poslednie resheniia'; Also, *Koms. pr.*, nos: 130 (June 1929) p. 4; 305 (late Nov. 1930) p. 3; 101 (late April 1931) p. 2; etc.
46. I. L., 'Interesy klassa i revolutsii vyshe zhalosti k staromu . . . Nash otvet komsomolke Kon', *Koms. pr.* (25 Apr. 1929) p. 4.
47. 'Sviataia professura', signed by a 'Neprosveshchensky', i.e. the 'Unenlightened one', *Bezbust.*, no. 3 (March 1929) pp. 6–7.
48. 'Materialy k istorii Akademii nauk', *Pamiat'*, a *samizdat* historical miscellany (Moscow, 1979) (Paris, 1981: YMCA Press) especially p. 476.
49. *Bezbust.*, no. 12 (1931) p. 19.
50. Ant. Zorsky, 'Dve demonstratsii', *Bezbozh.*, no. 8 (Feb. 1923) p. 2.
51. The 'angelic resolution' is the hymn, 'Glory to God in the Highest . . .'. See: M. Kostelovskaia, 'Khristos rozhdaetsia', *Bezbust.*, no. 12 (Dec. 1927) p. 2; 'Komsomol'skoe rozhdestvo', *Bezbozh.*, no. 11 (21 March 1926) p. 8; N. Amosov, an editorial on the LMG anti-Christmas campaign, *Bezbozh.*, fortnightly, no. 3 (Feb. 1930).
52. 'Shestvie bezbozhnikov na prazdnovanii 10-letiia Oktiabrskoi revolutsii', *Bezbozh.*, no. 5 (1928), p. 15.
53. *Koms. pr.*: 11 Apr. (1929) p. 4, 25 Apr. (1929) p. 4; 8 May (1929) p. 4; no. 101 (late April 1931) p. 2. The latter also complains that both the Orthodox and the sectarian clergy continue to attract young people to the detriment of lethargic LMG and Komsomol cells. No. 305 (late Nov. 1930) p. 3, writes that the Church and the sectarians counteract the Komsomol quite successfully with their *Khristomol* organizations. But all such religious groups were made illegal by the 1929 legislation. Does the paper infer underground activities of the Churches or is its information simply over a year outdated? Also: Oleshchuk, 'Protiv burzhuaznokulatskogo rozhdestva', *Bezbozh./illustr./*, no. 23 (Dec. 1931).
54. Oleshchuk, 'Za bol'shevitskii sev, protiv kulatskoi paskhi', *Bezbozh./newsp./*, no. 2–3 (Jan. 1933) p. 17.
55. M. Galaktionov, 'Itogi ianvarskogo plenuma TsKa i TseKaKa VKP (b)', *Bezbozh.*, no. 1 (1933) pp. 2–3; Amosov, n. 50 above.
56. Powell, *Antireligious Propaganda* . . . (a solid book otherwise), p. 38. See: 'Moskovskomu komitetu VKP (b) 'a resolution of the LMG C. Counc. which concludes by praising Stalin and 'Stalin's faithful disciple, Comrade Khrushchev', *Bezbozh.*, no. 9 (1936) p. 4. Several issues of the journal in 1939 carry a boring serialized article 'Stalin on Religion'. . . .

CHAPTER 3: PERSECUTIONS, 1921–41

1. These rebellions (including the great peasant rebellion of Siberia in the same year, the revolts of the Basmachi in Central Asia, etc.) were of more concern and embarrassment to the Bolsheviks than the war against the

Whites. The latter could be written off as 'class enemies', but the workers and peasants were the element in whose name and, allegedly, by whose efforts the Bolsheviks had seized power. Particularly embarrassing were the Kronstadt sailors who, along with the Latvian Sharp-Shooters, had been the only effective military force in bringing Lenin to power and protecting him in November 1917, and now they were demanding his and his party's resignation from power.

2. For details, see Pospielovsky: *Russian Church*, ch. 2; 'The Renovationist Schism in the Russian Orthodox Church', *Russian History*, vol. 9, parts 2–3 (1982) pp. 285–307.
3. Pospielovsky, *Russian Church*, ch. 4. Most of his new opponents protested not so much against the general posture of civic loyalty, which had been generally accepted by practically all churchmen at least since 1923, as against the mendacious assurances of the Declaration that there had never been any religious persecutions under the Soviets; these were seen as a betrayal of the martyrs.
4. Pospielovsky, *Russian Church*, ch. 3; Regelson, *Tragediia*, pp. 272–3, 278–84.
5. Regelson, p. 285.
6. Valentinov, *Shturm.*, p. 285.
7. ibid, pp. 56–77.
8. Pospielovsky, *Russian Church*, chs 2 and 3.
9. Valentinov, *Shturm.*, pp. 58–72.
10. Regelson, p. 285, cites the figures of an official Soviet author on church themes, Kandidov.
11. This was the case of the arrest of a Jewish Kiev worker, Beilis, in 1911, charged with a sadistic murder of a Christian boy. The anti-Semites tried to accuse Beilis of an alleged Jewish ritual murder of Christian children to use their blood in the preparation of *matsos*. The investigation and trial continued until 1913, when with the help of Russian Orthodox theologians it was proved that the legend of Jewish ritual murders was unfounded and that Beilis was innocent of the murder. Beilis was acquitted and released.
12. Polsky, *Mucheniki*, vol. 1, pp. 25–57 and vol. 2, pp. 293–4; Valentinov, *Shturm.*, pp. 67–8; M. Manuil, *Die russische orthodoxen Bischoefe von 1893 bis 1965. Bio-Bibliographie* (Erlangen: Oikonomia, 1981) vol. 2, pp. 142–5.
13. Valentinov, *Shturm.*, pp. 68–75. His cited examples include the sentencing of a bishop to eight years, another bishop to six years, and a church warden to eight years of imprisonment.
14. Valentinov, *Shturm.*, pp. 75–8.
15. The figures are for the period 1921 to 1923. See: Pospielovsky, *Russian Church*, ch. 1, n. 7; Polsky, *Mucheniki*, vol. 1, pp. 213–14 (details in Appendix 1); Struve, *Christians*, pp. 37–8.
16. Valentinov, *Shturm.*, p. 68.
17. Ironically, this had also been the aim of Leo Tolstoy. See, Arkhiepiskop Ioann (Shakhovskoi), *K istorii russkoi intelligentsii (Revolutsiia Tolstogo)* (New York: Ixoyc, 1975?) pp. 40, 42, *et passim*.
18. Bp. Leontii, *Political Controls over the Orthodox Church in the Soviet Union*

(New York: Columbia University, Butler Library, The Bakhmeteff Archives. Folder: Leontii. Collection: Research Program on the USSR) pp. 11–14. In more recent times the late Fr. Sergii Zheludkov was deprived of his licence to serve as priest by the Soviet authorities for having organized a pilgrimage of his parishioners to the site of an icon, or church-dome renovation. A similar case in Yugoslavia in the late 1940s resulted in the imprisonment of Fr. Valdimir Rodzianko, now Bp. Basil. The latter information was supplied by Fr. Valdimir to this author. The information on Zheludkov was supplied by Russian Orthodox Christians who had known him in the USSR.

19. 1926–8 letters from Russia in *Vestnik RSKhD*, no. 7 (July 1928) pp. 12–17; E. MacNaughten, 'Informal Report of Religious Situation in Russia', 3 October 1927, 2 (*Hoover Institution Archives*, Colton Collection, Box 6).
20. F. Svetov, 'Optina Pustyn' segodnia'; Anonymous, 'Zhizneopisanie ieromonakha Nikona'; both in *Nadezhda*, no. 8 (Russia 1981; Frankfurt 1982) pp. 10–311.
21. Polsky, *Novye*, vol. 1, pp. 203–17.
22. Pospielovsky, *Russian Church*, ch. 2; A. Levitin-Krasnov, *Likhie gody, 1925–1941* (Paris: YMCA Press, 1977) pp. 255–9; Levitin and Vadim Shavrov, *Ocherki po istorii russkoi tserkovnoi smuty* (Kuesnacht, Switzerland: Institut Glaube ind der 2 Welt, 1978) vol. 1, pp. 77–8.
23. Polsky, *Novye*, vol. 1, pp. 125–43.
24. Pospielovsky, *Russian Church*, chs 3 and 4. Regelson (*Tragediia*, p. 542) in his list of bishops arrested in 1926 forgets to include M. Sergii, Peter's locum-tenens and the future patriarch.
25. Nik. Shemetov, 'Arkhimandrit Tavrion (Batozsky)', *Vestnik RKhD*, no. 127 (Paris, 1978) pp. 253–5.
26. Regelson, *Tragediia*, pp. 568–74, particularly p. 570; MacNaughten ms., 1.
27. MacNaughten, 1–2.
28. Ibid, p. 599; Alexander Solzhenitsyn, *The Gulag Archipelago*, vols 3–4 (New York: Harper & Row, 1975) p. 72.
29. Struve, *Christians*, p. 48.
30. Regelson, *Tragediia*, pp. 534–6. The list does not include bishops and other clergy detained for short periods at a time (for less than one year).
31. Pospielovsky, *Russian Church*, ch. 2, pp. 73–6. Bp. Leontii, as an illustration of the distrust of the Ukrainian believers towards the self-proclaimed uncanonical Autocephalist Church, cites the case of the wife of M. Lypkivsky (like the Renovationists, some of the Autocephalists' bishops were married), who on her death-bed requested that a priest of the Patriarchal Orthodox Church administer the last rites to her and bury her. Her wish was fulfilled. Leontii, Political Controls 60.
32. Pospielovsky, *Russian Church*, ch. 2; Bp. Leontii, *Political* 5, pp. 23–37, and 44–65.
33. For example: Bp. Afansii (Sakharov) in *VRKhD*, no. 107, pp. 170–211; priests Piotr and Ierax, *VRKhD*, no. 124, pp. 269–98; the Elder Sampson (Sivers) in *Nadezhda*, no. 9, pp. 123–69; and others.
34. A case in point illustrating the arbitrariness of such taxes was that of The Holy Virgin Protection Church in Kiev. The authorities suddenly

declared that the church would be taxed 100 r. if a bishop served there. Then, on the eve of the Paschal night service they slapped on a 400 r. tax. The church committee refused to pay, so the state officials closed the church preventing the Easter all-night service from being celebrated. The church remained closed. MacNaughten ms., 4.
35. N. Orleansky, *Zakony o religioznykh ob'edineniakh RSFSR* (M.: Bezbozhnik, 1930) part 2, pp. 56–173.
36. Struve, *Christians*, p. 48; and Metropolitan Sergii's 1930 Memorandum to the Soviet Government protesting the hideous taxes, *inter alia* Struve, pp. 48–52. Also, a caricature on such 'unemployed' priests in rags surrounding a chapel with the caption: 'Employment Office for Pops', in *Bezbust.*, no. 18 (1929) pp. 14–15. A case in point is cited in Levitin's *Likhie* . . . , p. 72.
37. Kirill Shevich, 'Bor'ba za veru v SSSR', *VRSKhD*, vol. 1 (Jan. 1931) pp. 16–20.
38. *Vybory v sovety deputatov trudiashchikhsia* (M., 1938) pp. 49–60.
39. Chap. 2 in this volume and Shevich, 'Bor'ba . . . ' pp. 19–20.
40. Regelson, *Tragediia*, pp. 492 and 501; Levitin, *Likhie* . . . , p.210.
41. William C. Fletcher, *The Russian Orthodox Church Underground, 1917–1970* (London: Oxford University Press, 1971) pp. 51–81; Regelson, *Tragediia*, p. 477. Most probably Sergii was using early 1929 figures, because the ensuing rural chaos caused by the collectivisation precluded the procurement of any reliable statistics on the churches there, which were anyhow being closed by the thousands.
42. Levitin, *Likhie*, pp. 222–3, 245–328; Pospielovsky, *Russian Church*, ch. 5. On the liquidation of monasteries, see also: Curtiss, *Russian Church*, p. 267; Polsky, *Novye* . . . , vol. 2, pp. 168–70.
43. This is Levitin's estimate; according to another source there were no more than ten Orthodox churches in Moscow by early 1935. The discrepancy may be partly explained by the fact that Levitin, a former Renovationist, counted the seven Renovationist parishes also as Orthodox, which a strict Orthodox would not do. See: 'Rasstrel prot. A Ksenofontova i prot. N. Burdikova', *Vozrozhdenie* (A Russian Paris daily) 24 April 1936; Levitin, *Ocherki*, vol. 3, p. 346.
44. B. Sove, 'Sovremenoe polozhenie Rossiiskoi Tserkvi', *Put'*, no. 53 (April–June 1937) p. 68; data from *Izvestia*, 12 Aug. 1936, and *Pravda*. 15 Apr. 1937.
45. Levitin, *Ocherki* . . . , vol. 3, pp. 344–6.
46. Pospielovsky, 'More on Historic Preservation Policy in the USSR'. *Canadian Slavonic Papers*, vol. 17, no. 4 (Winter 1975) pp. 641–9; Polsky, *Novye* . . . , vol. 2, p. 240; Regelson, *Tragediia*, p. 505; Levitin, *Likhie*, p. 324; but in his *Ocherki* (vol. 3, pp. 344–6) Levitin contradicts himself by saying that of the Orthodox churches open in the 1920s, 95 per cent were closed by 1939, which should have left some 2000 functioning churches.
47. Regelson, *Tragediia*, pp. 550–7, 502, 557.
48. Levitin, *Likhie.*, pp. 322–3.
49. Ibid, p. 322; Kurt Hutten, *Iron Curtain Christians* (Minneapolis: Augsburg Publishing House, 1967), p. 11.
50. *Forever Flowing* (N.Y.: Harper & Row, 1972) pp. 143–4.

51. 'Chudo v Kalinovke' and other stories, see chap. 2 above.
52. *Uchebnik dlia rabochikh antireligioznykh kruzhkov* (M.: Bezbozhnik, 1930) p. 5; *Antireligioznyi krest'ianskii uchebnik* (6th edn, M.-L., 1931) pp. 8–9.
53. *Uchebnik . . . raboch.*, p. 5.
54. M. Kol'tsov, 'Kak stroiat tserkvi', *My – bezbozhniki*, pp. 44–50.
55. Z. A. Yankova, 'Sovremennoe pravoslavie i antiobshchestvennaia sushchnost' ego ideologii', *VIRiA.*, no. 11 (1963) pp. 72–80.
56. I. Blinov, 'Along the Path which Leads to the Crumbling of Religion', *Bezbozhnik*, no. 4 (20 Jan. 1931). Translated by the Russian Religious Press Service, Paris; Press release, The Bakhmeteff Russian Emigre Archives, Columbia University. Moreover, Yaroslavsky's estimate was based on the preliminary data of the discarded 1937 census, in which many believers concealed their faith out of fear, according to Fr. Polsky (*Novye . . .*, vols 2, 24) and Levitin (*Likhie*, p. 312).
57. Ya. Nemukhin, 'Perekhod k nepreryvnoi proizvodstvennoi nedele i antireligiozny front', *Bezbust.*, no. 18 (1929) p. 4; cartoon in the same issue, pp. 14–15; a similar cartoon of the failure of the feast of Christmas owing to the continuous work week, ibid, no. 2 (1930) front page.
58. *Bezbozh.*, no. 8 (1937) p. 14; no. 2 (1938) p. 13.
59. *Vybory v sovety deputatov trudiashchikhsia i antireligioznaia propaganda* (M.: Molodaia gvardiia, 1938) pp. 3–7.
60. P. Zarin, 'Religioznye obriady zaochno', *Bezbozh.*, no. 7 (1936) p. 4.
61. Polsky, *Novye . . .*, vol. 2 pp. 78–83. This is a perfect illustration of the use of the tax as a sledge-hammer to crush the Church.
62. Polsky, *Novye . . .*, vol. 2, pp. 70–126.
63. Regelson, *Tragediia*, pp. 597–600 (according to that source, Bp. Maxim was shot at the end of 1930); M. Artem'ev, 'Dva pravednika', *Vozrozhdenie*, 12 Dec. 1931; N. Shemetov, 'Pravoslavnye bratstva', *VRKhD*, no. 131 (1980) pp. 156–7.
64. For samples of his writings and encyclopaedic interests, as well as biographical and autobiographical material on him, see *VRKhD*, no. 114 (1974) pp. 149–92; no. 124 (1978) pp. 341–2; no. 135 (1981) pp. 39–96. Also see: *Bogoslovskie trudy* (M.: The Moscow Patriarchate) no. 12 (1974), no. 17 (1977), and others; *Nadezhda*, no. 7 (Russia, 1980; Frankfurt, 1982) pp. 275–97.

In his 1924 C. V. sketch, Florensky lists the following positions he has held in Soviet institutions (most of them simultaneously): 'lectures at the All-Russian Association of Engineers, the Russian Society of Electrotechnics and other associations . . . works for the All-Union Council of National Economy . . . lectures at the Superior Art Workshops and develops a course on the analysis of space . . . leads experimental work at the State Experimental Electrotechnical Institute and from 1924 is the head of the Laboratory for Material Testing there . . . is a member of the Central Electrotechnical Council . . . carries on experiments and publishes for the Special Conference on the Improvement of Production Quality'.

Among his non-theological publications were: *Analysis of Space in Art, The Number as a Form, On the Peculiarities of Flat Graph Lines . . . , Materials for the Study of the Language Spoken in the Kostroma Region, A Dictionary of*

Graphic Symbols, Lectures on an Encyclopaedia of Mathematics, The Technology of Dialectrics, Porosity of the Insulatory Ceramics and the Method of Calculation of the Surface of Irregular Bodies, Electro-integrator, etc. Florensky, 'Biographical Data', *VRKhD*, no. 135, pp. 58–9.
65. N. Sventsitskaia, 'Otets Valentin', *Nadezhda*, no. 10 (1984) pp. 183–220; Valentin Sventsitsky, 'Shest' chtenii o tainstve pokaianiia v ego istorii', and S. I. Fudel', 'U sten tserkvi', ibid, no. 2 (1979) pp. 105–78 and 233–4, respectively.
66. These are but a few typical illustrations. On Zhurakovsky: 'Sviashchennik Anatolii Zhurakovsky', *Nadezhda*, no. 10, pp. 19–82; *Sv. A. Zhurakovsky. Materialy k zhitiiu* (Paris: YMCA Press, 1984). On Mechev and his father, also a priest, who were among the most outstanding initiators and spiritual leaders of the semi-monastic and yet worldly church brotherhoods in Moscow, see, N. Shemetov, 'Pravoslavnye bratstva', *VRKhD*, no. 131 (1980) pp. 158–9.
67. Anonymous, 'Preosviashchennyi Manuil Lemeshevsky', *Vestnik RSKhD*, nos 93 and 94 (vols 3 and 4, 1969) pp. 112–29 and 154–67, respectively. His 'Who's Who' on Russian bishops, as referred to before, is being published at the time of this writing in Erlangen (West Germany) under the editorship of P. Coelestin Patock, OSA, by *Oikonomia*, at the rate of approximately one volume per annum. Levitin, *Slovo ob umershem*, MS. (M.: Samizdat, 2 June 1969).
68. Mark Popovsky, *Zhizn' i zhitie Voino-Yasentskogo, arkhiepiskopa i khirurga* (Paris: YMCA Press, 1979) pp. 595–6, 14–5, 223–8, 247–8, 299–320. Also, Arkhiep. Luka, 'Memuary', *Nadezhda*, no. 3 (1979) pp. 66–138.
69. Regelson, pp. 568–74; Pospielovsky, *Russian Church*, vol. 1, chs 4, 5 and 6; N.V.T., 'Episkop Afanasii (Sakharov)', *VRKhD*, no. 139 (1983) pp. 195–217; 'Krestny put' preosv. Afanasiia Sakharova', *VRSKhD*, no. 107 (1973) pp. 170–211.
70. Polsky, *Novye*..., vol. II, p. 148.
71. Ibid, pp. 182–3.
72. Ibid, p. 215.
73. Ibid, pp. 210–12.
74. 'Mucheniki khristianstva XX-go veka', *VRKhD*, no. 134, pp. 235–45.
75. Polsky, *Novye*..., vol. II, pp. 226–7.
76. Ibid, pp. 170–2.
77. 'Starets Sampson', *Nadezhda*, no. 9, pp. 123–69.
78. 'Matrenushka', ibid, no. 7, pp. 241–5.
79. 'The Baptist Spies. They Have Been Working for the Secret Service of Poland', *Koms. pr.*, no. 47 (26 Feb. 1929); cited from English translations ms., Colton Collection, Hoover Institution Archives, Box 6, Folder 'World Revolutions'.
80. See: Pospielovsky, *Russian Church*, vol. I, p. 178; L. Rakusheva, *Komsomol protiv religii* (L., 1939), p. 41; 'Zarubezhnaia popovshchina ...' and "Kontrrevolutsionery ... delo 'Promyshlennoi partii'", *Bezbozhnik*, no. 68 (10 Dec. 1930) pp. 1 and 2 resp. The Orthodox Church had no *officially* functioning theological institute in Leningrad in 1925, only unofficial continuing evening courses for former theology students.
81. Rakusheva, *Komsomol*..., pp. 34–45.

82. *Pravda*, no. 263 (23 Sept. 1935); translation, Colton Coll., Box 7, Folder 'Translations'.
83. 'Chernosotenets-ofitser-spekuliant-episkop', *Bezbozh.*, no. 17–18 (1932) pp. 22–3. The case is further obscured by the Patriarchate Synod's acceptance of Bishop Dometian's alleged court confession of 'crimes against chastity', suspending him until the time when he would be able to appear before an ecclesiatic court in person for a hearing on the moral issue. 'Po delu Episkopa Dometiana Gorokhova [of Arzamas]', *ZhMP*, no. 13 (1933), Paris Retyping, 3–4.
84. Rakusheva, pp. 40–1, quoting *Izvestia* of 22 Nov. 1937.
85. Ibid, p. 41. He was rearrested in 1937 and shot in 1938: 'Preosviaschennyi Manuil.', *VRSKhD*, no. 93, 124n.
86. Rakusheva, pp. 42–3.
87. *Vybory v sovety* . . . , pp. 47–8 *et passim*.
88. Levitin, *Ocherki*, vol. 3, p. 344.
89. *VRKhD*, no. 126, p. 249.
90. A list of known imprisoned bishops and priests up to 1930, dated Moscow, 10 March 1930, includes 197 bishops and 89 parish priests. The author stresses it is far from complete. It includes a description of the murder of Bp. Erofei (Afonin) on 23 April 1928. The bishop, who had a presentiment of his forthcoming arrest, was making archpastoral visits to his diocesan villages. In one of the villages the GPU arrived to arrest him. When they saw masses of villagers converging on the horse-cart in which they were hauling the bishop away, they simply shot him on the spot. Making use of the panic caused by the shooting, the GPU made a number of arrests of peasants, sentencing each to a prison or exile term, including the bishop's 16-year-old acholyte, sentenced to a three-year exile to the north. 'Spisok pravoslavnykh episkopov . . .', Ms., Nicolaevsky Collection, Hoover Inst. Archives, Box 144, Folder 1, Also: Konstantinov, *Gonimai 'tserkov'*, p. 17.

CHAPTER 4: AN 'INTERLUDE': FROM 1941 TO STALIN'S DEATH

1. Spinka, *Church in Soviet Russia*, pp. 80–87.
2. Regelson, p. 192.
3. Pospielovsky, *Russian Church*, vol. 1, chs 4 and 5, Ep. Afanasii, 'Dni i etapy moei zhizni', *Vestnik RSKhD*, no. 81 (1966) pp. 13–17; N.V.T., 'Ep. Afanasii', *Vest. RKhD*, no. 139 (1983) pp. 195–217; V.Ia. Vasilevskaia, 'Dva portreta', *V.RKhD*, no. 124 (1978) pp. 269–98; Regelson, pp. 568–74.
4. M. Polsky, *Novye mucheniki rossiiskie*, vol. 1 (Jordanville, 1949). In Regelson's *Tragediia* there are biographies of at least five other bishops who had survived into the 1940s without ever being allowed to return to their episcopal duties. Two of them, Metropolitan Kirill (Smirnov) of Kazan' and Bishop Amphilokhii (Skvortsov) never made peace with the Sergii-Alexii administration. The former died in prison or exile either in

1941 or 1944, the latter in retirement in 1946. The other three, Bishop Arkadii (Ostalsky), Archbishop Feodor (Pozdeevsky) and Bishop Gavriil (Abalymov) either made peace with the Patriarchate or had never been in opposition; yet none of them was allowed to function as a bishop: Arkadii died in the camps or exile in the 1940s, Feodor in retirement in the late 1940s, Gavriil as dean of the Balta Monastery in 1958. None of them at the time was older than many ruling bishops. Regelson, pp. 560, 566–7, 576, 577 and 604.

5. Nikolai Shemetov, 'Edinstvennaia vstrecha', *VRKhD*, no. 128 (1979) pp. 244–51.
6. V. Alexeeva, 'Vospominaniia o khrame sv. bessrebrennikov Kira i Ioanna na Solianke', *VRKhD*, no. 141 (1984) 214 n.
7. Levitin-Krasnov, 'Slovo ob umershem' (Samizdat: ms.), 1969 (?); another, incomplete, biography in *VRSKhD*, nos 93 (1969) and 94 (1969), pp. 112–29 and 154–67, resp.
8. Archb. Vasilii (Krivocheine), 'Pamiati episkopa-ispovednika', *VRKhD*, no. 116 (1975) pp. 255–9.
9. Pospielovsky, *Russian Church*, vol. 1, ch. 7; vol. 2, ch. 12.
10. Archb. Vasilii, 'Arkhiepiskop Veniamin (Novitsky)', *VRKhD*, no. 120 (1977) pp. 189–94.
11. See: Shemetov above, n. 5; and Sv. Dmitri Dudko, 'Pust' snova sazhaiut', *Posev*, no. 10 (October 1977) pp. 28–30.
12. Fr. Ilia Shmain's oral testimony to this author, Jerusalem, Israel, July 1983.
13. Pospielovsky, *Russian Church*, vol. 2, ch. 9.
14. N. Mikhailov, 'Kommunisticheskoe vospitanie molodezhi – glavnaia zadacha Komsomola', *Bol'shevik*, no. 23–24 (December 1946) pp. 11–15. He doesn't directly attack religion, but calls for an active ideological upbringing of youth, criticizing the Komsomol for relegating this function to schools and the school for limiting itself to strictly educational (informationally) functions. Also, Mark Popovsky, *Zhizn' i zhitie Voino-Yasenetskogo* (Paris: YMCA Press, 1979) pp. 414–21. By 1954 the number of open churches in Crimea was reduced to 49, despite Luka's energetic and desperate struggle. Popovsky, p. 469.

CHAPTER 5: RENEWAL OF THE INCENDIARY PROPAGANDA, 1958–85

1. 'Formirovanie nauchnogo mirovozzreniia i ateisticheskoe vospitanie', *Kommunist*, no. 1 (1964) p. 31.
2. Powell, *Antireligious . . .* , p. 87.
3. Ibid, p. 92.
4. Ibid, p. 92; G. Vasil'ev, 'Bogoslov – podstrekatel'', *NiR*, no. 10 (1966) pp. 25–6; Alla Trubnikova, 'Klikushi v pokhode', and 'Tainik v taburetke', *Oktiabr'*, no. 7 (1962) pp. 130–42, and no. 9 (1964) pp. 161–77, respectively.
5. P. Voskresensky, 'Dukhovnyi otets Vadima Shavrova', *NiR*, no. 5 (1960)

pp. 32–7. For Levitin's rebuttal, see his 'Moi otvet zhurnalu *Nauka i religiia*', (20 June 1960, *Dialog s tserkovnoi Rossiei* (Paris: Ixis 1967) pp. 43–69; E. Baller, 'Vospityvat' voinstvuiushchikh ateistov', *NiR*, no. 2 (Oct. 1959) pp. 78–9.

6. Voskresensky, 'Dukhovnyi ...', pp. 32–3; being a character assassination of the late Vadim Shavrov, a son of a Soviet general, himself a veteran and an invalid of the Second World War whom Levitin had baptized while they were in a concentration camp during Stalin's post-war purges. A. Shamaro, 'Tsvet stoiachei vody', and 'Krestonosnoe predatel'stvo', *NiR*, no. 9 (1960) pp. 45–50, and no. 3 (1961) pp. 38–43, respectively. There he attacks the clergy of the Orenburg Diocese at the time when, as he himself states, twenty-six priests have just been imprisoned; and the clergy of the Belorussian archdiocese for their alleged sell-out to the Nazis during the Second World War. In fact, the very reverse is true regarding Belorussia (see Pospielovsky, *The Russian Church*, vol. 1, ch. 7), while the Orenburg Diocese was being persecuted to frustrate the religious revival effected by its remarkable bishop-martyr, Manuil (Pospielovsky, *Russian Church*, vol. 1, pp. 58 and 111, vol. 2, ch. 10). Religious faith is again represented as a mental malaise. Edit., 'Dushevnobol'nye v roli sviatykh', *NiR*, no. 6 (1961) pp. 18–19.

7. L. Zavelev, 'Istoriia novogo Iova', *NiR*, no. 7 (July 1960) pp. 36–43; M. Khomenko, 'Zhitie vladyki Andreia', *NiR*, No. 8 (1962) pp. 62–9; V. Siuris, a former priest, 'Chomu ia zrixia dukhovnoho sanu?', *Voiovnychyi ateist*, no. 7 (July 1961) pp. 25–7; N. Kar'kov, 'K komu zhe idti ispovedovatsia?', *NiR*, no. 6 (1960) pp. 61–5. The fraudulence and fixed stereotypes of such publications and clergy character-assassinations are revealed particularly when well-known (alas, not for the average Soviet citizen) historical facts are thus twisted: for instance, the story of the 1921–2 famine and Patriarch Tikhon's attitude to it. Contrast: Unsigned, 'Padenie sviateishego patriarkha', *NiR*, no. 3 (1964) pp. 88–90; and Pospielovsky, *The Russian Church*, vol. 1, ch. 3. Attacks against Archb. Iov continued even after he had served his prison term and became a diocesan bishop once again. For example, V. Ushakov, *Pravoslavie i XX vek* (Alma-Ata: Kazakhstan, 1968) pp. 52–6. Had there been any substance in these accusations, neither of the bishops would have been reappointed soon after their release.

8. A. Osipov, 'Bitva za dushi chelovecheskie', *Oktiabr'*, no. 10 (1963) pp. 163–70.

9. 'S krestom na shee', *Lit. gaz.*, (2 Oct. 1962). Other similar slanderous material on monasteries and pilgrimages: three letters by former theology students, 'Podumaite o svoei sud'be!' and 'Dnevnik inokini', *NiR*, no. 4 (1962) pp. 27–33. Particular attacks on the Pochaev Monastery: Iu. Melmiichuk, 'V Pochaeve kolokola zvoniat', *NiR*, no. 2 (1960) pp. 57–9; O. Shamaro, 'Meshkantsi bratskoho korpusu', *Voi. at.*, no. 12 (Dec. 1961) pp. 18–24; Shamaro, 'Bessilie "chudotvornykh sviatyn"', *NiR*, no. 1 (1962) pp. 26–30; E. Maiat, I. Uzkov, 'Rushatsia monastyrskie steny', *NiR*, no. 9 (1961) pp. 22–31.

10. Levitin, *Zashchita very vs SSR* (Paris: IXΘYC, 1966) pp. 32–62.

11. 'Klikushi...', pp. 138–42. There is also an implied attack on the Church

Establishment when the author states that the Church only pretends not to render direct support to pilgrimages (p. 142). The decree in question is dated 16 March 1961: II, 10 (b) which forbids 'religious centres, religious associations, priests... to organize believers' pilgrimages to the so-called holy places'. *Zakonodatel'stvo o religioznykh kul'takh* (New York: Chalidze Publications, 1981) p. 80. The struggle against the Velikoretskoe pilgrimages has continued well into the 1980s. In 1981 the pilgrims were met by militia and the KGB troops, who enclosed the holy stream in barbed wire, banning all access. *Posev*, no. 11 (1981) p. 3.

12. 'Klikushi', p. 136; 'Tainik', p. 164,
13. For example, N. Proskuriakova, 'Marnovirstvo – voroh zdorov'ia', *Voiovnychyi ateist*, no. 7 (Kiev, 1963) pp. 12–15.
14. 'Formirovanie...', pp. 30, 38, and others.
15. 'Tainik', pp. 163–5 *et passim*. Similar slanderous stories on the Old Believer and 'True Orthodox' hideaways in: Shamaro, 'Vernopoddannye bezvozvratnogo proshlogo', *NiR*, no. 3 (1959) pp. 49–54; 'Na beregu chernoi magii', *NiR*, no. 1 (1963) pp. 21–9; L. Khvolovsky, 'Byvshie liudi', *NiR*, no. 7 (1964) pp. 24–32.
16. See Volume 1, chapter 4, and volume 2, chapter 7 of this present study.
17. *NiR*, no. 3 (1965) pp. 23–5.
18. L. Pinchuk, 'Otvechaem veruiushchim', ibid, p. 25. This idealization of the cave-man is a central anti-historical and nihilistic feature in Marxism (from Rousseau), contradicting its Hegelian historicism.
19. *Zhenshchina pod krestom* (L.: Lenizdat, 1966) pp. 6–27. Osipov prefers not to elaborate on the fact that this woman, a Soviet schoolteacher with full higher education, 'retired' in 1959 after only nineteen years of work as a teacher, the same year that Levitin-Krasnov and the late Boris Talantov were expelled from their teaching positions for their belief in God. This was the year of the purge of the teachers who practised their religious beliefs.
20. E. Sergienko, 'Sviatye pis'ma', *NiR*, no. 4 (1977) pp. 55–8.
21. A characteristic case is that of Levitin. Slandering him in 1960 (n. 5 and 6 above), the journal not only did not withdraw its statement after he had hand-delivered his true autobiography to its office, but continued slandering him six years later (n. 4 above).
22. Osipov, 'Bitva', pp. 166–9.
23. In the above report Il'ichev criticizes the atheist literature for being 'too academic'; he says that there should be a more direct attack – that is, he advocates propaganda that would stimulate and justify persecutions.
24. *NiR*, therefore, relegates the crudest hate propaganda to readers' letters. For example, the editorial in no. 12 for 1967, 'Otkrovennyi razgovor', cites *inter alia* a reader's letter: 'Our error is obvious: we sentimentalize, we fear to insult the believer's feelings ... Your position is that of pandering to the believers. *NiR* publishes most of its material with the aim of presenting atheists as creative optimists, working for the good of man, unselfish, hard-working, dedicated, while contrasting these with alleged opposite characteristics of religious believers, under the heading of 'The Spiritual World of Man', in almost every issue, at least in the 1980s.

25. L. Anninsky, 'Sila dukha i vera v Boga', *NiR*, no. 10 (1965) pp. 44–7; A. Ivanenko. 'Nad tsym varto zamyslytys', *Liudyna i svit*, no. 7 (July 1965); Larisa Kuznetsova, 'Na tikhoi ulitse', *NiR*, no. 1 (1974) pp. 44–9; V. Kharazov, 'Dosadnaia istoriia', *NiR*, no. 7 (1979).
26. Osipov, *Zhenshchina* . . . , pp. 64–70.
27. Material of this sort, reprimanding the official guides, began to appear under the heading of 'History and the Contemporary' on quite a regular basis from 1982: for example, no. 11 (1982) pp. 34–7, no. 1 (1983) pp. 39–44, no. 5 (1983) pp. 28–33, no. 7 (1983) pp. 30–1, no. 3 (1984) pp. 25–31, no. 6 (1984) pp. 31–5. One of them denounces a museum guide for being a religious believer, citing her explanation that the richness of colour and artistic mastery of an iconographer were inspired by his faith and the doctrine of the Church which he expressed in colour; whereas the line should have been the reverse: despite the doctrine which narrowed the possibilities of artistic expression, the artist was so great that *even* within the narrow confines of iconography he managed to achieve mastery (no. 3, 1984, pp. 26–7). Another guide said he personally was not a believer but he failed to appreciate the necessity of atheist propaganda: 'If God exists, . . . then the attempts to negate this are senseless; if He does not exist, then there is no one to struggle against.' (*NiR*, no. 5, 1983, p. 31).
28. A. V. Belov and A. D. Shilkin, *Ideologicheskie diversii imperializma i religiia* (M.: Znanie, 1970) p. 34.
29. M. Kosyv, 'Pokutniki – kto oni?', *NiR*, no. 8 (1975) pp. 56–7; L. Smirnov, 'Iavlenie bogomateri s pomoshch'iu nozhnits i kleia' (including the photo), *NiR*, no. 1 (1966) p. 95.
30. 'Stantsiia Bezbozhnik', *NiR*, no. 1 (1974) pp. 70–5.
31. Lev Ovalov, 'Pomni obo mne', *NiR*, nos 1–6 (1966), particularly nos 4 and 5, pp. respectively 80–93 and 77–89.
32. Michael Bourdeaux, *Patriarch and Prophets* (London: Macmillan, 1969); Pospielovsky, *Russian Church*, vol. 2, ch. 10.
33. Belov and Shilkin, *Ideologicheskie*, pp. 35–43; their *Diversiia bez dinamita* (M.: Polit. literatura, 1972) pp. 84–99, etc.
34. In addition to the above titles, see *inter alia*: Belov and Shilkin, *Religiia v sovremennoi ideologicheskoi bor'be* (M.: Znanie, 1971); V. V. Konik, *Tainy religioznykh missii* (M.: Molodaia gvardiia, 1980); Belov, *Sviatye bez nimbov* (M.: Sovetskaia Rossiia, 1983); Evgenii Vistunov, *Priglashenie v zapadniu* (L.: Lenizdat, 1984). The latter also contains a relatively detailed, if falsified, history of the Narodno-trudoroi soiuz (NTS), and descriptions (also falsified) of the Leningrad Christian-feminist movement and its participants. All of them, as well as several Soviet citizens who had co-operated with the NTS, are depicted as only using the label of Christians to camouflage their subversive activities.

NTS – or, in full, the Toiling Alliance of Russian Solidarists – is a patriotic Russian anti-communist organization working towards a 'national revolution' and moral renewal in Russia, since its foundation by Russian émigré youth in 1930. Its underground activities inside the USSR and among Soviet citizens abroad, its refusal 'to die' in accordance with the 'biological laws of emigrant communities', and its ability to

replenish itself from among the ranks of new waves of émigrés, make it particularly hateful to the Soviets, who constantly label it as a Western intellegence services' front organization.
35. Belov and Shilkin, *Ideologicheskie, Religiia v sovremennoi ideologicheskoi bor'be* (M.: Znanie, 1971), and *Diversiia*; V. V. Konik, *Tainy religioznykh missii* (M.: Molodaia gvardiia, 1980); and a multitude of other similar publications.
36. For example, the above-cited 'Otkrovennyi razgovor', *NiR*, no. 12 (1967), also quotes letters which say, for instance: 'I'm ashamed and deeply hurt that we are approaching . . . fiftieth anniversary of the Soviet power without having overcome religion.' A 1984 survey of readers' letters says that readers of the older generation express much concern that 'some young people . . . fall under the spell of religion'. For some it is a fad, in other cases 'the youth's interest in religion is not that superficial at all . . . to a considerable extent this interest is stimulated by some . . . [Soviet] works of literature, cinema, theatre, painting': 'Chitatel' i zhurnal', *NiR*, no. 9 (1984) p. 3.
37. *Mir cheloveka*, E. Romanov (ed.), (M.: Molodaia gvardiia, 1976, circ. 100 000) p. 14 *et passim*.
38. Cited from A. Babiichuk, 'Molodiozhy ideinuiu zakalku', *NiR*, no. 1 (1985) p. 10. It is interesting that the resolutions of that ideological plenum do not mention religion by name, but only ideological diversions and the necessity to struggle for a better ideological education of the Soviet people. Soviet 'religiological' publications constantly refer to that plenum, and cite excerpts from speeches, as in Babichuk's article, in the way of a guidance for the intensification of anti-religious struggle. In most such quotations it is merely declared, 'as stated at the plenum', thus giving the impression that such direct appeals were contained in one of its resolutions (or perhaps there was an unpublished secret resolution to this effect as well).
39. G. Belikova, 'Strannaia sud'ba Sashi Karpova', *NiR*, no. 9 (1984) pp. 37–40.
40. A. Shamaro, 'Delo igumenii Mitrofanii', *NiR*, no. 9 (1984) pp. 41–5; D. Koretsky and Shamaro, '"Sviataia" Nastia', *NiR*, no. 3 (1984) pp. 45–50; A. Shuvalov, 'Piushchee dukhovenstvo', *NiR*, no. 6 (1984) p. 40; F. Nikitina, 'V belom klobuke s zhandarmskim axelbantom', *NiR*, nos 11 and 12 (1982) pp. 41–3 and 42–4, respectively; N. Aleev, 'Ne ukradi, a sam ukral', *Pravda vostoka* (1 January 1970) p. 4.
41. 'Chitatel' i zhurnal', *NiR*, no. 9 (1984) pp. 4–5.
42. Vladimir Tendriakov, 'Chudotvornaia' (The Miracle-Working Icon), *Chrezvychainoe* (M.: Sovremennik, 1972) pp. 91–178; the story was first published in the early 1960s. M. G. Pismanik, *Lichnost' i religiia* (M.: Nauka, 1976) pp. 18–21.
43. In addition, there is the obligatory ideological dimension. The CPSU Central Committee may adopt a less aggressive policy towards religion for tactical reasons (as in East Germany, Poland, Hungary, for instance), but to abandon its principle of hostility would be tantamount to abandoning Marxism as the official doctrine.

CHAPTER 6: PERSECUTIONS UNDER KHRUSHCHEV

1. See his various speeches on ideological matters between 1954 and 1964, and the 1959 educational reform resolution, a Khrushchev pet project.
2. Bourdeaux, 'The Black Quinquennium: The Russian Church, 1959–1964', *Religion in Communist Lands* (henceforth *RCF*), vol. 9, no. 1–2 (1981) p. 18.
3. Levitin, 'Sviataia Rus' v eti dni' (Samizdat: 21 October 1964), AS 719, p. 15.
4. Popovsky, *Zhizu' i zhitie*, pp. 466–7, and the above 1954 Khrushchev speech.
5. According to a private report, when schoolchildren brought this story home and asked their grandmother why the cosmonaut Gagarin had not seen God, she replied: 'Of course he did not, for Jesus said only the pure in heart will see God.'
6. See the last section of this chapter.
7. Talantov, 'Bedstvennoe polozhenie Pravoslavnoi Tserkvi v Kirovskoi oblasti i rol' Moskovskoi patriarkhii' (Kirov: Samizdat, 1966–7), Keston College *Samizdat* archive (no. 739?) p. 1021; Bourdeaux, *Patriarch*, ch. 4. On Talantov, see Levitin-Krasnov, *Rodnoi prostor* (Frankfurt/M.: Possev, 1981) pp. 293–9.
8. Bourdeaux, *Patriarch*, pp. 121–2.
9. Ibid, p. 123.
10. F. Kovalsky, 'Pressure on the Orthodox Church in Belorussia' (Samizdat, 1965?), Keston Coll. Archives, SU Ort. 12/1; see also, Pospielovsky, *Russian Church*, vol. 2, p. 441.
11. Konstantinov, *Gonimaia Tserkov*, p. 290.
12. Ibid, p. 291; Bourdeaux, *Patriarch*, p. 121.
13. 'Pis'mo prikhozhanki gor. Zhitomira', *VRKhD*, no. 111 (1974) p. 241; 'Razrushenie khrama v Zhitomire', Ibid, no. 116 (1975) pp. 230–31.
14. Bourdeaux, *Patriarch*, p. 119.
15. I. A. Kryvelev, 'Preodolenie religiozno-bytovykh perezhitkov u narodov SSR', *Sovetskaia etnografiia*, no. 4 (1961) pp. 37–43.
16. I. V. Gagarin, *Religioznye perezhitki v Komi ASSR i ikh preodolenie* (Sykty'vkar, 1971) pp. 64–73.
17. V. M. Motitsky, *Staroobriadchestvo Zabaikal'ia* (Ulan Ude: Buriatskoe knigoizdatel'stvo, 1976) pp. 60–62. See also n. 28 below, on the growth of religious observances in the late 1950s to early 1960s.
18. Statements to the press in the West by Metropolitan Nikodim in 1964, for instance, as heard personally by the present author in London and as cited by Talantov, 'Bedstvennoe', pp. 26 and 27, from BBC Russian broadcasts of that year and of 8 October 1966.
19. Talantov, ibid, p. 26.
20. Talantov, 'Bedstvennoe', p. 28, citing the Soviet author G. Z. Anashkin.
21. Shafarevich, *Zakonodatel'stvo* . . . , pp. 60–1; Yakunin, 'O sovremennom polozhenii . . .', *passim*; V. Furov, 'Iz otcheta . . .', *VRKhD*, no. 130 (1979) pp. 275–7.
22. 'Rech' Patriarkha . . . Alexiia na konferentsii sovetskoi obshchestven-

nosti za razoruzhenie' (Moscow, 16 February 1960), *ZhMP*, no. 3 (1960) pp. 33–5.
23. 'Deianiia Arkhiereiskogo sobora Russkoi Pravoslavnoi Tserkvi', *ZhMP*, no. 8 (1961) pp. 5–29; 'Osnovnye voprosy deiatel'nosti Komissii sodeistviia pri ispolkomakh v raionnykh Sovetakh deputatov trudiashchikhsia po kontroliu za sobliudeniem zakonodatel'stva o kul'takh', *VRKhD*, no. 136 (1982) pp. 273–8. A more detailed discussion of this in my *Russian Orthodox Church under the Soviet*....
24. Talantov, 'Bedstvennoe', *passim*. As the testimony of Fr. Konstantin Tivetsky, a Moscow priest until his immigration to the USA in 1980 (oral testimony to this author, San Francisco, June 1980), and documents cited in the next chapter demonstrate, these high-handed practices continued to this day.
25. Talantov, 'Bedstvennoe', p. 32; and multiple documents on the persecutions at the Pochaev Lavra and other monasteries. Also, the oral testimony to this author of Iuri Kublanovsky, poet and historian, who had worked for six years as a church janitor in the Moscow area and also worked on artistic restoration in monasteries prior to his expulsion to the West in the autumn of 1982 (Paris, August 1983).
26. Talantov, 'Bedstvennoe', p. 34; 'Otkrytoe pis'mo sviashchennikov Nikolaia Eshlimana i Gleba Iakunina Patriarkhu Alexiiu', *Grani*, no. 61 (1966) p. 133.
27. Talantov, 'Bedstvennoe', p. 34.
28. Shafarevich, *Zakondatel'stvo o religii*..., p. 34 *et passim*.
29. Bourdeaux, *Ferment*..., pp. 20–1 *et passim*.
30. Michael Rowe, 'The 1979 Baptist Congress in Moscow...', *Religion in Communist Lands*, no. 3 (1978) pp. 188–200; Pospielovsky, 'The Forty-First All-Union Congress of the Evangelical Baptists...' *St. Vladimir's Theological Quarterly*, no. 4 (1975) pp. 246–53.
31. Rev. D. Konstantinov, *Gonimaia Tserkov'* (New York: Vseslavianskoe izdvo, 1967) p. 287; he cites the 1962 date. An inside source from Belorussia gives 1960 as the date of implementation of this measure in the Belorussian SSR: F. Kovalsky, 'Pressure on the Orthodox Church in Belorussia' (Keston College Archives, Su Ort. 12/1). As documents 713 and 717 (an appeal of four lay persons to the Eastern Patriarchs on behalf of the Pochaev Lavra, dated 1963; and an unsigned group address of lay Orthodox believers of the Ukraine and Belorussia to the World Council of Churches conference in Odessa, of 2 February 1964) cite 1961 as the year of the implementation of all these oppressive measures.
32. Talantov, 'Bedstvennoe...', p. 35.
33. ibid, pp. 35–6.
34. Oral information to this author by a Russian Orthodox wife of an American diplomat in Moscow. The above AS 713, and the L'vov resident Feodosia Varavva, persistently harassed by the Soviet authorities and the press with attempts to deprive her of parental rights owing to the religious upbringing of her children, state that children are permitted to participate in church services and to receive communion only in Zagorsk and Moscow to placate the many Western tourists, diplomats and journalists there. Varavva, 'Vostochnym patriarkham

Ierusalimskomu, Antiokhiiskomu, Konstantinopol'skomu i dr. i v Organizatsiiu Ob'edinennykh natsii' (L'vov. Keston College Archives, Su/Ort 11/10.3). Fr. Tivetsky maintains that pre-school special Te Deums for school children is a common practice in most Orthodox churches (oral testimony). The late Metropolitan Nikodim of Leningrad assured this author that in his diocese children were never prevented from coming to church or receiving communion.
35. Konstantinov *Gonimaia*, p. 305. The reason for so many clergy arrests in the Orenburg Diocese may have been the fact that Manuil (Lemeshevsky), its ruling archbishop, had continued Patriarch Tikhon's practice of secret ordinations of priests (unregistered and undeclared to the CROCA plenipotentiaries) as a security in case of mass liquidation of the overt clergy by the regime. See, Yakunin, 'O sovremennom polozhenii R.P.Ts....', *Vol'noe slovo*, no. 35–36 (1979) pp. 70–1.
36. Shafarevich, *Zakonodatel'stvo*, p. 64.
37. See in the following chapter the case of Fr. Pavel Adel'geim. Fr. Vitali Boiko, a church choir director at the Holy Virgin Protection church in Kiev was fired from the position by order of the Kiev CRA plenipotentiary in 1980 for having organized a youth choir in the church. The choir was likewise dissolved by the same order. *Khronika tek. sob.*, no. 60 (Moscow, 1980; New York, 1981) p. 73.
38. Talantov, 'Bedstvennoe...', pp. 21–2.
39. Ibid, pp. 22–3.
40. In 1964 the late Fr. Vsevolod Shpiller, a very prominent Moscow priest, assured this author that Patriarch Alexii had appointed Archbishop Ermogen to the nearby diocese of Kaluga in order to have the most steadfast and reliable bishops around himself in that dire moment of the regime's attack on the Church. A little more than a year later the same Ermogen was dismissed by the same patriarch and ordered to reside in the Zhirovitsy Monastery in Belorussia. His 'crime' was that he had led a delegation of eight bishops to protest to the Patriarch against the 1961 Church By-Laws as being uncanonical. Bourdeaux, *Patriarch*..., pp. 34 and 239–44.
41. Unofficial information from the Russian Church sources; Bourdeaux, *Patriarch*, p. 73; Archb. Vasilii (Krivocheine), 'Arkhiepiskop Veniamin (Novitsky) (1900–1976)', *VRKhD*, no. 120 (1977) p. 290; Konstantinov (*Gonimaia*, p. 304), erroneously states that Archbishop Veniamin was tried in 1961.
42. Konstantinov, p. 304.
43. Bourdeaux, *Patriarch*..., pp. 69–73 and 175; 'Russian Orthodox Church Ordeal' (from a Special Correspondent), *The Times* (London) Nov. 1960; Archb. Vasilii, 'Poslednie vstrechi s mitr. Nikolaem', *VRKhD*, no. 117 (1976) pp. 214–15, and his 'Arkhiep. Veniamin...', pp. 291–2.
44. Testimony to this author by Metropolitan Nikodim (London, 1966?). The Chernigov Cathedral, in fact, was closed in 1973, leaving only a small church in the suburbs for the faithful. *Christian Science Monitor*, 2 July 1973; *RCL*, no. 4–5 (1974) pp. 66–7.
45. See above: Eshliman-Yakunin and Talantov. Also: Talantov, 'O polozhenii Russkoi Pravoslavnoi Tserkvi v SSSR, o predatel'stve eio

upravleniia' (Kirov: Samizdat, August 1967 – March 1968; AS 745), 18 p.
46. Testimony of Fr. M., a former foreign student at the Leningrad Theological Academy, as told personally by Metropolitan Nikodim (testimony to this author, July 1983).
47. AS 717; testimony to this author by a leading official and priest of the Moscow Patriarchate (spring 1979). Such at least was the fate of the Minsk and Volhyhia seminaries. See also, 'Pis'mo arkhiep. Foedosiia Brezhnevu', *VRKhD*, no. 135 (1981) pp. 236 – 7.
48. The pre-1960 figures are from the Moscow Patriarchate's official statements (e.g., Konstantinov, p. 39). The 1972 figure quoted in a testimony to this author by a prominent priest in the Moscow Patriarchate (spring 1979).
49. Soviet authors admitted later that the clerical desertions had no effect on the faith of the believers, who retorted: 'The rascal had served us to make money, and now he serves you to make money; the more such priests go over to the atheists, the better for us.' D. Ushinin, 'Novye veianiia v ateisticheskoi propagande v SSSR', *Grani*, no. 60 (1966) pp. 214 – 15.
50. Talantov, 'Bedstvennoe . . .', pp. 36 – 40.
51. *Khronika tek. sob.*, no. 62 (M.: Samizdat, 1981; N.Y.C., 1982), p. 89.
52. Talantov, 'Bedstvennoe . . .', p. 40.
53. Decree No. 1159. 'O monastyriakh v SSSR', *Zakonodatel'stvo o religioznykh kul'takh* (N.Y.C.: 1981 Chalidze reprint from: Iuridicheskaia literatura, M. 1971) p. 36.
54. See, *inter alia*: the already cited AS 713 and 717; Bourdeaux, *Patriarch*, pp. 74 – 85, 87 – 8, 97 – 116, 173 – 5; A. Levitin-Krasnov, *Zashchita very v SSR*, Archbishop Ioann of San-Francisco, ed. (Samsidat reprint, Paris: IXΘYC, 1966) pp. 63 – 87; etc. On attacks on the Holy Trinity-St Sergius Lavra and the Pskov Monastery of the Caves, see also Levitin, *Dialog s tserkovnoi Rossiei* (Paris: IXΘYC, 1967) pp. 35 – 41, and *Zashchita very*, pp. 32 – 62.
55. Bourdeaux, *Patriarch*, p. 99; Kublanovsky, oral testimony to this author (Paris, August 1983).
56. Kublanovsky, 'V Pochaevskoi lavre', *Russkaia mysl'* (30 June 1983) p. 7. According to Kublauovsky's memoires, the monastic treasurer shouts to the restorers: 'Use a lot of gold, kids, don't be stingy; the monastery has got plenty of the stuff!' Levitin reminisces about how barbarously neglected and ruined was the St Sergius-Trinity Lavra when it was a state museum during his visit there in 1937. The Church received it back in 1945, when the country was tapped to the limit by the war. Yet within two years the whole complex was beautifully restored by the charity of the believers. Not a penny was spent by the state although the restoration work cost millions of rubles. *Dialog* . . . , p. 41.
57. Bourdeaux, *Patriarch*, pp. 99 – 101.
58. Ibid, p. 106.
59. Levitin, *Zashchita very* . . . , pp. 67 – 71.
60. A letter to V. M. Kamensky (a St Tikhon's Seminary professor and a former Lithuanian diocesan secretary) from the Soviet Union. The author, daughter of a deceased Orthodox priest in the region of Pochaev and Kamensky's friend, was 70 years old at the time of that writing in late

1964 or early 1965. See Kamensky's Files, The Bakhmeteff Russian Emigre Archives, Columbia University.
61. Levitin, *Zashchita* ..., pp. 70–1.
62. Bourdeaux, *Poctriorch*, pp. 102–14.
63. Ibid, pp. 98–116.
64. AS 713, p. 3.
65. Konstantinov, *Gonimaia*, pp. 301–2.
66. AS 713, AS 717; Bourdeaux, *Patriarch*, 164–82; Valentin Shkol'nyi, 'Brat i sestra', *NiR*, no. 6 (1965) pp. 42–5.
67. For example: 'Vsem detiam bozhiim', *Posev*, no. 11 (1969) p. 12; Bourdeaux and Katherine Murray, *Young Christians in Russia* (London: Lakehead, 1976) pp. 130–37.
68. A. Khvorostianov and B. Borovik, 'Izuver poluchil po zaslugam', *NiR*, no. 1 (1962) pp. 81–2.

CHAPTER 7: PERSECUTIONS AFTER KHRUSHCHEV

1. See Struve, *Christians*, 295–6; Marshall, *Aspects of Religion*, 133–4; Khrushchev's speech at the 22nd Party Congress; Il'ichev's report, chapter 3, current volume.
2. See D. Ushinin, 'New Currents in the Soviet Atheistic Propaganda', *Grani*, no. 60 (1966) pp. 198–230.
3. Archb. Feodisii, 'Letter to Brezhnev', *VRKhD*, no. 135 (1981) pp. 221–2. During the same years reports reached the West about the brutal closure and destruction of close to ten Orthodox churches, mostly in distant provinces, but some in major cities, such as The Holy Trinity church dynamited in Leningrad in 1966, or the Epiphany church in Zhitomir closed in 1973 and demolished the following year. This is a monthy newspaper, organ of the Orthodox Church in America (see Bibliography) *The Orthodox Church* (New York, April 1967) p. 3; *Khronika tekushchikh sobytii*, no. 53 (M.: Samizdat, August 1979; NYC reprint, 1980) pp. 128–9; Kathleen Matchett, 'Trends in Soviet Anti-religious Policy', *RCL*, vol. 2, no. 6 (1974) pp. 15–16.
4. On Baptists, see, Michael Rowe, 'The 1979 Baptist Congress in Moscow ...', *RCL*, no. 3 (1978) pp. 188–200. The Orthodox figure has been calculated by this author on the basis of data given in *ZhMP* in various issues between 1978 and 1983. Kuroedov's figure in 33 Orthodox churches newly opened or built during the same years. *Religiia i tserkov' v sov. obshchestve*, p. 144.
5. Reports in *Russkaia mysl'*, 26 January 1967; and *The Orthodox Church*, April 1967, p. 3.
6. 'Kogda plachut kamni', *VRSKhD*, No. 104–105 (1972) pp. 142–8.
7. *Khronika tekushchikh sobytii*, no. 54 (M., 15 Nov. 1979; N.Y., 1980) pp. 101–2.
8. *Khronika* ..., no. 53 (M., 1 Aug. 1979; N.Y. 1980) p. 129. *Khronika*, no. 63 (M., 1981; N.Y., 1983), however, reports a similar pogrom of a Uniate church in obviously the same village, but dates it 7 December

Notes and References 253

1977. This report (p. 112) states that since that time the believers have sent over 100 letters and eleven different delegations to various Soviet offices requesting the reopening of the church, but were told on each occasion that as long as they remained under Cardinal Slipyi ('the enemy of the Soviet state'), they would not be allowed to reopen their church. Since the first report spoke of delegations and petitions sent to Patriarch Pimen, it is probable that the village had two churches, one Orthodox and another Uniate (the latter unregistered). In the latter case the claim of a particular persecution of the Uniates and patronage for the Orthodox becomes questionable.

9. *Khronika*, no. 54, pp. 99–100.
10. Ibid, no. 53, pp. 128–9 and no. 54, pp. 100–1.
11. *Religion in Communist Lands*, no. 4–5 (1974) pp. 66–7.
12. *A Letter from 36 Gorky Orthodox Workers to ... Eugene Blake*, AS 197; *A Letter .... to U Tan* (UN General Secretary), AS 198; *RCL*, vol. 6, no. 1 (1978) p. 67; AS 3249 (USSR, 11 April 1978), a document of the Moscow Christian Committee for Defence of Believers' Rights.
13. Shafarevich, *Zakonodatel'stvo* ..., pp. 15–18. Also, oral testimony of a wholly reliable source close to the Zuckerman family, July 1983.
14. 1975–9 petitions signed by over 1200 persons requesting the opening of a church in the village of Bol'shoi Khomutets in the Lipetsk Province to serve a total of twelve churchless villages; 12 ex-monks of the Kiev Monastery of the Caves and 186 laymen signed petitions in 1978 requesting the reopening of that monastery closed by the state under Khrushchev (*Posev*, no. 2, Feb. 1979, p. 12). 1172 persons signed petitions requesting the reopening of a church in the town of Kotovo in the Volgograd Province; other groups have been requesting the opening or reopening of Orthodox churches in at least five villages in the Rovno Province, one village in the Kharkov Province, two in the Michurinsk Province (*Posev*, no. 3, 1980, p. 13; and no. 2, 1981, p. 9). 419 Georgian and Russian Orthodox believers forwarded several petitions requesting the reopening of at least one Orthodox church in at least one of the three districts of Azerbaidjan (Kakh, Belakan, Zakatal), where none of the more than fifty Orthodox churches is open for service, although 20 000 Georgian and 8000 Russian Orthodox believers reside there. Two ancient Orthodox churches were secretly blown up by dynamite there one night in 1965 (*Posev*, no. 2, 1981, p. 9).
15. 'Presledovanie staroobriadtsev v SSSR', *VRSKhD*, no. 91–2 (1969) p. 85.
16. *Khronika*, no. 24 (*Vol'noe sl.*, 4), pp. 19–20; and almost all subsequent issues of the publication. More detailed treatment is given in the journal, *Chronicle of the Lithuanian Catholic Church*.
17. *Khronika*, no. 60 (M., 1980; N.Y., 1981) p. 71; and no. 53, p. 125.
18. Ibid, no. 53, p. 126; *Posev*, no. 2 (1981) p. 9; Lithuanian *Samizdat* sources.
19. Safarevich, *Zakonodatel'stvo*, pp. 22–3; Bourdeaux, *Patriarch*, pp. 126–38 and 142.
20. *Khronika*, no. 48 (M., 14 March 1978) p. 111; no. 49 (M., 14 May 1978; N.Y., 1978) p. 53.
21. Ibid, no. 48, pp. 113–15 and no. 55 (M., 31 December 1979; N.Y. 1980) p. 43.

22. Oxana Antic, 'Persecution of Jehovah Witnesses Continues', *RDE-RL Research Bulletin*, RL 223/85 (9 July 1985).
23. O. F. Volkova, 'Zaiavlenie Podgornomu i Rudenko', n.d. but late 1972, AS 1229; two *samizdat* anonymous reports on searches in connection with 'the Buddologists Affair', AS 1229a and b; 'Zapis' protessa nad ... B. D. Dandaronom' (Ulan-Ude, December 1972) AS 1240; AS 1409, 1409a, b and c, and 1410. These consist of appeals by Dandaron's associates (including those pronounced psychotic) on theirs and his behalf, a xerox copy of a slanderous article from the Russian language *Pravda Buriatii* of 21 Jan. 1973, and a translation of a similar slanderous article on Dandaron in the Buriat language newspaper, *Buriaad Unen* of 18 Jan. 1973 by A. Motsov and S. Sadoshenko. See also, *Delo Dandarona* (Firenze, Italy: Edizioni Aurora, 1974) *passim*.
24. 'The Yogi with Blue Eyes or the Real Face of Krishna Devotees', *Sotsialisticheskaia industriia*, 24 Jan. 1982, in *Current Digest of the Soviet Press Abstracts*, vol. 34, no. 13 (1982).
25. Multiple oral testimonies to this author by Soviet Christian neophytes, including Elena and Yuri Olshansky (New York, June 1981).
26. Lithuanian *samizdat* and many issues of *Khronika* ... , including nos 49, p. 54, and 54, pp. 92–8; also documents on the unofficially ordained priest, Sigatas Tamkiavichus, AS 5024 and 5025 (Lithuania, 3 April 1983; RL, *Materially samizdata*, 5 August 1983).
27. Bohdan Bociurkiw: (i) 'The Catacomb Church: Ukrainian Greek-Catholics in the USSR', *Religion in Communist Lands*, vol. 5, no. 1 (1977); (ii) 'Religious Situation in Soviet Ukraine', *Ukraine in a Changing World*, Walter Dushnyk, ed. (N.Y.: Ukrainian Congress Committee of America, 1977) pp. 173–90. 'Samizdat Sources Reveal Religious Persecution', *Radio Liberty Dispatch* (April 23 1971) pp. 4–5. An anonymous Ukrainian *samizdat* tract, 'From the Life of the Ukrainian Catholic Church' (18 pp., Jan. 1980), recounts the story of the suppression of the Uniates in the Ukraine (Galicia in 1946, Carpatho-Ruthenia in 1949), and adds details on the continuing harassment and closure of unregistered Uniate churches opening sporadically or continuing to exist semi-clandestinely all these years. See *Khronika*, no. 63, pp. 111–2, and other issues. On the Soviet 'interpretation' of the Uniate story, see, for instance, P. A. Petliakov, *Uniatskaia tserkov' – orudie antikommunizma i anti-sovetizma* (The Uniate Church Is a Tool of Anticommunism and Antisovietism), (Lvov: Vyshcha shkola, 1982) *passim*.
28. For example: *Khronika*, no. 49, pp. 56–62; Council of the All-Union Church of the Free Adventists, 'The Last Days of V. A. Shelkov', *Russkaia mysl'* (30 Oct. 1980) p. 6.
29. 'Believers Are Appealing for Defence against Lawlessness', *Posev*, no. 43 (27 October 1967) pp. 5–7; Bourdeaux, *Religious Ferment in Russia* (London: Macmillan, 1968) pp. 95–124.
30. For example: *Khronika*, no. 43 (M., 31 Dec. 1976; N.Y., 177) p. 69; no. 42, p. 69.
31. Eugene Pushkov, 'Something More than Music' and editorial comments, *Prisoner Bulletin*, vol. 5, no. 3 (International Representation for the Council of Evangelical Baptist Churches of the Soviet Union, Elkhart, tr.

Ind.) pp. 6–11.
32. *Vedomosti Verkhovnogo Soveta RSFSR*, no. 12 (390) p. 219.
33. 'Believers...', *Posev* (weekly), 27 Oct, 1967, pp. 6–7.
34. 'Baptisty: uspekhi i poteri', and 'Khronika', *Posev*, nos 8 (Aug. 1983) and 11 (Nov. 84), pp. 4 and 3 respectively.
35. *Khronika*, no. 42, pp. 70–1.
36. Ibid, p. 69.
37. V. Tishchenko, 'Under Cover of a Lie', *Trud*, 21 May 1981, p. 4; cited from *The Current Digest*..., vol. 33, no. 31 (1981).
38. 'Prisoner Update: Dmitri Miniakov', *Prisoner Bulletin*, vol 5, no. 3, 4–5; *Khronika*, no. 47 (30 Nov. 1977) pp. 58–9; no. 61 (16 March 1981) p. 49; no. 63 (31 Dec. 1981) p. 110. On Graham: 'U veruiushchikh eto vyzovet razocharovanie...', *Russkaia mysl'*, no. 3538 (11 Oct. 1984) p. 7; and other sources.
39. *Khronika*, no. 44 (M., 16 March 1977; N.Y., 1977) p. 71.
40. For example: *Khronika*, no. 39, p. 54; no. 41 (M., 3 August 1976; N.Y. 1976) pp. 20–1; no. 52 (M., 1 March 1979; N.Y. 1979) p. 108; no. 55, pp. 42–3; no. 56 (M., 30 Apr. 1980; N.Y., 1980) pp. 93–4.
41. *Khronika*, no. 44, p. 72. On the imprisonment of Jehovah's Witnesses for their conscientious objection: *Khronika*, no. 54, p. 104; M. Derimov, 'Jehovah's Witnesses in Brooklyn Nets', *Pravda Ukrainy* (January 21, 22 and 23, 1983).
42. *Khronika*, no. 44, p. 71; a 1983 report of the Christian Committee for the Defence of Believers' Rights to the WCC IV General Assembly (Vancouver, Canada), 24. VII, 1983, AS 5037.
43. The Christian Committee for the Defence of Believers' Rights in the USSR, 'To the Delegates and Participants of the VI WCC General Assembly in Vancouver' (M.: Samizdat, 24 July 1983), *Materialy samizdata* (12 Aug. 1983), AS 5037.
44. The International Human Rights Society in Frankfurt/Main West Germany, has 895 names of Soviet prisoners of conscience currently in camps, jails, and psycho-prisons (183 cases). Of these 352 have been incarcerated entirely for their religious activities. The Society believes that the real number of Soviet prisoners of conscience, including those imprisoned for their faith, may be more than ten times the above numbers. 'Mrachnaia Statistika', *Novoye Russkoye Slovo* (New York) 9 March 1986, p. 3.
45. 'Persecution of Believers' and 'Letters of Pochaev Monks', *VRKhD*, no. 135 (1981) pp. 250–2; 'Attack on the Pochaev Lavra', ibid, no. 136 (1982) pp. 260–1; *Khronika*, no. 63, pp. 112–13.
46. 'Persecution of Believers', *VRKhD*, no. 132 (1980) pp. 209–11; 'Reports from Russia', *Rus. m.*, 20 Nov. 1980.
47. For example, interview with Larisa Volokhonskaia (New York, 16 Apr. 1980), baptized in this fashion in 1972.
48. Archbishop Feodosii, *Letter*, pp. 220–49.
49. CRA Report to the CPSU Central Committee, *VRKhD*, no. 130 (1979) pp. 311–26.
50. 'Fr. Vladimir Rusak's Open Letter to the... VI WCC General Assembly in Vancouver' and his 'Lenten Sermon', *Russkaia mysl'*, nos 3476 (4 Aug.

1983) and 3484 (29 Sept. 1983) respectively; also, AS 5017 and 5031. In October 1983, Fr. Rusak received a warning that unless he found a secular job by 24 November he would be tried for parasitism. But a clergyman has no labour passport in the USSR; without this no one may be employed. *Rus. m.*, no. 3493 (1 Dec. 1983) p. 7.

51. Archbishop Feodosii, *Letter*, pp. 220–49.
52. *VRKhD*, no. 130, pp. 279–99.
53. Oral testimony to this author, 1982.
54. This point was stressed to this author in 1983 by a non-Russian Orthodox cleric who had received his education at a theological academy in the USSR, but who preferred to remain anonymous.
55. *Khronika*, no. 60, p. 73. The fact that the priest served merely as a church choir director indicates that this was not the first time he was in trouble with the Soviet authorities.
56. *Khronika*, no. 63, pp. 112–13; *VRKhD*, no. 136, pp. 167–9.
57. *VRKhD*: no. 117, pp. 240–62; no. 130, p. 370; no. 112–113, pp. 261–81; no. 131, pp. 285–6; no. 132, pp. 230–32; no. 133, p. 293. For the full text of Dudko's TV 'confession' see *Izvestia*, 21 June 1980.
58. CRA Report for 1968 (Keston College: Samizdat Archive Ms.), 9p.
59. The same Moroz later repaid the priest by harassing him, and instigating his equally fanatical but apparently more athletic friend Ivan Hel' to beat up the priest in a Mordovian concentration camp, as part of their campaign to intimidate Ukrainians and put an end to their friendship and co-operation with the Russian and Jewish political prisoners. Subsequently an unofficial comrade court of political prisoners of different nationalities, including Ukrainians, deprived Moroz and Hel' of the status of political prisoners and declared them boycotted. See: *Khronika*, no. 47 (1977) pp. 98–9; 'The Valentyn Moroz Saga: A Conspiracy of Silence', *Student*, Canada's Newpaper for Ukrainian Students, vol. 12, no. 61 (February 1980) pp. 8–10. Moroz now resides in the USA.
60. Fr. Sergii Zheludkov on Fr. Vasilii Romaniuk, and other documents on him, *VRKhD*, no. 117 (1976 – *samizdat* documents) pp. 232–9; Romaniuk's letter, *VRKhD*, no. 129, pp. 281–3.
61. Oral testimony of Mr Lev Yudovich, currently professor at the US Army College of Modern Languages and Area Studies, Garmisch, West Germany. For the Soviet line, see: V. Efimov, 'From the Life of "Saint" Paul', *Pravda Vostoka*, (Tashkent, Uzbekistan, 12 July 1970); V. Alexeev and N. Dmitrieva, 'Father Paul without a Mask', ibid (26 July 1970). For an independent analysis of the Soviet press on the subject, see, V. Deriugin, 'What is the Guilt of Fr. Adelgeim?', *VRSKhD*, no. 97 (1970) pp. 157–63.
62. *Khronika*, no. 25 (5 March 1972; reprint: *Vol'noe slovo*, no. 4, 1972) p. 39; *Khronika*, no. 34 (Samizdat, Feb. 1975; N.Y. 1975) pp. 52–3; Vestnik *RSKhD*, no. 106, pp. 320–38.
63. *Khronika*, no. 58 (M., 1980; N.Y., 1981) pp. 21–3, and other *samizdat* documents. Over 200 Soviet citizens signed letters protesting his incarceration and sentence.

64. Alena Kozhevnikova, 'Interview with Vadim Shcheglov' (a member of the Christian Comm.), *Rus. m.*, no. 3476 (4 Aug. 83) p. 7.
65. *Russk.m.*, no. 3481 (8 Sept. 1983) p. 2.
66. Lenin's letter to Gorky, November 1913, *Collected Works* (M.: Progress Publishers, 1966) vol. 35, pp. 133–3.
67. 'K "delu" ieromonakha Pavla', *VRKhD*, no. 144 (1985) pp. 226–43.
68. *Posev*, no. 10 (October 1983) p. 12; *Russk. m.*, no. 3481, p. 2.
69. *Khronika*, no. 63, p. 113.
70. *Khronika*, nos 51, pp. 121–6, and 57 (M., 3 Aug. 1980; N.Y. 1981) p. 66. Documents on persecutions of the monastics and clergy, *VRKhD*, nos 135, pp. 250–2, and 136, pp. 260–9.
71. *Posev*, no. 2 (February 1984) p. 3.
72. Fr. Gleb Yakunin, 'On the Contemporary Situation of the ROC and the Prospects of Religious Revival in Russia'. Report to the Christian Committee (M., 15 Aug. 1979). *Vol'noe slovo* (reprint), no. 35–36 (1979) pp. 12–13, 81–2, *et passim*.
73. 'A Holy Place Desecrated' (a *samizdat* letter dated April 1983 and signed 'Orthodox Christians'), *Russk. m.*, no. 3476 (4 Aug. 1983) p. 6.
74. Yuri Kublanovsky's oral testimony to this author (Paris, August 1983). Kublanovsky, one of Russia's most talented poets of the young generation (born in 1946), and adult convert to Orthodoxy, spent most of his free time during his last decade in Russia as a 'working pilgrim' in monasteries and convents, not only praying, but also living there, and doing different jobs including restoration work for them. Also, his 'O Pochaevskoi lavre' (On the Pochaev lavra), *Russk. m.*, no. 3471 (30 June 1983) p. 7.
75. See note 67 above.
76. D Dudko, 'The New Martyr', *VRKhD*, no. 129, p. 280.
77. *Khronika*, no. 63, pp. 102–3; Natalia Gorbanevskaia, 'Interviews with Valeri Smolkin', *Russk. m.*, no. 3471 (30 June 1983) p. 6.
78. Sidney Bloch and Peter Reddaway, *Russia's Political Hospitals* (London: Futura Books, 1977) pp. 23–45. On p. 44, the authors state, on the basis of authentic data: '25 percent of the medical curriculum is devoted to political studies: ... bases of Marxism-Leninism, political economy, dialectical materialism, historical materialism, history of the CP, and Scientific Atheism.'
79. *Khronika*, no. 62 (M., 1981, N.Y., 1982) p. 156; no. 53, pp. 40–1; The Christian Committee ..., *An Appeal* (M.: Samizdat, 24 April 1979) AS 3581.
80. *Khronika*, no. 45 (M., 25 May 1977; N.Y., 1977) pp. 61–2; no. 46 (M., 15 Aug. 1977; N.Y., 1977) p. 78; no. 47 (M., 30 Nov. 1977; N.Y., 1978) p. 142; no. 51 (M., 1 Dec. 1978; N.Y. 1979) p. 148.
81. *Khronika*, no. 34 (M., 31 Dec. 1974; N.Y., 1975) p. 35; no. 45, pp. 62–4.
82. *Khronika*, no. 21 (M., 11 Sept. 1971; repr. in *Vol'noe slovo*, no. 1, 1972) p. 27.
83. *Khronika*, no. 49, pp. 37–8; no. 63, pp. 212–13.
84. Ibid. no. 48, p. 87; no. 53, pp. 105–6.
85. Ibid. no. 53, p. 107; no. 54, pp. 84–5.

86. Ibid, no. 43, pp. 60–3; N. A. Trushin, 'Religion in the USSR: New Believers, New Persecutions', *Russkaia mysl'*, no. 3119 (30 Sept. 1976) p. 5.
87. 'A Letter to Fillip Potter, General Secretary of the WCC from Seven Russian Orthodox Christians' (M.: Samizdat, 16–31 July 1976), AS 2602a; 'Six Documents on Alexander Argentov' (M.: Sanizdat, 16–31 July 1976), AS 2608; Eduard (George) Fedotov's Letter to Potter (M.: Samizdat, Sept. 76), AS 2771; *Khronika*, no. 41, pp. 12–14; no. 42, p. 68.
88. His and similar other extensions of concentration-camp terms are based on a new law adopted in 1983, on 'Malicious Disobedience in Labour Camps and Punitive Colonies'. Oxana Antic, 'Vladimir Poresh – a Victim of the Law of "Malicious Disobedience" in Soviet Camps', *RFE-RL Res. Bul.*, RL 72/85 (6 March 1985); 'Est' vysshii zakon, kotoryi trebuet ot nas spravedlivosti v otnosheniiakh drug s drugom', *Russk. m.*, no. 3 (January 1985) p. 7.
89. *Khronika*, nos: 41, p. 14; 43, pp. 60–3; 46, pp. 41–2; 51, pp. 124–5; 55, p. 35; 56, pp 51–5; 57, p. 65. Also: 'The Testimony of a Witness', *Russk. m.*, no. 3324 (4 Sept. 1980) p. 6; Georgi Fedotov, 'Letter to Titiana Khodorovich' (Samizdat, 13 Oct. 1976), AS 2747b; 'The Christian Seminar', a collection of documents from *samizdat*, *Vol'noe slovo*, no. 39 (1980) *passim*. On 23 October 1984, Poresh was re-tried on fraudulent charges, and his sentence prolonged by an additional three years at a strict regime camp. *Posev*, no. 1 (Jan. 1985) p. 8.
90. On 19 January 1980 another branch of the *Khristianin* Publishers was discovered by the KGB in the Dnepropetrovsk Prov. (Ukraine); *Khronika*, no. 56, pp. 89–90.
91. The trial ended on 6 December 1982. When searching for religious literature printed by the defendants, among their main recipients and probably secondary distributors were found not only priests and nuns, but also a doctoral student in the history of the CPSU and a militia (police) officer. 'On Religious Samizdat', 'A Chronicle of the Country', 'The Trial of a Group of Orthodox Christians' – all in *Posev*, respectively nos 6 (1982) pp. 6–7; 1 (1983) p. 9; 6 (1983) p. 5. 'A Report from Moscow', *VRKhD*, no. 136, pp. 277–8, unfortunately takes the official version at face value, namely that the defendants were black-marketeers with pecuniary aims. Subsequent information proved this version to be wrong.
92. Felix Svetov, 'An Open Letter to Russian Writers'; 'Zoia Krakhmal'nikova Sentenced' – both in *Posev*, resp. no. 10 (Oct. 1982) pp. 3–5, and no. 5 (May 1983) pp. 5–6. Also: 'Interview with Shcheglov', *Rus. m.*, (4 Aug. 83) p. 7; Pospielovsky, *Russian Church*, vol. 2, ch. 12. Nos 8–10 of *Nadezhda* had reached the West after her arrest; and nos 11 and 12 were 'published' in 1983–5 by her unnamed successors.
93. Oxana Antic, 'Member of a Christian Rock Group on Hunger Strike', *Radio Liberty Research* (RL 233/85) 17 July 1985. Release information supplied by Keston College.
94. *Khronika*, no. 54, pp. 104–5.
95. Michael Bourdeaux and Katherine Murray, *Young Christians in Russia* (London: Lakeland & Keston, 1976) pp. 130–40; *Khronika*, no. 48,

p. 119, and multiple other *samizdat* sources, including AS 3955 (March 1980) p. 3, reporting the deprivation of a Pentecostal family of parental rights.
96. Art. 66 of the 1977 Soviet Constitution states that it is the duty of Soviet citizens to raise their children as 'worthy members of the socialist society', that is of the Soviet Union. But Art. 6 says: 'The leading and guiding force of Soviet society, the core of its political system, its state and social organizations, is the Communist Party ... Armed by the Marxist-Leninist teachings. Art. 25 adds that 'the unified system of education ... serves the communist upbringing' of the citizens; therefore in the context of these three articles the constitutional duty of Soviet parents is to raise their children as communists. The Communist party statutes stipulate active struggle against religion as one of the duties of a party member.

The Family Code spells it out even more clearly. Art. 52: 'Parents are duty-bound to raise their children in the spirit of the moral code of the builder of communism. Art. 59 clarifies: 'Parents ... can be deprived of their parental rights if ... they effect a harmful influence on their children ... by antisocial behaviour.' This, by implication includes dedication to a religious belief, since social behaviour means active support for the building of atheistic communism. *Kodexy* (M.: Iuridicheskaia literatura, 1979) pp. 242–3.

Epilogue

1. See the speeches from the floor at the Eighth Writers' Congress. *Lit. gazeta*, 2 July 1986, particularly those of D. Likhachev and A. Voznesensky. Also Valentin Rasputin's novella *Pozhar* (The Fire) and Victor Astafiev's novel *Pechal'nyi detektiv* (A Sad Detective Story), first published respectively in *Nash sovremennik*, no. 7 (July 1985) and *Oktiabr'*, no. 1 (January 1986).
2. *Lit. gazeta*, 19 November 1986.
3. E. Pylilo in *Literatura i iskusstvo* (Minsk) 5 September, 1986; response in *Kom. pravda*, 3 October 1986. As cited by Vera Tolz, 'Soviet Writers Criticised for Christian Lenings', *Radio Liberty Research*, 5 November 1986.
4. Both in *Kom. pravda*, 10 December 1986. Cited in Fr. Kirill Fotiev, 'Sud'by kul'tury i khristianstva', *Russkaia mysl'*, 30 January 1987, p. 6.
5. G. Razumikhina, Al. Razumikhin, 'O delakh semeinykh', *Nash sovremennik*, no. 12 (December 1986), p. 150. The quotation within the citation is from V. Belov, a leading ruralist writer.
6. A. Tursunov, 'Ateizm i kul'tura', *Pravda*, January 1987.

Bibliography

ARCHIVES, DOCUMENTS, AND OTHER PRIMARY SOURCES

Hoover Institution Archives. Hoover Institute, Stanford, California.
'Kamensky Files', *The Bakhmeteff Russian Emigre Archives.* Columbia University, New York.
Kovalsky, F. 'Pressure on the Orthodox Church in Belorussia'. Russia: Samizdat, 1965 (?), Keston College Archives.
Leontii, Bishop. *Political Controls over the Orthodox Church in the Soviet Union.* 'Leontii collection: Research program on the USSR', The Bakhmeteff Archives.
MacNaughten, E. 'Informal report of religious situation in Russia', 3 October, 1927. 'Colton Collection', Hoover Institution Archives.
Ostraia luka. Samizdat ms, Keston College Archives.
Samizdat Archives. Radio Liberty, Munich.
Samizdat Religious Archives. Keston College, Keston, Kent, England.
'Spisok pravoslavnykh episkopov ... Nicolaevsky Collection', Hoover Institution Archives.
Talantov, B. Bedstvennoe polozhenie Pravoslavnoi Tserkvi v Kirovskoi oblasti i rol' Moskovskoi patriarkhill'. Kirov: Samizdat, 1966–1967, Keston College Archives.
——, 'O polozhenii Russkoi Pravoslavnoi Tserkvi v SSR, o predatel'stve eio upravleniia'. Kirov: Samizdat, 1967–1968, Samizdat Archives. Radio Liberty, Munich.
'N. Tsurikov Collection'. Hoover Institution Archives.
Ugolovnyi kodex RSFSR. Moscow: Iuridicheskaia literatura, 1979.
Varavva, Feodosia, 'Vostochnym patriarkham Ierusalimskomu, Antiokhiiskomu, ...'. L'vov: Samizdat, Keston College Archives.
Zakonodatel'stvo o religioznykh kul'takh, 2nd ed. Moscow: Iuridicheskaia literatura, 1971. 'Only for Internal Use'. New York: Chalidze Publications (Reprint), 1981.

SERIAL PUBLICATIONS

Antireligioznik, monthly. Moscow, 1926–1941.
Bezbozhnik illustrated, monthly/bimonthly. M., 1925–1941.
Bezbozhnik newspaper, irregularly, M., 1922–1941.
Bezbozhnik u stanka, monthly. M., 1923–1932.
Bogoslovskie trudy, once or twice annually. M., since early 1960s.
Bol'shevik, monthly. M., 1923–1952.
Buriaad Unen, daily. Ulan-Ude, Buriat ASSR.
Christian Science Monitor, daily. Boston.
Chronicle of the Lithuanian Catholic Church, irregularly. Lithuanian SSR: Samizdat, since early 1970s.

Current Digest of the Soviet Press, weekly. Columbus, Ohio.
Grani, quarterly. Frankfurt am Main, since 1946.
Izvestiia, daily. Moscow.
Khronika tekushchikh sobytii, irregularly. M.: Samizdat, since 1968. Reprinted: Frankfurt an Main: Possev, 1968–1972; New York: Chalidze publications, since 1973.
Kommunist, 18 issues annually. M., since 1952.
Komsomol'skaia pravda, daily. M.
Krokodil, thrice monthly. M.
Literaturnaia gazeta, weekly. M.
Liudyna i svit, monthly. Kiev: Znanie, since 1967.
Nadezhda: khristianskoe chtenie, irregularly. M. Samizdat, since 1977. Reprinted: Frankfurt am Main: Possev.
Nauka i religiia, monthly. M., no. 1, 1922 and since 1959.
Novoye Russkoe Slovo, daily, N.Y., since 1910.
Oktiabr', monthly. M.
The Orthodox Church, monthly, Syosset, N.Y., since 1965.
Posev, weekly/monthly. Frankfurt am Main, 1945–1968.
Pravda, daily. M.
Pravda Ukrainy, daily. Kiev.
Pravda Vostoka, daily, Tashkent, Uzbekistan.
Prisoner Bulletin, bi-monthly. Elkhart, Indiana.
Put', monthly. Paris, 1925–1940.
Radio Liberty Research Bulletin, weekly. Munich, since mid-1950s.
Religion in Communist Lands quarterly. Keston, Kent, England, since 1973.
Revoliutsiia i tserkov' irregularly/monthly. M., 1919–1924.
Ruskaia mysl', weekly. Paris, since 1947.
Saint Vladimir's Theological Quarterly. Crestwood, N.Y., since 1957.
Sovetskaia etnografiia, bi-monthly. M., since 1931.
Student, Canada's Newspaper for Ukrainian Students, monthly. Edmonton.
The Times, daily. London.
Trud, daily. M.
Vedomosti verkhovnogo soveta RSFSR., weekly, M., since 1936.
Vestnik russkogo studencheskogo khristianskogo dvizheniya (Vestnik RSKhD, or VRSKhD), and since issue no. 112–113, 1974 – *Vestnik russkogo Khristianskogo dvizheniya (Vestnik RKhD, or VRKhD)*, presently thrice annually. Paris, since 1926.
Voiovnychy ateist, monthly. Kiev 1960–1967.
Vol'noe slovo, 4–6 times annually. Frankfurt an Main, 1972–1981.
Voprosy istorii religii i ateizma. M., until 1964.
Vozrozhdenie, daily. Paris, 1918–1940.
Zhurnal Moskovskoi Patriarkhii, monthly. 1931–1943.

BOOKS AND ARTICLES

Antic, Oxana, 'Members of a Christian rock group on hunger strike', *Radio Liberty Research Bulletin*, RL 233/85, 17 July, 1985. Munich.
——, 'Persecution of Jehovah Witnesses continues', *RL Research Bulletin*, RL 223/85, 9 July, 1985.

—, 'Vladimir Poresh, a victim of the law on 'Malicious Disobedience' in Soviet Camps', *RL Research Bulletin*, RL 72/85, 6 March, 1985.
Antireligioznyi krest'ianskii uchebnik, 6th rev. ed. Moscow: Moskovskii rabochii, 1931.
Belov, A. V. *Sviatye bez nimbov*. M.: Sovetskaia Rossiia, 1983.
—, and Shilkin, A. D. *Diversiia bez dinamita*. M.: Politicheskaia literatura, 1972.
—, *Ideologicheskie diversii imperializma i religiia*. M.: Znanie, 1970.
—, *Religiia v sovremennoi ideologicheskoi bor'be*. M.: Znanie, 1971.
Benningsen, Alexandre A. and Wimbush, Enders S. *Muslim National Communism in the Soviet Union*. Chicago: University of Chicago Press, 1979.
Bloch, Sidney, and Reddaway, Peter. *Russia's Political Hospitals*. London: Futura, 1978.
Bociurkiw, Bohdan, 'The Catacomb Church: Ukrainian Greek-Catholics in the USSR', *Religion in Communist Lands*, vol. 5, no. 1, 1977.
—, 'Religious situation in Soviet Ukraine', *Ukraine in a Changing World*, Dushnyk, Waltered. New York: Ukrainian Congress Committee of America, 1977.
Bourdeaux, Michael (ed.), *Patriarch and Prophets: Persecution of the Russian Orthodox Church Today*. London: MacMillan, 1969.
— (ed.), *Religious Ferment in Russia*. London, 1968.
— and Katherine Murray. *Young Christians in Russia*. London: Lakenhead and Keston College, 1976.
Curtiss, John. *The Russian Church and the Soviet State, 1917–1950*. Boston: Little, Brown, 1953.
Delo Dandarona. Firenze, Italy: Edizioni Aurora, 1974.
Dunn, Denis J. *The Catholic Church and the Soviet Government, 1919–1949*. N.Y.: Columbia University Press, Monograph No. XXX, Keston Book No. 10.
Flerov, I. A. ed. *My bezbozhniki*. M.: Gosudarstvennoe antireligioznoe izdatel'stvo, 1932.
Fletcher, William C. *The Russian Orthodox Church Underground, 1917–1970*. London: Oxford University Press, 1971.
Golosovsky, S. and G. Krul'. *Na manyche 'Sviashchenn'; Sektanskoe dvizhenie sredi molodezhy*. M.: Molodaia gvardiia, 1931.
Konik, V. V. *Tainy religioznykh missii*. M.: Molodaia gvardiia, 1980.
Konstantinov, Prot. Dimitri. *Gonomaia tserkov'*. N.Y.: Vseslavianskoe izd., 1967.
Kuroedov, V. A. *Religiia i tserkov' v Sovetskom obshchestve*. M.: Polit. lit., 1984.
Lenin, V. I. *Collected Works*, vol. 35. M.: Progress, 1966.
Levitin-Krasnov, A. *Dialog s tserkovnoi Rossiei*. Paris: ΙΧΘΥΣ, 1967.
—, *Likhie gody, 1925–1941*. Paris: YMCA, 1977.
—, *Rodnoi prostor*. Frankfurt am Main: Possev, 1981.
—, *Slovo ob umershem*. M.: Samizdat, 2 June 1969.
—, 'Sviataia Rus' v eti dni'. Russia: Samizdat, 21 October 1964/Munich: RFE/RL, AS #719.
—, *Zashchita very v SSSR*. Archb. Ioann of San-Francisco, ed. Paris: Ιχογς, 1966.
Levitin-Krasnov, A. and Shavrov, V. *Ocherki po istorii russkoi tserkovnoi smuty*.

Kuesnacht, Switzerland: Institut Glaube in der 2 Welt, 1978.
Luka, Archb. 'Memuary', *Nadezha*, no. 3, 1979. Russia: Samizdat.
Manuil, M. *Die russische orthodoxen Bischoefe von 1893 bis 1965. Bio-Bibliographie*. Erlangen: Oikonomia, 1981.
Marshall, Richard H. Jr (ed.), *Aspects of Religion in the Soviet Union, 1917–1967*. Chicago: University of Chicago Press, 1971.
'Materialy k istorii Akademii nauk', *Pamiat'*. M.: Samizdat/Paris: YMCA, 1981.
Motitsky, V. M. *Staroobriadchestvo Zabaikal'ia*. Ulan Ude: Buriatskoe Knigoizdatel'stvo, 1976.
Nepluev, N. N. *Kratkiia svedeniia o Pravoslavnom Kresto-vozdvizhenskom trudovom bratstve*. Chernigov: tipografia Gubernskogo pravleniia, 1905.
——, *Trudovye bratstva . . . i Khristianskoe gosudarstvo*. Leipzig: Beer & Hermann, 1893.
N. N. Nepluev, Podvizhnik zemli Russkoi. Sergiev Posad: tipografia Sv.-Tr. Sergievoi Lavry, 1908.
Orleansky, N. *Zakony o religioznykh ob'edineniakh RSFSR*. M.: Bezbozhnik, 1930.
Osipov, A. *Zhenshchina pod krestom*. Leningrad: Lenizdat, 1966.
Petliakov, P. A. *Uniatskaia tserkov' – orudie antikommunizma i antisovetizma*. Lvov: Vyshcha shkola, 1982.
Pismanik, M. G. *Lichnost' i religiia*. M.: Nauka, 1976.
Pol'skii, M. (ed.) *Novye mucheniki rossiiskie*. Jordanville, N.Y.: Holy Trinity Monastery Press, 1949.
Popovsky, M. *Zhizn i zhitie Voino-Iasentskogo, arkhiepiskopa i khirurga*. Paris: YMCA, 1979.
Pospielovsky, Dimitry, 'The forty-first All-Union congress of the Evangelical Baptists', *ST Vladimir's Theological Quarterly*, no. 4, 1975. New York: St Vadimir's Seminary.
——, 'More on historic preservation policy in the USSR', *Canadian Slavonic Papers*, vol. 17, no. 4. Winter 1975.
——, *The Russian Church Under the Soviet Regime, 1917–1982*, 2 vols. Crestwood, N.Y.: St Vladimir's Seminary Press, 1984.
Powell, David E. *Antireligious Propaganda in the Soviet Union: a Study of Mass Persuasion*. Cambridge, Mass.: MIT, 1975.
Prokhanov, Ivan. *In the Cauldron of Russia, 1869–1933*. N.Y.: 1933.
Putintsev, F. *Politicheskaia rol' i taktika sekt*. M.: 1935.
Rakusheva, L. *Komsomol protiv religii*. Leningrad, 1939.
Razvernutym frontom. O zadachakh i metodakh antireligioznoi propagandy. M.: Izd-vo aktsion. ob-va Bezbozhnik, 1929.
Regel'son, Lev. *Tragediia Russkoi tserkvi, 1917–1945*. Paris: YMCA, 1977.
Romanov, E. (ed.), *Mir cheloveka*. M.: Molodaia gvardiia, 1976.
Rowe, Michael, 'The 1979 Baptist Congress in Moscow', *Religion in Communist Lands*, no. 3, 1978.
Shakhovskoi, Archb. Ioann. *K istorii russkoi intelligentsii – Revolutsiia Tolstogo*. N.Y.: Ixoyc, 1975.
——, *Vera i dostovernost'*. Paris, 1982.
Sheinman, M. M. and Yaroslavsky (eds), *Antireligioznyi krest'ianskii uchebnik*. M.: Moskovskii rabochii, 1931.

Solzhenitsyn, Alexander. *The Gulag Archipelago*. N.Y.: Harper & Row, 1975.
Sovetskaia istoricheskaia entsiklopediia, 16 vols. M., 1961–1976.
Spinka, Matthew. *The Church in Soviet Russia*. N.Y.: Oxford University Press, 1956.
Struve, Nikita. *Christians in Contemporary Russia*. London: Harvill Press, 1967.
Sventsitskaia, N. Otets Valentin, *Nadezhda*, no. 10. Russia: Samizdat, 1984.
Sventitskii, Fr. Valentin. 'Shest' chtenii o tainstve pokaianiia v ego istorii', *Nadezhda*, no. 2, 1979.
Svetov, F. 'Optina Pustyn' segodnia', *Nadezhda*, no. 8. Russia: Samizdat/Frankfurt am Main, 1982.
Tendriakov, Vladimir, 'Chudotvornaia', *Chrezvychainoe proisshestvie*. M.: Sovremennik, 1972.
Uchebnik dlia rabochikh antireligiozykh kruzhkov. M.: Bezbozhnik, 1930.
Ushakov, V. *Pravoslavie i XX vek*. Alma-Ata, Kazakhstan, 1968.
Ushinin, D. (pseudonym of D. Pospielovsky), 'New currents in the Soviet atheistic propaganda', *Grani*, no. 60. Frankfurt am Main, 1966.
Valentinov, A. A. ed. *Chernaia Kniga/Shturm nebes*. Paris, (1925?).
Vistunov, Evgenii. *Priglashenie v zapadniu*. L.: Lenizdat, 1984.
Volkov, A., 'Vskrytie moshchei prepodobnogo Sergiia Radonezhskogo', *Nadezhda*,no. 5. Russia: Samizdat/Frankfurt am Main: Possev Verlag, 1981.
Vybory v sovety deputatov trudiashchikhsia i antireligioznaia propaganda. M.: Molodaia gvardiia, 1938.
Yaroslavsky, E. 'Speech at the Second LMG Congress', *Razvernutym frontom*. M.: Bezbozhnik, 1929.
Zalygin, M. *Solenaia Pad'*. M.: Voenizdat, 1981.
'Zhizneopisanie ieromonakha Nikona', *Nadezhda*, no. 8. Russia: samizdat 1981/Frankfurt am main: 1982.
Zhurakovsky, Fr. Anatolii, Biographical:
 (1) *Materialy k zhitiiu*. Paris: YMCA Press, 1984.
 (2) 'Sviashchenik Anatolii Zhurakovsky,' *Nadezhda*, no. 10, 1984.
Zybkovets, N. F. *Natsionalizatsiia monastyrskikh imushchestv v Sovetskoi Rossii, 1917–1921*. M.: Akademiia Nauk SSR, 1975.

Index

Academy of Sciences 43
Adventists 31, 180, Appendix 2
  Church of Seventh Day
    Adventists 157–8
  Legal Defence Group 174
  True and Free Seventh Day
    Adventists (AUCTFSDA)
    156–9
Alexii, Patriarch 79, 92, 128, 231 n.37
All-Union Council of Evangelical
  Christians and Baptists *see*
  Baptists
Andropov, Yurii 145
Antireligious decrees, resolutions,
  legistlation, and Church laws
  213–14
  Decree of 23 Jan. 1918 –
    Separation of Church and
    State x, 1, 12–13, 16, 62
  Decree of 1 March 1919 –
    Liquidation of the cult of
    corpses and mumies 19
  Soviet Constitutions of 1918 and
    1924 61
  under Stalin 61–3, 70, 150, 207–8
  under Khrushchev 105, 121–2, 127, 129, 135–6
  under Brezhnev 150, 157, 159–60, 163–4, 169, 186–7, 259 n.96
  under Gorbachev 188
Antireligious education 42, 102
Antireligious parades, meetings 44–5
Antireligious propaganda
  antireligious serial publications
    45, 91, 99, 189: *Antireligioznik* 30–1, 34; *Bezbozhnik* 19, 31, 34–5, 37–8, 42–3, 45, 71, 98; *Bezbozhnik u stanka* 29, 35–7, 42–3, 98; *Science and Religion* (*Nauka i religiia*)
19, 24, 26, 98–102, 104–5, 108–16; *Revolution and the Church* (*Revoliutsiia i Tserkov'*) 19–20, 23, 30; *World of Man* 117
  and religion in art, culture, and literature 112–14, 117, 189–92
  religion as a drug 36, 37
  religion as a mental disorder 36
  and religious revival 117
  in serial publications:
    Komsomol'skaia Pravda 28, 37, 43, 87; *Krokodil* 37, 95, 113; *Soviet Ethnography* 127
  support of Renovationist schism 24, 27
  tactics, debates over methodology: pre-Khrushchev 36–7, 42, 44–6, 56, 64, 69; under Khrushchev 99, 101–4, 106–7; post-Khrushchev 108–11, 114
  and youth and religion 71, 108, 117, 125
Antireligious propaganda – attacks on
  'anti-semitism' of Orthodox Church 28
  Baptists 30, 85–6, 114, 161–2
  Bishops 87–8, 103, 134
  Buddhists (Hare Krishna) 155–6
  Christian scholars 43
  Christians in *kolkhozy* 32, 35, 89
  Church holidays 37, 44–5
  Church in connection with famine relief 24–7
  Church for alleged involvement in intelligence organised criminal and blackmarket operations 85–9, 111, 111–17

Antireligious propaganda – attacks on – *continued*
  Church as scapegoat for economic problems 34–5, 36, 45, 85
  clergy 28, 30, 42, 50, 69, 71, 86–7, 88, 103
  hierarchical structure of Church 23–5, 28
  Jehovah Witnesses 111, 114, 155–6
  Judaism 27–9, 44, 106
  Loyalty of Church 28–9
  Lutherans 87
  miracles 21–3
  monasteries 50, 105, 142, 177
  Moslems 27, 34, 89, 106
  Old Believers 115
  Pilgrimages and pilgrims 105–6
  Renovationists 27, 33
  those refusing to recognise Renovationists 52
  Roman Catholic Church 44, 86–7, 95–6
  Saints 19–20
  Sectarians 30–4, 42–3, 87, 108
  Sergii, Patriarch 28
  theological academies and seminaries 23, 86
  Tikhon, Patriarch, 24, 26–7, 50, 87
  'True Orthodox' 106–8, 115–16
  Ukrainian Uniates 114
Antireligious serial publications *see* Antireligious propaganda
Antireligioznik *see* Antireligious propaganda
Anti-Sergiite schism *see* Schism – on the right Antonov rebellion 47
Argentov, Alexander 181–182
Arkhangelsk City Union of Orthodox Clergy and Laity 11–12
Arrests x, 59
  of Bishops 2, 52, 77–79, 88; in connection with
    Renovationist schism 58
    under Gorbachev 188
Art and religion *see* Culture
Atarbekov 8

Baptists 30, 85–6, 131, 144, 146, 180
  All-Union Council of Evangelical Christians and Baptists (AUCECB) 131–2, 159, 162
  Central Council 31
  Council of Churches of the Evangelical Christians and Baptists (CCECB/ Initsiativniki/Unofficial Baptists) xiv, 132, 154, 156, 159–62, 183–4, 186, 188, Appendix 2
  Council of Relatives of the Imprisoned Christian Baptists 184, Appendix 2
  'Khristianin Publishers' 183–4, Appendix 2
Barinov, Valerii 186, 216
Beilis case 53–4
Beletsky, S. 4
Believers – statistics on numbers 45, 70–1, 127
Belkov, 24, 52
Bezbozhnik *see* Antireligious propaganda
Bezbozhnik u stanka *see* Antireligious propaganda
Bishops, Archbishops, and Metropolitans
  Afanasii (Sakharov), and 'Sakharovites' 78–81, 91–3
  Alexander (Petrovsky) 73–4
  Alexii, Metr. (Gromadsky) of Kiev 103
  Alexii 76
  Alexii, Metr. (Ridiger) 189
  Andrei, Archbp. (Sukhenko) of Chernigov 102–3, 134
  Andronik, Archbp. of Perm 6, 229–30 n.11
  Antonii, Archbp. of Arkhangelsk 75

Bishops, Archbishops, and
  Metropolitans – *continued*
Antonii, Metr. (Mel'nikov) 189
Antonii, Metr. of St Petersburg 9
Arkadii (Ostal'sky) 74
Dometian (Gorokhov) 87–8
Efrem 4
Ermogen, Archbp. of Tashkent 134
Feodosii, Archbp. of Poltava 164–5, 168–70
Filaret, Metr. of Kiev 167, 171
Filaret, Metr. of Minsk 189
Germogen, of Tobolsk 2, 3, 6
Illarion, Archbp. (Troitsky) of Krutitsy 58
Illarion (Belsky) 75–6
Ioakim, Archbp. of Nizhni Novgorod 3
Ioann, of Kirov 136
Iov, Archbp. (Kresovich) of Kazan 102–3, 134
Joseph, Metro. 76
Konstantin, Metr. (D'iakov) 74
Kornilii, 12
Korobov, of Vetluga 89
Leontii, of Astrakhan' 8
Luka (Voino-Yasenetsky) 78–80, 84, 97
Makarii, of Viaz'ma 7
Manuil (Lemeshevsky) 78–9, 93–4
Maxim (Ruberovsky) 74
Maxim (Zhizhilenko) 76–7, 79, 84
Nikodim, of Belgorod 7–8, 9
Nikodim, Metr. (Rotov) 134–5
Nikolai, Metr. 128–9, 134
Nikolai, Metr. of Rostov-on-Don 75
Onufrii (Gagaliuk) of Elisavetgrad 75
Peter, Metr. (Poliansky) 58, 73, 210
Pimen, Metr. of Kharkov 74
Pitirim, Archbp. 167
Planton (Kulbush) of Tallin 10
Purlevsky, of Sergach 89
Roman Catholic Bishops: De Ropp, Archbp. 13;
  Sladkiavichus 153;
  Steponavichus 153
Serafim, Metr. (Ruzhentsov) 88
Serafim, Metr. (Meshcheriakov) of Belorussia 75
Sergii, Metr. (Voskresensky) of Vilnius Appendix 1
Stefan (Nikitin) 84–5
Varfolomei (Remov) 76
Venedikt, Archbp. 134
Veniamin, Archbp. (Novitsky) of Irkutsk 94, 134
Veniamin, Metr. of Petrograd 17, 51–5
Victor (Ostrogradsky) of Glazov 73
Vladimir, Metr. of Kiev 9–10
Bishops – consecration *see* Consecration
Bishops – numbers of 46, 67–8
Blokhin, Nikolai 185, 217
Borisov, Prof. 43
Budarov, Sergei and Vladimir 185, 217
Buddhism 155–6
  Hare Krishna 156, 188, Appendix 2
Bukharin, Nikolai, and 'Bukharinites' 45, 87, 89
Burdiug, V. 184–5, 217
Burtsev, Vladimir 183

Chaikovsky 12
Chapaev 2
Chernenko, K. U., and religion 117
Christian Committee for the Defence of Believers' Rights (CCDBR) 173–4, 180, 181
Christian Communes of Sobriety 32
Churikov, and Churikov sect 31–2, 85
Church
  attendance 18, 45
  and the Civil War x, xi, 1–6, 16, 27–8, 69

Church – *continued*
  denials of persecutions 28–9, 59, 99, 128
  and Renovationist schism 49, 52, 58, 77, 79
  and the 1905 Revolution 9
  under German occupation 91–3, 125, 193, 197–9, Appendix 1
Church and State
  and baptisms 14, 164–5
  and burials 14, 73, 164
  and famine relief 24, 26–7, 48–53, 55
  general history *see* Introduction, Appendix 1
  and marriages 12–14, 73, 164
  and miracles 21–3, 56
  reapprochment during 1914–18 91
  and saints 19–20, 56, 136
Church publicity *see* Religious publishing
Churches
  desecration of 9, 15, 38
  destruction, closure – pre-Khrushchev ix–x, 1, 15, 22, 38, 40–1, 57, 64, 66, 69–70, 73–4, 83, 97, 121; of anti-Sergiite Churches
  destruction, closure – post-Stalin 123–8, 133–4, 136, 146–9, 169–70, 199; in Kirov diocese 122–4, 126, 136, 153; of Baptist prayer houses 160–1; of Pentecostal prayer houses 163; of Roman Catholic churches 126, 152–4
  numbers of churches remaining open ix, 46, 64, 66–67, 70, 124, 126–7, 135, 146, 149, 169; of Roman Catholic churches 152
  preservation of as cultural, historical or architectural monuments 38, 190–1; Fund for the Restoration of Historical Monuments 170;

VOOPIK – All-Russian Association for the Preservation of Historical and Cultural Monuments 191
  re-opening of, construction or enlargements of churches and similar attempts 70, 83, 93, 121, 145–6, 148–51, 169–70; During 1939–45; of old Believers churches 152; of Roman Catholic churches 153–4
  resistance to destruction and closures of Churches 1, 22, 74, 116, 123–5, 134, 147–8
Churches and monasteries – transformation for alternative uses 38–9, 57, 64, 176; of Roman Catholic churches 153–4
Civil War and the Church x, xi, 1–6, 16, 27–8, 69
Clergy, monks and nuns (Orthodox)
  Adelgeim, Fr Pavel 172–3
  Alimpi, Archimandrite 176
  Alipii, Fr 139, 177
  Amvrosii, monk-priest 10
  Amvrosii, Fr 176–7
  Antonii, Fr Esner-Foiransky-Gogol 83
  Boiarsky, Fr 53
  Boiko, Fr Vasilii, 170
  Chel'tsov, Fr Mikhail 82
  Dimitri, Fr 10
  Dragozhinsky, Fr 8–9
  Dudko, Fr Dimitri 94, 171
  Eshliman, Fr Nikolai 116, 135, 173
  Florensky, Fr Pavel 77
  Fonchenkov, Fr Vasilii 173
  Gainov, Fr Nikolai 173
  Gapon, Fr Georgii 86–7
  Gavriil, Abbot 177
  Gavril, Fr 83–4
  Golovanov, monk 140
  Ilarii, monk-priest 138–9

Clergy, monks and nuns
  (Orthodox) – *continued*
  Ivasiuk, Fr Nikolai 178
  Izrail, monk 10
  Kochurov, Fr Ivan 3
  Konin, Fr Lev 179
  Makeev, Valeria, Nun 179
  Mechev, Fr Sergii, 78
  Medved', Fr Roman 76–7
  Mikhailov, Fr Iosif 179
  Miliutinsky, Fr Alexei 5
  Mokovsky, Fr 8
  Nektarii, elder 57
  Nikon, monk-priest 57
  Ornatsky, Filosof, Fr 3
  Pavel, Fr. Lysak 174
  Perestoronin, Fr T.G. 133–4
  Pitirim, monk 176
  Pivovarov, Fr Alexander 174
  Podolsky, Fr Alexander 5
  Polsky, Fr 73, 81–2
  Prigorsky, Fr Ivan 5
  Rasputin, Fr 12
  Roman Catholic clergy: Bubnis,
    Fr Prosperas 153;
    Krapiwnicki 13;
    Lauriniavichius, Fr Bronius
    178; Lutoslawski 24;
    Zavalniuk, Fr 154;
    Zdebskis, Fr 153
  Romaniuk, Fr Vasilii 171–2
  Rusak, deacon Vladimir 166–8
  Sampson, elder 84
  Serafim, Fr Batiukov 93
  Simonov, Fr 128
  Surtsov, Arch-priest 12
  Sventsitsky, Fr. Valentin 77–8
  Tavrion, monk 59
  Trubetskoi, Fr Nikolai 92–3
  Unka, Grigori, monk 140
  Vladimirov, Fr Iakov 11
  Vostorgov, Fr 3–4
  Yakunin, Fr Gleb 116, 135, 173,
    227–8
  Zdriliuk, Fr 170–1
  Zhurakovsky, Fr A. 78
Clergy Conference of Siberia 50
Clergy consecration *see*
  Consecration

Clergy – deregistration of 123,
  129, 133, 167, 171
Clergy – numbers of 46, 68, 135,
  152, 165
Closure of churches and
  monasteries *see* Churches
Collectivisation x, 42, 62–4
Communes, Christian agricultural –
  attacks on 15, 30–3, 42–3,
  230–1 n.31
Concentration camps 60, 73–5,
  81, 83
Confiscation of church property
  1, 15
Confiscation of church valuables
  for famine relief 24, 26, 47–
  51, 55, 69
  arrests and trials in connection
    with 49–50, 53–5
  resistance to 49, 55
Congresses, Party
  8th 69
  10th 47
  15th (1928) 42
  21st (1959) 122
  27th (1986) 190
Consecration of new bishops and
  clergy 121, 168
Council of Churches of the
  Evangelical Christians and
  Baptists *see* Baptists
Council of Relatives of the
  Imprisoned Christian Baptists
  see Baptists
Council for Religious Affairs
  (CROCA or CRA) 97, 123–4,
  128–32, 141, 146, 149–50,
  156, 163–6, 168–70, 172, 177
Culture – art, literature, traditions
  . . . and religion xiv, xii, 112,
  189–92
Culture Fund 190–1

Desecration of churches *see*
  Churches
Destruction of churches,
  monasteries *see* Churches
Destruction, closure, of Holy Places
  136

Ermolaev, Sergei 183
Executions and murders 3-4, 7, 78, 82
  of believers x, 1-4, 6, 10, 12, 59, 81-3, 141, Appendix 2; in connection with famine relief 50, 55
  of bishops 3-4, 6-8, 15, 55, 60, 68, 74-6; Andrionik, Archbp. 6; Germogen 2-3, 6; Maxim (Zhizhilenko) 76-7; Nikolai, Metr. 75; Platon 10; Varfolomei (Remov) 76
  of Churikovites 32
  of clergy 3, 5, 8, 10-12, 15-16, 68, 74-5, 82, 84, 178, 183; Kochurov, Fr 3; Mechev, Fr Sergii 78; Medved', Fr Roman 76-7; Ornatsky, Fr 33; Vostorgov, Fr 4; in camps 82-3; in connection with famine relief 50, 55-6; in connection with schism 58; of Lutheran clergy 10; of Roman Catholic clergy 4, 178
  of monks and nuns 10-11, 15-16, 54, 141; Alimpi, Archimandrite 176; from Caucasus underground monastery 175; in Kazan 82; in Rostov-on-Don 75; in connection with famine relief 55-6

Fedotov 181-2
Fudel, S. I. 93
Fund for the Restoration of Historical Monuments see Churches — preservation of
Furov 165-6, 168-9, 171-2, 177

Galiev, Sultan 34
Galliamov, Sergei 180-1
Gerasimchuk, Maria 141
Germans and Church see Church under German occupation
Gorbachev, Mikhail – and religion 188, 190
Gorbachev, Raisa 191
Gorev-Galkin, Mikhail 19, 27
Graham, Billy 162
Grossman, Vasili 68-9
'group of twenty' 204-7
Gurovich, Ya.S. 52-4
Gzhevskaia, Marfa 141

Hare Krishna see Buddhism
Henry, Maurice 99-100
Holy Places — destruction, closure of see Destruction
Hope: Christian Readings see Samizdat

Il'chev, Leonid 99, 104, 107
Il'insky, Captain N. S. 155
Imprisonment
  of believers 2, 55-6, 60, 82, 93, Appendix 2
  of bishops 15, 56, 58, 60, 68, 73-5, 79-80, 84-5, 87-8, 92, 94, 134; Afanasii (Sakharov) 80-1, 92; Andrei, Archbp. (Sukhenko) of Chernigov 134; Veniamin, Archbp. (Novitsky) 94
  of clergy 15, 56, 68, 73-4, 77-8, 92, 133, 153, 174, Appendix 2
  numbers imprisoned for faith (including in psychiatric hospitals) 160, 163, 184
Industrial Party 86
Initsiativniki see Baptists
Intelligentsia, religious revival ix, 117, 156, 179

Jehovah Witnesses and Jehovists 154-5, 222
Jesus Regiments 16
Journal of the Moscow Patriarchate see Moscow Patriarchate
Judaism and Jews 13-14, 28, Appendix 2

Kagan 14

Kalinovsky 24
Kaltakhchian 191
Kaplan 43
Karlovci 28
Kerensky 33
Khvostov, A. 4
'Khristianin Publishers' *see* Baptists
Khrushchev, Nikita, and religion x, 46, 121–2, 145
 reaction from West 98–9, 121
Kirov 8
Kollontai, Alexander 17
Komsomol – anti-religious activity of 38, 44, 68–9, 97, 132, 164, 170
Korolenko, Iustina 141
Kostelovskaia 42
Krakhmalnikova, Zoia 185–6, 220
Krasikov, Piotr 30, 32–3
Krasnitsky 24, 52–3
Krokhin 185
Kronstadt rebellion 47
Kryvelev 189–91
Kuntsevich, Lev Z. 6
Kuvshinov, I. A. and son 59
Kuz'kin, Alexander 183

League of Militant Godless 28, 31, 33, 36–9, 44, 64, 68, 71
Leagues of Laymen 17
Legal Defence Group *see* Adventists
Legislation *see* Antireligious decrees, resolutions, *etc.*
Lenin
 and NEP 47
 and religion 1, 24, 26, 36, 49, 57, 174
 Turanian movement 34
Leningrad liberation organization 86
Levitin-Krasnov 65–7, 101–2
Ligachev, L. N. 190
Likhachev, D. S. 190–1
Literature and religion *see* Culture
Lithuanian Catholic Committee for the Defence of Believers' Rights *see* Roman Catholic Church

Lithuanian Helsinki-Watch Group *see* Roman Catholic Church
Living-Church *see* Renovationists
Lockhart, Bruce 87
Leginov, Anton 37–8, 42
Lunacharsky 42
Lunin, A. 28–30
Lutherans 13, 87
Lypkivskyites *see* Ukrainian Autocephalist Church

Maklakov, N. 4
Mariamov, B. 109
Martynov, Evgenii 180
Marxism and Christianity/religion 1, 9, 29, 33, 49, 107, 110, 122
Mensheviks 6
Metropolitans *see* Bishops
Miniakov 188, 222
Miracles 20–3, 56, 84–5
Monasteries and convents, and attacks against them 10, 50, 82, 134–6, 164, 175–6; Alexander-Nevsky 17; Optina 57; Pochaev-Lavra 105, 137–42, 164, 176–7; Pskov Monastery of the Caves 105, 177; St Sergius-Trinity 174, 176–8
 destruction, closures of, and similar attempts x, 1, 15, 57, 65, 82, 134, 136–42, 177
 numbers of monasteries and monks 136; in Pochaev-lavra 176
 resistance to closure of 134; in Pochaev-lavra 137, 141–2
 transformation for alternate uses *see* Churches
Monastic working communes 15, 57
Monks *see* Clergy, monks, etc.
Moor 99
Moroz, Valentyn 172
Morozova, Maria 141
Moscow Patriarchate 128, 136, 167, 196–7, 212
 Journal of the Moscow Patriarchate 102, 167, 188

Moslems and Islam 13, 18, 27, 34, 89, 106
Murders see Executions
Music, religious rock music – 'Trumpet Call' 186, 216

Nationalism xiv–xv, 60
  Turkic 34
  Ukrainian 9, 86, 157, 172
Nauka i religiia see Antireligious propaganda
Nechytailo, A. 168–70
New Economic Policy 47
New Israel Sect 30–3
Nikolaev 146–7
NTS – Toiling Alliance of Russian Solidarists 116, 246–7 n.34
Nuns see Clergy, monks and nuns

Ogorodnikov, Alexander 181–2, 186, 188
Old Believers 115, 127–8, 151–2
Oleshchuk, F. 39, 64, 71, 88–9
Osipov, Alexander 103–4, 105, 110–12

Paris Peace Conference 11–12
Party Congresses see Congresses
Peace Fund 170
Pectoral Crosses 90
Pentecostals xiv, 143–4, 154, 156, 162–3, 180, 186, 188
Persecutions of see also Arrests; Executions; Imprisonments; Appendix 2
  Adventists 158–9
  Anti-Sergiites 48, 60, 65, 67, 73, 75–8, 91–3
  Baptists 144, 159–62, 180, 184, 186, Appendix 2
  Buddhists 155–6, Appendix 2
  Christian Committee 173
  Christian scholars 43
  Clergy ix–x, 1, 3, 57, 62, 73, 81, 133–4, 167, 170–3, Appendix 2
    for 'collaboration' during 1939–45 92–4, 97
  Jehovah Witnesses and Jehovists 155, Appendix 2
  laity ix–x, 1, 81, 143–4, 181–2, Appendix 2
  monks and nuns ix–x, 1, 65, 81, 105, 137–42, 175–9, Appendix 2
  official admissions of xi, 70–1, 73, 127–8
  parents of religious youth 142–3, 186
  Pentecostals 143–4, 162–3, 180, 186, Appendix 2
  religio-philosophic seminar 181–3
  those refusing to recognize Renovationist schism 47–8, 58, 80
  Uniates 157
  youth, seminarians, and students 133–5, 180–2; Moscow University religio-philosophic study group 94–6, 181
Pilgrimages and pilgrims 105–6, 130, 135–7, 140–1, 164, 175–6
Pimen, Patriarch 177–8
Platonov, Sergei 43
Plekhanov 141
Poliakov, Igor 183
Popkov, Viktor 183
Poresh, Vladimir 182–3, 223–4
Powell, D. 101
'Prayer for Bolsheviks' 76–7
Preservation of churches see Churches preservation of
Priests see Clergy
Prokhanov, Ivan 18
Protests
  religious processions 2–3, 6, 12, 17
  sermons 7–8
  Western – against religious persecutions 64–5
Provisional Government 3
Psychiatry and psychiatric hospitals, and their use against believers 36, 140, 156, 178–81
publishing, religious see Religious publishing

Purges 43
Pushkov, Pastor Eugene 159
Pylilo 191

Radek, K. 13
Ratushinskaia, Irina 188
Rebellions against Bolsheviks 47
Regelson, Lev 67–8
Religio-philosophic seminar 181–3, 186
Religious publishing 183–5, 217
Religious revival Introduction, 70–1, 96, 117, 131, 156, 179, 181–2
Renovationist – Living Church x, 24, 27, 47, 54, 58, 66–8, 74–5, 79–80, 194–5, 211
and campaign for confiscation of church valuables 49
and Patriarchal Church 49, 52, 58, 77, 79
putsch 49
and State 24, 27, 33, 49, 58, 88
Republican associations for the preservation of historical and cultural monuments *see* Churches, preservation of
Revoliutsiia i tserkov see Antireligious propaganda
Roman Catholic Church 13, 152–4, 156–7, 189
persecutions of Roman Catholics 13, 24, 153, Appendix 2
Lithuanian Catholic Committee for the Defence of Believers' Rights 174
Lithuanian Helsinki-Watch Group 178
Rublev, Andrei 112
Rumachik, Peter 225
Rutgaiter 14

Saints 19–20, 56
Sakharovites *see* Bishop Afanasii (Sakharov)
Samizdat xi–xiv, xiin, 110, 144
'Holy Letters' 110–11
Hope: Christian Readings (Nadezhda) 185, 220

Khristianin Publishers 183–4
Schism – on the right 48, 60, 65, 67, 73, 76, 78–81, 91–3
Schoolteachers – attacks on 42, 56, 102, 153
Science and Religion see Antireligious propaganda
Seminaries *see* Theological academies
Sergii, Patriarch 58, 65, 67, 73, 77, 79, 81, 91, 210
and loyalty to State x, 28–9, 48, 59–60, 65, 73, 76, 79, 81, 194–5, 211
and Stalin concordat (1943) 68, 78, 91
Services – disruption of 15, 45
Seven Year Plan (1959), and religion 122
Shamaro 109, 115
Shcheglovitov, I. 4
Shchipkova, Tat'iana 182–3
Shchors 2
Shelkov, V. A. 158, 159, 215, 225
Shevchuk 85
Shipilov, Vasilii 180
Shmain, Ilia, Fr 95–6
Shpitsberg, 20
Shuia Clash 49
Sidorov 184
Skrebets, Olga
Smirnov, Afanasii 12
Smolkin, Valeri 178
Snezhnevsky and other schizophrenia theories as applied to believers 36, 178–9
Sobor, All-Russian 1917–18 4, 6, 12
Stalin, Joseph – and religion xi, 42, 64–5, 88, 93, 95–6
concordat with Sergii 68, 78, 91
State Famine Relief Commission 51
State and religious youth 131–3, 142–4, 186
Students *see* Youth; Theological academies
Sverdlov, Yakov 5–6

Talantov, Boris 122–5, 128, 131, 133, 135–6
Taran 141
Taxation, rents – and clergy, churches and monasteries 62–4, 74, 136, 205
Theological academies, seminaries, and seminarians 121, 133, 180
 closures of 135, 168
 harassment and control of students by CROCA 165–6, 168–9
 Moscow Theological Seminary 165
 numbers of seminaries and students 135, 152
 Volhynia Seminary in Lutsk 168
 unofficial 76
Theophanes the Greek 112
Tikhon, Patriarch 2, 12, 13, 24, 28, 50, 58, 79, 87
 anathema to Bolsheviks 1, 6
 arrest of 49, 52
 and the Civil War 16
 and famine relief 26–7, 48, 55
 and loyalty 28, 59, 194
 and Renovationist schism 58
Timokhin Sergei 186, 216
Toiling Alliance of Russian Solidarists see NTS
Tokmakova, Lydia 141
Tretiakov, E. 156
Trials see also Appendix 2
 of Ostal'sky, Bishop Arkadii 74
 of Sergii, Archimandrite 54–5
 of Veniamin, Metropolitan of Petrograd 51–5
 of Roman Catholics 50
 of Jews 50
 of Zoia Krakhmalnikova 185–6
 in connection with confiscation of church valuables 49–50, 53–5
 for religious publishing 184–5
 re-trials in camps 175, 182–3, Appendix 2
 show trials: Industrial Party 86; Leningrad Liberation Organization 86; Union for the Liberation of the Ukraine 86
Trotsky, and Trotskyites 45, 87, 89
Trubnikova 105–6, 109, 115, 117
True Orthodox 106–8, 115–16, 127
'Trumpet Call' see Music
Turanian Movement 34

Ukrainian Autocephalist Church 60, 86
Ukrainian nationalism 9, 86, 157, 172
Ulianov, G. 109
Underground Church 79, 92, 127, 145
Uniate Church 95, 114, 157
Union for the Liberation of the Ukraine 86
Union of Russian People 53

Valentinov, A. A. – *Black Book* 2, 4–5, 8, 14, 50, 55
Varavva, Feodosia 143–4
Vatican 86
Vins, George 161
VOOPIK see Churches, preservation of
Vvedensky, Metr. A. 24, 52, 53
Vyshinsky, Andrei 89

War Communism 1, 47
World Council of Churches 174
World of Man see Antireligious propaganda
Work week – continuous, and banning of days off on church feast days 56–7, 71, 72, 91

Yankova 70
Yankovich, Alexander, 180, 228
Yaroslavsky, E. 16, 36–7, 42, 45, 69, 70–1
Yevtushenko, E. 191
Youth, students and religion 71, 102, 117, 131, 133, 135, 180–2, 186

Youth, students and religion –
continued
   Moscow University student
     religio-philosophic study
     group   94–6, 181
   religio-philosophic seminar
     181–3, 186

Zaichenko, Grigorii   185
Zhurnal Moscovskoi Patriarchii   *see* Moscow Patriarchate
Zinoviev, and Zinovievites   87
Zuckerman, Dr Boris   151
Zyrianov, Khristofor   115

GPSR Compliance
The European Union's (EU) General Product Safety Regulation (GPSR) is a set of rules that requires consumer products to be safe and our obligations to ensure this.

If you have any concerns about our products, you can contact us on

ProductSafety@springernature.com

In case Publisher is established outside the EU, the EU authorized representative is:

Springer Nature Customer Service Center GmbH
Europaplatz 3
69115 Heidelberg, Germany

www.ingramcontent.com/pod-product-compliance
Ingram Content Group UK Ltd.
Pitfield, Milton Keynes, MK11 3LW, UK
UKHW041416180426